Japan's
Foreign Policy
Since 1945

Japan's Foreign Policy Since 1945

KEVIN COONEY

An East Gate Book

M.E.Sharpe
Armonk, New York
London, England

An East Gate Book

Copyright © 2007 by M.E. Sharpe, Inc.

Library of Congress Cataloging-in-Publication Data

Cooney, Kevin J.
  Japan's foreign policy since 1945 / by Kevin J. Cooney.
    p. cm.
  Includes bibliographical references and index.
  ISBN-13 978-0-7656-1649-4 (cloth : alk. paper); ISBN-13 978-0-7656-1650-0 (pbk. : alk. paper)
  ISBN-10 0-7656-1649-1 (cloth : alk. paper); ISBN-10 0-7656-1650-5 (pbk. : alk. paper)
  1. Japan—Foreign relations—1945– I. Title.

DS889.5.C68 2006   327.52—dc22

Printed in the United States of America

To My Parents, Jerry and Arliss Cooney
You raised me right and taught me to
love all the peoples of this world.

Contents

List of Figures and Illustrations

Maps

Acknowledgments

I am deeply indebted to so many people for all their help and encouragement, without which this text would not have been written. As always, the final responsibility for this book and its contents rests solely with me. Nevertheless, I am especially grateful to all those who have helped me with this project, and I would like to express special thanks to the following people:

To my mentor, Dr. Sheldon Simon of Arizona State University, and his wife Charlann, for all their past and continuing advice, support, and help to me and my family.

To my friend, Dr. See Seng Tan of the Institute of Defence and Strategic Studies, Nanyang Technological University in Singapore, for his friendship and advice over the years as well as the Christian fellowship you have provided.

To my friend Scott Thompson for letting me bounce ideas off of you and for keeping in touch.

To the Sakurai and Takagi families for all your help during the field research for this text.

To my editor, Patty Loo, thank you for all your faith, patience, and confidence in me. I look forward to working with you on many more projects in the future. You are a brave woman and an inspiration.

To the administration, faculty, and staff of Union University, especially the members of my department and my department chair, Dr. Stephen Carls and his wife Dr. Catherine Carls, for supporting this effort and their friendship. I would like to express a special thanks to my student worker, Jenny Buffington, for all her efforts in proofing and indexing the final draft and providing me with a student's perspective on the text. Congratulations on your upcoming wedding. You have a wonderful future ahead of you, *carpe diem ad majorem dei gloriam.*

To my friends Jay Haugen, Shaun Orchard, and Kris Putrasahan and your families, thank you for your friendship and love over the years. Each of you is so important to me in a special way. I miss seeing all of you but I am grateful for free minutes at night and on weekends that help keep us connected.

My penultimate and deepest thanks go to my family both here and in Japan. To Mama and Papa Sano *arigato gozaimashita* for blessing me with a part of Japan that I will never stop loving. Thank you also for spending time with your daughter and grandchildren here in America while I was writing this book. Thank you to my brothers and sisters (both natural and in-law) for keeping me humble and connected to family, but especially to Damien for defining what it really means to be family, I cannot imagine life without you as my brother. To Dad and Mom, thank you for raising me (and all of us) right and to love God. I hope to follow your example with your grandchildren, my children. I am especially thankful for and proud of my two children, Aiyana and Kian. You are both so special to me. I love you dearly. Daddy will spend more time at home now. To Atsuko, my wife, thank you so much for all your support and patience with me as I worked long nights and weekends to finish this book. I love and appreciate you and will do so forever. You are the best.

My final thanks go to God, who makes life worth living and through whom all good things come.

Kevin Cooney
Union University

List of Acronyms and Terms

amae: dependence on and concern for other people

APEC: Asia-Pacific Economic Cooperation

ASDF: Air Self-Defense Forces

ASEAN: Association of Southeast Asian Nations

ARF: ASEAN Regional Forum

BMD: Ballistic Missile Defense

Comfort Women: A euphemism used by the Japanese military during World War II to describe women (mostly Korean and Chinese but including some Western women interned or held prisoner by the Japanese) who were forced to work as sexual slaves to "service" Japanese soldiers before going into battle.

CPJ: Communist Party of Japan

Democratic Peace Theory (DPT): The Democratic Peace Theory states that because no two democratic nations have ever gone to war with each other no two democracies are likely to ever go to war with each other.

Diet: The Japanese Parliament. The Diet is the legislative body in Japan. It has both an upper house, the House of Councillors (*Sangin*), and a lower house, The House of Representatives (*Shugin*). The lower house is primary in that it may override a vote of the upper house by a two-thirds majority. The prime minister and the cabinet usually come from the lower house, but they may come from either.

DMZ: Demilitarized Zone

DPJ: Democratic Party of Japan

DPRK: Democratic People's Republic of Korea (North Korea)

DSP: Democratic Socialist Party

EU: European Union

G4: Japan, Germany, Brazil, and India, which are all seeking permanent status on the U.N. Security Council.

G7: The term used to describe the meeting of seven leading economic powers (in the 1970s) that evolved into a major annual economic and political meeting hosted by each nation in turn. Its members are Japan, the United States, Canada, Great Britain, France, Germany, and Italy.

G8: The G7 plus Russia. Russia participates in the political discussions but not the economic ones.

gaiatsu: Foreign, and in particular American, pressure.

gaijin: foreigner

GATT: General Agreement on Tariffs and Trade

GNP: Gross National Product

ICBMs: intercontinental ballistic missiles

Iishi: Literally "men of high purpose." This group of late-nineteenth-century Japanese elites made it their purpose to learn Western ways and secrets and to modernize Japan whether it wanted to or not.

JCP: Japan Communist Party

JDA: Japan Defense Agency

KEDO: Korean (Peninsula) Energy Development Organization (now defunct)

kenpou: The Japanese constitution.

kiretsu: Monopolistic Japanese business cartels.

Komeito: A Buddhism-based political party in Japan currently allied with the ruling LDP party.

LDP: Liberal Democratic Party. Its Japanese name is *Jiminto.*

MAD: mutual assured destruction

manga: Japanese comic books read by both children and adults.

MITI: Ministry of International Trade and Industry

MSDF: Maritime Self-Defense Forces

Meiji Era: Meaning "enlightened rule." Named for the Emperor Meiji, it lasted from 1868 to 1912. During this period the Meiji Restoration took place in which Japan modernized faster than any nation had ever modernized and became a major military power. The Meiji constitution implemented during that era was in effect until the end of World War II. It centered the power structure in Japan around the upper-class feudal lords and the military.

MOFA: Ministry of Foreign Affairs

naiatsu: internal pressure

NBR: National Bureau of Asian Research

NCO: non-commissioned officer

NPR: National Police Reserves (predecessor to the SDF 1950–52)

NSF: National Safety Forces (predecessor to the SDF 1952–54)

nemawashi: Japanese term for the consensus building process.

ODA: Official Development Assistance

OEF: Operation Enduring Freedom

OIF: Operation Iraqi Freedom

on: indebtedness

ox walk tactics: The tactic used by the SDP during the passage of the PKO Law. In protest, the SDP members of the Diet walked as slowly as possible to cast their ballots, thus delaying the final outcome.

P5: The permanent five members of the U.N. Security Council with veto power (China, France, Russia, the United Kingdom, and the United States).

PKF: peacekeeping forces

PKO: peacekeeping operations

PLA: People's Liberation Army (China)

PPP: purchasing power parity

PRC: People's Republic of China (Mainland China)

RMA: Revolution in Military Affairs. A concept used to signify technological leaps that require a rethinking of military tactics. High technology is accelerating the frequency of RMAs.

ROK: Republic of Korea (South Korea)

Sangin: Upper house of the Japanese Diet; the House of Councillors

SCAP: Supreme Command (or Commander)/Allied forces–Pacific

SDF: Self-Defense Forces

SDP: Social Democratic Party

SDPJ: Social Democratic Party of Japan, the predecessor to the current SDP.

SLOC: sea lanes of communication

Shugin: The lower house of the Japanese Diet, the House of Representatives.

TMD: Theater Missile Defense system

UNESCO: United Nations Educational, Scientific, and Cultural Organization

UNITAF: United Task Force (created by the U.N. Security Council)

UNPKO: United Nations Peacekeeping Operations

UNSC: United Nations Security Council

UNTAC: United Nations Transitional Authority in Cambodia

wa: harmony

WTO: World Trade Organization

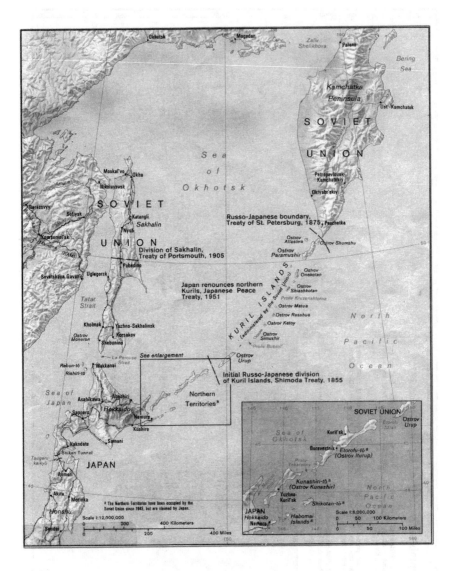

Disputed Kurile Islands/Northern Territories

Japan's
Foreign Policy
Since 1945

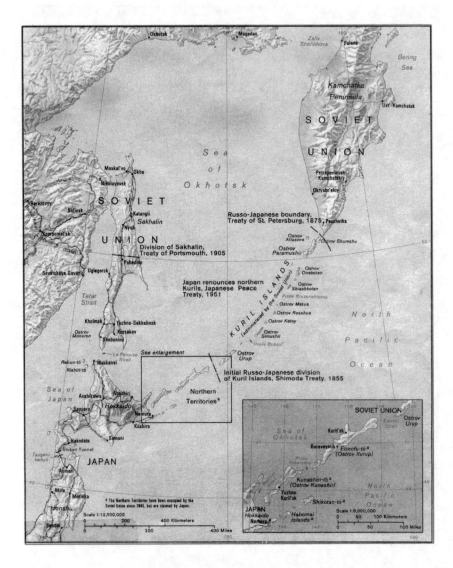

Disputed Kurile Islands/Northern Territories

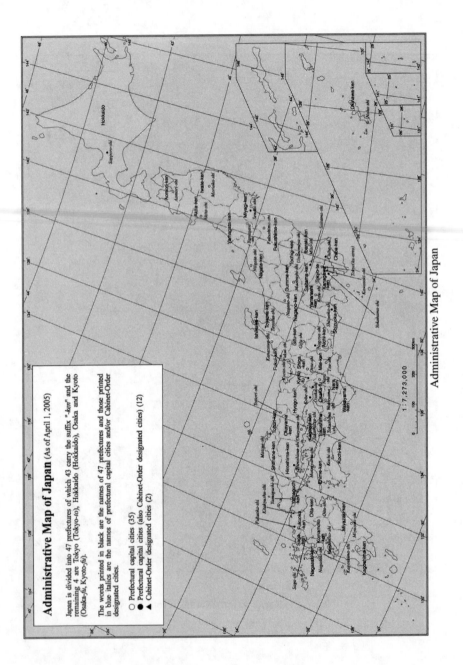

Administrative Map of Japan (As of April 1, 2005)

Japan is divided into 47 prefectures of which 43 carry the suffix "-ken" and the remaining 4 are Tokyo (Tokyo-to), Hokkaido (Hokkaido), Osaka and Kyoto (Osaka-fu, Kyoto-fu).

The words printed in black are the names of 47 prefectures and those printed in blue italics are the names of prefectural capital cities and/or Cabinet-Order designated cities.

○ Prefectural capital cities (35)
● Prefectural capital cities (also Cabinet-Order designated cities) (12)
▲ Cabinet-Order designated cities (2)

1:7,273,000

Administrative Map of Japan

xx

Japan's Foreign Policy Since 1945

1

Introduction

The Story of Japan after World War II

*. . . the political organism is always experiencing both continu-
ities and change, and thus is always in motion, slipping behind,
moving ahead, holding fast, or otherwise adjusting and changing
in response to internal developments and external circumstances.*
—James N. Rosenau[1]

Japan, as a nation, is in the midst of change, much of it brought about by the
end of the Cold War. The current manifestation of this change is evidenced
by the fact that Japan is sending troops overseas into combat zones (in a noncombat role) for the first time since the end of World War II; the nation is
very anxious to demonstrate that it can make a "human" contribution to the
world community and to its American allies, in spite of its constitutional
limitations. Japan is also attempting to step out of the larger shadow of the
United States into greater partnership with that nation as an equal and to take
its place alongside the other great powers. At the same time, Japan is coming
to terms with the fact that, in spite of its great economic strength, it is vulnerable to both international and domestic economic turbulence and to its own
structural problems. It is additionally coming to terms with the reality that it
is a major power on the world stage; as such it can be a tempting target for
extremists. An instance of this vulnerability is the Peruvian embassy hostage
incident that lasted from December 1996 though April 1997.[2] The role of
Japan's Self Defense Forces (SDF) in Iraq and elsewhere has now made the
country a potential target of Islamic terrorist groups.

In previous writings, I have argued that Japan is in the midst of a maturation process in which it is seeking to present itself as a great power. This
argument will be continued in this book. I will further argue that a process is
under way in the Japanese Diet (legislature)[3] to transfer power from the powerful bureaucracies in Japan to the elected legislative leadership of the Diet.
More important, significant political elements within the ruling Liberal
Democratic Party (LDP) are seeking to escape the constitutional constraints

3

imposed by Article Nine by amending or rewriting Japan's postwar constitution. Article Nine being the most important barrier to Japan's becoming a normal nation will be closely examined in chapter 2.

This text will thus be a narrative about political leaders in Japan, their foreign-policy choices, and my quest to understand the shifts and changes in their foreign policy. The book is, moreover, an account and exploration of the people in leadership positions and the way they view the world. It is also the story of the Japanese foreign-policy leadership, based on my conversations and interviews with these leaders. The basic thesis of this book is that people make policy while institutions administer the policy that is made by leadership. It is for this reason that people—or agents, if you will—will be the primary focus of this book. This will be a study of the human element in politics and specifically in foreign policy. The conclusions will primarily be based on trends in observed behavior and attitudes rather than on statistical data or institutional analysis. The study of structure or institutions will be included, but it will be secondary.

This book will also be an invitation to the reader and to the student of Japanese foreign and security policy to think about the issues facing Japan's leaders. It is assumed that Japan's leaders do have the nation's best interests in mind. The question thus becomes, what are the best foreign and security policy choices for Japan? Ideology plays an important role here. The realist would make choices that differed from those made by the idealist or the intuitionalist in similar situations. I recognize my own realist inclinations, but I will present scenarios from differing perspectives and schools of thought. Each chapter has questions for thought, discussion, and debate, as there is no one simple answer as to what is in Japan's best interest.

A further goal of this book will be to introduce the reader and student to the background and history of modern Japan's foreign-policy issues and to place them in the context of the present. It will particularly focus on the recent choices in foreign and security policies brought about by the end of the Cold War and the role its neighbors play in shaping Japan's foreign-policy choices. To put this aim succinctly, this book will be an empirical examination of changes in Japanese foreign policy brought on by the end of the Cold War and a study of what the Japanese political leadership believes that Japan's role in the world should be. Japan is a major player, and its growing power on the world scene and changes in its foreign policy frequently impact the rest of the world. Furthermore, studying change in Japan provides students of foreign policy with an excellent case study of a major power engaged in foreign-policy change during an extended period of global uncertainty. To begin our examination of Japanese foreign policy, we will look at the event that changed the post-World War II foreign policy for all nations: the end of the Cold War.

The Catalyst for Change

As in Virgil's phrase, "a new order for the ages," so the "New World Order" rang in the end of the Cold War, and as in Virgil's Roman Empire, the post-Cold War world of *Pax Americana* has witnessed wars and uprisings on all fronts. For Japan, the simple world it knew during the Cold War had become complex. Choices were no longer clear. Decisions became much more difficult, complicated, and far-reaching.

It is said that some nations live by the sword and perish by the sword. Since World War II, Japan has lived by the dove of pacifism and must now choose whether to let its role in the world dwindle, perish by its self-imposed pacifism,[4] or take up the sword and risk the casualties and enemies it has avoided since the end of World War II.

Japan was not alone in feeling the effects of the sudden and unpredicted end to the Cold War. That event brought about profound changes in the foreign policy of many nations. The bipolar conflict that had governed the post-World War II era ended in such a way that no nation was fully prepared to deal with a world turned upside down. The new situation also created new problems, ones that had been unthinkable during the Cold War, such as the total disintegration of the Soviet Union and collapse of full control over the Soviet stockpile of weapons of mass destruction. The United States/Soviet conflict nevertheless left a residue of structures, institutions, and policies that continue to shape and govern the foreign affairs of many nations in the so-called New World Order. Japan was one of the nations whose foreign policy was particularly affected by the end of the Cold War. This situation was due in many ways to the unique-ness[5] of Japanese foreign policy and the country's constitutional restraints.

During the occupation of Japan by the United States after World War II, the Occupation Government, headed by General Douglas MacArthur, wrote and gave Japan its postwar constitution. This constitution has been called The Japanese Peace Constitution. The key foreign-policy peculiarity of Japan's constitution is Article Nine of Chapter II: The Renunciation of War. It states:

> Aspiring sincerely to an international peace based on justice and order, the Japanese people forever renounce war as a sovereign right of the nation and the threat or use of force as a means of settling international disputes. In order to accomplish the aim of the preceding paragraph, land, sea, and air forces, as well as other war potential, will never be maintained. The right of belligerency of the state will not be recognized.[6]

Article Nine was written shortly before the onset of the Cold War and is fundamental to the understanding of Japanese postwar foreign policy.

As a result of the onset of the Cold War, Japan was pressured by the United States into establishing the SDF, an entity that was to have only *defensive* capabilities and was to provide a domestic defense against foreign invasion. The linchpin of this arrangement is the United States-Japan Security Treaty, which promises United States support if Japan is ever attacked, thus negating the need for Japanese force projection (offensive) capabilities.

The long-term effect of Article Nine was that Japan had a constitutional excuse *not* to act as a "normal" nation in international affairs. The primary architect of Japan's foreign policy under Article Nine was then-Prime Minister Shigeru Yoshida.[7] His foreign-policy strategy or agenda became known as the Yoshida Doctrine. During much of the Cold War, Japanese foreign policy was based on this doctrine, which permitted Japan to focus on economic development while depending on the United States for its national security needs. The great benefit of this was that Japan did not have to spend much of its gross national product (GNP) on defense and on other needs related to national security. The cornerstone of the Yoshida Doctrine (as of the SDF) was the Japan-United States Security Treaty in which the United States guaranteed Japanese security. Japanese foreign policy, in turn, was largely based on loyalty to and support for the United States.

This policy worked well until the end of the Cold War and the Gulf War that followed. The Gulf War took Japan, politically, by surprise; "like a bolt out of the blue."[8] Iraq's invasion of Kuwait on August 2, 1990, and the subsequent war had a major impact on the politics of Japan.[9] Japan was forced to face the true reality of its economic superpower status for the first time in a major international crisis. Initially, Japan sprinted out of the blocks, only to stumble and be left dazed and bewildered when it realized that the Cold War was over and the rules had changed. Japan was asked to participate at a level that was commensurate to its economic status in the world. This demand meant a human or military contribution to the war effort, and Japan was not prepared to comply. Japan's "checkbook" diplomacy—the policy by which it contributed financially to international actions by the United States and the United Nations but never made a "human" contribution by putting the SDF in harm's way. This policy caused Japan to be severely criticized abroad, especially in the United States. The Yoshida Doctrine that had served it so well was in desperate need of revision.

At the core of the problem was the old constitutional question of Article Nine. The question was whether Japan could send troops overseas even if they were under United Nations command. Japan was not ready to answer this question, but the world was waiting for a reply. Japan was still in the middle of trying to come to terms with the end of the Cold War and its impact on United States-Japanese relations and on the United States-Japanese Security Treaty. Japan was searching to find its new place in the world when the Gulf War forced Japan to make some hard choices. These choices, though inadequate in the eyes of many, started a debate within Japan that has forced it to attempt to reconcile its economic superpower status with its constitutional obligations.

As a result of the external pressures brought on by the Gulf War and its aftermath, on June 15, 1992, the Japanese Diet passed the Law Concerning Cooperation in U.N. Peacekeeping and Other Operations (otherwise known as the PKO Law), which went into effect on August 10 of that same year. This law marked the most significant change in Japan's postwar foreign/ military policy since the creation of the SDF in the 1950s. It also signaled a fundamental shift in the course of Japanese foreign policy, because for the first time since World War II, Japanese soldiers could be sent on missions outside Japan, except that this time, they would be under United Nations command. The Japanese government reserved the right to send or recall the troops but could not command their missions.

The Problem and the Questions

The problem for Japan is that while its constitution renounces war and prohibits the maintenance of military forces, it is a global economic power. It is the second-largest donor to the U.N. budget, yet it exists in a global political environment that requires a human contribution involving risk by the major powers to global peace. The questions that are being asked are: "What is Japan's new role in the world? What accounts for the gradual change in the role of the SDF? What are the domestic driving forces behind these changes? What is Japan's long-term foreign-policy agenda?"

In the following chapters, we will look at the causes and implications of foreign-policy changes in Japan since the end of the Cold War. I recognize that the restructuring of Japanese foreign policy does not represent a fundamental change in that policy, because Japan is not fundamentally changing its loyalties; rather, the nation is working to establish a fuller partnership with the United States while at the same time protecting its vital interests in the face of a China rising as a regional rival to Japan and a global rival to Japan's ally, the United States. Under the constraints imposed by Cold War interpretations of Article Nine, Japan limited its foreign policy under the Yoshida Doctrine out of the need to impress upon the United States that it was a loyal and dependable ally. In the post-Cold War era, Japan is seeking to enlarge its foreign-policy role to that of a normal nation. Normal nations have independent foreign policies and more important an independent military prerogative or option. Japan, under Article Nine, does not have an independent military option. At the same time, changes in Japanese foreign policy are not merely incremental course corrections, but also major shifts in national policy. Japan is undergoing a period of maturation in foreign policy in which Tokyo is stepping out of the larger shadow of the United States and taking its own place as a more equal and normal partner in the international arena.

This study of Japanese foreign-policy maturation is largely based on the literature dealing with changes in foreign policy that can be applied to Japan. It looks at this topic from three different levels of analysis.[10] These are: the level of the international system, the level of the individual, and the level of the state. The importance of the choice of these levels of analysis is that Japan operates as a major player within the international system, but it is Japanese societal values and their influences that dictate Japan's state-to-state relations. The first level of analysis used is the international system within the theoretical framework of neorealism.

The end of the Cold War brought about many changes in the international system. The bipolar world was replaced with a unipolar one, headed up by the United States as the unchallenged global hegemon. This situation presented new opportunities for Japan as well as for many other nations. In the next few chapters we will look at these changes in the international system from the point of view of Japanese foreign policy, the object being to show how Japan is reacting and adapting to changes in the international system and the opportunities that these changes present.

The second level of analysis that will be used is the individual/societal level. It is this level on which this book will primarily focus. I will examine the rise of new values and ideas in Japan's younger generation of leadership, a group that matured after World War II, and contrast this mindset to the attitudes of Japan's older generation of leaders that lived through the war. This section employs existing survey data, interviews with Japanese policy makers, and secondary literature to assess changes in the attitudes and values within Japanese society as they relate to foreign policy and the role of the armed forces. It also looks at the formation of foreign policy within the major political parties as reflective of these societal dynamics.

The third level of analysis is the state. This level looks at and determines whether Japanese foreign policy is undergoing a maturation process or is merely a continuation of past policy. By using the term "maturation," I ask whether Japan is directing its foreign policy to act as a "normal nation" with interests independent of its ally, the United States. In other words, is Japan really trying to step out of the larger U.S. shadow and its Yoshida Doctrine–based foreign policy and to act as an independent player? The state level also examines Japan's larger role in the world vis-à-vis other states. It particu-

larly looks at Japan's role in the world political economy and regional security. The security issue offers a range of questions and possibilities for Japan,
such as whether the nation will attempt to establish an independent naval
presence in East Asia and whether the nations of East Asia, and particularly
China, will accept a larger Japanese role. There is also the link between its
economic dominance and a possible future regional security role through the
Asia-Pacific Economic Cooperation forum (APEC) and Association of Southeast Asian Nations (ASEAN) Regional Forum (ARF).[11]

The Literature

As in any new study, it is important to review past work in order to place the
new work in context. The relevant literature for this study includes the literature on changes in foreign policy and on Japanese foreign policy. First, we
will look at the literature on restructuring, to be followed by the literature on
the making of Japanese foreign policy. As previously mentioned, even though
I acknowledge that Japan is not changing its basic foreign policy, I recognize
that its foreign policy is undergoing a maturation process for which the literature on the restructuring of foreign policy provides an explanation. Some
nations, such as China, reasoning from their own perspective, see Japan as
restructuring. Other nations see simply minor course corrections.

The concept of foreign-policy maturation helps us to deal with this problem of perspective by giving us a different angle to study. Since the 1991
Gulf War, there has been a fundamental change in Japanese foreign policy,
as evidenced by its dispatch of SDF troops overseas under U.N. command;
but there has been no reorientation of foreign allegiances, which is typically
the basis for defining foreign-policy restructuring.[12] The key to understanding the case of Japan is that under Article Nine, Japan has not been behaving
as a "normal" nation. The changes exemplified by the PKO Law demonstrate
that Japan is attempting to change its foreign policy so that it can take its
place among normal nations.

Foreign-Policy Restructuring

The literature involving foreign-policy restructuring began in the 1980s with
James N. Rosenau. His book was followed in the mid- to late 1980s by the
works of Kal Holsti, Kjell Goldmann, and Charles Hermann. These efforts
are important but are in no way conclusive; and they uniformly issue invita-
tions for more scholarly work on the issue of foreign-policy restructuring.

The seminal work is James Rosenau's *The Study of Political Adaptation*,
published in 1981. This book is a set of essays on the subject written and

published throughout the 1970s. The basic argument that Rosenau makes is that

> our understanding of politics can better be deepened and broadened by treating political phenomena as forms of human adaptation. . . . the political organism is always experiencing both continuities and change, and thus is always in motion, slipping behind, moving ahead, holding fast, or otherwise adjusting and changing in response to internal developments and external circumstances.
>
> Therefore, . . . to analyze how the adjustments are made, the changes sustained, and the continuities preserved is to engage in the study of political adaptation.[13]

What Rosenau specifically does is postulate that foreign policy is essentially a mechanism for a nation to adapt to or deal with changes in the world around it.

Rosenau's work was furthered by Kal Holsti as the editor of the book, *Why Nations Realign: Foreign Policy Restructuring in the Postwar World* (1982). This work takes the form of a collection of essays by Holsti and others looking primarily at examples of foreign-policy change in the Third World and in small states. Foreign-policy change in the First World is acknowledged by Holsti as being difficult to handle, but cases of change are examined from Canada and France. There is the beginning of a theoretical element of foreign-policy change in this work. Rosenau describes what he sees as happening to nations when they made changes in foreign policy, but Holsi begins to theorize as to what is happening when nations adjust their foreign policy. Thirteen types of foreign-policy restructuring are identified by Holsti as possible changes a nation-state can make over time. These thirteen types are subsumed into four ideal kinds of foreign policies. They are: isolation, self-reliance, dependence, and nonalignment-diversification.[14] The framework of his model focuses on the roles of external factors, domestic factors, background historical and cultural factors, and factors within the policy-making process itself.

Holsti concludes that we cannot explain from a foreign-policy point of view why some states restructure and others do not when faced with similar circumstances. In spite of this problem, Holsti was able to give us an understanding of certain conditions that would predispose a state to change its foreign policy. He also found that it was easier for a nation to declare its intent to change foreign policy than to implement the announced change. This last aspect of change has an interesting application to the Japanese case in that some current aspirations for change are not being implemented as the result of both overt and covert international opposition. Holsti's study provides an excellent opportunity to examine the factors that can prevent foreign-policy change at the state level. On the other hand, Holsti's work deals almost exclusively with threat-based change rather than with situational or environment-based change, which would be more applicable to the Japanese case. It is for this reason that this book does not rely primarily on the model developed by Holsti for foreign-policy restructuring.

In his 1988 book, *Change and Stability in Foreign Policy: The Problems and Possibilities of Détente,* Kjell Goldmann looks at the patterns of political action to understand the process of détente. He looks at the pressures for change and the pressures, on the other hand, for continuation of previous policies.[15] Goldmann lays out a "theoretical sketch" for the stabilization of foreign policy that demonstrates whether a foreign policy will continue or change. His strength is in the cataloging of ways in which foreign policy can undergo change and in which stability could be undermined. The application of Goldmann's "theoretical sketch" to my inquiry is limited in that the research does not look into the stabilization of Japanese foreign policy. Rather, the book examines change and the causes of change in Japanese foreign policy since the end of the Cold War.

Charles Hermann's 1990 presidential address to the International Studies Association is particularly useful in that it looks at redirection of foreign policy incrementally. The title of his address/paper is "Changing Course: When Governments Choose to Redirect Foreign Policy." It is Hermann's model that is used for my research because Hermann's model, more than Holsti's or Goldmann's, allows for the continual change in foreign policy that is always happening, as noted by Rosenau. Furthermore, Hermann notes, "Change is a pervasive quality of governmental foreign policy."[16] Hermann investigates the study of foreign-policy change and finds that the "decision making process itself can obstruct or facilitate change."[17] Thus there is the argument that change always exists in foreign policy and that the studies of foreign-policy restructuring are one and the same. Hermann, however, disagrees with this argument and I concur that there is a difference. This difference requires a close examination of change in the decision-making process, which is one element of this discourse.

According to Hermann, "Changes that mark a reversal, or at least, a profound redirection of a country's foreign policy are of special interest because of the demands their adoption pose on the initiating government and its domestic constituents and because of their potentially powerful consequences for other countries."[18] Wars may begin or end because of foreign-policy changes. It is for this reason that some scholars conclude that, because of the effort needed to change foreign policy, regime change may be the only way to facilitate it. However, as Hermann points out, when we reflect on this we find cases where the same government that started a foreign policy was the one responsible for its reversal or replacement.

The question that Hermann is asking in general and that I am asking with respect to Japan is, "Under what circumstances do these kinds of changes occur in which an existing government recognizes that its current course is seriously inadequate, mistaken, or no longer applicable? What are the conditions under which self-correcting change may arise?"[19] The answers to these questions can and will have significant impact on the study of foreign policy, not only because foreign policy changes are for the better (because often they are not), but rather for the consequences they generate and pose for the country's people and institutions as well as for other countries.

Hermann is concerned with the fundamental redirection of a nation's foreign policy. Hermann deals with his focus through a four-level graduated description of foreign policy change. The four involve increasing levels of change: (1) adjustment changes, (2) program changes, (3) problem/goal changes, and (4) international orientation changes. This last change involves a basic shift in the international actors' roles and activities in which not just one policy but many policies are simultaneously changed. This change typically, but not invariably, involves a shift in alignment with other nations or a major shift in the role that a nation plays within an alignment.

The conditions for change based on Hermann's research into different academic disciplines beyond political science—such as political psychology, psychology, sociology, education, and others—are fourfold. First, domestic political systems may affect foreign policy. For example, (1) issues become a centerpiece in the struggle for political power; (2) the attitudes and beliefs of a dominant domestic constituency undergo a profound change; and (3) a realignment of the essential constituency of a regime occurs, or a revolution or other transformation takes place.[20] The second is bureaucratic decision making, the third is cybernetics, and the fourth is learning.

Hermann further develops his model by selecting from his review of the literature two elements necessary to effect change in a domestic political system's foreign policy. They are: first, that there must be change in that system and, second, that systemic change must trigger a change in the government's foreign policy.[21] The agents of change are labeled as leader-driven, bureaucratic advocacy, domestic restructuring, and external shock.[22] The interaction of these with the decision-making process can be seen in Figure 1.1. Of course there is likely to be interplay between these agents of foreign-policy change.

The rest of Hermann's article deals with the various phases of foreign-policy decision making and will be examined more closely in chapter 4 of this book. Next, we will quickly look at the various sources about Japanese

Figure 1.1   **The Mediating Role of the Decision Processes Between Change Agents and Degree of Policy Change**

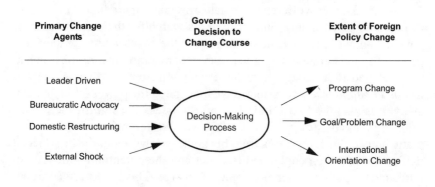

Source: Charles Hermann, "Changing Course: When Governments Choose to Redirect Foreign Policy." *International Studies Quarterly* 34 (1990): 13.

domestic and foreign policy that will provide the foundation for this analysis of the recent changes in Japanese foreign policy. These works relate to the literature on changes in foreign policy and Hermann's model in that they examine unique cultural factors and Japanese attitudes toward foreign policy. They also give us a greater understanding of the various agents of change at work in the creation of Japanese foreign policy.

Japanese Foreign Policy

Gerald L. Curtis, a leading expert on Japan, in his book *The Japanese Way of Politics* (1988), provides a good foundation for our study of the Japanese political system. Curtis explores the foundations of the Japanese postwar political system and the establishment of the Liberal Democratic Party. He also looks at the main opposition party, the Socialists, and its role in perpetual opposition. The interaction of these two parties is explored in the context of Japanese political decision making. Curtis furthers this study of domestic politics by looking at the changing nature of the Japanese voter, a change that has accelerated rapidly since the book was published. He updates his earlier study with *The Logic of Japanese Politics: Leaders, Institutions, and the Limits of Change* (1999) in which he examines the end of one-party dominance in Japanese politics. Three other excellent works dealing with the inner workings of the Japanese political system are *Japanese Politics: Fixed and Floating Worlds* by Timothy Hoye (1999), *Japan's Dysfunctional Democracy* by Roger W. Bowen (2003), and *Introduction to Japanese Politics* (4th edition, 2004) by Louis D. Hayes.

Probably the most comprehensive work on the role of Japanese domestic political power is Karel van Wolferen's *The Enigma of Japanese Power* (1993). Van Wolferen systematically takes apart almost every area of Japanese political and public life in his search for the core of Japanese power. Van Wolferen's conclusion is that the main source of Japanese power is in the bureaucracy rather than in democratic institutions such as the Diet and to a lesser extent the Prime Minister's Office. While *The Enigma of Japanese Power* may have overstated the power of the bureaucracy, it is also the first scholarly work to assess the significance of the Japanese bureaucracy in detail.[23] While van Wolferen focuses on bureaucratic power, this book gains from his book's views about the interface of that power and the people, and the Diet and the potential application of bureaucratic power as a major agent of change. This book further argues that foreign-policy-making power is slowly shifting away from the Ministry of Foreign Affairs (MOFA) to the Diet.

Another book by Gerald Curtis that deals directly with the topic of foreign policy is an edited volume called *Japan's Foreign Policy After the Cold War: Coping with Change* (1993). This volume was the first work to look at Japan's post-Cold War options. It analyzes Japan's diplomatic style, economic needs, security concerns, and relations with its neighbors; most importantly, it looks at Japan and the new multilateralism. It provides state-of-the-art thinking on Japanese foreign-policy making.

Curtis furthers this in his edited 1994 work, *The United States, Japan, and Asia*, a collection of papers exploring the current status of Japan in relation to the United States and the rest of Asia. Military concerns, such as the stability of the United States-Japan Security Treaty and ways the differing regional powers and groupings, such as China and ASEAN, view it are examined in detail. More importantly, the economic tensions between the United States and Japan are examined with an eye toward the future role of Japan in the world.

Reinhard Drifte, another leading expert on Japanese foreign policy, also takes a look at the future of Japan's foreign policy in his 1998 book, *Japan's Foreign Policy for the 21st Century: From Economic Superpower to What Power?* Professor Drifte sees Japan as increasingly willing to act as a major power, having come to terms with the end of the Cold War. He views Japan's position in the world as having increased to the point that even nonaction by the Japanese government can have a major effect on other nations.[24] Furthermore, Japan is seen as having not yet fully established its "ideological, intellectual and moral leadership" resulting in a "leadership by stealth."[25]

In "Cultural Norms and National Roles: A Comparison of Japan and France" (1987), Martin W. Sampson III and Steven G. Walker provide a basic examination of cultural norms that govern Japanese politics. This survey and its comparison with France's political workings highlight the central thesis of this book, to the effect that Japan is changing the direction of its foreign policy and that of its role in the world. Fritz Gaenslen, in his 1992 paper "Decision Making Groups," further explores the theoretical application of group decision making, an examination that is very valuable in the case of Japan in that nearly all decisions of consequence are made by groups. This group dynamic is an especially interesting application for Hermann's model.

Several works by such scholars as Takashi Inoguchi, Warren Hunsberger, Akitoshi Miyashita, and Yoichi Funabashi further this study of Japan's foreign-policy agenda. Overall, the available secondary literature provides good background for this text. The history of Japanese foreign policy is covered in detail, along with an informative and useful discussion of Japanese decision-making norms. What is lacking is any empirically based study of why the PKO Law was passed over the strong objections of the opposition and how the law relates to future Japanese foreign policy objectives. This book partially fills this gap in the literature by examining the intentions and opinions of relevant members of the Japanese Diet and the Foreign Ministry. It is hoped that these will provide the reader with an opportunity to glimpse the direction and future goals of Japanese foreign policy.

Elite Interviews

The empirical core of this text is based on a series of field interviews I conducted with members of both houses of the Japanese Diet, Foreign Ministry officials, members of the Japanese press, cabinet officials, and Defense Agency officials. Because there are 512 members in the lower House of Representatives and 252 members in the upper House of Councillors, the interviews concentrated on Japanese members who focus on foreign policy or sit on foreign-relations or defense-related committees in the Diet. Interviews with Diet members who possess expertise in foreign policy from every major party were conducted. Senior Foreign Ministry officials, who deal with day-to-day issues in Japanese foreign policy as well as with ongoing issues, were also interviewed.

Japanese politicians often confide in members of the press in exchange for their silence on an issue until the matter is resolved. Once the issue is resolved, the reporters are free to chronicle the events that transpired from the knowledge they had gained from first-hand interviews. Given this unique relationship between press and politicians, two interviews were conducted with members of the press corps who specialized in foreign policy. Defense Ministry officials were also interviewed to gauge their reactions to changes in Japanese foreign policy.[26]

The interviews were in Japanese or in English, as required for the comfort of the interviewee. The interviewee was also given the opportunity to remain anonymous if he or she so chose. This offer helped to elicit answers that were more frank and honest than might be expected from party or government positions. Any comments by those who chose to remain anonymous are so cited.

Two separate but similar questionnaires were constructed for the interviews; both were in Japanese and English. One was designed for Diet members and the other for government officials and academics. A special set of open-ended questions was designed to probe the Diet members for the reasons that caused them to support or oppose the PKO Law and for their personal thoughts on the future direction of Japanese foreign policy. I probed the individual members' feeling on the need for change in policy by asking, "Why do you feel that the government felt it necessary for Japan to pass the PKO Law?" This query was posed to elicit the government's reasoning, behind the scenes, as to why they lobbied Diet members to pass the PKO Law and the differing perspectives by political party. This question was followed by another asking whether the member agreed or disagreed at the time and why.

A follow-up question asked the Diet members if they would change their vote now if they could, and if so, why? This question was to check for any realignment or change of opinion. The questions thus give us both past and present perspectives.

The second questionnaire reflected Hermann's change paradigm by looking for the primary change agents and the extent of foreign-policy change that they bring about. Some of the questions concerned the following: What did the interviewee believe the goals of Japanese foreign policy should be? What needs to be done to achieve these goals? What are the obstacles to these goals? How should Japan deal with these obstacles? How does such a plan fit with Article Nine? What role, if any, should Japan seek in international security forums? If Japan does take on a larger role, how will it deal with its history in East Asia? What could or would be the domestic consequences of this larger role? Who or what groups are pushing for foreign-policy change? What are the forces outside Japan that are pushing for change? The questions were designed to build on each other. For example: Where do you feel that Japan is going in the future with its foreign policy? Do you feel this is the right direction? Why, or why not? If not, where would you like to see it go in the future?

As with any research based on elite interviews, the validity of the results depends on the integrity of the answers given by the interviewees. Internal validity will be a problem only in the author's translations from Japanese and the codification of the results. To avoid the issue, the translations were cross-checked with others in order to control for the potential problem, so that the reader can be assured that quotations in the text are accurately translated from Japanese. The criterion-related, or predictive, validity of the interviews that can be applied to the direction of Japanese foreign policy in general is reasonably strong. As Japanese society revolves around consensus, so does the nation's decision making. Even with a highly controversial issue, the PKO Law, the Diet still had to forge a majority consensus. The Foreign Ministry, for all its power, still needs the Diet to change or reinterpret constitutional law. Thus the opinions of the Diet members, officials of various ministries, and the press do matter, and they will matter in any future foreign-policy legislation.

The main threat to the validity of any research project or text is current events. Political events with global implications are always happening and will continue to happen. The trick is to appropriately capture the essence of what is happening and to create a framework by which the reader can interpret these events as they unfold. Nations act and react in an ever-changing world. During the writing of this text, there have been several major events within Japanese foreign policy that have potential long-term implications. If there are any events that happened after the survey relating to the PKO or Japanese national security, and in particular, if these events are bad (that is, if a squad of Japanese soldiers is killed while serving in Iraq or on a PKO mission), the future of the SDF in Japanese foreign policy could look dramatically different from its appearance at the time of this writing.[27] These types of problems are impossible to control for; and both I and the reader need to be aware of and acknowledge the dynamic nature of writing on current policy.

One of the main threats to reliability of the answers given in interviews is that they would not necessarily be the same as answers given to a Japanese scholar. The reasoning behind this disparity is that the Japanese as a whole tend to be very private about what they consider to be internal matters. Consultation and research yielded no definite conclusion concerning the type of answer that would be given to a *gaijin*[28] studying Japanese foreign-policy making. Conventional wisdom is that the survey would result in true answers and possibly even clearer answers than those a Japanese would receive under similar circumstances.[29] The actual interview experience seemed to uphold this hypothesis, and several illustrations of this confirmation are given through out the text.

The Variables

As in any social- or political-science research project, there is a need to acknowledge the variables and focus on and control the direction of the research.

For this text, the end of the Cold War and the First Gulf War are seen as the initial independent variables for Japan's foreign-policy maturation, because these are watershed events that clearly demonstrated the need for change in Japanese foreign policy. The PKO Law was the first major effort to deal with the realization that change was needed in Japanese foreign policy in the aftermath of the First Gulf War. The PKO Law is thus a dependent variable representing the change brought about by these independent variables. From the time of its enactment, the PKO Law can be seen as a new independent variable for foreign-policy change, accounting for the changes in the role of the SDF on U.N. peace-keeping missions. The reason for this change is that the PKO Law permitted Japan to send troops overseas for the first time since World War II. This new ability took Japan a giant step forward in its quest to be a normal nation.

Furthermore, one can see the end of the Cold War as an independent variable, accounting for the dependent variable of the September 1997 revision of the United States-Japan Defense Guidelines. These guidelines spell out major changes in Japanese foreign and security policy vis-à-vis the United States. For example, in the event of a crisis or war, Japan will now provide ports and airports for U.S. forces. It will also provide minesweeping, and it is prepared to receive refugees from war zones as needed. This change is not without opposition. The Japanese Maritime SDF was to be given the right to enforce any U.N. embargo on the open sea by boarding ships to inspect their cargos; however, the bill authorizing this readiness was withdrawn from consideration in the Diet under heavy criticism, and this right of boarding ships under U.N. auspices is not part of the revised Guidelines. (An amendment in 2000 enabled ship-boarding for the first time.) Significantly, Japanese forces still cannot enter into combat or operate in a combat zone. However, SDF forces on U.N. peacekeeping missions can now act in self-defense as units rather than as individuals. How a combat zone is defined in any future conflict, such as one on the Korean peninsula, will also mark a significant foreign-policy challenge for Japan. The interaction between the different variables is illustrated in Figure 1.2.

This being said, the principal independent variable for this book is the PKO Law, because it marks such a significant change in what had been Japanese foreign policy. A secondary independent variable is the end of the Cold War, because it is the primary event that created the need for change in Japanese foreign policy. The principal dependent variable is foreign-policy change. The elite interviews, combined with the research in secondary sources, measure the direction of foreign-policy change. Further dependent variables are support for and attitudes toward foreign-policy changes. The elite interviews along with existing poll data expose attitudes toward the quantity of and level of support for change in Japanese foreign policy among elites and the general public.

Figure 1.2 **Variables**

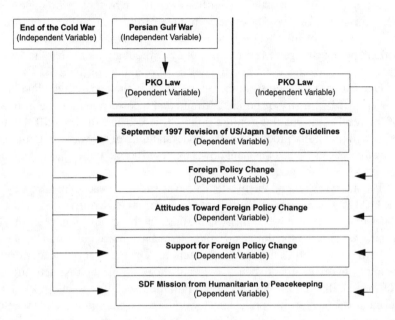

The elite interviews reveal a dichotomy based on party affiliation, with some overlap based on members who have switched parties or who simply changed their opinions. The study found that a majority supports the PKO Law on varying grounds relating to Japan's role in the world. The right wing in Japanese politics strongly supports it on the grounds that it was passed at a time when Japan asserted a more active military role. Those of a moderate bent welcome it with softer language than the right but with the same desire to get the proverbial "monkey" of World War II and Article Nine off their backs. Still others see it simply as a chance for Japan to give to the world by helping the United Nations. There seems to be consensus on the direction Japanese foreign policy should take, even though the reasons for that consensus differ.

A strong minority, coming mostly from the Socialist Party and other left-leaning groups, oppose Japan's continued participation in peacekeeping and a more active role in world affairs for two reasons, the first being Japan's past role as a military aggressor. Members of this group feel that elements within Japan are fueled by a desire to see the nation become a great power again through military might. The other grounds for rejection of the PKO Law are based on the simple principle that it violates the "pacifist constitution" of Japan and that a remilitarized Japan is a step in the wrong direction. One or both of these reasons were often cited to me by those who oppose the PKO missions, but there also seems to be a resignation on the part of most that the future of the PKO missions were "set in stone" and that there was little hope for change or reversal of policy without a major event that would promote public outcry, such as the deaths of members of the SDF.

One surprise gleaned from the interviews was the apparent decline in the power of the Ministry of Foreign Affairs and a corresponding rise in power of the the Diet in making foreign policy. It is because of this shift that this book will hopefully produce a better understanding of the way foreign-policy decisions are made in Japan and how Japanese foreign policy has changed in the post-Cold War period.

The interviews found that while there was strong bureaucratic advocacy for the PKO Law, the real push for the law's passage was leader-driven. The external shock of the Gulf War was primary in the push for this change. The research also discovered other factors for change that Hermann's model did not account for.

Furthermore, all of the differing potential "change agents" (leader-driven changes, bureaucratic advocacy, external shock, domestic restructuring), as Hermann calls them in his model, go into the decision-making process and result in various foreign-policy changes in Japan (see Figure 1.1). One of the intentions of this book is to shed light on the strength of the various agents of change in the Japanese decision-making process that results in shifts in Japanese foreign policy. Often there are multiple agents of change at work at any given time. Each agent is trying to influence foreign policy to some extent and may vie with other agents. For example, the bureaucracy might choose to advocate small or incremental program changes; at the same time, some political leaders might push for an international change of orientation, and domestic sources of restructuring might be advocating no change at all. When balanced by the various strengths of the competing interests, the resulting change might result in a simple change in policy goals or redefining of the problem reflecting the strength of the leadership and the relative weakness of domestic influences for change.

In sum, the elite interviews helped to clarify the Japanese process of foreign-policy change and to test the utility of Hermann's model for Japan. To be useful, political-science models should help us understand the real world, and this book provides an example of this process through Herman's model.

Objectives and Expected Significance of the Book

The conventional wisdom had been that Japan was a rising hegemon that was presenting itself as a challenger to the current and seemingly declining hegemon, the United States, as well as to China.[30] However, Japan's sustained economic slump and the meteoric rise of China have led many, both inside and outside of Japan, to question the idea that Japan is capable of achieving hegemony. Some have even mockingly asked, "Is Japan number one or number twenty-three?" Given Japan's potential to pull itself out of its own economic slump and its position as the second-largest economy in the world, the question that should be asked is, "Does Japan desire to be a hegemon?" And if so, are the recent changes in its foreign policy a sign of this goal or merely a reaction to the end of the Cold War by implementing a "goal/problem change"? Or are the recent changes a sign that Japan is radically changing its foreign policy, undergoing an "international-orientation change"? In other words, there are three possibilities. The first is that Japan wants to become a hegemon. The second is that Japan does not want to take a more significant role in the world and is merely trying to raise its standing in the world by attempting to provide humanitarian assistance through the United Nations. The third is that Japan is trying to become a more important or larger player or partner with the United States without hegemonic aspirations. The following chapters explore these alternatives.

The objective of this book is to present the changes in Japanese foreign policy to the reader, along with my analysis of what Japanese elites and the Japanese public believe to be their country's best global security role. The significance of this study is twofold in that, first, it contributes to a better understanding of Japan's foreign policy and, second, that the nature and causes of foreign-policy change can be better understood. It will also hopefully stimulate further research, so that scholars can continue to study the decision-making methods that determine Japanese foreign policy and will contribute, in a wider sense, to our understanding of foreign-policy change in general.

Outline of the Book

In order to provide the context of Japanese foreign policy for the book, chapters 2 and 3 look at the history of Japan's postwar foreign policy and its implications for current foreign policy. The fourth chapter examines the theoretical framework for the research in detail in light of international-relations theory and the literature on foreign-policy change within the present context. This chapter also attempts to clarify and theoretically further Hermann's model in light of observed Japanese foreign policy. The fifth chapter looks at Japan's state-to-state relations with an eye on national and regional security. Special attention will be paid to Japan's options regarding security and alliances within East Asia. The sixth chapter examines Japan's place in the international system and addresses the question of Japanese hegemony. It also examines the domestic societal level of Japanese attitudes toward foreign policy, with a focus on what I call the myth of *gaiatsu* (foreign pressure). Existing survey data are extensively used in both chapters 5 and 6, along with the results of the interviews I conducted in the field. The seventh chapter will look at China and North Korea as challengers and rivals to Japan in Northeast Asia. The final chapter attempts to be predictive of the future direction of Japanese foreign policy as described in the fifth and sixth chapters and draws the conclusions of the book as well as details the needs for future research.

2

The Legacy of the Occupation

An "Abnormal" Foreign Policy

> *. . . land, sea, and air forces, as well as other war potential,*
> *will never be maintained.*
> —Article Nine, Constitution of Japan[1]

There are three major periods of modern foreign-policy change in Japan: the opening of Japan and the Meiji Era up to World War II, the Cold War, and now the post-Cold War time. Each of these periods saw significant events and foreign pressure for change dictate the foreign policy that would develop in Japan. Each time, Japan responded in its own unique way to adapt to the world around it. This chapter will examine the development of Japanese foreign policy in the modern era in order to show how Japan got to where it is today.

The arrival of Commodore Matthew Perry in 1853 marked the opening of Japan to the modern world, the beginning of Japan's first period of modern foreign policy, and an attempt to integrate itself into the world system. This period culminated with the Meiji Era (1868–1912), which saw Japan change from a feudal society to a modern industrial nation that could compete with the powers in Europe. The driving force for this change was the realization on the part of Japan that it needed to industrialize or it would be colonized by more powerful, modern nations.

The driving force that led Japan to modernize was fear—fear that Japan would be dominated by foreigners. This anxiety can be seen as foreign-driven, in the sense that if foreigners had stayed away from Japan, then Japan might still be a feudal society today. There were, of course, internal elements that pushed for reform in Japan, such as the Iishi, a small group of Japanese elites who banded together and made it their cause to drag Japan (kicking and screaming) into the nineteenth century. In the end, however, fear of foreign influence was the driving force for change; thus, the pressure for structural change came from outside Japan.

An important development during this period was the establishment of a democratic constitution. The Meiji Era constitution was implemented in 1889 in response to popular demand by the people of Japan for democratic reforms. At the time, the Japanese government was run by a small group of bureaucrats who wanted to keep control centralized rather than diffused to the people in a democratic system. To this end, they created the Diet and developed a constitution (based on the German constitution instituted by the German Chancellor Bismarck) that kept power centralized in their hands while giving minimal power to the people. The lack of real power in the hands of the people through their democratically elected representatives in the Diet eventually led to military rule and the disaster of World War II.

The importance of a constitution and a democratic form of government to our study of Japanese foreign policy comes from the Democratic Peace Theory. The Democratic Peace Theory states that since no two democratic nations have ever gone to war with each other no two democracies are likely to ever go to war with each other. American Presidents Bill Clinton and George W. Bush have made promoting democracy a foreign policy priority for their administrations as a way to promote world peace. The lack of a true popular democracy in Japan is seen by the proponents of the Democratic Peace Theory as the reason behind Japanese military aggression in the early twentieth century.

The second major period in modern Japanese foreign policy was the rebuilding of Japan after the destruction of the nation during World War II and the Cold War period. This period included the rewriting of Japan's Meiji Era constitution. This newly rewritten constitution would dictate and greatly limit Japan's foreign policy.

During the U.S. occupation of Japan after World War II, the occupation government, headed by General Douglas MacArthur, in concert with Japan's cabinet, rewrote and revised Japan's constitution. This postwar constitution has been nicknamed the Japanese Peace Constitution, a reference to Article Nine of Chapter II, the renunciation-of-war clause. This article states:

> Aspiring sincerely to an international peace based on justice and order, the Japanese people forever renounce war as a sovereign right of the nation and the threat or use of force as a means of settling international disputes. In order to accomplish the aim of the preceding paragraph, land, sea, and air forces, as well as other war potential, will never be maintained. The right of belligerency of the state will not be recognized.[2]

Article Nine was written before the onset of the Cold War. As a result of the Cold War, Japan was pressured by the United States into establishing the Self-Defense Forces (SDF), which were to have defensive capabilities only. For example, the Air SDF could have fighter planes but not bombers or mid-air refueling capabilities that would permit it to take any conflict to the attacker's home soil. The linchpin of this arrangement is the United States-Japan Security Treaty, which promises U.S. support if Japan is ever attacked, thus making the need for Japanese force projection (offensive) capabilities unnecessary. The parties of the left wing in Japanese politics, particularly the Communist Party, have never accepted this arrangement as constitutional, and it has been part of their party platforms to dissolve the SDF if and when they come to power.[3] Japanese politics in general tends to be governed by consensus, which is often the result of cultural norms. The Japanese view of the role of the nation is clearly demonstrated by Walker and Sampson in their comparative study of Japan and France.[4] The Japanese basic organizational motif is the group. Group consensus is primary in most areas of Japanese life. All sides of an issue are given extensive consideration in a process called *nemawashi,* which serves the purpose of building consensus within the group at an early stage as to not break the harmony (*wa*), indebtedness (*on*), and dependence on and concern for other people (*amae*).[5] This institutional group harmony within the Diet[6] was broken with the passing of the PKO Law by the LDP over the strenuous objections of the principal opposition party, the SDP.[7]

The very fact that the *wa* was challenged was a significant sign of a major change in the direction of Japanese politics. The LDP obviously felt that the passing of the PKO Law was more important to Japan than the maintenance of general harmony within the Diet. The opposition felt that to support this law would be detrimental to Japan and to the integrity of the constitution. The result was two differing attitudes as to the correct direction Japan should take in the coming years and the role of its foreign policy on the world scene. The LDP policy toward the United Nations and peacekeeping is now a priority in Japanese foreign policy, and it has been enlarged to include a highly visible campaign for a permanent seat on the U.N. Security Council.

Since World War II, Japan has not posed a threat to the region through military power and, in spite of its modern military, it continues to be basically a defensive power. The possibility that Japan could rearm itself offensively very quickly if the United States-Japan Security Treaty ever fails is of concern to Japan's Asian neighbors.[8] Japan has even been called a virtual nuclear power because of the general consensus that Japan has the technology and resources to develop, produce, and deploy nuclear weapons in a relatively short period of time.[9] The questions being asked by those who study Japan are these: Where is Japan, as a nation, headed in relation to its role in the world? Does Japan wish to be a great power again? How will its role in the United Nations be perceived by its neighbors?

Japan's neighbors, China and South Korea in particular, have voiced concern over Japan's new, more activist approach to foreign policy, and more significantly, there are a large number of internal domestic questions as well. The *New York Times* noted in an editorial that "Japan is slowly overcoming decades of reticence about building and using military forces. This change in attitude carries important implications for Asia and the United States."[10] Some, like Professor Emeritus Kazuo Ota of Rakuno Gakuen University,[11] wonder whether there is a clear, coherent, and definite agenda to Japan's foreign policy or whether it is merely a reflection of the norms of the foreign policy of democratic states.[12] Will Japan's foreign policy swing to domestic demands? How important are domestic concerns to the formation of Japanese foreign policy? Will domestic fears of war and militarism prevent Japan from becoming a hegemon? Critics have alleged that the PKO Law is just a pretext for securing the legitimacy of the SDF by invoking the name of the United Nations and capturing Japan a place in superpower diplomacy.[13] There is a strong fear that if the government is permitted to use the SDF as a tool in its foreign policy, Japan will repeat the mistakes of its past.[14] The *New York Times* in August 1999 wrote: "[I]in recent months, Tokyo has shown a new willingness to stand up to North Korean bullying, deflect criticism from China and involve itself in regional defense arrangements."[15]

This chapter will start to deal with these questions within the larger issue of whether Article Nine violates the sovereignty of Japan and prevents Japan from acting as a sovereign nation (or as a normal nation). We will start this process by examining the historical background of the Japanese "Peace" Constitution and Article Nine. Next, Japan's Cold War foreign policy will be addressed. In chapter 4, the Gulf War and its impact on Japanese foreign policy will be examined as the causal change agent for the redirection of its foreign policy. This discussion will be followed by a view of the political and legal issues surrounding the PKO Law and the Japanese quest for a permanent seat on the U.N. Security Council. It is in this context that the potential for Japan's role as a world leader will be stressed in particular.

Historical Background

In the closing days of World War II, the Allied leaders met in the Berlin suburb of Potsdam to plan for the post-World War II world. During this meeting, they issued the Potsdam Declaration, which set forth the terms for the surrender of Japan as unconditional and laid out the goals for the occupation of Japan. The primary purpose of the occupation "was to eliminate the authority and influence of the old order that had misled the Japanese people into a war of conquest, with a view toward establishing a new order of peace, security, and justice."[16] The Allied policy declared:

The ultimate objectives of the United States in regard to Japan, to which policies in the initial period must conform, are

a. To insure that Japan will not again become a menace to the United States or to the peace and security of the world.
b. To bring about the eventual establishment of a peaceful and responsible government [which] should conform as closely as may be to principles of democratic self-government but *it is not the responsibility of the Allied Powers to impose upon Japan any form of government not supported by the freely expressed will of its people.*[17]

It is important to note that the Potsdam Declaration wanted popular reforms that would last beyond the occupation. The Allies, though, were determined to destroy Japan's dominant "military establishment with a new constitution that imposed a new relationship between the people and their leaders."[18] Many historians consider the ability of the military to control the Cabinet to have been the major defect of the Meiji constitution.[19] General MacArthur believed that the Japanese themselves should come up with the constitutional reforms of the Meiji Era constitution, but he put a high priority on reform of the constitution (called *kenpou* in Japanese) by requesting that the government draft a revised constitution.[20] This push for the alteration of the constitution seems to reflect the belief that if power were placed in the hands of the people, Japan would no longer be a threat, the idea behind this democratic objective being what the democratic peace theory would later postulate: that democracies do not fight each other.[21] The will of the people is the primary factor in any democratization effort. John Mensing, commenting on Japan's occupation and democratization, wrote: "[The evidence] clearly shows how democratization, or the promise of it, was embraced by the Japanese people as a benefit for themselves, as something that many people aspired to, or quickly recognized as something they desired."[22]

The first draft of the revised constitution presented to the occupation authorities by the government of Japan was totally unacceptable to General MacArthur and his staff; it contained only cosmetic changes of no real substance, and it made no real changes to the old order of elite control. The requirements of the Potsdam Declaration would not have been fulfilled under this draft.[23] After a second attempt by the Japanese government resulted in only further cosmetic changes, General MacArthur ordered his staff to draft a model constitution for the Japanese government to follow.

It is in this model draft that Article Nine first appeared. The exact origin of Article Nine is unknown and may never be known.[24] Many have incorrectly assumed that it came from General MacArthur and the victorious

Allied powers. It is virtually certain that it came neither from official Washington sources nor from internal political debate within Japan, but rather from less official sources.[25]

The importance of the origin of Article Nine centers on the question of whether it violates Japanese sovereignty and prevents it from acting as a truly sovereign nation. If Article Nine is of Japanese origin, it is not a violation of Japan's sovereignty because it represents a feeling that emerged from Japanese representatives, even if it came under the occupation. On the other hand, if its origin is with the United States and the victorious Allied powers or General MacArthur, then it does violate Japanese sovereignty, in the sense that Japan is not and was not able to determine its own destiny as any truly sovereign nation has the right to do. This second possibility does not mean that Article Nine should automatically be revoked. If it has gained the support of the majority, its current status reflects the will of the people.

Such would seem to be the case given the current interpretation by the government and courts of Japan.[26] I would also argue, based on the evidence presented by the late Colonel Charles Kades, a member of the government section of General MacArthur's staff, and Kenzo Takayanagi, the distinguished chairman of Japan's Commission on the Constitution, that the origin of Article Nine is indeed Japanese. Kades makes a strong case, and Takayanagi's research concurs, that Article Nine was suggested to General MacArthur by then Japanese Prime Minister Kijuro Shidehara during a private meeting. Takayanagi wrote:

> Shidehara behaved as if Article 9 were proposed by MacArthur, although he never clearly said so. If he had said that the proposal was his and not MacArthur's, it might have been rejected by the Cabinet. Shidehara was diplomatic enough to know this. So Cabinet Members who attended the meeting, including Yoshida and Ashida thought that the proposal was made by MacArthur and not by Shidehara. After this [Cabinet] meeting, Shidehara told a number of his close friends that "Article 9 did not come from abroad" and that it was his own proposal. Neither Yoshida nor Ashida was aware that the original proposal was made by Shidehara. They thought, as I did at the time, that it was imposed by the Allied Powers. These events account for the difference between Ashida's public statement at the plenary session and his private opinion in his pamphlet, and Yoshida's written memorandum sent to the Commission on the Constitution which denied that the article was Shidehara's.[27]

Kades goes even further by noting the possibility that Article Nine may have had its origin with Emperor Hirohito himself and Shidehara merely passed on the emperor's idea.[28] Major General Frank Sackton, USA (Ret.), then Col. Frank Sackton, who was one of MacArthur's chief aides during the occupation and was also present in SCAP (Supreme Command/Commander Allied forces-Pacific) headquarters during the writing of the constitution, has a contrary opinion on this issue. In an interview, General Sackton stated that he believed it must have been MacArthur who had written Article Nine because it fit MacArthur's personality to do something that had never been tried before, such as taking away a state's right to wage war. General Sackton disputed the idea that the emperor could or would have come up with such a radical idea, one that would potentially undermine Japanese power in the future. Furthermore, General Sackton stated that he doubted that Shidehara could have come up with such a radical concept by himself because he lacked the "intellect" for such an original idea.[29] This is possible, but in hindsight, Article Nine is arguably the most significant element of the constitution. However, its significance would have been very difficult to predict. Problems with the limitations imposed on Japan by Article Nine cropped up as early as 1950, with the Korean War. The United States wanted to rearm Japan and it could not, because it failed to adequately foresee the Cold War when it permitted Japan to have Article Nine as part of its constitution.

It is important to note that during the occupation, the Japanese leadership wanted to limit as much as possible the damage to elite political institutions. At the same, time the Allies, grateful that they had been spared the need for an invasion of the Japanese home islands, feared losing control of occupied Japan to a popular uprising if they instituted radical changes that upset the populace.[30] It is for this reason that SCAP, under MacArthur, desired to keep the imperial system. It was feared that if the imperial system were abolished, the people would revolt. At the same time, the Allies wanted to strip the elites of their power and to place it in the hands of the people. In many ways, they were attempting to play the people against the elites.

Japanese leaders, on the other hand, feared that SCAP was planning to abolish the imperial throne, knowing that after Japan's surrender, the people were fairly ambivalent toward the imperial system. This is a classic case of both sides not knowing the intentions and fears of the other. Had they understood the American fears, the Japanese leadership might not have been as willing to make the proposals and concessions that the leaders did.[31] They are unlikely to have proposed Article Nine to MacArthur. It is more likely that it was the result of a maverick individual (such as Shidehara or a person close to him who gave him the idea) or small group than its conception by any consensus within the Japanese leadership. At the same time, it is strange that if MacArthur did author Article Nine, he did not mention such a radical idea to anyone before proposing it. But given MacArthur's personality,[32] it is not unthinkable that he could have come up with the idea. The occupation government put a similar constraint to the people of Japan that Article Nine does to the nation as a whole when it took away the right to personal self-defense from Japanese citizens, which has also remained a part of Japanese law since then.[33]

In summary, Kades does note, and Sackton agrees, that no one knows for sure where Article Nine came from.[34] It was just assumed for many years that it was a United States/MacArthur product, when in reality it was not something that the victorious Allies had planned in any formal way.

A second argument as to the legality of Article Nine is that the whole constitution was imposed on Japan against its will and that thus the Japanese need not abide by it. The imposition of a constitution against the will of the Japanese *people* was never the American intention at all from MacArthur's point of view. The will of the Japanese people was foremost, in this regard, in the minds of the occupation forces. They realized that unless the reforms enacted were reflective of the will of the Japanese people, they would be useless once the Allies ended the occupation and left. For this reason, MacArthur's staff emphasized very clearly to the Japanese government that this draft was not being forced on the Japanese. Evidence of this assurance is contained in a memorandum by Jiro Shirasu who was present when General Courtney Whitney presented the government section's draft of the proposed constitution. Shirasu summarized General Whitney's remarks as follows:

a. The Japanese Government draft has been rejected as "totally unacceptable."
b. The SCAP (Supreme Commander for the Allied Powers) draft is "acceptable" to all the Allied Nations and to SCAP.
c. *This draft is not being forced on Japan.*
d. The United States believes the Japanese people *want* this draft.
e. SCAP has supported the Emperor. This draft supports the Emperor and is the only way for protecting the Emperor System from those opposing the Emperor.
f. It is better if the Japanese conservatives moved far to the left.[35]

Genkichi Hasagawa, who was also present at the meeting, concurred with this summary in his notes when he wrote, "Whitney said neither the form nor the contents were being forced on Japan. . . . He said he believed the SCAP draft met the wishes of the Japanese people."[36]

This last point, involving the will of the Japanese people, is of primary importance in understanding Article Nine and its origins. The Japanese cabinet originally resisted the SCAP draft and Article Nine, but General MacArthur threatened to take the draft directly to the Japanese people if the Diet refused to consider it. This insistence demonstrates how much the Allies had tapped into the popular mood of the nation. They had every confidence that the

Japanese people wanted this constitution, which would permit them to have a measure of control over their government that they had lacked before. The Japanese people were sick and tired of the horrors of war that they had suffered and were eager to renounce war and the military.[37] Alfred Oppler, who was involved in the reforms of the occupation, wrote: "One only had to read the newspapers and speak to the man on the street . . . to realize that there were powerful movements among the people of enthusiastic support of Occupation objectives."[38]

These occupation objectives were established in the new constitution as fundamental principles. John M. Maki of the University of Massachusetts, in his introduction to *Japan's Commission on the Constitution: The Final Report,* notes these components that have made the Japanese constitution an enduring constitution. They are:

1. The three basic principles of the constitution: popular sovereignty, pacifism, and the guarantee of fundamental human rights;
2. No single crippling defect in the constitution surfaced;
3. The constitution is functioning effectively in practice as a fundamental law for Japanese society based on the principles of democracy;
4. No matter what the outcome on the question of revision, one inevitable result would be a deep scaring of the body politic;
5. No revision, whether on a large or small scale would be quick or easy.[39]

There are probably other reasons for the constitution's stability and almost certainly foremost among these reasons is that it captured the hearts and minds of the people who were weary of war and desired peace, especially the peace that was offered by Article Nine.[40]

Further specific support for Article Nine is shown in a poll taken by the *Mainichi Shimbun* newspaper in May 1946. The poll found that 70 percent of those polled supported Article Nine and the renunciation of war. Only 28 percent opposed it.[41] Tesu Katayama, who would later become prime minister, told a plenary session of the House of Representatives that the reason that the Socialist Party was endorsing the new constitution was that "sovereign power is in the hands of the people," and because of Article Nine, which "has by no means been given or dictated from outside but is an expression of a strong current of thought which has been running in the hearts of the Japanese people."[42]

During the Diet debate[43] on the new constitution, several changes were made to Article Nine, with the consent of SCAP. First was the total ban on self-defense that would have clearly outlawed the current SDF. The second was the Ashida Amendment, which in essence opened the door for the SDF in the future by adding the phrase "In order to accomplish the aim of the preceding paragraph" to Article Nine. This extra wording made it possible for the formation of the SDF as long as it did not violate the previous line about the right to war being renounced. Self-defense became an option. It is important to note that the purpose of the ambiguous language in the Ashida Amendment was not clear to those who voted for it or for the new constitution.[44] Many at this time thought that Article Nine banned the military forever. When asked why Japan had not expressly reserved the right to self-defense, then-cabinet minister Yoshida noted,

> Of late years most wars have been waged in the name of self-defense. This is the case of the Manchurian Incident, and so is the War of Greater East Asia. The suspicion concerning Japan today is that she is a warlike nation, and there is no knowing when she may rearm herself, wage war of reprisal and threaten the peace of the world. . . . I think that the first thing we should do today is to set right this misunderstanding . . . it cannot be said there is no foundation for that suspicion.[45]

It is very important to note this lack of provision for self-defense as well as the absolute outlawing of self-defense because with the outbreak of the Cold War and the Korean War, the priorities of the United States and its requirements from Japan changed drastically. The United States wanted Japan to provide for its own self-defense and to ally itself with the United States against the Communist bloc. This idea caused a domestic debate within Japan to break out; one that is continuing to this day over the constitutionality of this issue. General MacArthur from his command of the United Nations forces in Korea and again in his memoirs stated that he had never intended the Japanese to be without a means of self-defense.[46] But as Kades notes, what General MacArthur and those in the occupation forces thought was no longer as relevant as it had once been and is currently totally irrelevant. However, Japan is a sovereign nation and it is *its* interpretation of *its* constitution under *its* laws and courts that is relevant.[47]

Still, the San Francisco Peace Treaty of 1952 had yet to be signed, and the United States, in its role as the principal occupying power, instructed the Japanese to organize a 75,000-man National Police Reserves (NPR) in 1950. This organization was, in reality, a mere disguise for a new Japanese army, according to Colonel Frank Kowalski of the United States Army, who as Deputy Chief of Civil Affairs (1950–52) assisted in its organization.[48] The NPR was justified as being essential to internal security following the transfer of SCAP forces to Korea.

The hurried signing of the San Francisco Peace Treaty ended the occupation of Japan a decade earlier than originally planned. The United States wanted to make Japan into a Cold War ally and cajoled many other nations into signing the treaty without fully dealing with all the leftover issues of the war that continue to haunt Japanese foreign policy to this day. Issues such as a formal apology to its neighbors in East Asia for World War II and compensation for "comfort women" forced into sexual slavery during the war. The term "comfort women" was a euphuism used by the Japanese military during World War II to describe women (mostly Korean and Chinese but including some Western women interned or held prisoner by the Japanese) who were forced to work as sexual slaves to "service" Japanese soldiers before going into battle. In recent years some of the surviving women have come forward with claims against the Japanese government for their mistreatment during the war. To this date, Japan claims that the peace treaty ended all claims for reparations from the Japanese government and some within Japan have gone so far as to claim that the women were all volunteers. The treaty was, at best, a rushed effort by the United States, reflecting the realities of the Cold War at the time and left many issues unsolved, both known and unknown at the time. Several war criminals who had escaped capture and thus punishment were able to return to their lives in Japan without fear because of the treaty.

Japanese Foreign and Security Policy 1952–1990

Challenges to the SDF

In April 1952, the NPR was renamed Japanese National Safety Forces (NSF), headed by Prime Minister Yoshida himself. The NSF contained both ground and maritime elements. In 1954, with the passage of the Defense Agency Establishment Law, Japan began building the Ground Self-Defense Forces, and the NPR received its third name, the Self-Defense Forces, or SDF, as it is known today.

Each of these incremental changes was challenged in the courts and in the public arena of debate as violating the constitution and Article Nine. The Japanese public recognized, on the one hand, the need for self-defense because of the Korean War. On the other hand, the Japanese passionately disapproved of any military capability that could be deemed offensive in nature.[49] Pacifism had taken root in Japanese culture. Royer cites an example of this in a note by Fukui that stated:

> Pacifism represented and popularized by Article 9 rapidly developed into a *popular cult*. Pacifism became the object of fervent devotion among large

> numbers of Japanese. It became deeply instilled in their hearts incomparably faster than did any of the democratic principles of government also proclaimed by the new Constitution. During and immediately following World War II, the people of Japan experienced destruction, hunger and death directly, physically and personally, not just abstractly and intellectually. Thus, the post-war Japanese were emotionally devoted to the ideal of *peace at almost any cost.*[50]

In an interview, Jiro Kodera advanced this argument when he described the Japanese people as believing that peace simply exists and that one need not fight in order to have it. Kodera described the Japanese people (in general) as being so pacifist that they largely had no concept of the work and vigilance it takes to maintain peace.[51] While this may be an overstatement, it illustrates that pacifism is the norm in Japanese culture. Another example of the Japanese people's devotion to the principles of pacifism contained in Article Nine occurred when Prime Minister Ichiro Hatoyama tried to gain approval for amending the constitution in 1955 by calling a general election. The left and right wings of the Socialist Party successfully united and prevented any attempt at amending the constitution by winning over one-third of the seats in the Diet. It is important to note that the constitution has yet to be amended or revised since its original form adopted in 1947.

After this event, successive governments have refrained from attempting to amend the constitution; rather, they have reinterpreted the constitution to fit the needs of the times. The result has been a greater and greater liberalization of the meaning of "self-defense" capabilities and "offensive" capabilities (see the earlier quote from Prime Minister Yoshida). What was defined as offensive capability by one cabinet may not reflect the opinion of another cabinet's interpretation of "self-defense." An example would be when Director General Jungo Kimura, who succeeded Yoshida in the Safety Ministry, was asked to name something that would be definitely forbidden as constituting "war potential." Kimura replied that "[a] jet airplane would constitute war potential."[52] Kimura had no idea that by the 1980s the Air Self-Defense Forces would be flying the F-15, the most advanced fighter in the U.S. Air Force at the time.[53] Times had changed and so had the interpretation of Article Nine.

Another example is the well-known cabinet policy statement of 1967, which announced the "three non-nuclear principles." Japan pledged that it would not possess, manufacture, or permit nuclear weapons to be brought to Japan.[54] What is not so well known is the 12 March 1959 statement that was made by Prime Minister Nobusuke Kishi to the House of Counselors: "The Government intends to maintain no nuclear weapons, but speaking in terms

Photo 2.1 **Japanese F-15 Fighter** (*Source:* U.S. Air Force photo by Airman 1st Class Justin Weaver. www.af.mil)

of legal interpretation of the Constitution there is nothing to prevent the maintaining of the minimum amount of nuclear weapons for self-defense."[55] A week later the Kishi Cabinet issued an official statement that read:

> In the event that an attack is waged with guided missiles and there are no other means of defense, counter attacks on enemy bases are within the scope of self-defense. With the right of self-defense retained as an independent nation, the Constitution does not mean for the nation to sit and do nothing and await its death.[56]

With each broadening or change in the interpretation of Article Nine came a new challenge to the government from the left-wing political parties and from individuals, often in the form of court challenges to the constitutionality of the SDF. The Japanese courts, in deference to the government, have consistently upheld the constitutionality of the SDF.[57] Lower courts have, at times, ruled the SDF to be unconstitutional, but all of these decisions have been overturned by higher courts or the Supreme Court (the *Saikosaibansho,* in Japanese).[58] Under the Meiji constitution, the Japanese court system was responsible to the executive. The new constitution tried to separate judicial and executive power, but to a large extent, it has failed in reality.[59] The use of judicial review is scant, and the *Saikosaibansho* has made no attempt in the last forty years to establish itself as an activist court, especially in the area of constitutional issues.[60] This situation has resulted in the government's having nearly free rein in the area of constitutional interpretation. The conservative LDP's uninterrupted rule from 1958 to July 1993 and from June 1994 to the present has offered consistency to this arrangement; one party was continuously interpreting Article Nine.

The Yoshida Doctrine

As a nation without the ability to go to war or to threaten war, Japan had to adapt its foreign policy to the limitations imposed on it by the constitution. One of the founders of the LDP was Prime Minister Yoshida. It was Yoshida who first discovered that Article Nine could be used in Japan's favor.[61] With the presence of United States forces and nuclear umbrella to protect Japan and the constitutional ban on (offensive) military forces, Japan was free to pursue rapid economic development without the added economic weight of having to maintain a standing military that would drain resources badly needed to rebuild the economy. This became known as the Yoshida Doctrine and essentially permitted Japan to be a "free rider" living in the shadow of American security and the U.S. nuclear umbrella throughout the Cold War at no real cost to itself. Japan had only to maintain a minimal level of self-defense capability in order to please the United States while most of the time following the United States lead in foreign policy.[62]

The key component of this arrangement is the United States-Japan Security Treaty, which was first signed in 1952 and revised in 1960 amid great controversy and debate within Japan. The two versions are, in essence, two totally different treaties, even though the 1960 version is only called a revision of the original treaty signed during the occupation. The 1952 version essentially gave the United States carte blanche access to Japan for military purposes. The 1960 version required consultation between the two nations and was much more equal in nature. The United States-Japan Security Treaty is Japan's only formal military alliance,[63] making the United States Japan's only formal ally. The treaty has taken on an increasingly vital role in the maintenance of peace within the Pacific Rim and can be compared in importance to NATO for the United States.[64]

The Security Treaty helps to alleviate fears within the Pacific Rim of a remilitarized Japan, especially among nations that were occupied by Japan during World War II. The reasons for these fears touch on potential future problems for Japanese foreign policy and will be discussed in later chapters.

It is important to note the role of the United States in the process of the formation of the SDF into its current state. U.S. pressure is an issue that runs throughout the formation of Japanese defense and security policy. Japanese politicians have been able to explain many of their bolder actions regarding the SDF by referring to pressure from the United States.[65] This "American pressure" is called *gaiatsu*. This can literally be translated as "pressure from the outside" and is a common term in any newspaper report on the subject.[66] Thus, the official Japanese explanation for many of Japan's defense and security policy decisions is essentially that "the Americans made us do it."[67]

As the strain of the Cold War grew, the Americans were "making Japan do" more and more in terms of its own defense. Even with the 1 percent GDP limitation by 1990, the size of the Japanese economy raised the Japanese defense budget to the third-largest in the world, behind the United States and the former Soviet Union's.[68] The Japanese SDF is, currently, one of the most modern and well-equipped forces in the world—in a nation that is not even supposed to have an army, navy, or air force when one interprets its constitution in the most literal sense. The LDP has always managed to "amend" the constitution by reinterpretation[69] and created an armed force that exists even though it is severely limited in what it has been authorized to do.

The limitations on the SDF will be discussed in the following chapter, but the question of sovereignty arises whenever one mentions that the "Americans made us do it." I would argue that if Article Nine is of Japanese origin (and I believe that the evidence indicates that it is), then it can be said to represent the antimilitarist, antinationalist aspirations in Japan. The militarist, nationalist elements within Japan could be said to have been at their weakest during the occupation period. The popular imposition of constitutional reform, including Article Nine, by the Allied powers, serves as a check on right-wing nationalistic forces within Japan. Foremost in people's minds, in the immediate postwar period, was a prevention of a repeat betrayal by political and military leaders. So much was sacrificed during World War II for nothing but defeat and humiliation in the end. The left wing, which best represents, in the political sense, the fears of a reappearance of military expansionism, has been able to use the opportunity created by Article Nine to its advantage in preventing a repeat of the mistake of World War II. It has done this by inhibiting the SDF, so that it can never become the war machine that the imperial armed forces were. Thus, Article Nine does not represent a loss of sovereignty; rather, it is a domestic check against the potential rise of militarism in Japan once again.

For over sixty years, Japan has, in essence, attempted to live within the spirit of Article Nine. The choices that it has made regarding the SDF reflect the choices of a sovereign nation. The United States might have influenced these decisions, but in the end, they were the decisions of a popularly elected government about what it believed to be best for Japan. With the end of the Cold War, many things changed for Japan. The following chapter will look at how the Gulf War shaped changes in Japan's foreign and security policy.

3

The Gulf War Requires Change

The purpose of all war is ultimately peace.
—Saint Augustine

On June 15, 1992, the Japanese Diet passed *The Law Concerning Cooperation in U.N. Peacekeeping and Other Operations* (otherwise known as the
PKO Law), and it went into effect on 10 August of that same year. This law
marked the most significant change in Japan's postwar foreign and security
policies since the creation of the Self-Defense Forces (SDF) in the 1950s.
When interpreted narrowly or at face value, the constitution would seem to
prohibit the maintenance of any military forces. The sending of SDF troops
overseas was an extremely controversial change in policy for the Japanese
government. The fact that this law was passed in spite of Japan's constitutional renunciation of war was a direct response to the political fallout of the
Persian Gulf War. In this chapter, we will look at the politics behind this
radical shift in Japanese policy and some of its long-term implications, such
as the demise of the Yoshida Doctrine.

The Gulf War and Japanese Foreign Policy

Politically, the Gulf War took Japan by surprise, "like a bolt out of the blue."[1]
Iraq's invasion of Kuwait on 2 August 1990 and the war had a major impact
on the politics of Japan,[2] which was forced to face the reality of its economic
superpower status for the first time in an international crisis. Japan's foreign-
policy establishment sprinted out of the blocks at the start of the crisis, only
to stumble and be left dazed and bewildered when it realized that the Cold
War was over and that the rules had changed. Japan was asked to participate
at a level that was equal to its economic status in the world, and Japan was
not ready to do so. Japan's checkbook diplomacy caused it to be severely
criticized abroad. The Yoshida Doctrine, which had served Japan so well,
was in need of revision. At the core of the problem was the old constitutional
question of Article Nine. Could Japan send troops overseas even if they were
under United Nations command? Japan was not ready to answer this question, although the world was waiting for an answer. Japan was still in the

middle of trying to come to terms with the end of the Cold War and its impact on the United States-Japan Security Treaty. Japan was searching to find its place in the world when the Gulf War forced it to make some hard choices. These choices, though inadequate in the eyes of many, started a debate within Japan that has made it come to better terms with its economic superpower status and its constitutional obligations. How Japan reacted to the Gulf crisis gives us an enhanced insight into the foreign-policy debate on this issue and into the overall foreign-policy-making process within Japan.

Japan's historical relations with the Middle East before the late twentieth century were almost nonexistent. Japan's first major foreign-policy crisis with the Middle East was the 1973 oil crisis and the OPEC oil embargo. Its second encounter was the 1980 oil crisis. Neither of these crises affected Japan militarily. The Gulf crisis was different in that Japan was expected to be a full-fledged partner in the war efforts.[3] The Japanese government did not want to go this route, instead wishing to contribute in other ways, primarily financial.

It is to Japan's credit that it was unusually swift in responding to the invasion of Kuwait by initiating its own economic embargo against Iraq even before the United Nations did so. This move is in contrast to the way Japan stumbled through almost every other issue that it dealt with during the Gulf War.[4]

The first stumble that Japan made was when the United States called on its allies to support and contribute to the Gulf crisis/war effort in any way possible. Japan initially pledged $400 million to the effort. This was raised a few days later to $4 billion, but not before the damage was done. The question was, "Why not $4 billion in the first place?"[5] Japan was perceived as being stingy. Japan, which imported 90 percent of its oil from the Middle East, had more at stake with the potential loss of oil imports than most Western nations, yet it was perceived as willing to make only a token contribution. The final financial contribution pledged by Japan toward the Gulf effort was $13 billion, making Japan the second-largest financier of the war behind Saudi Arabia, but the earlier image of tokenism remained.

In the meantime, President George H. W. Bush was using his now famous style of telephone diplomacy to raise a multinational force. For the first time, Japan was asked to make a military contribution. Before the Gulf crisis, no Japanese politician had ever voiced the idea of SDF serving overseas.[6] Now, it was receiving intense *gaiatsu* from the United States and the international community to send troops to the Gulf. Japan needed to make a "human" contribution, not just a financial one, to the maintenance of international order.[7] If other nations were sending their men and women to fight and possibly die in a foreign war, then it was reasonable that Japan should do the same as a nation that benefited more than most from Persian Gulf oil.

The problem was Article Nine and domestic opposition, both in the Diet and in the public in general, to involvement in any kind of military conflict. It would prove to be a very difficult decision for the government to make. It was a no-win situation for Prime Minister Toshiki Kaifu,[8] who was basically faced with three choices:

1. Recognize the constitutional prohibition against sending troops abroad imposed by Article Nine and refuse to participate militarily in the Gulf.
2. Make sending troops abroad for U.N. purposes legal by enacting a constitutional amendment [very difficult if not impossible].
3. Make sending troops abroad for U.N. purposes legal by extra constitutional means; that is, amending the SDF law or enacting a new deployment-authorization law.[9]

Kaifu chose the third option. On 27 September 1990, he announced a plan to send a "United Nations Peace Cooperation Team" to Saudi Arabia. This team would be made up of "civil service personnel and members of the Self-Defense Forces."[10] Its purpose was to sidestep Article Nine by creating a non-SDF contingent to send to the Gulf. What the government could not do was sidestep popular opposition. On the day the proposal was submitted to the Diet, 23,000 people gathered in protest.[11] The bill had to be withdrawn from the Diet in November of that year, but it served as a forerunner to the PKO Law, which was passed two years later.

In the end, Japan was able to send only minesweepers to the Gulf conflict after the fighting had ended. This maneuver was accomplished by reinterpreting the constitution to permit the Maritime Self-Defense Forces to protect Japanese (and, in reality, other) shipping in the Gulf from mines sown by the Iraqis. This small flotilla performed very well in Japan's first overseas "military" venture since the end of World War II.[12] The seeds were sown, though, for changes in Japan's foreign, security, and defense policies.

The Peacekeeping Operations Law (PKO)

The Gulf War or crisis made Japan rethink its foreign, defense, and security policies. This rethinking led to two bills being brought before the Diet. The first was the Kaifu Bill, which failed and the second was the bill brought by his successor, Kiichi Miyazawa. Both bills generated an intense debate that in many ways continued for years after the law passed. This debate, both in the domestic and the international sphere, asks what Japan can and should do in maintaining international order and stability. Aside from the question of the overall constitutionality of the SDF, the question that needs to be asked is whether the fears of a rearmed Japan were justified. Even the Socialists (SDP), who traditionally pledged to dismantle the SDF, gave up their pledge when they were part of the coalition Morihiro Hosokawa government in 1993 and 1994 and when their leader, Tomiichi Murayama, became prime minister in the summer of 1994. Not only did they not push for dismantling, they did not even push for scaling back the SDF. Rather, they moved to formally accept it as legitimate.

Legal Issues

The legal issues that surround this debate center on how far one can stretch the interpretation of Article Nine's ban on military forces. They also address Japan's legal obligations to the United Nations. In the 1950s, Japan had a stated United Nations-centered diplomacy upon which it wished to base its foreign policy. The problem is that the United Nations Charter requires members:

1. to be "a peace loving state";
2. to "accept the obligations contained in the present Charter"; and
3. to be "able and willing to carry out these obligations."[13]

Of importance to this discussion is the requirement to "carry out these obligations" because two of these obligations are:

1. "All Members shall give the United Nations *every assistance* in any action it takes in accordance with the present Charter"; and
2. "the Members of the United Nations *agree to accept and carry out* the decisions of the Security council in accordance with the present Charter."[14]

Japan's constitution runs into direct conflict with these provisions when it comes to military peacekeeping and enforcement of United Nations Security Council resolutions. In the past, Japanese cabinets have stated that they could not participate in United Nations' peacekeeping or peacemaking efforts. After the Gulf War, this situation changed. Driven by the desire to make a human contribution and to normalize Japanese foreign policy, the conservative LDP actively sought to legalize Japanese participation in U.N. peacekeeping efforts. To accomplish this end without violating the constitution, the PKO law needed to guarantee that the SDF peacekeepers sent from Japan would not be involved in any situation that would require the use of force. The ban on the use of force even included the ability to participate if other U.N. peacekeepers come under fire. This ban does not prevent *individual* SDF troops from shooting back if they come directly under fire during a U.N. peacekeeping effort because this "use of weapons" in self-defense would be justifiable.[15] To achieve the goal of never having the SDF use their weapons, five conditions were set down in the PKO Bill to minimize the chances of the SDF's becoming involved in a conflict that would require the use of force. They are:

1. Agreement on a cease-fire shall have been reached among the parties to the conflict.
2. The parties to the conflict, including territorial State(s), shall have given their consent to the deployment of peace-keeping forces and Japan's participation in such forces.
3. The peace-keeping forces shall strictly maintain impartiality, not favoring any party to the conflict.
4. Should any of the above guideline requirements cease to be satisfied, the Government of Japan may withdraw its contingent.
5. The use of weapons shall be limited to the minimal necessary to protect personnel's lives, etc.[16]

This policy has its strong critics, who claim that the legalization of SDF participation in U.N. peacekeeping is nothing less than an attempt to mobilize the SDF on the international stage. Making contributions to the international community is not the primary objective but rather a secondary one, according to these critics.[17] The primary objective would be to finally shake off the constraints of Article Nine by making the SDF a *fait accompli* on the world stage. These critics represent the fears of those within Japan who feel that Japan has not learned from its past and is attempting to travel down the road toward militarism again. Under the postwar constitution, the tendency of Japan has been to revert back as much as possible, under the restraints of the new constitution, to the old Meiji constitutional style of governing. The Meiji style of governing being to centralize power with a select elite rather than the people as democracy demands. This tendency has been strongly evidenced in the development of bureaucratic politics in Japan during the postwar era.

The left wing of Japanese politics, which has spent most of the last fifty years out of power, worries about the desire of the right wing to control the SDF and to use it as a tool of Japanese foreign policy if it gains status as a military again. Thus, at the core of this issue is whether civilian control of the SDF can be maintained during peacekeeping operations[18] and whether Article Nine will be rendered null and void by the deployment of the SDF overseas. One way of dealing with this problem was by the placing of SDF troops solely under U.N. command and control during all stages of peace-keeping operations. It can be argued that Article Nine can remain in effect and Japan/the SDF can participate in U.N. peacekeeping operations if under U.N. command.[19] Thus, Japan can contribute but does not have to exercise power over its contribution. This would prove to be the best course for Japan to follow with respect to inter-Asian relations and domestic politics. Any attempt to revoke Article Nine for the purpose of greater participation would bring instability and friction to all of the above with unpredictable consequences.

Many critics of government attempts to weaken the constitutional controls on the development of armed forces see Article Nine as a check on the Japanese political system. This check, not intended by its framers, is a product of practices within the Japanese political system. Article Nine prevents conservative forces within Japan from establishing a military power base. The ability of the left to prevent the revocation of Article Nine prevents conservative forces from the total domination of Japanese politics and creates a balance of power between the left and the right. The majority of the PKO Law critics come from within Japan, but many are also from without; which brings us to the next debate.

International Politics and the PKO

Western nations basically do not fear Japan militarily, but many Asian nations have concerns based on their own historical experience with Japanese militarism. Western nations would prefer that Japan be an active player in the world scene, while many inside Japan and Asia feel that Japan is not ready for this role. With regard to Japan, the world can basically be divided into those who believe that Japan has something to offer the international community and those who do not. There are those who trust Japan and those who do not.[20] Japan's aggression during the 1930s and early 1940s left deep scars in many of the Pacific Rim nations of East Asia.

China is a prime example of this attitude. When LDP General Secretary Obuchi Keizou visited China in August 1991 seeking understanding for the PKO Bill, Chinese Communist Party General Secretary Jiang Zemin indirectly voiced his concern by calling on Japan to educate its people about the enormous harm the Japanese military caused China.[21] Prime Minister Kiichi Miyazawa met with a similar reception in January 1992, during a visit to Seoul. South Korea's president, Roh Tae Woo, stated that, while he understood the reasons behind the PKO Law, many nations would like to see Japan focus on economic contributions and nonmilitary assistance. The Philippines has also expressed concern that the PKO legislation would nudge Japan toward militarism.[22]

Of those who supported Japan's efforts to legalize the overseas deployment of the SDF for peacekeeping, the most prominent in Asia was Cambodia's premier, Hun Sen. Cambodia wanted SDF participation in UNTAC (United Nations Transitional Authority-Cambodia) under U.N. control. This was the only case of outspoken support for Japan within Asia with the exception of Malaysia and Thailand.[23] Japan has been urged to make a "human" contribution to world peace and stability, and because of its past history, is having to proceed very cautiously as not to upset its Asian neighbors. Singapore's senior minister and former prime minister, Lee Kwan Yew, expressed the feelings of Asians and condensed the international debate on this issue when he spoke at a February 1992 business seminar in Kyoto. He said, "unlike the Germans, Japan has not been open and frank about the atrocities and horrors committed in World War II. By avoiding talk about it, the victims suspect and fear that Japan does not think these acts were wrong, and that there is no genuine Japanese change of heart."[24]

The Political Debate

The Japanese government's first attempt under Prime Minister Toshiki Kaifu to legalize the sending of troops on U.N. peacekeeping activities failed miserably, both in the Diet and with the public. The second attempt a year and a half later, under the new prime minister, Kiichi Miyazawa, was able to pass the Diet, but it took the actual deployment of SDF troops to begin the process of public acceptance of the SDF's new role.

The Kaifu Bill and Why It Failed

Against the backdrop of heavy *gaiatsu* from the United States, the first peacekeeping bill was presented in September of 1990. The Kaifu Bill, as it is now called, was basically doomed from the start. There were so many questions about it: Did it violate the constitution? Does it permit the SDF to exist? Can the SDF be sent abroad? Will the SDF be able to use force?[25] These questions and others made the bill extremely unpopular. Only 12.2 percent of the population supported the bill, with over 66 percent of the population opposing it.[26]

Prime Minister Kaifu made four major mistakes in attempting to make a human contribution to the Gulf War or crisis.[27] The first was that he miscalculated how strong popular opposition to the bill would be. The Japanese people in general, based on their severe experience in World War II, wanted nothing to do with sending their sons to any kind of armed conflict. During his questioning on the bill before the Diet, Kaifu was at times at a loss to explain what the SDF would do in certain situations. The government also made several flip-flops in its policy position. These reversals were perceived as waffling and further alienated those who opposed the bill.

The second major mistake was that Kaifu was overly hasty in submitting a bill of this magnitude. He broke the conventional practice of making decisions based on broad consensus. He was attacked for this haste by both the opposition and his own party. Japanese decision making takes time and is quite unlike the presidential system in the United States, where decisions can be made quickly.

Kaifu's third mistake was to base his position on cooperation with the United States. Kaifu and the foreign ministry seemed to be focusing only on pleasing the United States, giving the appearance that Japan was a puppet of the Americans. The problem was that in the court of American public opinion, American soldiers were ready to defend international justice (and Middle East oil) with their lives and all Japan had was its checkbook.

The fourth major reason the Kaifu Bill did not pass was that the prime minister failed to provide firm guidance. If the bill had been explained well and clearly to the nation and the Diet, it might have been able to garner support. As it was it was destined to fail. It was withdrawn from consideration in November 1990 without ever having been voted on.

The Miyazawa PKO Bill

In December 1991, the new prime minister, Kiichi Miyazawa, submitted a revised PKO Bill to the Diet. This time the consensus of the Diet was not ignored. The LDP needed support from one or two of the opposition parties to get the PKO Bill through the House of Counselors, where it did not control a majority. The LDP was able to secure an alliance with the Democratic Socialist Party (DSP) and *Komeito* (Clean Government) parties. The Socialists, on the other hand, were doing all they could to stop the bill. The government made sure that the final version of the bill did not require future Diet approval for PKO missions.[28]

The bill was railroaded through the House of Representatives as the opposition tried to stall the vote. In July 1992, the bill was introduced into the upper house. The opposition tried every possible maneuver to stall the vote. In the end, it resorted to "ox walk" tactic, which delayed the vote for several days and was shown in the international media.[29] The bill passed in the end and became law a few days later, when it was passed by the lower house.

The final law was a compromise, and it has many flaws that will make life difficult for the SDF, though many of these flaws have subsequently been eliminated in future laws reauthorizing and amending the PKO Law every three years. It is, though, a dramatic change for Japan and one that was debated (but not at the same intensity) again in July 1995, when the law came up for the required three-year review. The final draft of the law has ten basic provisions, which are:

1. The prime minister does not need Diet approval to send the SDF to take part in activities such as transportation, communication, construction, international humanitarian assistance, election supervision, administration, and police functions.
2. SDF participation in activities such as monitoring cease-fires, supervising the disarmament or withdrawal of troops, patrolling a buffer zone, defining a cease-fire line, and assisting in the exchange of prisoners is frozen until separate legislation is passed authorizing such activities.
3. When the freeze is lifted, the prime minister must receive Diet approval each time he wishes to send the SDF to engage in activities outlined in point 2, which clearly carry the risk of armed confrontation and shots being fired in anger.
4. Local conditions must be conducive to the success of the peacekeeping operation: a cease-fire must be in place and the parties involved must accede to the participation of the SDF.
5. The peacekeeping operation must be politically neutral. It cannot be at the service of any party to the dispute.
6. When the government wishes to extend a peacekeeping operation beyond a two-year limit, it must seek renewed Diet approval.
7. No more than 2,000 personnel will take part in either type of peacekeeping operation.
8. In unavoidable situations, personnel on peacekeeping missions can only use small arms to defend themselves "within a rational limit dictated by circumstances."
9. The government must review the entire law within three years.
10. Without Diet approval, the government may use SDF trucks, ships, and planes for humanitarian purposes in connection with a peacekeeping operation, such as refugee evacuation. It may also sell to the United Nations goods necessary for peacekeeping operations at lower than market levels, or it may donate these goods outright.[30]

The First Three Missions: Cambodia, Mozambique, and the Golan Heights

Japan's first two U.N. peacekeeping assignments were to Cambodia and Mozambique respectively. The third is an ongoing mission to the Golan

Photo 3.1 **Prime Minister Koizumi Speaks to SDF Troops on a UNPKO Mission in East Timor** (*Source:* Photo courtesy of the Office of the Cabinet Public Relations, Cabinet Secretariat, Japan)

Heights. In Cambodia, the SDF worked for UNTAC and earned high praise as a professional force.[31] During the time Japan was in Cambodia, two Japanese were killed. One was a civilian worker and the other was a policeman. There were fears at the time that this would lead to calls for the withdrawal of Japanese peacekeepers. It generally did not. In fact, general public support started to grow as it began to better understand the nature of peacekeeping. A certain level of national pride began to grow among the Japanese public because Japan was finally making a human contribution to world peace.

The operation in Mozambique also went well, and there was no loss of life. Japan continues to volunteer for future peacekeeping roles, but only those that fit its rules. One such mission is the current ongoing one to the Golan Heights and a subsequent mission in East Timor.

An example of the rules Japan has placed on its SDF forces is that (until recently) under Japanese law, officers and non-commissioned officers (NCOs) were not permitted to order their troops to fire or withhold fire. This rule effectively prevented the SDF troops from acting as a unit in any combat situation, thus destroying their effectiveness. The reality of the situation was that the commanders in the field ordered their troops to fire only when ordered to do so. If an incident occurred, the field commanders took full responsibility for violating Japanese law. The field commanders were told by their superiors that they would be protected as much as possible but that they might have to take the fall if the incident caused a backlash.[32] No incident ever took place, and in the spring of 1999 the Japanese Diet amended the law to permit its troops to act as a normal military unit for self-defense.

It is important to note that originally, the government decided that the SDF would participate in "peacekeeping operations" only and not with "United Nations-authorized" forces, such as the coalition deployed for the Gulf War or UNITAF (United Task Force) in Somalia.[33] However, in order for Japan to help out its American ally in Iraq, Prime Minister Junichiro Koizumi deployed the SDF to Iraq to help rebuild the country after the United States–led invasion. Japanese troops serving in Iraq have come under attack on several occasions but have not needed to fire back. Both Dutch and Australian forces have been deployed (with much controversy in their own countries over this "babysitting" role) to keep the SDF safe and out of direct combat.

However, in spite of all the restrictions, the SDF have thus begun their transformation from a defensive force within the United States-Japan Security Treaty to the force of a nation that is sharing the task of guaranteeing international security.[34] With the PKO Law, Japan as a nation has come a long way toward normality, but it still has a ways to go if it chooses to stay on the same path that it has been traveling.

Toward a Security Council Seat and Beyond

The Gulf War gave Japan the excuse to do what had been unthinkable since the end of World War II: send troops overseas. Japan has now expanded this newfound freedom into a desire for a permanent United Nations Security Council seat. Japan has sat on the Security Council as a nonpermanent member nine times, and it currently holds that position.[35] To gain a permanent seat, the Charter of the United Nations would need to be amended and the support of all five current permanent members gained. Of these, only China has expressed opposition to Japan's elevation to permanent-member status. The other four have at varying times expressed open support for the election of Japan to this elite group, and numerous regular members of the United Nations have expressed support for Japan. However, vocal opposition by China and South Korea has put a strong damper on Japan's aspirations. Japan is currently trying to bypass China's opposition by linking its efforts to the so called G4 nations (Japan, India, Brazil, and Germany), all of whom are also seeking permanent membership on the Security Council in the next round of expansion or reform. The problem for each G4 member is that each as a strong opponent with veto power over any reform.

The fact that Japan is being considered for this position is testimony to

Japan's economic power and influence internationally. Domestically, on the other hand, power and influence are split. Japan is a much divided country. Some political observers have called this condition "divided politics" or "cultural politics."[36] The division was strong in the postwar years but has weakened in recent years. There are two basic platforms. The right-wing policy platform has stressed:

1. Alliance with the United States, greater expenditure and role for [the] Self-Defense Forces, and anticommunism.
2. National identity, traditional morality, and the emperor.
3. Production, efficiency, and innovation.
4. Protection of and subsidies to socially weak sectors.

And the left-wing policy platform has stressed:

1. Neutrality or nonalignment, light defense posture, and antihegemony nationalism.
2. Civil freedom, egalitarian norms, and democracy.
3. A better working and living environment and protection of consumers.
4. Social welfare, education, and public expenditure.[37]

Since the end of the Cold War, this basic political divide has been undergoing dramatic changes as the political parties search for new ground. The election for the lower house of July 1993 shattered the LDP's long hold on power and led to electoral reform in Japan designed to make the system more fair and to permanently break the LDP's stranglehold on power. Succeeding elections have been under the reformed electoral system, and if there is one thing that the LDP is good at it is finding a way to win elections. When it has not had an absolute majority in one or both houses, the LDP has been able to hang on to power through a series of coalitions. On September 11, 2005, Prime Minister Koizumi led the LDP to a landslide victory by promising reform. When Koizumi's postal-reform bill failed to pass in the Diet, he called a snap election. Most political observers described his actions as political suicide; however; Koizumi defied the odds and won a resounding victory over the main opposition, the Democratic Party of Japan (DPJ).

What direction the next government will take in foreign policy is also open to speculation. Japanese hawks and such nationalists as Ichiro Ozawa and Shintaro Ishihara are clearly committed, along with Prime Minister Koizumi, to making Japan as powerful and as assertive a nation as possible on the world stage. They seek respect and power for Japan, though probably not through foreign conquests as in the past.[38] As those with like-minded opinions are elected, Japan will continue to take on a more assertive role on the world stage.

This possibility brings us to another question: is Japan to be feared? It can be expected that, combined with Western pressure and the softening of public opinion against *all* military action, the principles of pacifism, which have begun to erode, will continue to fade. While nationalist remilitarization of Japan is probably not likely to occur, it is important that we not ignore the possibility. As several commentators have noted, it is possible that the Japanese know their own national psyche better than we do, and it would be important to listen to them.[39] An example of Japanese fears of the military outlook of some members of the SDF is given by Yoshitaka Sasaki. He recounts:

> A telling dinner conversation of a few years ago between admirals of the Maritime Self-Defense Force and the U.S. Navy exposed the thinking of members of Japan's military circle. According to well-informed sources, the U.S. admiral proposed that Japan build a large hospital ship. Why not dispatch the ship off the coasts of areas around the world stricken by natural disasters or armed conflicts and have doctors trained at the National Defense Medical College treat those affected, he suggested. The Japanese admiral instantly retorted: If we had the money, we would build an aircraft carrier.[40]

Until Japan's economic crisis of the last fifteen years, many, both inside Japan and internationally, saw Japan as a potential future hegemon, to replace a seemingly declining United States. A disturbing side effect of this assumption is the way renewed military conflict between the United States and Japan is often portrayed in the Japanese media and in *manga*, or comics, that are read by so many Japanese.[41] Given the sporadic fractious nature of United States-Japanese relations that usually surround trade issues, if the current United States-Japan Security Treaty were to be abandoned, there is the possibility (however small) of hostile Cold War-like conflict developing between the United States and Japan. In trade disputes that have strong nationalistic undercurrents, both sides have demonstrated that they are capable of demonizing the other.[42] Posturing by both sides may leave no room for either to back down or compromise.

It is not in Japan's (or the United States') best interest to see conflict of this nature arise. Neither is it in the interest of Japan to see a premature decline of the hegemony of the United States in the near future.[43] Japan depends too much on the *Pax Americana* or the hegemonic stability that the United States currently provides the world. Japan is in much the same position as it was before World War II. The nation imports raw materials and exports finished products; if this flow is interrupted, there is little that Japan can do about it by itself except to appeal to the United States. The SDF just does not have the global reach needed to keep the sea lanes of communication (SLOCs) open.

Japan's economy can easily suffer from international instability. Japan is especially vulnerable to the loss of Middle Eastern oil, because it imports over 90 percent of its oil needs. This vulnerability is in many ways no different from the sanctions that Japan faced before its attack on Pearl Harbor in World War II. U.S. sanctions on Japan in 1941 for its actions in China, cutting off oil to Japan, were causing its economic collapse and undermining, if not destroying, its military efforts in China.[44] The same vulnerability exists today; Japan needs open SLOCs. Furthermore, Japan has one major potential adversary in East Asia—China. China is developing the capability that could threaten or interrupt Japan's trade. Japanese national security needs and economic needs can thus be said to be synonymous. Japan is in no way ready to take on the role of a hegemon *at this time* or in the foreseeable future. It still needs and desires that the United States continue to be engaged in East Asia as a protector of East Asian stability and its own economic well-being. The risk of going it alone outweighs any benefit of total independence from the influence of U.S. hegemony.

There are many questions that can be asked about the debate over what Japan can, should, and will do. Questions such as: Why all the debate? Why all the fuss about Japan's doing what any normal sovereign nation should be able to do any time it wants to—that is, contribute to global security through the United Nations? In the end, everything really comes down to two questions that many, both inside and outside of Japan, ask: Has Japan learned from the outcome of World War II, and What has it learned? Can Japan be trusted to act as a civilized nation and not resort to militarism again? The answer to this last question is probably "Yes," but there are obviously doubts about the correct answer inside Japan.

There are also concerns about this possibility abroad. Much of the concern comes from the failure of Japan to come to terms with World War II in a public way. Japan needs to deal with this situation and accept the facts of its history. It will be difficult to do so, given the Japanese reluctance to admit that mistakes were made by their predecessors and the fact that many of Japan's senior political leaders served in World War II or had friends and loved ones who died during the war. There is a generational issue here; to admit that Japan was wrong would be to admit that the Japanese who died during the war died in vain. Thus, confronting the past will cause severe embarrassment and loss of face. This situation is compounded by the need to admit to wrongs committed against Korea and China, whose people, many conservative Japanese feel, are racially inferior to Japanese.[45] Japan has yet to make amends with its neighbors who suffered horrendously under the heel of Japanese military occupation during World War II.

Furthermore, Japan needs to come to terms with its own people, especially its children, about the events that transpired during the war. Germany has done penance for the crimes of the Nazis during World War II, teaching their young people so that history will not be repeated. All German schoolchildren are taught about the Nazi past. In Japan, little is taught about Japanese imperialism.[46] Thus, the youth of Japan do not know of the past; thus, the fear of its Asian neighbors.[47]

There is also the ongoing issue of history textbooks, which whitewash the atrocities committed by Japan during World War II. The Ministry of Education has recently been approving these textbooks for use in Japanese public schools. Only a handful of Japanese school districts within Japan have elected to use these controversial texts that rewrite history; however, their approval has caused diplomatic tensions between Japan and South Korea and China, and the books have come to symbolize Japan's lack of remorse for World War II. Annual visits by various prime ministers and cabinet members, including Prime Minister Junichiro Koizumi, to the Yasukuni Shrine where several "class A" war criminals are enshrined, have sparked anti-Japanese riots in China and protests in Korea. These visits serve no purpose in enhancing Japanese foreign policy. However, they do cater to the sentiments of the right wing of the ruling LDP's political base.

In essence, Japan needs to apologize, not necessarily to the United States, but to the nations of East Asia. The United States was attacked by Japan and in the ensuing war, defeated and occupied Japan. Anything that the United States needed from Japan in the form of an apology should have been achieved during the occupation. Furthermore, the United States does not place a strong cultural significance on apologies. This is not so with the nations of Asia that Japan invaded. Culturally, Asia needs an apology because the East Asian nations better understand the cultural significance of an apology from Japan. Without an admission of guilt there can be no forgiveness for the past, and without forgiveness, Japan will never have credibility as a normal nation. The Japanese government's use of the SDF will continue to have strong opposition both at home and abroad. James Auer, director of the Center for United States-Japan Studies at Vanderbilt University and an expert on United States-Japan foreign policy and defense issues, feels that "[u]ntil Japan truly comes to grips with its global responsibilities; it will continue to find itself unable to obtain the prestige of a permanent Security Council Nation."[48]

The absence of an acceptable national apology for its actions in World War II is hindering Japan's foreign policy. Many in Japan's foreign policy community seem to have an "ostrich with its head in the ground" mentality about the need for an apology. Ryozo Kato, former director general of the Foreign Policy Bureau of the Ministry of Foreign Affairs (MOFA) and current ambassador to the United States, is typical. In the context of discussing the late Iris Chang's book, *The Rape of Nanking,* he stated, "If we can just hold off [apologizing] for ten to twenty more years, everyone who lived through it [World War II] will be gone and it will all be forgotten."[49] This was said at the same time that the former Yugoslavs were killing each other in a centuries-old conflict whose instigator no one can remember but that each side wants to end on its own terms. If Japan allows the generation that committed and suffered the atrocities of World War II to die off with no apology, then future apologies will ring hollow to succeeding generations.

It is interesting to note that younger Japanese politicians tend[50] to desire that Japan apologize now rather than later, so that they can rid themselves of this burden. They see the lack of an apology as a hindrance to Japanese foreign-policy goals. Politicians who espouse this attitude include Councillors Kei Hata and Ichita Yamamoto.[51] The older generation sees a sincere apology as anathema, even if it is better for current foreign policy and for future generations for them to apologize to those who survived the atrocities of Japan's war of conquest and colonization in Asia. The reason why it is better for the World War II generation to apologize, rather than leave the apology to future generations, is that if the generation who suffered under the Japanese can forgive those who committed the atrocities, then it will be much more difficult for future generations to hold Japan responsible for actions that the victims themselves forgave.

If Japan wants to claim any moral leadership, it is important to offer a sincere apology—not the kind of "apology" the Diet issued on 6 June 1995 in Tokyo. This resolution used the word *hansei,* which means "reflection" or "remorse," much the way school kids might express themselves about forgetting to do their homework. Neither the word nor the resolution gives any indication of who is responsible or who should be sorry. The words *kokai* and *shazai,* which mean "remorse and regret" and "apology" respectively, were not used.[52] Only 230 Diet members out of 511 voted for this resolution, which was a political compromise forced through the Diet by the Socialist prime minister, Tomoiichi Murayama. The resolution did not express the acceptance of responsibility that is needed by Japan's World War II enemies. Japan did apologize in a more sincere way in the fall of 1998 to South Korea for actions taken during its long occupation of the Korean Peninsula; however, the textbook situation and ongoing Yasukuni Shrine visits have undermined much of the goodwill established by the 1998 apology, which came out of the necessity to work with South Korea as an ally in dealing with North Korea as a "rogue" state.

In conclusion, Japan is a sovereign nation that must make its own decisions, and these carry their own consequences. Japan is searching for respect among nations. To achieve the ends of those within Japan who wish to see Japan take a leadership role, the very thing they do not want to remember must be dealt with. Japan, as Germany did, must come to terms with its history if it wants to reclaim its sovereignty in the minds of others. The hardest thing in this context is the need to humble itself about its past and apologize. Japan is very good at getting what it wants politically over time because of its general farsightedness. If this farsightedness is combined with the needs of the community of nations, Japan may receive the respect it seeks.

Japan is currently caught between the West, which expects it to show leadership, and East Asia, which objects to its leadership. Japan needs to show the world that it is willing to learn from its past and apply those lessons to the future. Japan is not likely to become a superpower, but it is more likely to continue to be a great power. The PKO is just the beginning for Japan. Many people in Japan fear the PKO Law because they are not confident that their will is reflected in its democratic institutions. The Japanese government needs to bring its people into the decision making process if they really want to be a sovereign nation that is united in purpose.

The need to bring the Japanese people into the decision-making process is based on the fact that MOFA has bureaucratic control of the foreign-policy-making process that has limited the role of the elected Diet in directing foreign policy. In a democratic society, foreign-policy decisions should reflect the will of the people or their elected representatives, not the wishes of an unelected elite serving in MOFA. MOFA controls much of the decision-making process because of a general lack of interest by Diet members in foreign affairs. However, interest in foreign policy is developing with a new younger generation of Diet members who are taking a more active hands-on approach to foreign policy. The next several chapters will look at this restructuring trend, among others, in order to explore current developments in Japan and its prospects for the future in East Asia and the world.

4

Theoretically Speaking

Realism and Alternative Security

> *We are in a period of profound change in*
> *international relations and foreign policy.*
> —Charles F. Hermann[1]

In any study in political science and international relations, it is important to place ideas and observations of state behavior in the context of theory. This chapter will place this case study of Japan in the context of the established international-relations and foreign-policy theories. Political theory helps to explain the reasons why nations make the choices that they do, and it helps us to better predict state behavior. The chapter describes Japan's adaptation to the changes brought about by the end of the Cold War through the application of a foreign-policy-restructuring model developed by Charles Hermann. The model is applied to Japan's foreign-policy restructuring after the Cold War.

This chapter will also look at the alternative security choices that Japan faces because of the limitations imposed on it by Article Nine. Observed reactions to field interviews with Japanese foreign policy makers themselves will also be examined in detail. The overarching purpose of this chapter is to build the theoretical framework for the rest of the book. Detailed analysis of the overall direction of Japanese foreign policy and conclusions are saved for the final chapters.

Any study attempting to understand Japanese foreign and security policy since World War II must recognize the impact of Article Nine of Japan's constitution. It cannot be underemphasized, since the article gives up Japan's "right" as a sovereign nation to wage war and maintain a military.[2] The realities of the Cold War and the world we live in required Japan to "interpret" Article Nine to permit self-defense. This revised view led to the creation of the Self-Defense Forces (SDF) as a form of traditional security. The problem for Japan, particularly in the post-Cold War era, is how to employ the SDF without violating the constitution.

Given the constitutional limits placed on Japanese security in the post-

Cold War world, Japanese security policy has grasped at nationalist elements within Japanese society in attempts to "securitize" itself by means of a foreign policy independent of the United States. While the political right in Japan has proved more capable than the political left of securitizing its issues, most of these attempts give Japan little more than a psychological feeling of pride rather than any true security benefit in the classical sense. However, when looked at in the wider sense of alternative security, Japan is making gains in terms of its security situation.

The following section will review Japan's limitations.[3] This will be followed by a review of what is meant by alternative security and securitization, based on the study by Buzan et al. We will next examine theoretical foundations of Japanese foreign policy by looking at what international-relations theory teaches us about the way states behave when they are faced with potential threats. Specifically, the chapter will examine the difficulties Japan faces in dealing with potential threats in traditional ways as a result of the limitations Article Nine imposes on Japan.

As stated previously, Japanese foreign policy revolves around the interpretation of Article Nine of the constitution. Nothing in Japanese foreign policy can be understood without a fundamental understanding of what is considered constitutional under Article Nine. Over the years, Japan has managed to modify its constitution through reinterpretation rather than through the more traditional method of straightforward amendments. To date, the constitution and Article Nine have managed to establish themselves as sacrosanct, and any serious attempt to amend Article Nine is likely to result in a political uproar that the Japanese government does not want to see.[4] As mentioned in chapter 2, this rigidity is largely because Japanese bureaucrats and politicians tend to be sensitive to public displeasure because of the Asian cultural desire to have a balance in the *wa*.[5] The *wa* is the cultural concept of balance and harmony in one's public and private life that is so important in many Asian cultures. Direct public conflict is not desirable. Politicians strive to maintain a balance, which means the absence of open conflict. Establishing a consensus is important. Public support—or rather, the lack of opposition—is crucial for too many Japanese politicians.[6] Nevertheless, it is important to note that while political consensus is helpful, it is not always required—witness the passage of the original PKO law. The public supported the LDP's efforts in general because the Social Democratic Party of Japan's (SDPJ)[7] "ox walk" tactics backfired when the international broadcast of the tactic caused national embarrassment. The result was a solidification of Japanese public support for the LDP on this issue, regardless of personal feelings about the PKO Bill, and a silencing of those who opposed the bill as a result of the embarrassment.[8]

Japanese Limitations

As a nation, Japan is realistic about its political power. It cannot ever truly hope to compete with the United States one-on-one in any meaningful way. Japan simply does not have the resources or the population to be a true hegemon. That is, it does not have the ability or resources to both seize power and to maintain it. Japan is a great power, but not a superpower. One of the reasons for this situation is that the same problem that plagued the country during World War II is still with it today: Japan is a country that is poor in natural resources. It is therefore required to import raw materials and to export finished products, something that it is very good at, given Japan's status as the second-largest economy in the world. However, Japan's economic status may be short-lived as other nations, such as China, are poised to surpass it in the near future.[9] Part of the problem is that Japan's population is aging at a remarkably rapid rate. Within the next few years, over half of Japan's population will be over sixty-five. Japanese live longer than any other nationality in the industrialized world; life expectancies for men and women are eighty-two and eighty-six years respectively. Japan is already facing the severe financial task of providing retirement incomes and medical care to a growing population of retirees, who are living longer and longer after retirement. The Japanese social-security system is projected to run out of funds by 2010.[10] Fewer and fewer workers are supporting those on government pensions. At the same time, Japan has the highest debt ratio of any developed nation; the government is deep in debt. In 2005, Japan's population began to shrink as recorded deaths surpassed recorded births and immigration in number for the first two quarters of the year. This situation had not been projected to happen until 2007 at the earliest. Local government officials are struggling to find ways to create incentives for Japanese families to have more children, but so far, they have not had much success. Japan must already import foreign workers to do "dirty" jobs that Japanese will not do. This importation of workers may also begin to change the social structure of Japan as Japanese intermarry with foreigners, diluting Japan's racial homogeneity. Japan has also begun to expand its industrial base overseas, partially because of the lack of workers at home.[11]

There will be a tremendous burden on the youth of Japan to support its aging population, especially when the ratio of workers to retirees is projected to reach 1:1.4 by the year 2020.[12] Japan has more citizens over the age of sixty-five than under the age of fifteen.[13] The Japanese people themselves are acutely aware of the problem. Eri Kimura, aged twenty-three, who works in insurance sales, is an example of how the younger generation is worried about Japan's future because of its aging population. She says, "The number of young people paying for the older generation is causing a strain on our taxes. . . . And the number of children being born is decreasing so it's become a serious burden."[14]

Technology has given Japan the ability to be a powerful nation, but it does not give it the global military reach that is needed by a true hegemonic power. So many Japanese couples have only one child or are choosing not to have any children that Japan's already shrinking population is expected to contract to less than 100 million (from the 128 million today) within the next century. With so few children to grow up to serve in the armed forces, Japan, like the United States (for different reasons), is likely to be very risk-averse.[15] Japan's primary vulnerability is not to invasion, but to interruptions or the closing of the sea lanes of communication (SLOCs). Japan must trade to survive and prosper.

Japan does not now, and will probably never, have the resources to be a world power (in the traditional sense). Japan is much better served by working as a great power within the world community and using its economic strength as the basis of its power. Japan will continue to have conflicts with the current hegemon, the United States, but these disputes should remain moderate in the larger scope of things.

Since World War II, Japan, recognizing its own limits, has remained in the shadow of the United States through its judicious use of the Yoshida Doctrine. With the end of the Cold War and the unwillingness of the United States to permit Japan to continue to be a free rider and to use its position under U.S. hegemony to its economic advantage, Japan must decide what role and position it should hold in the world. At the same time, there are those within Japan on the right wing, such as former LDP member Ichiro Ozawa, who advocate a more independent Japan. There are even some in academia outside of Japan, such as Professor Chalmers Johnson, who advocate a more independent Japan, free from the constraints of the United States-Japan Security Treaty and the U.S. military presence that comes with it. There are also those on the left, such as the traditional old guard in the SDP and the Japan Communist Party (JCP) who desire the same outcome, but they envision a more neutral or isolationist Japan rather than an activist or assertive one.

The obvious reality is that across the political spectrum, Japan does desire a more independent or autonomous role in international security and is caught between what it desires and its constitutional restraints. A major problem for a more independent Japan is that it has no friends in the region, only rivals. However, Japan has an extraordinary advantage because of its one-way security relationship with the United States. It is to Japan's economic benefit to stay as close to the United States as possible. One might even go so far as to describe Japan as being addicted to its relationship with the United States under the Yoshida Doctrine. It can be compared to a benign addiction, as one might have to chocolate, rather than to drugs or alcohol. One can stop eating chocolate at any time—but why stop, when it tastes so good and gives one so much pleasure?

The difficulty for Japan is that it needs an active and, in many ways, more independent foreign policy to show that it is a great power, capable of independent action. As mentioned previously, Japan has an increasing industrial presence overseas, and it needs to protect it. Traditionally, nations have used military power or the credible threat of military intervention to protect foreign economic interests. Japan will need a more dynamic foreign policy to protect its interests for which it currently depends on the United States. Milton Ezrati writes in *Foreign Affairs:*

> A more active foreign policy will become unavoidable as the overseas expansion of Japanese industry establishes connections in the rest of Asia that Japan will need to secure. Though such a move goes against present Japanese instincts, no nation, including Japan, can afford to locate its production facilities abroad and not develop the capability to at least threaten to project power to protect those sources of wealth. This new security perspective will be all the more radical because it will run counter to Japan's long standing reliance on U.S. protection of Japanese interests.[16]

The problem for Japan is the constitutionality of power-projection capability. Japan depends on the United States to protect its interest overseas because of Article Nine and the Yoshida Doctrine. When U.S. interests and Japanese interests coincide, this arrangement works well. As Japan and the United States find themselves competing against each other for world markets, and as the United States finds itself increasingly distracted by the war on terror, Japan will need to develop constitutionally acceptable options to protect its interests.

Part of the problem for Japan, if it takes on a more independent role, is that Japan derives so many benefits from its relationship with the United States that losing this relationship would cause Japan immediate hardship, even if it can somehow be beneficial in the long run. Cutting itself loose from the United States would force Japan to radically change its foreign and security policy, but it would not necessarily make Japanese foreign policy any better or the nation more secure.

The following illustration should help to clarify Japan's options. The American "father" is trying to raise the Japanese "son."[17] The father, having raised the son, can set the son loose at "eighteen" and allow the son to become independent, or the father can continue to support, educate, and nurture the son into a more equal relationship/partnership.

The son, on the other hand, can choose independence, or he can continue to permit himself to be nurtured. This quandary raises the question of whether the son, if he permits himself to be nurtured, will become an equal partner and a united force with the father, in a bond that makes them stronger than either would be alone. Alternatively, the son can remain dependent on the father and never truly become independent. Thus, the son would be a proverbial "loser" who has no real ambitions and never leaves the nest; Japan is clearly not in this category.

If the son chooses independence, he makes his own way in the world. While he becomes independent, he is free to rejoin the father at any time, provided that the reunion or reconciliation is mutual. A historical example of this situation is the Anglo-American relationship, in which the United States fought for and won independence from the British, but during the course of two world wars the United States established a "special" relationship with Britain through a common heritage that eventually led the British to acquiesce to United States hegemony. This peaceful transfer of power is historically unprecedented, and in my opinion it represents a bond of culture and heritage that made or helped to make the British see the transfer of power as something that was acceptable because power remained "in the family."

In the United States-Japan relationship, the situation is more abstract. There is no common language, culture, or heritage. In many ways, one can hardly find two more different nations. There is, however, a common recent history, particularly since World War II, when the United States gave Japan its democratic process and institutions and helped to promote and develop Japan's capitalist economic system.[18] The United States-Japan Security Treaty cemented this "adoptive" relationship in which the United States took a willing (Yoshida Doctrine practicing) Japan under its wing and helped it to rebuild.

Japan is now at a choice point of whether it stays with the United States or goes its own way. Within Japan, the debate on this issue is rising. There are activist governors, such as the former governor of Okinawa, Masahide Ota, and the current governor of Tokyo, Shintaro Ishihara, who want the United States military out of Japan or at least to remain with a greatly reduced role.[19] The ruling LDP and MOFA are inclined to stay with the current United States relationship, but they have failed to chart, in many ways, a coherent course for the continuation of the United States-Japan relationship. The September 1997 Guidelines, which attempted to clarify the relationship and responsibilities of both Japan and the United States under the treaty, are in many ways a temporary patch but not a long-term course change or strategy. In many ways Prime Minister Koizumi has tightened Japan's relationship with the United States through his close personal relationship with President George W. Bush.

Photo 4.1 **President Bush and Prime Minister Koizumi Throw a Baseball for Reporters at Camp David** (*Source:* White House Photo)

Nevertheless, there are very few within Japan who have articulated a long-term direction for Japanese foreign policy, and no one in a position of direct leadership has voiced international goals for Japan over the long term (five to ten years in the future). The only prominent new goal Japan is pursuing is its quest for a permanent seat on the U.N. Security Council and a continued use of the SDF in international missions in noncombat roles.

In field interviews with MOFA officials, most of those interviewed demonstrated a clear lack of even moderate-range (three to five years) goals for the future.[20] Exceptions to this reluctance were the former minister of defense, Hideo Usui, Councillor Keizo Takemi, and Ukeru Magosaki, director general of the Intelligence and Analysis Bureau of MOFA, who articulated specific objectives. Representative Usui's goal is to start a serious debate on foreign and security policy issues. He stated his desire for me to interview others in leadership positions (more on this below) because he felt that the questions would make others in leadership positions think about Japan's choices in a changing world and realize that Japan's future foreign policy was of interest to others outside of Japan.

Councillor Takemi expressed a desire to make the Diet a source of foreign-policy debate. He is focusing on educating his fellow Diet members on foreign-policy issues by bringing them into the foreign-policy-making structure through the use of committee hearings. He is also working to change the structure of the committee system in the Diet by adding subcommittees to facilitate this objective.[21] Director General Ukeru Magosaki's paper, "New Diplomatic Challenges in East Asia" (1998), is an overview of Japan's position in the post-Cold War era and an analysis of Japan's future foreign policy options.[22] While Japan is currently content to continue its close relationship with the United States, it is exploring alternative security possibilities. The following section describes what is meant by alternative security and its potential for Japan.

Alternative Security

Barry Buzan et al., in their 1998 book, *Security: A New Framework for Analysis,* examine the "wide versus narrow" debate in security analysis.[23] The "wide" debate deals with the tendency of some to view everything as a security matter. An example would be the "War on Drugs" in the United States, in which stopping the flow of drugs into the United States is viewed as a matter of national security. The "narrow" debate focuses almost exclusively on traditional military concerns, such as the balance of forces and the need to protect the territorial sovereignty of the state. This chapter examines the "wide" debate in relation to Japan's security policy. The basic argument is that, by focusing on the "narrow" traditional security issues, we will find it difficult to come to a fuller understanding of Japanese foreign and security policies. However, Buzan et al. caution against the "intellectual and political dangers of simply tacking the word security onto an ever wider range of issues."[24] There needs to be a balance in any examination of nontraditional security issues. Thus, there is a requirement for some kind of connection or thread to traditional security issues that links to the alternative issue. Issues relating to traditional security concerns will largely be ignored in this section (except as they link to alternative issues) to allow us to focus on the alternative issues that are important to Japanese security. According to Hans J. Morgenthau, traditional security encompasses protection of a state's people, territory, and economy from outside attack.[25] For Buzan et al., alternative-security issues can be much more wide-ranging (with the caveat about the need for caution against attaching security to too many issues). Issues involving environmental, societal, and political sectors can be incorporated as critical security issues. Furthermore, domestic economic issues that are not subjected to traditional international threats can and should also be included in what Buzan et al. call the securitization process. Buzan et al. describe securitization as "the exact definition and criteria of securitization is constituted by the intersubjective establishment of an existential threat with a saliency sufficient to have substantial political effects."[26] To put it simply, a security threat exists when and if the state recognizes or perceives the threat in a way that has political consequences. For Buzan et al., the danger lies in looking at security in too narrow a perspective. Traditional approaches to security, as well as alternative approaches, must be incorporated in any examination of security. However, security is much more than any specific threat or problem. Such threats or problems may be only political in nature.[27]

It is also important that the issues being securitized are perceived as security issues both by those inside a state and by those outside it. An issue is not securitized until it is accepted as securitized, both internally and externally. The previously mentioned "political consequences" thus need to be apparent both domestically and internationally. Furthermore, there needs to be a "speech act" in which an issue is securitized. The danger must be spoken of in terms of the threat that, if not dealt with, will potentially cause harm to the state. This harm can be ad hoc or institutionalized. However, according to Buzan et al., an issue has not been successfully securitized until those on the outside have perceived the speech act as securitizing the issue. There also needs to be a consideration of the side effects of securitizing an issue that may lead to making the issue a greater threat than previously assumed. In these situations, desecuritization may be the ideal choice.[28] That is to say that the state may want to proclaim that a previously announced threat is no longer a threat. A historical example of this type of desecuritization would be the World War II alliance between the United States and the Soviet Union. The previous nontraditional threat from the ideology of Communism was abandoned because of the need to deal with the immediate and mutual threat of Nazi Germany.

When looking at alternative security issues, we must recognize that the nation-state does not exist in a vacuum. In terms of security, a nation-state is part of the larger community of states with which it interacts politically, economically, culturally, and adversarially. It is common to perceive these sectors as being independent rather than interdependent. To consider a wider security agenda, we must consider the interlinking of the security sectors and the ways they affect the overall security of the state. Splitting the sectors into their own subunits is helpful for analysis but troublesome when one needs to examine a state's overall security environment.

Alternative security issues have been made ever more important as the result of the erosion of Western military, economic, and political power by the forces of globalization. Protecting the state is not the same as it once was. Classical security issues of military comparison between border states may be a thing of the past. Relations between states over a host of issues that can be securitized are now normative in their application. As Buzan et al. state, "All of the states in the system are enmeshed in a global web of security interdependence."[29] However, insecurity is often associated with proximity because of the fact that security threats do not travel well.[30] States worry more about their neighbors than they do about distant potential threats. This circumstance creates what Buzan et al. call "security complexes," which are regionally based clusters "whose security perceptions and concerns are so interlinked that their national security problems cannot reasonably be analyzed or resolved apart from one another."[31] These security complexes are "miniature anarchies" that operate as a fully functional subset of the larger system.[32]

When we look at Japan in light of the arguments of Buzan et al., we can see that Japan sits in what may be called a Northeast Asian security complex. The players in this security complex are Japan; China, including Taiwan; the two Koreas; Russia; and the United States. How these players have reacted and are reacting to Japan's securitizations efforts are of vital importance. The primary focus of alternative security analysis in this and subsequent chapters will be the domestic economic securitization of Japan and the economic subsets of rice and the environment in the Sea of Japan. The political and foreign-policy issue of Japanese commercial and research whaling in light of alternative security, and Japan's efforts at tsunami relief in Southeast Asia, will also be looked at. However, before focusing on these issues, we need to examine what international-relations theory tells us about Japan's situation and the limits placed on Japanese policy by Article Nine. International-relations theory can teach us about what a state hopes to *gain* by the process of securitization and its motives for engaging in the process of alternative security.

The Theoretical Foundations of Foreign-Policy Restructuring

The question is whether Japan can *politically* restructure its foreign policy. And if it can, the form it will take. As to the question of whether Japan can restructure its foreign policy the answer is easy—Yes, it can. There is general consensus, particularly within the Diet, that Japan needs to be doing something, but the form of that something is a matter of debate. Some of the more charismatic Japanese political leaders have clear ideas about a more independent Japan. Examples are former LDP politicians, such as Ichiro Ozawa, whose ideas are expressed in his book *Blueprint for a New Japan: The Rethinking of a Nation*,[33] and Shintaro Ishihara, who wrote *The Japan that Can Say "No."*[34] The problem is that often many of these "charismatic" foreign-policy agendas concentrate on immediate gains and (in many ways) petty gratification while long-term implications are not addressed.[35]

As the late former American speaker of the house, "Tip" O'Neill, once said, "All politics are local" and Japan is no exception. The slogan widely used during President Bill Clinton's 1992 campaign, "It's the economy, stupid!" rings true in Japan as well as in the United States.[36] Economic welfare and domestic needs drive voters in Japan just as they do in the United States. As one MOFA official depressingly put it, "the voice for foreign policy change *will* come from those who emphasize domestic politics *first.* This is probably a mistake and against Japanese interests and it could even be a disaster for Japan."[37] The implication here is that the Japanese voter will elect political leadership that will solve Japan's domestic economic problems, regardless of those leaders' foreign-policy agenda. The fear on the part of the MOFA official is that an ideologue could seize the foreign-policy reins and take Japan in an ill-conceived direction that would risk Japan's standing in the world by pursuing personal gains at the expense of absolute gains for the nation. An example of such a disaster could be a "nationalist" foreign policy that terminates the United States-Japan Security Treaty in order to assert Japanese independence, forcing Japan to go it alone or to seek other possible alliances in which Japan would be the dominant player but at the same time leaving Japan internationally weaker without the hegemonic backing of the United States.

This is not to say that Japan has ever ignored its own domestic needs. In fact, since World War II, under the Yoshida Doctrine, Japan has pursued a foreign policy governed by domestic needs. Since the end of the occupation, Japan has concentrated on a foreign policy based on realism or "self-help."[38] Realism, as described by Joseph M. Grieco,

> encompasses five propositions. First, states are the major actors in world affairs (Morgenthau 1973: 10; Waltz 1979: 95). Second, the international environment severely penalizes states if they fail to protect their vital interests or if they pursue objectives beyond their means; hence, states are "sensitive to costs" and behave as unitary-rational agents (Waltz 1986: 331). Third, international anarchy is the principal force shaping the motives and actions of states (Waltz 1959: 224–38; 1979: 79–128; Hoffmann 1965: 27, 54–87, 129; Aron 1973a: 6–10). Fourth, states in anarchy are preoccupied with power and security, are predisposed toward conflict and competition, and often fail to cooperate even in face of common interests (Aron 1966: 5; Gilpin 1986: 304). Finally, international institutions affect the prospects for cooperation only marginally (Waltz 1979: 115–16; Morgenthau 1973: 512; Hoffmann 1973b: 50).[39]

Japanese realistic foreign policy has not been the traditional power-based realism of Hans J. Morgenthau.[40] Rather, realist Japanese foreign policy has been largely based on a realistic assessment of Japan's foreign-policy limitations under Article Nine. Article Nine's constitutional limitations have meant that Japan has been forced to *realistically* pursue an institutionalist-neoliberalist[41] foreign policy.[42] Institutionalists would say that Japan is simply following an institutionally based foreign policy; not realism. However, the institutionalists are wrong, as Grieco argues—and I concur:

> [I]n fact, neoliberal institutionalism misconstrues the realist analysis of international anarchy and therefore it misunderstands the realist analysis of the impact of anarchy on the preferences and the actions of states. Indeed, the new liberal institutionalism fails to address a major constraint on the willingness of states to cooperate which is generated by international anarchy and which is identified by realism. As a result, the new theory's optimism about international cooperation is likely to be proven wrong.[43]

Japan has depended on the United States-Japan Security Treaty[44] and the Untied Nations for its security needs. This institutionalist approach to its foreign policy is not based on a belief in institutionalism, but on a realistic assessment of its options, which are few.

The premise underlying this argument is that realism *dominates or influences* all calculations concerning relations between nations. This argument runs counter to the ideas of many political scientists who hold that there are multiple theoretical explanations for the behavior of nation-states. As Sheldon Simon states in his 1995 paper, "International Relations Theory and Southeast Asian Security":

> Students of international politics have debated the efficacy of alternative theories of state behavior for decades. Among the most prominent of these debates is the question of whether world politics is a zero-sum conflict in which all state-actors view one another as unmitigated competitors versus the less gloomy vision of a world in which states can best achieve security and prosperity through cooperation rather than conflict. Put simply, advocates of the first school see international politics as a struggle for *relative gains* in which the power and the status of states are determined hierarchically. The second school disagrees, insisting that all members of the system benefit when absolute gains are achieved across the system, virtually regardless of their distribution. Those who follow the first approach are called realists; their more optimistic rivals take the label: *neoliberalists*. These alternative visions currently compete for the attention of many statesmen in the post-cold war world, who are searching for policies to secure and advance their governments' fortunes.

While realists concede that states may be concerned in the long run with absolute gains, they insist that immediate survival needs take precedence and require independent military and economic capabilities that attenuate cooperation. Neoliberals counter that strong empirical evidence of cooperation in international politics and the creation of institutions to facilitate cooperation show that states do not necessarily concentrate on relative gains exclusively.

Theoretically, under zero-sum conditions, there is no basis for international cooperation regimes because one actor's gain is another's loss. Indeed, in the realist world, a hegemonic state determines the structure or rules of international relations.[45]

Simon argues in his article that both realism and neoliberalism are evident in Southeast Asian security policy. I do not question this finding; rather, I offer an alternative hypothesis for why nations pursue an alternative or institutionalist foreign policy. An institutionalist foreign policy is a policy based on the use of multilateral forums, such as the United Nations and the ASEAN Regional Forum, (ARF) for security rather than traditional alliances. I will also explain why nations accept absolute gains in cooperation with other states rather than competing over relative gains.

Realists argue that as the current dominant hegemon, the United States, declines,[46] other nations will vie for the right to be top dog. Neoliberals argue that states with an investment in the current hegemon's regime will have an interest in preserving or creating frameworks that will continue the rules and regulations imposed by the reigning hegemon.[47] This second neoliberal argument is seen as nothing more than an attempt by nation-states to augment their power through institutionalism. Nations are motivated by the need for "self-help," but the realities of the post-Cold War world are forcing them to pursue *relative gains* through *absolute gains*. States see the competition to be "top dog" as resulting in a net loss in terms of *relative gains* for themselves. Part of the reasoning behind this belief is that, as Grieco writes, "For realists, a state will focus both on its *absolute and relative gains* from cooperation, and a state that is satisfied with a partner's compliance in a joint arrangement might nevertheless exit from it because the partner is achieving relatively greater gains."[48] With survival foremost on their minds, nations practicing realism choose *absolute gains* over a net loss in *relative gains*. States will return to relative gains only when they are more profitable than absolute gains.[49] With the world becoming more interdependent, nation-states are less likely to find themselves pursuing *direct relative gains* when *absolute gains* offer so much more.

To illustrate this concept of relative versus absolute gains, let us look at the

Figure 4.1   **A Diagram Illustrating Why a Nation Practicing Realism Might Choose Other Options for Realist Reasons**

case of Japan. As states are maneuvering for "top dog" status, Japan realizes that it is not in a position to be a serious contender for hegemony because of its limitations under Article Nine, among other reasons. Realizing its limitations, it tries to position itself for relative gains through absolute-gain methods. Japan needs the stability offered by the regime of the current hegemon, the United States, to continue in order to pursue relative gains. This need requires that Japan pursue a neoliberal approach to its foreign policy and the resulting absolute gains. Japan's calculations tell it that *absolute gains* will give it a *greater relative gain* than if it pursued only *relative gains*. That is, the *absolute gains* from the relationship with the United States outweigh any conceivable *relative gains* from abandoning the relationship.

A nation may thus choose to pursue a purely realist path or not. It may choose to follow a liberal path because it is the rational thing to do. This is a kind of "localized rationality" on the part of Japan.[50] Part of this logic is based on the belief that people and nations must have incentives to work for goals and interests beyond their immediate selfish needs and agendas. Thus, the behavior of nations can be explained in realist terms, no matter what form of policy they seem to be practicing. The circumstances in which they make a "realist" choice may reflect a view of mankind in which a nation can choose to work for the common good because it is in the nation's particular interest. Figure 4.1 diagrams this concept.

This argument adds to the ongoing debate between Joseph Grieco and Robert Powell over the issue of relative versus absolute gains in international relations theory.[51] Neoinstitutionalists argue that states are interested only in their own gains and do not care about the gains of other states. Grieco[52] disagrees with this assessment and argues that nations will pursue relative gains over absolute gains *if* they can. Powell[53] tries to marry both these schools of thought by arguing that the choice of relative or absolute gains is situational in nature. A nation will pursue relative gains from a state that it fears as a security threat. If it does not harbor this fear, it will pursue absolute gains. What I am arguing, particularly in the case of Japan, is that in this process, there is a simultaneous element: states will pursue relative gains in any given situation, even when, on the surface, they appear to be pursuing absolute gains. If a state does not have the option or ability to pursue a realist or neorealist strategy, it will attempt a neoliberal strategy, focused on absolute gains in economics and security. In the case of Japan, its economics are strong but its security options are weak, because of its limitations. It thus rationally pursues a pragmatic strategy of diplomacy in order to make relative gains in terms of intangibles, such as goodwill and influence. On the surface, Japan is currently pursuing absolute gains by using a neoinstitutionalist strategy, but underneath, it is seeking relative gains in the form of intangibles, since it cannot make relative gains in the traditional forms of economics and security because of its limitations.

For example, Japan needs open SLOCs. If Japan cannot trade internationally, it will starve. To keep the SLOCs open, it must either do so by military force (which, constitutionally, it can only do to a limited extent, if at all) or it must work with other nations through institutions to keep the SLOCs open. Japan's need to keep the SLOCs open is self-centered, but it carries a benefit for other nations as well, because cooperation in most cases is better than conflict. In realist terms, considering Japan's limitations, collaboration with the United States is Japan's best option. Furthermore, in realist terms, security cooperation adds to Japan's power by strengthening it as a nation through goodwill and economics, thus giving it status or influence as a power of a kind that it would not have been able to achieve by military means. Japan has made a relative gain by letting other nations gain in absolute terms. In sum, I am arguing that Japan's security policy can be explained through realist doctrines. If one looks at Japanese options and limitations, one can see a realist strategy governing Japan's foreign policy, even when, at first glance, it appears to be an institutionalist policy (which on the surface it is).

In Japan's case, after the occupation, it was forced to deal with the reality of Article Nine. Without the constitutional ability to raise an army, wage war, or threaten to wage war, Japan was forced to pursue an institutionalist foreign policy. During the Cold War, Japan institutionalized its foreign policy through the United States-Japan Security Treaty and, to a lesser extent, through the United Nations. Since the end of the Cold War, Japan is still following an institutionalist foreign policy, again with the United States-Japan Security Treaty as the centerpiece.

At first glance, the United States-Japan Security Treaty is simply a "self-help" effort on the part of Japan. The treaty allies Japan with the current hegemon, the United States, by providing Japan its security guarantee. The treaty, however, serves other purposes for Japan. In addition to guaranteeing Japan's security, it legitimizes Japan's role in East Asian security by assuring other Asian nations that the "Japanese genie" will be kept "in the bottle." Furthermore, the treaty provides stabilization for East Asia as it keeps the United States deployed in a forward direction and engaged in the region.

However, the significance and importance of the United States-Japan Security Treaty has declined (but has not been eliminated) since the end of the Cold War. Japan is not as crucial an ally to the United States as it was during the Cold War, when the United States was trying to contain Communism. The end of the Cold War reduced Japan's leverage vis-à-vis the United States because Japan was no longer seen as an essential ally in the fight against Communism. Benefits from the relationship are now tipped in favor of the Japanese, in that Japan's relative gains are greater than the United States gains, even though both sides share absolute gains.[54] The full impact of this situation is that Japan is more vulnerable to abandonment by the United States if the Americans ever wished or felt it necessary to abandon Japan. Fear of such a development is rife in Japan, particularly on the right wing of Japanese politics.[55] One result is that Japan has been searching for new options to raise its stature and increase its power and thus its importance to the United States and the rest of the world.

Japan has been increasingly focusing on a United Nations-centric policy, at the same time participating in such regional forums as ASEAN, Asia-Pacific Economic Cooperation (APEC), and the ASEAN Regional Forum.[56] It is also championing a larger role for itself within the United Nations. Its quest for a permanent seat on the Security Council is supplemented by the championing of its nationals for important positions within the United Nations. Japan has also been accused of using its economic power to allegedly "purchase" important positions within the United Nations for Japanese. An example is the "checkbook" campaign that, according to an article in Le Monde, Japan waged on behalf of the head of UNESCO, Ambassador Koichiro Matsuura.[57] In these cases, money becomes a foreign policy tool to increase Japan's political influence in international bodies.

Alternative Views of Japanese Security

The events of 9/11 and the emergence of the North Korean threat in the minds of the Japanese public have embarked Japan on its most radical foreign and security policy changes since the end of the Cold War. The SDF supported Operation Enduring Freedom (OEF) and is now serving as part of the reconstruction effort in Iraq as part of Operation Iraqi Freedom (OIF).

Japan has come a long way from being the nation that, until the end of the Cold War, was content to sit on the sidelines of international conflict. However, as Japan increases its role globally, its regional security complex is growing increasingly critical. First and foremost is Japan's need to securitize its domestic economy.

Japan's current status as a major world power is based entirely on the size and strength of its economy. In the late 1980s, Japan was on top of the world. It was seen as the up-and-coming challenger to the reigning hegemon, the United States. Its economy was the second-largest in the world behind the United States. The Japanese yen was strong and stable. People around the world were studying Japanese as the "it" language for movers and shakers who wanted to succeed. At the same time, trouble was brewing for Japan. Land speculation had led the Tokyo metropolitan area to achieve a paper value greater than that of the forty-eight contiguous United States. The Japanese "bubble economy" was about to burst. Soon after that event, the Japanese economy began to stagnate. This stagnation continued throughout the 1990s. So, while the United States and most of the world boomed during the decade, Japan sank deeper into recession and suffered from a deflationary spiral until March 2006 when the consumer price index in Japan rose for the first time in nearly a decade.

The major blame for the continued stagnation of the Japanese economy has been placed on Japan's unwillingness to implement meaningful economic or political structural reform. The Japanese government has continued to prop up bankrupt firms and financially insolvent banks, while implementing stimulus package after stimulus package, none of which ever work. Currently, the political leadership in Japan is fighting an uphill battle against cultural and political norms to implement structural reforms needed to bolster its sagging economy. A series of prime ministers, culminating with the current prime minister, Junichiro Koizumi, have all promised structural change, but all have failed to muster the political capital needed to break down the existing structures.

The recognition of the need for Japan to securitize its economy has been very slow in coming, but the economic rise of China has caused Japan to move forward more aggressively than it has done in the past to spell out the terms of its security need in the global context. Japan's November 28, 2002, executive report to the prime minister on strategies for the twenty-first century highlights this need. It states:

> Japan will be more directly influenced by Chinese economic development than any other country and has a responsibility to articulate a national economic vision under this new paradigm. *The essential first steps will be to*

*quickly dispose of nonperforming loans and at the same time reform the
economic structure itself.*

The promotion of science and technology will be an absolute prerequi-
site to achieving this. *Nor can regulatory reform be avoided.* Japan must
rectify high-cost structures, enhance educational facilities, and accept more
foreign students, with the ultimate aim of attracting direct investment from
overseas in high value-added areas such as high technology industries and
research and development.

Structural reforms in the agricultural sector are also essential. Japan
must study mechanisms to mitigate the impact on domestic agriculture and
to ensure food security.[58]

This acknowledgment of the need to reform its economy in light of the
challenge from China is remarkable in view of Japan's economic problems of
the last fifteen years and its slowness in dealing with its structural problems.

During the last round of GATT (General Agreement on Tariffs and Trade),
Japan (along with South Korea) attempted to negotiate an exemption for rice
as a staple food in which Japan felt the need to remain self-sufficient. Successive crop failures in the early 1990s dispelled the myth that Japan could
ever be self-sufficient in rice. The political need to protect domestic agriculture remained. Japan is a nation that cannot feed its population without food
imports. Japan imports over 40 percent of its domestic food consumption.
Much of the 60 percent it does not import comes from the seas surrounding
Japan, particularly the Sea of Japan. It is for this reason that environmental
issues in the Sea of Japan should be of the highest priority for Japan. However, Japan has largely failed to prioritize this area as an essential issue. Instead, it has chosen to focus on the recently ratified Kyoto Protocols that,
without the participation of China, the United States and India, the three
largest polluters, seem meaningless. While the Kyoto Protocol focused on
greenhouse gases, the Sea of Japan faces the twin threats of both growing
Chinese industry and the resulting pollution and the nuclear waste disposed
of by the Soviet navy in the Sea of Japan during the Cold War.

Japan's strategies for the twenty-first century include a focus on the creation of an international framework that would include the establishment of
"environmental rules in Asia, particularly for Chinese companies," which it
sees as potentially the largest polluters.[59] Notably absent from this recommendation is any mention of Russia. This omission may, in part, be due to
the continuing dispute over the ownership of the Kuril Islands, which both
Japan and Russia claim as their own (more on this dispute in later chapters)
and the economic need for diversified oil resources. Over 90 percent of Japanese oil currently comes from the Middle East. Japan is looking to Russian

oil as an alternative to Japanese dependency on the Middle East. To this end the Japanese have lobbied strenuously, and seemingly successfully, for an oil pipeline to be built from the Siberian oil fields to the Siberian coast of Russia rather than having it run through China and Manchuria. Japan does not want to trade dependency on the Middle East for dependency on China, a potential rival within its security complex.

A second area of securitization for Japan that is of interest for those study-ing alternative security is the area of culture. Japan imports massive amounts of Western culture and, for the most part, it is like the United Kingdom and the Scandinavian countries in permitting that culture to be absorbed without hin-drance. The issue of whaling is different, however; time and time again, Japan has stood up in international forums to support a dying and economically un-essential (whale meat is stockpiling in storage freezers as most Japanese seem uninterested in consuming it) and unneeded industry, claiming the need to preserve the traditional culture of whaling in Japan. This reasoning is basically false in that the whaling that is being fought for today is the product of Japan's post-World War II need to feed itself.[60] However, as Akitoshi Miyashita and Yoichiro Sato argue in their book, *Japanese Foreign Policy in Asia and the Pacific,* Japan is willing to fight for continued whaling for primarily political, rather than economic, reasons. First, Japan is looking for ways to prove to the world that it can stand up to international pressure and not give in. Second, it wants to demonstrate that it can have a foreign policy independent of the United States. Third, it worries that, if it gives in on the whaling issue, other Japanese sea-based industries might begin to face international pressure to shut down.[61] It wants to draw a line in the water, if you will, to protect its dependence on the sea for much of its national food supply.

Japan is willing to spend international goodwill in order to protect what it considers a vital area for its security: its food supply. At the same time, it feels that it needs a more internationally assertive foreign policy in order to boost its standing in the world. This attitude can be likened to a new kid in school picking a fight with the biggest guy in school. The object is not to win, but to gain the respect of his peers by demonstrating his toughness. Japan is trying to demonstrate its willingness to stand virtually alone on an international issue. The issue is high-profile, but the consequences are not strategic in the long term.[62]

A third area of alternative security is international goodwill, augmented by the assets of the SDF. The December 26, 2004, tsunami (also called the Boxing Day Tsunami), that struck the Indian Ocean in Southeast Asia pro-vided Japan with an opportunity to demonstrate its abilities to be a major player in disaster relief through the use of the SDF as well as its famous "checkbook diplomacy."

Photo 4.2 **A Japanese Air Self-Defense Forces C-130 Delivering Aid**
(*Source:* U.S. Air Force photo by Tech. Sgt. Bob Oldham. www.af.mil)

On January 1, 2005, Prime Minister Koizumi pledged a half-billion dollars in aid (the largest pledge at the time, but since passed by others) to the
stricken region. However, much of the aid is being targeted at Indonesia,
which, while being the hardest-hit nation, is also the nation within the
region that Japan most wishes to build stronger relations with. More significantly, however, is the fact that Japan was able to quickly deploy over
1,000 SDF personnel to the region, along with multiple Maritime SDF
ships, which were soon followed by much-needed helicopters. The incredible abilities of the Japanese SDF and other military forces (most notably,
American) to render aid and assistance quickly and efficiently shocked
traditional relief workers. The two greatest needs were transport and fresh
water. Naval ships contain desalinization plants that can turn seawater into
fresh drinking water in massive quantities. The helicopters from naval bases
provided transportation of workers and supplies to areas where local land-
based transportation could no longer go.

Through its efforts to alleviate the suffering from the Boxing Day Tsunami, Japan was able to securitize its goodwill efforts. Japan had a need to
demonstrate its abilities as a nation so that it could be taken more seriously
in international forums. To use an old adage of the late President Theodore
Roosevelt, Japan wants to speak softly but carry a big stick—the "big stick"

being its ability to demonstrate the capabilities that most nations lack when it comes to rendering aid. Japan's efforts are in marked contrast to its regional rival, China, which, in spite of it now being the world's second-largest economy (in purchasing power parity terms), was able only to give paltry sums of aid (in comparison to others) and virtually no military assistance because of its lack of a blue-water navy. Japan is looking to build up goodwill internationally as a world power that deserves to be recognized. Japan's quest for a permanent seat on the United Nations Security Council is using this goodwill to boost support for its bid. A permanent seat on the Security Council brings with it, not only prestige, but also the security of always having a voice in times of international crisis.[63] Furthermore, other states would need to consult and work with Japan to achieve international goals. Japan would thus have the added security of being able to prioritize its security needs vis-à-vis potential threats.

In conclusion, this chapter has looked at the meaning of alternative security and what it means to securitize (or not to securitize) an issue. Furthermore, we have examined Japan's security limitations imposed by Article Nine and the effects of these limitations on Japan's ability to make *gains* in traditional ways. Because of these limitations, Japan has explored alternative security issues as part of its overall security strategy. In terms of alternative security, Japan is just beginning to examine its options and to prioritize them. Domestic economic issues are rightly at the forefront, with whaling close behind. Japan is nothing without its economy. If it can securitize and then fix its domestic economic problems, Japan has the potential to be a player of consequence in the twenty-first century. The world already recognizes Japan's economy as essential to Japan's security and is waiting for Japan to take the needed actions in order to fix the problems that have lost it a decade of international progress. The risks of doing nothing are great for Japan, considering China's rising economic and military power.

The issue of Japan's only partially securitizing its environment presents a great challenge for Japan in light of alternative security issues. Pollution in the seas around Japan will continue to grow unless Japan, the nation most affected by the pollution, creates a securitized awareness in the Northeast Asian security complex. There are competing interests that Japan must weigh in light of the dynamic nature of East Asian security in the coming years. However, in spite of its limitations, Japan is moving forward to deal with its future and its role in the world community.

5

Foreign-Policy Restructuring in Japan

*By this I mean that a political society does not live
to conduct foreign policy; it would be more correct
to say that it conducts foreign policy in order to live.*
—George F. Kennan[1]

For the most part, Japanese politicians believe revision of the constitution and the removal or amending of Article Nine to be a political impossibility because of the disruption such an action would cause and its dubious chances for success. Prime Minister Junichiro Koizumi's September 11, 2005, landslide election victory may embolden constitutional reformers as the LDP and its coalition partner, *Komeito*, now have a clear two-thirds majority in the lower house of the Diet. While Prime Minister Koizumi might see constitutional revision as beyond the scope of his mandate, there certainly will be some impetus to at least attempt constitutional reform at some level. Nonetheless, even without a wholesale revision of the constitution, change is taking place in Japanese foreign policy. Five sources of this change are seen in Japan as having caused this restructuring.

The first and most obvious is the end of the Cold War and the repercussions this end brought to the world system. The influence of this event on Japanese foreign policy after 1990 cannot be overemphasized. It alone, without the other four, can be seen as a causal factor for change in Japanese foreign policy.

The second is the 1994 internal rule changes within the Japanese electoral system, which loosened the stranglehold rural interests held on Japanese politics by establishing a better proportional electoral system.[2] This change resulted in changes in the type of representation and the orientations and interests of elected Diet members. Traditional-style politicians began losing ground to politicians from urban Japan. The current populist government of Prime Minister Koizumi is evidence of this trend as factions within the ruling LDP continue to lose influence to popular and more dynamic politicians.

The third causal factor for change is a byproduct of the second. A new, younger generation of leaders is emerging in the Diet. This generation is more likely than not to have been at least partially educated overseas, and these Diet members desire to see Japanese politics and policy reflect the elected leadership they have seen in other countries, rather than the bureau-cratic leadership that has prevailed for so long in Japan.

The fourth causal factor for change is the Persian Gulf War and the result-ing criticism that Japan suffered for its role in it (or the lack of a human role in it). This factor produced its own result in the form of the PKO Law and continual revisions, which are giving Japan a much more normal role in U.N. peacekeeping missions. Major Takashi Motomatsu, a former commander of an SDF PKO mission to the Golan Heights, describes how difficult and pro-fessionally embarrassing it was when he had to explain the exceptionalism of the SDF in a combat situation to his Polish U.N. commander in the field. The Polish officer responded by asking Major Motomatsu, "What kind of military force are you?"[3] Recent changes in the PKO Law have made such conversations less necessary, but the earlier confusion illustrates the prob-lems Japan faces when attempting to adapt its foreign-policy limitations to the realities of the post-Cold War world, when Japanese must still live with the legacy of Article Nine.

The fifth causal factor of Japanese foreign policy restructuring was the events of 9/11 in the United States. Japan's ally was attacked, and even though the United States-Japan Security Treaty specifically exempts Japan from aiding the United States, Japan felt that the time had come to raise the level of its human contribution. Japan deployed the Maritime SDF in support of Opera-tion Enduring Freedom (OEF). The MSDF ships supported and refueled American warships in the Indian Ocean in support of combat operations there. The SDF have been assisting the United States in the rebuilding of Iraq and have pledged to continue this assistance through a least the end of 2006. However, given the strength of Prime Minister Koizumi's September 2005 electoral victory, it is very likely that the SDF mission to Iraq will continue into 2007 and beyond as long as the SDF remains casualty free.

A Model of Foreign-Policy Restructuring

As Charles Hermann notes, "We are in a period of profound change in inter-national relations and foreign policy."[4] Hermann wrote right after the Cold War ended and the Berlin Wall fell. Every nation was revisiting its foreign policies to reflect the disintegration of the Iron Curtain. Japan was no excep-tion. Some nations were quicker to adapt than others, but Japan was not one of the early ones. It took the Persian Gulf War to wake Japan up to the reality of its new position in the post-Cold War world. Since that time, Japan has been attempting to restructure its foreign policy to tackle the realities of a post-Cold War world while living with the one element that makes Japan unique in the entire world, Article Nine.

Charles Hermann's 1990 paper, "Changing Course: When Governments Choose to Redirect Foreign Policy," and the model it contains are applied to these causal factors or independent variables of change listed in the previous section. The reason for this is that Hermann's model allows for the continual change in foreign policy that is always happening, as noted by James N. Rosenau and cited in chapter 1. Furthermore, Hermann notes that "change is a pervasive quality of governmental foreign policy."[5] Additionally, Hermann's investigation of foreign-policy change finds that the "decision making process itself can obstruct or facilitate change."[6] Thus, change *can* be seen as always existing in foreign policy and the study of foreign policy and restructuring can be one and the same. Both Hermann and I disagree with this argument, and we argue that there is a difference—the difference being that the study of foreign policy focuses on the continual stream of policy, the incremental adjustments that are continually being made, and the actions of decision makers. On the other hand, foreign-policy restructuring focuses on the need to change policy because the old policy did not work, is not working, or has been rendered obsolete by events.[7] An important factor here is that those who are restructuring the policy are, in essence, the same people who developed the policy in the first place. The change is not merely the reflection of a new government's differing ideology from the previous ones. This difference requires a close examination of change in the decision-making process, which is one element of this discourse.

A quick review of Hermann's argument is warranted here. According to Hermann, "changes that mark a reversal, or at least, a profound redirection of a country's foreign policy are of special interest because of the demands their adoption pose on the initiating government and its domestic constituents and because of their potentially powerful consequences for other countries."[8] Wars or other conflicts may begin or end because of foreign-policy changes. It is for this reason that there is a tendency to conclude that as a result of the effort needed to change foreign policy, there is a need for regime change as the only way to facilitate this change. But as Hermann points out, when we reflect on this situation, we find cases in which the same government that initiated a foreign policy was the one responsible for its reversal or replacement.

The question that Hermann is asking in general, and we are asking in relation to Japan is, "Under what circumstances do these kinds of changes occur in which an existing government recognizes that its current course is seriously inadequate, mistaken, or no longer applicable? What are the conditions under which self-correcting change may arise?"[9] In the case of Japan, it was the end of the Cold War and the ensuing Persian Gulf War that began this process of change. This change continues through changes within the Diet and the makeup of its members.

Japan has not fundamentally changed its orientation vis-à-vis the rest of the world. It is still a solid democracy, and the strongest democracy in Asia. It has no real intention of going head to head with the United States. Japan is not considering aligning itself against America, and it steadfastly desires to continue to have cordial relations with the United States. What it is doing is exploring its options. With the Cold War over, Japan realizes that it can no longer depend on the United States the way it did during the Cold War, because U.S. priorities have changed and with these changes, Japan's position in America's priorities.

Japan wants options in an ever-changing world. It realizes that during the Cold War, all of its eggs were kept in one basket, and that basket was the United States. It was a calculated gamble, and Japan won it. There is a saying in Japan, "Japan is always lucky." Japan was lucky, but it also does not want to press its luck. There is also a barely spoken, but very real, fear of abandonment in Japan.[10] It is worth repeating Grieco here, "For realists, a state will focus both on its absolute and relative gains from cooperation, and a state that is satisfied with a partner's compliance in a joint arrangement *might nevertheless exit from it because the partner is achieving relatively greater gains.*"[11] This last aspect—a partner's exiting from a relationship—is a very real fear for Japan. Japan can easily be seen as getting far more from its relationship with the United States than the United States does. Thus, according to Grieco and realist theory, Japan is a *possible* candidate for abandonment by the United States. As a nation that uses realism as its principal foreign-policy framework, Japan clearly realizes this possibility and hence fears abandonment.

This apprehensiveness is a fundamental problem for Japan, in that it does not want to have to go it alone. Japan is looking to expand its sphere of influence without jeopardizing its relations with the United States.[12] Japan also realizes that the United States wants a more independent Japan. The United States would prefer to deal with Japan on a more "normal" basis— "normal" meaning the way it works with allies such as the United Kingdom, France, and Germany. The problem with this wish is, again, Article Nine.[13]

Japan is basically searching for a way to be "normal" while still living with Article Nine. The Yoshida Doctrine was adopted by the LDP, which has ruled Japan continuously since 1958, with only an eleven-month interruption in 1993–94. The LDP is the same party today that is responsible for foreign policy in Japan. That is to say that the same political actor that created, adapted, and used the Yoshida Doctrine as the centerpiece of Japan's postwar foreign policy is now attempting to change it. This condition fits within Hermann's and the literature's definition of foreign-policy restructuring. First, there needs to be a change in the system, and that change needs to motivate a government to change *its* foreign policy.[14] In the case of Japan, the end of the Cold War and the ensuing Persian Gulf War[15] provided the change that stimulated the Japanese leadership to pursue alternatives to its Cold War foreign policy. Foreign-policy changes in Japan are continuous and ongoing, but they are still driven by the same stimulus: the need for Japan to find a new role for itself in a post-Cold War world. It is to this situation in Japan that Hermann's model is applied, as a case study, with the hope that it can teach us more about how nations restructure their foreign policy. It is also hoped that there can be an expansion of Hermann's model (to be described below) that will give us a clearer picture of the foreign-policy decision-making process.

Hermann's model is concerned with the fundamental redirection of a nation's foreign policy. Defining the type of change or redirection is very important, and Hermann deals with it through a four-level graduated description of foreign-policy change. The four involve increasing level of change: (1) adjustment changes, (2) program changes, (3) problem/goal changes, and (4) international orientation changes. This last change involves a basic shift in the international actors' roles and activities, in which not just one policy but many are simultaneously changed. This change typically, but not always, involves a shift in alignment with other nations or a major shift in the role that the nation in question plays within an alignment. As noted previously, this kind of shift is not what is happening in Japan, because Japan is showing no signs of changing its loyalties vis-à-vis the United States and other liberal democracies.

The first change, adjustment change, requires a change in the recipients of a foreign policy rather than a change in the foreign policy itself. This adjustment clearly does not apply to Japan. The second change, program change, requires qualitative changes and new instruments of statecraft, although the purposes stay the same. In Japan's case, this kind of change may reflect the changes since the passage of the PKO Law. But it is the third change that best describes the restructuring Japan undertook after the Cold War.

The problem/goal change requires the purposes of the original policy to change. The original purpose of the Yoshida Doctrine was to support Japan's economic rebuilding by permitting it to deemphasize its own defense by relying on the United States-Japan Security Treaty. At the same time, it permitted Japan to deal with the constitutional limitations imposed by Article Nine. Japan found this policy unworkable in the "New World Order" that came about after the demise of the Iron Curtain. The purposes of the Yoshida Doctrine needed to be replaced with new purposes that reflected Japan's new place in the world. Japan no longer needed to rebuild its economy, it is an economic giant. It desires to come out from under the United States shadow and be seen as a power unto itself. Clearly, it is Hermann's second and third levels of change that are most applicable to Japan. For the purposes of this text, and for the sake of consistency, foreign-policy changes will be described in the same terms that Hermann uses. Program changes will be described as changes in means, and goal problem/changes as changes in ends. As Hermann notes, the differences between means and ends are difficult to empirically define, other that in what has already been described.[16] As Hermann writes:

> In program change, however, one would expect to find changes in the configuration of instruments, in the level of commitment, and probably in the degree of expressed affect. All these developments, plus policy statements and policy actions incompatible with prior goal or problem stipulations—if not open rejection of prior goals—accompany goal/problem changes. International reorientation involves dramatic change in both words and deeds in multiple issue areas with respect to the actor's relationship with external entities.[17]

The conditions for change based on Hermann's research are fourfold. First, domestic political systems may affect foreign policy. For example, (a) issues become a centerpiece in the struggle for political power; (b) the attitudes and beliefs of a dominant domestic constituency undergo a profound change; and (c) a realignment occurs of the essential constituency of a regime, or a revolution or other transformation takes place.[18] In the case of Japan, only the first two (a and b) are seen to have taken place. The LDP and the SDPJ made the PKO Law a divisive issue that shattered traditional harmony. This dispute had the effect of changing party loyalties in the domestic constituencies of both parties. Furthermore, the public in Japan has grown to accept the need for Japanese troops to take part in U.N. PKO missions. This acceptance was caused in part by the Persian Gulf War and the effect it had as a prime-time war on Japanese television. The Japanese public saw Japan as a major power that was not sending its soldiers to a major conflict being fought by its allies.

The second area is bureaucratic decision making. This area of study examines the bureaucrats who work in government agencies, to see whether their roles support or oppose changes in foreign policy. It takes into account the variables of perception and personality. For Japan, this is a (if not the) critical area of analysis. Japanese bureaucrats wield tremendous influence and are extremely powerful when compared to other nations. The recognition within MOFA that change was needed was a major factor in the passage of the PKO Law. It is for this reason that elites in the relevant bureaucracies, the Ministry of Foreign Affairs (MOFA) and the Japan Defense Agency (JDA), were studied intensively during the field research to be described later in this chapter.

The third area is cybernetics, which is the science of communication and control,[19] and deals with the agent. It attempts to monitor and examine a complex stream of variables over time. Hermann states:

> An essential feature of [cybernetic] approaches is that the agent, attempting to pursue some standard or goal, continuously monitors a select stream of information from the environment that indicates where he is in relation to that goal and how the relation has altered across intervals of time. The agent engages in incremental self-corrective action in an effort to close on the goal or remain in close proximity to the standard. This process accounts for the association of cybernetics with the concepts of information (feedback) and control (steering).
>
> The elaboration of such a process would appear to be attractive for interpreting adjustment changes in policy. The system of control might also be extended to cover program changes as well.[20]

The area of cybernetics that Hermann notes as having the most promise for foreign-policy restructuring is the part that looks closely at the fact that agents deal with the highest priorities first.[21] For example, policy makers will probably focus on national survival and then move on to political survival, ideology, or personal goals. This aspect is less enlightening in the case of Japan, but it is still important, particularly when one compares the priorities of the different agents involved in the decision-making process. The differing priorities of MOFA and the politicians in the Diet are fascinating, as is the apparent lack (when compared to the other two) of fervor on the part of the JDA to the change process.

The fourth and final area is learning. This area is defined by nations' responding, not out of principle, but in response to some kind of reward or punishment. Change, Hermann notes, does not always imply learning.[22] In Japan's case, learning can be seen as a causal feature for change. Japan's lack of ability to make a contribution of personnel to the Persian Gulf War earned it worldwide condemnation and awakened Japan to the fact that its foreign policy was no longer adequate. Japan learned that the next time an international crisis occurred, the country needed to be better prepared to respond in a way that would be acceptable to the international community and commensurate with its status as a major economic power.

Hermann further develops his model by selecting from his review of the literature two things necessary to effect change in a domestic political system's foreign policy: first, there must be change in that system, such as the end of

Figure 5.1   **The Mediating Role of the Decision Processes Between Change Agents and Degree of Policy Change**

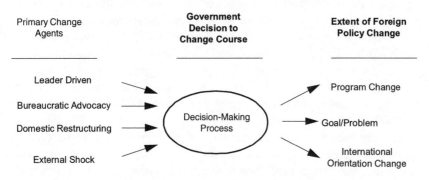

Source: Hermann, "Changing Course: When Governments Choose to Redirect Foreign Policy." *International Studies Quarterly* 34 (1990): 13.

the Cold War; and, second, systemic change must trigger a change in the government's foreign policy, such as the passage of the PKO Law in direct response to Japan's inability to adapt quickly to the end of the Cold War.[23] Major change, according to Hermann, "depends on mobilizing sufficient specialized human talents to overcome or circumvent the organizational structures and processes committed to the maintenance of existing policy."[24] It is for this reason that most studies of foreign-policy change center on changes in leadership or in governments. New leaders or governments are often much better able to make changes because they can change organizations. Such was not the case for Japan with the PKO Law. In the aftermath of the Persian Gulf War, existing leadership redirected Japanese foreign policy. The leaders in Japan had to form a coalition from the bureaucracy and the Diet in order to gain enough support to push through the PKO Law. The abhorrence that many Japanese elites and the public felt for sending troops overseas had to be overcome. The combination of advocacy by both the leadership and the bureaucracy (MOFA) helped pass the PKO Law. These two groups were the agents of change. The agents of change that Hermann lists are labeled as leader-driven, bureaucratic advocacy, domestic restructuring, and external shock.[25] The interaction of these with the decision-making process can be seen in Figure 5.1.

Leader-driven change is often authoritative in nature. In the case of Japan, it was the strong leadership under Prime Minister Miyazawa, as opposed to the weaker leadership of Prime Minister Kaifu, that the PKO Law was passed. Without strong pressure by the party leadership on the LDP rank-and-file members, no bill would have passed the Diet.

Hermann's second change agent, bureaucratic advocacy, would seem to be a contradiction in terms. Bureaucratic groups are known for their resistance to change, but they can be open to change when it has a positive influence on their power—especially when the advocates for change are high-ranking officials within the bureaucracy itself. Such was the case in Japan. As noted above, the bureaucracies in Japan are exceptionally powerful, and they often write policy and present it to lawmakers. In Japan's case, elites within MOFA, such as former Vice Foreign Minister Shunji Yanai, played a strong advocacy role in the writing and lobbying (behind the scenes) for the PKO Bill.

The third agent of change, domestic restructuring, refers to a political segment within a society on which the regime is dependent in order to govern. If this segment loses its influence or the ability to elect members to the national body, the regime may be freed to pursue its own policies or forced to abandon policies that are no longer sustainable. In many countries, this situation can be caused by redistricting. In the case of Japan, domestic restructuring had no effect on the passage of the PKO Law, but it is having an effect on the ongoing process to adopt a post-Cold War foreign policy. The restructuring and redistricting of the Diet in 1994, for the first time since the end of the occupation, has removed much of the LDP's rural power base as apportionment has become more equitable. This change has given urban voters a greater voice in national affairs, resulting in a new, younger generation of leadership in the Diet. (This younger generation will be discussed at the end of this chapter.)

The fourth agent of change is external shocks. This is when serious international events spur foreign-policy change. The events need not be distressing ones. In this case, it was the Persian Gulf War in the aftermath of the Cold War that drove Japan to restructure its foreign policy. External shock is always a factor in foreign-policy change, but not a constant one. The test firing, by North Korea, of the Taepodong-1 missile over Japan solidified support for the Theater Missile Defense system (TMD), which is a small but significant foreign-policy change for Japan.

It was originally thought that for Japan a fifth level of change would be foreign pressure, or *gaiatsu*. This can be seen in Figure 5.2. As we study Japan, it becomes clear that this pressure is the case. Foreign pressure plays a critical role in the foreign-policy decision-making process, and it can be considered as a fifth agent of change. In Japan's case, foreign pressure plays a special role. *Gaiatsu* is an influential factor in propagating change in Japanese foreign policy, not only as an agent of change, but also as a tool used by the other primary change agents to justify and "sell" their decisions to the public at large. (The political implications of this use of *gaiatsu* are explored in subsequent chapters.)

Figure 5.2 **Hermann's Model Plus External Pressure**

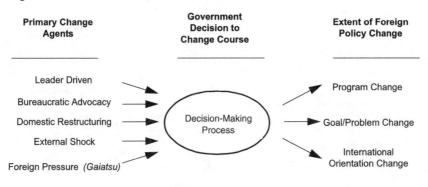

Of course, there is likely to be interplay between these agents of foreign-policy change. External shock can rouse a government into action and result in the agents of change interacting with each other to change policy. Sometimes this change will be dramatic, and sometimes it will be nonexistent, as a government realizes that there is nothing that it can do. Hermann's model stops at this point, but I believe that he overlooked an important factor in his model of the restructuring process. This factor is a series of constants that intervene in the decision-making process. These constants can take the form of laws, values, cultural norms, physical limitations, and the like, that are unique to any particular nation. An illustration of this state of affairs can be seen in Figure 5.3. In the case of Japan, there are the obvious limitations imposed by Article Nine. There are also the pacifist norms held by the population in general, which work to limit what Japan can do internationally.

The decision-making process part of Hermann's model can best be described as a matrix that contains preexisting factors controlled by no one, or which at least are virtually uncontrollable by the government trying to make the decision. It is into this matrix that the influence of the primary change agents enters and proceeds to mix with the existing influential norms to produce some form of change or to block change from occurring. If we are ever truly going to be able to understand the decision-making process, we need to understand, not only what goes into the process, but also what already exists in it. This is because the sum of what goes into the process *does not always equal what comes out*. A change takes place in this matrix that fundamentally controls the direction of foreign-policy change.

In the case of Japan, this direction can be seen in the effect of Article Nine on the decision-making process. One cannot understand Japanese foreign-policy decisions without taking into account Article Nine. We can discern no logic to

Figure 5.3 **Hermann's Model Plus Intervening Variables**

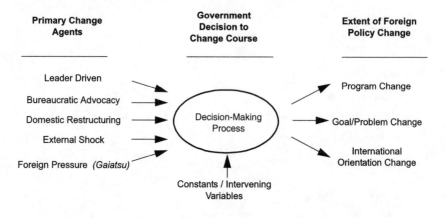

the results unless we understand Japan's limits under Article Nine. No policy change can happen without this question being asked and answered: How does Article Nine affect this policy? Furthermore, in Japan's case, pacifist attitudes that are part of the cultural norm in Japan are also part of the equation.

The rest of Hermann's research deals with the various phases of the foreign-policy decision-making process. The most important of these is that Hermann notes that the process is *not* linear. Decision making often takes place in cycles, with pauses, and it is not an orderly process.[26] Hermann suggests seven stages in which developments must occur in order for major change to take place. They are:

1. Initial policy expectations.
2. External actor/environmental stimuli.
3. Recognition of discrepant information.
4. Postulation of a connection between problem and policy.
5. Development of alternatives.
6. Building authoritative consensus for choice.
7. Implementation of new policy.[27]

Each of these seven stages can clearly be seen in the Japanese decision to pass the PKO Law.[28]

Talking to the Policy Makers Themselves

In the course of writing this book, I conducted field research by interviewing some of the Japanese foreign-policy makers themselves. In order to explore the process of restructuring in Japanese foreign policy in the post-Cold War era, a questionnaire was designed to probe this process. The purpose of this questionnaire was to explore, through a series of personal interviews, the opinions, insights, and aspirations that Japanese elites have for Japanese foreign policy. The principal tools used for the interviews were two questionnaires, in both Japanese and English. One set of questions was designed for Diet members and government ministry officials, and another set was designed for academics and journalists. The questionnaires asked basically the same questions but from the different perspectives of those inside and outside of government.

The interview questions were based on Hermann's model and designed to invite an exploration of values on the part of the interviewee. The questions about goals imply values, and values imply beliefs. The purpose was to elicit discussion about issues that elites often cannot explore, because so much of their public persona is devoted to meeting the expectations and assumptions of others. As diplomat and historian George F. Kennan observes in his memoirs about a particular incident in United States-Soviet affairs during the interwar years:

> This episode has remained in my mind as the first of many lessons I was destined to receive, in the course of a diplomatic career, on one of the most consistent and incurable traits of American statesmanship—namely, its neurotic self-consciousness and introversion, the tendency to make statements and take actions with regard not to their effect on the international scene to which they are ostensibly addressed but rather to their effect on those echelons of American opinion, congressional opinions first and foremost, to which the respective statesmen are anxious to appeal. The question, in these circumstances, became not: how effective is what I am doing in terms of impact it makes on our world environment? But rather: how do I look, in the mirror of domestic opinion, as I do it? Do I look shrewd, determined, defiantly patriotic, imbued with the necessary vigilance before the wiles of foreign governments? If so, this is what I do, even though it may prove meaningless, or even counterproductive, when applied to the realities of the external situation.[29]

What Kennan rightly observed about American diplomats can be applied generally to elites in democratic polities, especially in this modern age of media, in which image is everything. Elites often say what others want to hear or what will make them look good. The questionnaire was designed to help elites speak frankly about their genuine hopes for Japan. There was also the possibility that the elite's fears and frustrations with Japanese foreign policy would be expressed. Questions that examined Japanese history helped to explore the elite's experience and conscience regarding Japan's role in World War II. These questions were particularly useful in getting the elite to open up. Overall, the questionnaire seemed to elicit more ingenious responses from the elites who were interviewed. Notable exceptions to this result were older, more experienced elites, such as former Foreign Minister Yukihiko Ikeda, who skillfully controlled the interview and the direction of the answers so as not to reveal too much in the way of personal opinion.[30]

The Questions

In preparation for the field interviews in Japan, the questions to be asked had to be designed very carefully in order to elicit interest in the questions themselves in such a way that it would encourage the interviewees to give open answers. The next few pages describe the questions and the general responses to the questions. This description is included here to help us gain a better understanding of policy makers and their thinking on foreign policy.

The first question asked why the interviewees believed that the government felt it necessary to pass the PKO Law and whether the interviewee agreed with the government or not at the time and currently. This question was designed to measure the impact of the Persian Gulf War and its impact on Japanese foreign policy, even though the war was not mentioned in the question. I wanted to test the effect of the war as an independent variable by not mentioning it and seeing how often it was listed as a primary factor in the government's decision to pass the PKO Law. As anticipated, nearly all of the interviewees mentioned the Persian Gulf War immediately in their answers. The follow-up questions were designed to assess political attitudes toward the PKO Law and changes in attitudes since the law was passed. These questions were most significant for those who opposed the law. The level of acceptance that was accorded the law, even by those who had opposed it, was surprising. The Socialists were the most significant opponents of the PKO Law at the time of its passage, however the Socialists I interviewed were not as concerned with the PKO Law six years later, possibly reflecting their role as part of the governing coalition with the LDP.

The second question asked about the differing interests that supported and opposed the PKO Law. It was expected that most would name MOFA, the parties, or factions involved in lobbying for or against the law. The purpose of this question was to explore whether there were any significant interests that were pushing or opposing the law that had not been widely reported. As expected, most named the obvious parties or party factions responsible for the passage of the PKO Law and those who opposed it. Some, however, named significant individuals and their agendas. This question thus probed the identity of the change agents involved in the decision-making process.

These two questions were asked first because they set the agenda for the rest of the interview. They subtly reminded the interviewee that change had taken place in Japanese foreign policy.[31] This understanding led to the third question. The third question and its subsidiary parts asked what the respondents felt to be the long-term goals of Japanese foreign policy and whether they felt that these were the right long-term goals. Having been reminded that change had taken place, the interviewees were now asked where they thought the direction of that change was going and whether that change was felt to be positive. The interviewees were permitted to ponder the implications of change in Japanese foreign policy by being asked why they felt the way they did about the changes. This aspect of question three resulted in many long pauses, as clearly many of those interviewed appeared to have given little thought to why they felt the way they did about foreign policy.

The fourth question asked for the interviewees' opinion of what they personally thought the goal of Japanese foreign and security policy should be. This question was asked in order to permit the interviewees to express their own agenda for foreign policy and to allow the interviewer to place the interviews in the context of the respondents' own political beliefs. Follow-up questions asked what domestic and international obstacles there were to their goals and how Article Nine fit into these goals. These subsidiary questions were partially designed to study how well the persons had thought out their agenda, particularly in light of Article Nine, which is so central to Japanese foreign policy.

The fifth question asked what kind of role Japan should seek in multilateral security forums. This question was designed to test attitudes and thinking about institutionalism on the part of Japan. It was also used to test whether Japan saw itself in a leadership role or in a participatory role in multilateral forums. Most respondents had to be prompted with examples of multilateral forums—an indication that they did not think of foreign policy in terms of multilateral efforts.

The sixth question asked the respondent to list the top three security and top three foreign-policy concerns for Japan. This question was designed to test awareness on the part of the elite of Japan's position in the world and the threats that it faces. This proved to be a very sensitive question to most, because it required them to list their concerns. Many respondents asked that their answers to this question be kept off the record, and even with these assurances, they were very careful in their answers. For example, many would list Korea as a security threat rather than name North or South Korea specifically. Those interviewed in MOFA were inclined this way, more so than were

Diet members. On the other hand, some Diet members were very frank and blunt in their assessment of Japan's security threats, with several listing the United States as Japan's number-one security threat! One Diet member, Representative Eisuke Mori, was especially frank and insightful when he listed Japan's top three security threats as "the economy, the economy, and the economy."[32] His realization that *without* its economic power, Japan would be just another country, without any real global significance, was extremely insightful. Japan's power and world position are directly tied to its economy. In the absence of military power and strength, Japan must use its economy as the basis of its claims to power. The ten-year recession in Japan has taken its toll on Japan's influence in the world.

The seventh question inquired into the September 1997 revisions of the United States-Japan Defense Guidelines and their implications for Japan. This question was designed to probe the respondents' understanding of the strengths and limits of Japanese foreign policy within the context of the United States-Japan Security Treaty and Article Nine. A follow-up question asked about the obstacles to the implementation of the 1997 revisions. It was hoped that this follow-up question would elicit insight into Japan's internal politics when dealing with foreign-policy change as a legal issue.

The eighth question asked about the role of the SDF and the limits that should be placed on it. This question was designed to elicit attitudes toward the SDF and the desire to see Japan as a more normal nation in terms of military power. In many ways, it was also a test of whether old militarist feelings would arise in the conversation, thus betraying a predisposition toward a more aggressive Japan. It was also hoped that this question would explore the limits of what elites in Japan see as the potential for the SDF.

The ninth question asked about how Japan should deal with its history in East Asia if it took on a larger role in world affairs. This question was designed to get at Japanese perceptions of how the Japanese see others who are viewing Japan. Japan's history in East Asia is very significant for China and Korea in particular. Any action that could be interpreted as Japan's taking on a more militaristic role in the world is likely to be met with opposition. China has been especially vocal in opposition to Japan's PKO missions, believing that these missions are setting a dangerous precedent. The question tested the level of awareness among Japanese elites of how Japan is viewed by other nations. It also tested Japanese attitudes toward the other nations of East Asia.

A follow-up question asked about the domestic consequences of a larger role for Japan. Given the pacifism that took root in Japan after World War II, it is thought that domestic opposition to Japan's increased military activity might be a major factor in Japan's deciding not to pursue certain foreign-policy goals. This question was designed to understand how elites viewed the domestic political situation.

The tenth question asked about domestic sources of foreign-policy change. It asked about the alliances and lobbying groups within the Diet and within Japanese politics that are pushing for change. The question was designed to uncover motives and agendas for change within the Japanese political world.

The eleventh question asked essentially the same thing at the international level. Its purpose was to gain an understanding of how elites view *gaiatsu* as part of Japanese foreign policy. As stated earlier in this chapter, *gaiatsu* was thought to be a major factor in the decision-making process of Japanese foreign policy. As the research progressed, however, it became clear that *gaiatsu* was not a major factor at all. Many of those interviewed were dismissive of the concept of *gaiatsu*. As one MOFA official stated, "Do you really think we would do anything that was not in our best interest?"[33] Remarkably few named the United States as a source of pressure for change.

The twelfth question dealt directly with Article Nine by asking whether it should be revised in the future and what form the revisions should take. The purpose of this question was to see if there was any movement to amend the constitution and to rid Japan of the proverbial burden of Article Nine. Such a move would mark a radical change in Japanese foreign policy. The removal of Article Nine would normalize Japanese foreign policy and make it similar to that of other nations. The answers to this question split sharply along party lines, with the LDP taking the forefront among those arguing for revision. (It is noteworthy that the LDP had, just a few weeks before the start of the interviews, convened a committee to discuss whether there was a need to create a committee to plan constitutional reform.)[34]

Question number thirteen asked about the Japanese commitment to bear the costs of world order. It questioned whether Japan was ready and willing to sacrifice itself for the good of the world. The purpose of this question was to ask whether Japan was ready to pay the price to be a world leader. Japan is often seen as motivated to act only if such an action furthers its own objectives. It has not given much indication, beyond its financial commitments through its Official Development Assistance (ODA), that it possesses the largess to be frequently involved in international situations, the way the United States. and other Western powers have.

The fourteenth question asked about the proposed revisions to the PKO Law that were before the Diet. This question brought the interview full circle and tested whether there was the resolve to push for more change. The PKO Law marked a significant change in Japanese foreign policy, and the law's revisions are the next step. The question asked about the probability of passage; interviews with Diet members asked how they intended to vote on the revisions. It was hoped that with this question, the interviewee could be drawn into a discussion of future changes in the PKO Law.

The fifteenth question was asked only of academics and not of journalists. It simply asked the academic to place Japanese foreign policy into a theoretical paradigm. This was done in order to measure how Japanese intellectuals conceptualize their country's role. This question, surprisingly, resulted in the most refusals to answer. When asked this question, most of the respondents proceeded to complain about the American fixation with theory as opposed to substance. "American academics are too theoretical!" they often complained. The few that did answer this question placed Japan in the realist or institutionalist paradigms.

At the end of each interview, the interviewee was thanked and asked if he or she would refer or recommend someone else for an interview. Most were very helpful in this respect, and some were very enthusiastic. For example, the former defense minister, Hideo Usui, was so excited about the questions being asked that he got on the phone himself and asked several other high-ranking officials in the Diet, MOFA, and the JDA to let me interview them, and he set up the appointments himself! He said that he wanted me to ask them my questions so as to get them thinking about these kinds of issues, as he had been trying to raise the same issues for quite a while.[35]

The Respondents and the Rationale

A total of fifty-six interviews were conducted in Japan, with Japanese elites from both houses of the Diet, Prime Minister's Office, the JDA, MOFA, and academia. The questions were asked in both Japanese and English. The rationale for interviewing the Diet members was twofold. First, the constitution places the ultimate decision-making power in their hands along with the opinion of their elected leader, the prime minister. Second, as a result of reapportionment, the Diet is gaining significance as a major source of Japanese foreign policy. Interviews were actively sought with both younger Diet members and with older, more senior Diet members to gain insight into any possible generational differences between Diet members.

The rationale for interviewing the career bureaucrats in MOFA is that in Japan, the ministries wield tremendous power over all aspects of their jurisdiction. An illustration of this power is the fact that even academy-based think tanks must seek approval of the relevant ministries in order to operate. A foreign-policy think tank must have the permission of MOFA to function under Japanese law. This power gives MOFA control over the terms of debate on any issue and, more strikingly, control over what is discussed. Furthermore, MOFA has often presented policy in finished form to the Diet for its approval or rubber stamping. The mindset of MOFA officials and their attitudes concerning change were seen as potentially very important with respect to the foreign-policy restructuring process in Japan.

The JDA is probably one of the politically weakest agencies in the Japanese bureaucracy because of the sensitivity to military affairs. Officials who serve in the JDA are often on loan from other ministries, such as the Ministry of Finance. Thus, the JDA does not have the same internal dynamics as other bureaucracies in Japan. Because of Article Nine and the overall sensitivity in Japan to the very existence of the SDF, the JDA tends to keep a lower profile when it comes to policy advocacy.[36] The relevance of interviewing members of the JDA is important to this research in that the SDF is the organization that is charged with carrying out the PKO missions, and JDA members' opinions and input into the change process is seen as significant.

Academics were interviewed because they observe Japanese politics up close every day, and their advice is often sought in matters of policy making. It is for this reason that academics with close ties to government or politicians were particularly sought; however, academics far from the centers of power were also sought out for interviews. The reason was to check for feelings and opinions away from the capital. As mentioned, many academics in Tokyo have close ties to politicians or the various ministries. I felt that, to be proportional, I needed to interview those who looked at Tokyo politics from afar. These interviews confirmed the perspectives being given to me in Tokyo, but they also gave the added insight of how "the man on the street" felt, as opposed to how the power brokers felt.

Interviews with journalists were included because Japanese journalists often have special contact with policy makers. Policy makers will often tell journalists things that they do not want published immediately. The policy makers give background interviews on the process as it occurs, on condition that the information not be printed or broadcast until after the matter in dispute or negotiation is finalized. These special relationships give journalists much deeper inside stories when they finally do publish them. Interviewing journalists would be a way of checking the accuracy (and honesty) of answers given by politicians. Unfortunately, only one journalist was interviewed.

Over all, nine interviews were conducted with MOFA officials. There were five interviews with JDA officials. Twenty interviews were conducted with Diet members. Six of the interviews were with members of the upper house, and fourteen were with members of the lower house. Four members of the prime minister's office were interviewed. Five government-sponsored researchers were interviewed, and thirteen other academics were interviewed. One journalist was interviewed. One political candidate for the Diet was also interviewed. (He lost.)

The interviews lasted from twenty minutes (the shortest) to three hours (the longest). Most interviews averaged forty-five minutes to an hour. In interviews with Diet members, strict attention to time had to be paid because of their busy schedules, but often, as a result of the questions, the member extended the interview into their next appointment because they found the questions so fascinating (and useful to themselves?). There seemed to be an appeal to the questions that made the elites think about matters they were not used to thinking about. This situation illustrates that maybe the questions that were asked in the interview are not being asked enough in Japan.

In summary, given the natural tendency of political elites to guard their personal opinions carefully, the questions gave a creative tension to the interview process. Answers to questions that challenged their values or their party's positions helped to gauge an understanding with respect to the assumptions underlying those values. A deeper question concerns these elites' underlying values. The response to this question is important in that ultimate beliefs often provide the perspectives that lead to decisions. The question is: Can ultimate values and realities be explored, maybe even realized, in ways not imagined by the current situation or under current policies? In many ways it is hoped that the answer is, "Yes, these values can be explored," but it will take time and the building of relationships to do so.

One immediate result of the interviews is insight into what Japan can offer the world and the United Nations that is more appropriate and more unique than military force. Some of the elites, especially the Socialists, tried to think outside the box of military power and the use of institutionalized violence. They welcomed the interviews as a chance to explore new ways of thinking.

Hermann's model allows for the attitudes and beliefs of a political system's constituency. These attitudes and beliefs are not so easily discovered by pollsters who look for current positions on issues. Yet some such convictions were uncovered in the interviews simply through inferences from the responses. The questions were open-ended and permitted follow-up questions that helped to clarify meanings. The overall picture gave insight into how the foreign-policy restructuring process takes place in Japan. The next section will give an overview of the results of the research and the insight that it gives us into foreign-policy restructuring.

What Are the Foreign-Policy Makers Thinking?

The field research proved fruitful. Many insights were gained from personal contact with decision makers that could not have been gained from written questionnaires. Personal interviews provided me with insight into the personal struggle many of these decision makers went through in order to come up with policy. The interviews also provided insight into the process of Japanese foreign-policy decision making and the obstacles to its restructuring.

The intellectual and institutional base for foreign-policy making in Japan is MOFA, where some of the brightest and most intelligent people in Japan work.[37] It would be a grave error for any nation to underestimate MOFA. Nevertheless, a power shift is taking place by which the Diet will direct foreign policy toward great powers and issues, leaving policy toward small nations and issues in the capable hands of MOFA in any given administration. Younger Diet members are looking to the Diet to be the principal source for foreign policy. While MOFA welcomes raising the profile of foreign-policy issues, it will most certainly resist the erosion of its power. However, some MOFA officials see this change as beneficial because the level of debate over foreign policy at the popular level has dropped to near zero in Japan.[38]

In the foreign-policy change matrix, as in most institutions, there is a generational propensity for change. In MOFA, this propensity is not as evident because of the strictness of the hierarchical structure in the ministry. While not an anathema, change does not seem to be desirable unless it can be contained. This can be seen by the rote answers, to interview questions given by MOFA members. For example, when asked about the long-range goals of Japanese foreign policy, most MOFA officials singled out "the safety and betterment of life for the Japanese people."

This response is in contrast to answers given by the Diet members, who could clearly name short-term goals, even when they struggled to name specific long-range goals. In particular, newer, younger Diet members seem frustrated by the slow pace of change. They seem to be pushing hard for change in the foreign-policy decision-making process. In some ways, their desire is to truly reflect democratic change, in which the "people" or their representatives are making, or at least influencing, the foreign-policy process on a regular basis.

Karel van Wolferen, in his book *The Enigma of Japanese Power,* describes Japan as basically run by bureaucrats, who have an inordinate amount of influence in a country that is supposed to be a democracy. Many of the younger generation of Diet members seem to chafe at the level of control exercised by the various ministries. They wish to see Japanese foreign policy reflect the elected leadership in Japan, rather than mirroring career officials in MOFA. Many of these younger Diet members have studied overseas and have observed the foreign-policy-making process in other countries, especially the Western democracies. They would like to see Japan have a similar foreign-policy-making process. The problem for Japan seems to be that most Diet members do not think enough about foreign policy, and MOFA itself fails to think originally about foreign policy. MOFA's group mindset dominates and seems to crush individual or independent thinking. This lack of originality in thinking is stunting the maturation of Japanese foreign policy in the post-Cold War world.

It is because of the bureaucratic mentality on the part of MOFA that the largest obstacle to restructuring may be the institution of MOFA itself. The legislature may attempt reform, but MOFA may choose to fight it, in an attempt to preserve its power over foreign-policy making. In "Structural 'Gaiatsu': International Finance and Political Change in Japan," T. J. Pempel makes the argument that institutional change is difficult without crisis.[39] While Pempel makes his argument in the area of economic reform, I would argue in the area of foreign policy. A crisis such as the Gulf War and the end of the Cold War gave Japan the push to make changes. In the absence of a crisis, future restructuring will be slow. The crisis of the Persian Gulf War pushed Japan to restructure, but it lacks a coherent plan beyond a general desire not to be seen as doing nothing in future conflicts. Japan has yet to answer the question (for itself) of where foreign policy is going. With no crisis to provide impetus, Japan is drifting.

An example of the problems facing Japan as a world power is its inability to *act* as a military power alongside the United States. Japan struggles to define the role of the SDF in peacetime as well as in wartime.[40] As Col. Noboru Yamaguchi pointed out in an interview, Japanese law currently requires tanks to stop at all traffic lights, even when engaged in combat (reality and common sense would dictate that the law would be ignored).[41] Japan simply has no detailed plans or contingencies for truly dealing with crises. In the event of a crisis, the Japanese government would still be debating about its policy responses while other nations are acting. This lack of planning is not confined to foreign and security policy but is also seen in other areas, as witnessed by the Japanese government's slow response to the Kobe earthquake.

Another problem is the debate over Japan's foreign-policy independence from the United States. Because of the use of *gaiatsu* as a source for Japanese actions, many in Japan feel that Japan has given in to the United States too many times.[42] Ryozo Kato, director general of the Foreign Policy Bureau of MOFA, stated that in a normal bilateral relationship, each side gives in about 50 percent of the time. In the United States-Japan relationship, Japan gives in 100 percent of the time; and there is a need for Japan to "win" once in a while.[43] Dissatisfied decision makers are looking for ways to "show" Japan's independence by disagreeing with the United States. What they ignore is that, for most of the Cold War, it was the United States that accommodated Japan.[44] According to Kato, Japan is suffering from a kind of interdependent fatigue syndrome and needs to start looking inward rather than outward.[45] Many in Japan want to see a more independent Japan vis-à-vis the United States. The problem for Japan is that going against the United States is not easy when often what is good for America is good for Japan, too.[46] There seemed to be a belief on the part of many respondents that Japanese restructuring should increase the country's independence from the United States.[47] This attitude is reminiscent of the earlier illustration, which described the United States and Japan in a father-son relationship. Some just want to see Japan break away from the United States and be independent for the sake of independence, regardless of how this change would affect Japan in a longer time frame.

Old versus New

Belief systems raise the question of whether the older generation in Japanese politics can change its way of operating and invest in the future with new thinking. The younger generation in the Diet is champing at the bit to raise its level of influence in the Diet. It is hindered by a seniority system that rewards seniority over competence. Moving up in leadership was likened by one youthful Diet member to climbing a pole with a person above you and below you. The only way to move up was for someone to fall from above you; there is no chance of passing people above you.

There is clear evidence of a generational gap in the Diet.[48] The younger generation is looking for new ways, while the older leadership wants to follow traditional methods. Many of the younger generation in the Diet have had foreign educations and are much more knowledgeable than the previous generation. Time is on the side of the younger generation, but the question is whether the needs of the nation for change will be met in the near future. There is a battle for influence going on in the Diet. Most members of the younger generation are attempting to climb the leadership pole as quickly as possible without alienating the older members, but this is a very difficult task, given Japanese societal norms, which demand respect for one's elders and those in senior positions.

The youth are making an impact on Japanese foreign policy. An interesting story was related to me by an academic in Japan about the friction within the LDP during the drafting of the PKO Law. It would seem that Representative Hajime Funada (one of the younger members of the Diet) was in a meeting where many of the older members of the party opposed to the PKO Bill were in attendance. These party elders were set to let the bill die a legislative death as had happened to the Kaifu Bill. Representative Funada stood up and physically blockaded the door, refusing to let any of the members out until they agreed to back the PKO Bill. In the end, the older members relented and backed the bill in the full Diet. This example of Representative Funada and his actions during the debate on the PKO Bill illustrate this growing influence of young Japanese legislators on Japanese foreign policy.

This younger generation often speaks English or some other foreign language well and have traveled and/or lived abroad for work or education. They are also doing the very thing that they need to do to influence Japanese policy: they are getting reelected.[49] They are persuading the older generation to make some changes. The interaction between the two generations is the key to understanding leader-driven change coming out of the Diet as a primary change agent. This interaction occurs in what I call the *interflux*[50] *of change.* Change occurs, not in a vacuum, but in a dynamic, ever-changing process. Younger Diet members are in a constant maneuver with the older generation to influence the direction of policy. There is no straightforward pattern that explains what the outcome of these maneuvers will be. The interflux of change, as it affects our theories for foreign-policy restructuring, and Hermann's model is illustrated in Figure 5.4. Part of this generational gap is due to Japan's history. Many older right-wing Diet members oppose an apology of any kind to the nations of East Asia, especially China.[51] The conservative right wing in Japan is in a state of denial about Japan's image vis-à-vis the rest of the world. Its steadfast opposition to apologies in general, and to China in particular, for actions taken during World War II has led to continued mistrust of Japan and its intentions. This mistrust is a major obstacle to an independent Japanese foreign policy. A valuable lesson that these right-wing elements within Japan could learn is from the positive results of Japan's apology to South Korea.

Part of the problem is that in many ways, Japan still behaves like a defeated nation. People in Japan want something to be proud of, and they do not want to have to think about all that they have to be ashamed of. Most nations seek pride in themselves through military might, through victories, and/or through heroes. This personhood, if you will, projects the power of the nation onto its citizens, much as sports fans personalize their association with their favorite team. An example applicable to Japan would be the recent Japanese movie *Pride,* which was so popular in Japan.[52]

Japan's Aspirations

Economic power does not carry the same status as military power. The desire is to be rich *and* powerful, not just nouveau riche. Japan's right wing sees economic power as being middle class, not upper class. Pervasive class attitudes about Japan's position in the world plague Japanese thinking. An ex-

Figure 5.4 **The "Interflux of Change" as it Affects Our Theories of Foreign-Policy Restructuring and Hermann's Model**

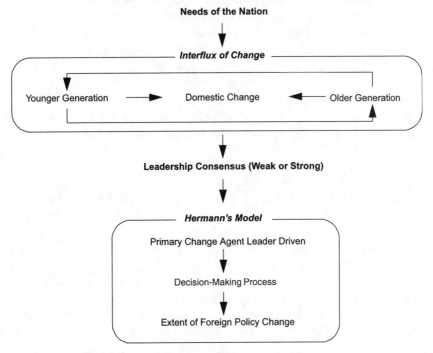

ample of this viewpoint is the book by Ezra Vogel, *Japan as Number One.*[53] Japan does not want to be seen as second class. First class is the only goal. Equality with others is a myth. Rank is primary. An example of how ingrained this desire is in Japanese society is the educational system, in which everyone must have the same opportunity, but it is test scores and class rank that dictate the future.

The problem with right-wing aspirations for a more independent Japan is that Japan is doing well overall without having to resort to militarism. Japan is using its prestige and reputation to establish its position and role through international institutions. If it chooses to confront the U.S. hegemony outright, it will win some battles at first, but in the end, it will lose as a result of lack of resources that could sustain its own hegemony. This is not to say that Japan would not choose to pursue hegemony; rather, it is in its own best interest not to do so. This argument depends on the logic of Japanese leadership to foresee the misconception of pursuing hegemony.

Remember the central focus of this chapter and book—finding the answer to the questions of how Japan's situation helps our understanding of foreign policy restructuring and decision making, and where Japan as a nation is headed. In the interviews, most respondents did not even realize what a multilateral forum was until they were given examples. In a given situation or crisis, consideration of options depends on knowing what those options are. Many in the Japanese hierarchy of foreign-policy leadership failed to consider or even know what options were available. When faced with a crisis, Japanese leaders behave as realists. Their understanding of the situation is based on a worldview that historically has tended to be realist in nature. They may consider other options, such as neoinstitutionalism, but they do so from a realist perspective. If you combine Japanese domestic conditions and international options, Japan's realism is, overall, very predictable. Japan will react to an external event based on its own capabilities and options, as realist theory predicts.

Thus, external events have the greatest potential to dictate foreign-policy changes for Japan, but these external events must still filter through the matrix of domestic opinion. Witness the August 1998 testing by North Korea of the Taepodong-1 missile over Japan. Several of the Diet members that I interviewed contacted me after my return to the United States to voice their concern and ask my opinion on the issue. The test firing of this missile also caused the Japanese public to acknowledge the North Korean threat to Japan (more on this subject subsequently). According to a poll taken by *Yomiuri Shimbun* (a leading Japanese newspaper), 70 percent of Japanese are worried about the outbreak of war, and nearly 60 percent feel that Japan will be attacked by military force.[54] North Korea's testing of the Taepodong-1 and planned testing of the Taepodong-2 missile in August or September of 1999, but postponed indefinitely under international pressure, has led the Japanese government to pursue the purchase of airborne-refueling capability for the Air Self-Defense Forces (ASDF). The idea being that if a missile fell in Japan or possibly violated its airspace, Japan would use the ASDF to preemptively destroy the North Korean launch site in "self-defense." This new attitude marks a huge change for Japan and its interpretation of the constitution. The idea that Japan could take offensive action for defensive reasons would have been totally unthinkable several years ago. Additionally, in direct response to the North Korean threat, Japan is pursuing Theater Missile Defense system research with the United States. We see that Japan is once again restructuring its foreign policy (yet another reinterpretation of Article Nine) as a result of an external crisis. Japanese reaction is dependent on public support or the lack of it. Japanese officials believe that the public would support a prime minister who ordered the destruction of the North Korean launch site if a missile fell on Japan.[55] In the absence of an overarching policy that would otherwise focus Japan's external orientation, these external crises have the greatest ability to initiate change in Japanese foreign policy. Basically, this chapter has argued that change takes place at two levels. At one level, there are the agents of change as described in Hermann's model. On the other level, there are the normative preconditions for change that govern and regulate change. These preconditions limit the change process. Without understanding these intervening variables, it is difficult to understand or predict policy change.

The next several chapters will examine Japan's security options in the post-Cold War world in East Asia. The following chapter examines Japan's place in the international system and looks more closely at Japanese aspirations for hegemony. Included in this chapter will be an examination of how *gaiatsu* is used as a tool of the other Japanese agents of change. Data from the field research and further analysis of Japan's foreign-policy restructuring will be woven throughout all of the following chapters.

6

Planning for Japan's Future Security

. . . security is more than the objective physical state of being free from physical threat. It is also psychological: we are free from fear to the extent that we lack a feeling of fear.
—Donald Snow[1]

Former Japanese Defense Minister Hideo Usui describes Japanese national security as the number-one priority of Japan's foreign policy.[2] Yet, as Masashi Nishihara of the Japanese National Defense Academy writes,

> Today, political leaders rarely talk about *comprehensive* national security. Instead they talk about how to defend Japan and cope with emergency situations around Japan and in East Asia. Security debates are dominated by subjects such as surveillance satellites, theater-missile defense systems, in-flight refueling devices for jet fighters, antiterrorist units in the SDF and the police organization, and the need for emergency laws. This is a clear indication that the Japanese have shifted their priority in national security.[3]

In light of the high priority that Japan seems to be placing on national security, this chapter will examine Japan's national-security options beyond its alliance with the United States. Fundamental to this examination will be the fact that Japan needs to consider and is considering options beyond the framework of its alliance with the United States. This is not to say that Japan wants to sever its relationship with the United States (in fact, it can be said that the relationship is now as strong as it has ever been), but rather that Japan needs to be considering alternatives—a "plan B," if you will—should Japan ever be abandoned by the United States or feel the need to demonstrate its independence from the United States by ending the United States-Japan Security Treaty. Diet member Shigeru Ishiba noted that "Japan cannot afford to be without allies, and who can it really trust except for the United States? Why? The U.S. bases here in Japan have proven America's commitment to Japan."[4] The problem for a Japanese "plan B" is that Japan has no real friends in the region. Thus, the question is

whether Japan should be doing more to cultivate friendships within its security complex.

As mentioned previously, Japan has a very real fear of abandonment.
During the Cold War, the United States's number-one priority was security.
When trade or economic conflicts between Japan and the United States oc-
curred, U.S. security concerns took precedence over economic concerns. With
the end of the Cold War, Japan cannot count on the security concerns of the
United States distracting it during trade conflicts. Japan's significance to the
United States is much less important in the post-Cold War era than it was
during the time of the Cold War. The fear in Japan is not just that the United
States might abandon it, but that its role it the world will be ignored or deemed
insignificant by the nations of the world.

The origins of this fear go back to the world community's reaction to
Japan's nonparticipation in the Gulf War. Japan was at the pinnacle of its
economic power, and yet its contribution to the war effort, while significant
in economic terms, was deemed insignificant by Japan's allies because there
was no human contribution. When the Gulf War was fought, Japan was sitting on the sidelines. There is even a Japanese term for this irrelevance that
describes what Japan has been feeling. It is called *"Japan passing."*[5] The
concept deals with Japan's fear that the world is passing it by and ignoring it
as irrelevant. While these fears may be overstated because Japan has such
tremendous economic influence; it does have a real fear of abandonment. In
particular there is the fear by many in Japan that Japan will be abandoned by
the United States in favor of China.

Part of the foundation for this fear came during the Clinton administration,
when it was alleged that Clinton's campaign had received contributions from
sources in China, giving rise to the appearance that the Clinton administration
was beholden to China. While in the United States it may seem outlandish, or
at best unproven in legal terms, that the Clinton administration traded influence for campaign contributions; outside of the United States it would seem
foolish for other nations, particularly such allies in the region as Japan, to
assume that the Clinton administration was not beholden to China. Common
sense dictates that they must at least consider this possibility and factor it into
their foreign-policy calculations. Japan is no exception to this rule.

This fear of undue Chinese influence was reinforced by Clinton's refusal
(at China's request) to stop off in Japan after visiting China in the summer of
1998 to brief the prime minister of America's most important ally in the
Pacific on the summit with China's leaders, as had been the custom of American presidents returning from summits in China before Clinton.[6] The Clinton
administration's increasingly close ties to China were noted outside of East
Asia. As Ted Galen Carpenter wrote in *Foreign Affairs:*

The increasingly cozy U.S.-Chinese relationship—described by President Clinton and Secretary of State Madeleine K. Albright in terms like "strategic cooperation" and "strategic partnership"—has alarmed Taiwan, unsettled longtime U.S. allies *Japan* and South Korea, and prodded India to unveil its nuclear weapons program. Such reactions will have long-term repercussions for Washington's political and military roles in Asia."[7]

While no Japanese leader would ever directly accuse an American administration of being unduly influenced by a foreign government, prudence would dictate that Japan's leaders consider the possibility and that Japan must be prepared to deal with such an eventuality as abandonment if it should ever happen.[8] The advent of the George W. Bush administration in the United States and the ensuing close ties between Japanese Prime Minister Koizumi and President Bush has helped alleviate Japanese fears of abandonment for the time being. However, abandonment could be only one American election away. It is in Japan's best interest to at least consider the possibility and lay the diplomatic groundwork for such an eventuality. Japan's national security depends on the abilities of its leaders to plan for multiple eventualities and possible setbacks.[9] As Ken Yamada wrote in the *Mainichi Shimbun,* quoting "high-level" diplomatic sources in Japan, "Tokyo might be forced to review its strategy and become a political superpower that could contend with the United States and China."[10] Former Prime Minister Morihiro Hosokawa went so far as to argue that the U.S. military presence in Japan needs to be reduced and that "Japan plays a far more vigorous role in the alliance."[11] The Japanese leadership is concerned and worried about Japan's national security and is exploring its options. This chapter will look at these options to see how they stack up against the dominant realism that is believed to be guiding Japanese foreign policy as described previously. In order to examine carefully Japan's foreign and national security options, we must first look at the current status of Japanese national security.

Japan's National Security

National security has traditionally been determined by a nation's political, military, and economic capacity.[12] Japan stacks up very well in each traditional area. It has capable domestic and foreign policy leadership, a very solid political system that espouses free and fair elections, and a strong, respected constitution that has given Japan a stable government.[13] During the last decade of the Cold War, under the United States-Japan Security Treaty, Japan's responsibility was to secure the sea lanes of communication (SLOCs) around Japan up to a thousand miles out. Thanks in large part to this responsibility, Japan has built a very modern and technologically advanced air and maritime defense force that is well able to protect the Japanese home islands. Japan's status as an island nation makes it considerably less vulnerable to conventional threats, such as invasion. Furthermore, the Ground Self Defense Forces (GSDF) is a modern, well-equipped fighting force generally capable of repulsing almost any attempt by an existing potential foreign invader to invade the Japanese home islands.

Beyond Japan's ability to defend itself is the question of its ability to protect its interests abroad. Protecting one's interests abroad requires an ability to project power. Japan does not currently have military power projection capabilities beyond the defense of the home islands. Japan lacks the power to militarily enforce its interests beyond the areas surrounding Japan. Under the terms of the United States-Japan Security Treaty, Japan depends on the United States for this capability.[14]

At the same time, Japan does have influence far beyond its military strength; largely because of its economic power and capabilities. However, it is very difficult to measure power outside of the terms of traditional military power. Japan obviously has power far beyond the reach of the SDF, but it is difficult to quantify or to measure. As Donald Snow wrote:

> *Measuring Power*—Although the concept of power is so pervasive and attractive for describing the operation of the international system, its precise measurement remains elusive. The difficulty has two bases.
>
> The first is finding physical measures that adequately describe the abilities of states to influence one another. A common effort has been to try and find concrete, physical measures, such as the size or sophistication of the armed forces or the productivity of states' industrial bases that should indicate which is the more powerful country in any head-to-head confrontation. The problem is that such measures work only part of the time; there is, for instance, no physical measurement to compare national capacities that would have led to the conclusion that North Vietnam had any chance of defeating the United States in a war, but they certainly did.
>
> The second problem is that measures cannot get at the psychological dimension of will and commitment. How can an outside observer determine, for instance, when a clash of interests is clearly more important to one party to a dispute than it is to an adversary (at least before the fact)? Once again, the Vietnam War is illustrative; the outcome of that conflict (unification of the country) was clearly more important to the North Vietnamese and its southern allies than its avoidance was to the United States. That is clear in retrospect; it was not at all clear before and even during the conduct of hostilities. Being able to see clearly in retrospect is of very little comfort to the policymaker.[15]

In economic terms, Japan is second only to the United States in terms of gross national product (GNP). Its industrial and technological prowess is world renowned.

It is partially due to Japan's strength in these traditional areas that define national security that Japan has experienced no direct threat to its national security outside of the possible threat from North Korea, if a Korean conflict were to spill over into Japan, and possibly the regional, hegemonic aspirations of China. A total breakdown of government in Russia might cause a refugee crisis for Japan, but this would probably not be a direct threat to its territory.

All of these concerns take into account the traditional definition of national security, but as Donald Snow also wrote:

> . . . security is more than the objective physical state of being free from physical threat. It is also psychological: we are free from fear to the extent that we lack a feeling of fear. Different people have contrasting notions about what makes them feel safe or secure; security will thus always, to some extent, be subjective. We may all agree on certain core conditions, primarily physical in nature, that define security, but there will also be areas where we disagree on what enhances or diminishes security. It is largely these disagreements that divide the traditionalists from the contemporary school.[16]

The contemporary school referred to takes into account areas of national security that have not been traditionally defined as national security. This larger definition of national security is often called *comprehensive security* or *alternative security*[17] as we noted earlier in relation to Buzan et al. In the aftermath of the end of the Cold War there is a need for Japan to consider how it stacks up in terms of alternative security. Alternative security takes into account such divergent issues as narcotics, the environment, illegal immigration, and the strength of the national economy. These issues are increasingly considered threats to national values, as well as to "the security and prosperity of the nation," to use the often repeated phrase given by MOFA to describe Japanese national goals.[18]

The concept of "comprehensive security" is actually of Japanese origin. In 1978, in the aftermath of America's defeat in Vietnam and the Middle East oil shocks, Prime Minister Masayoshi Ohira commissioned a private study group in the Nomura Research Institute to study Japan's foreign-policy options. Up to that point, Japanese foreign policy had been very unidirectional. The shocks of the 1970s showed Japan how dependent it was on foreign energy sources and raw materials and that the United States, its only formal ally, was not omnipotent and was seemingly in decline. The Nomura Institute came up with a concept it called comprehensive security. The idea was that, in light of its constitutional limitations, Japan should provide for its own security on a "holistic basis." In other words, Japan was attempting to define itself in terms of its own internal stability, national development, and social harmony (*wa*).[19] Japan would focus on more than just the military and aspects of national security but would also look at its national security from the perspective of its national needs in their entirety.[20] This wider outlook led Japan to pursue a more active role in the United Nations. It also began to take a more activist role in such international organizations as the World Trade Organization (WTO) in order to lobby for issues such as the continuation of the Japanese ban on imported rice.[21] Japan has also worked hard internationally to protect Japanese worldwide fishing rights and to preserve whaling, as well as to preserve the environment in Japanese ocean fisheries.[22] These concerns reflect, not only Japan's economic national security, but also cultural values and needs that go beyond the traditional concepts of national security.

In terms of comprehensive security, Japan does not do as well as when only traditional terms are examined. Japan has an illegal-immigration problem from China and Iran.[23] Though Japan's problem is not on the scale of the American illegal-immigration problem, it is affecting the culture of Japan. Japan's population is now declining, and most Japanese no longer wish to do the hard, dirty work that immigrants are willing to do. This situation has led to an influx of immigrants, both legal and illegal, into Japan, starting a slow dilution of Japanese ethnic homogeneity.[24] Homelessness, crime, and drugs are on the rise in Japan as traditional values break down and the economy remains stagnant. The state of the domestic economy, which is just attempting to emerge from a nearly fifteen-year-long recession, means that Japan is more heavily dependent on its international economy, and thus on the SLOCs, which facilitate its international trade, than ever before to keep the country economically sound.

In terms of comprehensive security, the greatest potential threat to Japan is economic, in the form of an interruption of commerce. It is for this reason that it is a very critical priority for Japan to maintain a strong allied relationship with the United States, whose power has a global reach that can extend to areas that Japan cannot touch. Without the United States, Japan would find itself exposed and its economic power stretched and potentially vulnerable.[25] This vulnerability is due to Japan's extensive investments abroad, with no real means of protecting it except diplomacy. The alliance with the United States helps to create a stability that protects Japanese economic investments and trade from foreign interference. Without the United States, Japan would need to protect its own trade, and its inability to do so makes it vulnerable. Japan worries about abandonment by the United States because of this economic vulnerability.

When asked in interviews to name the top three security threats to Japan, Japanese foreign-policy elites demonstrated a clear understanding of tradi-

Figure 6.1   **Security Threats to Japan as Named by Foreign-Policy Elites**

Threat	Countries	# of Times Mentioned	% of Respondents Listing in Top Three
1	North Korea	26	48%
	Korean Peninsula	23	43%
	North Korea First Response	33	61%
	Named Total:	49	91%
2	China	25	
	China/Taiwan	6	
	Total:	31	57%
3	Russia	14	26%
4	U.S. Abandonment	13	24%
4	Nuclear Proliferation*	13	24%
6	Economy	10	19%
7	Oil/Middle East	8	15%
8	Natural Disaster	6	11%
9	Collapse of Multilateral Cooperation	4	7%
10	Constitutional Limitations	3	6%
10	None	3	6%
10	Falling Behind in Technology	3	6%
10	U.S. Bases in Okinawa	3	6%
14	Food Supply	2	4%

Question asked: What are Japan's top three security threats or concerns?

Total responses: 162 (N=54). Note: Some respondents listed four responses as they could not prioritize the third threat. Three respondents listed only one answer (None). Two respondents refused to answer the question.

*There is a possible time bias here in that both India & Pakistan tested nuclear weapons during the period (May–June 1998) that the interviews were conducted. Under normal circumstances it might not have been this high. It is also very interesting to note that considering the time bias that only 20 percent of the respondents listed it as a top three foreign policy concern and only 24 percent listed it as a security threat.

tional threats and comprehensive threats to Japan's security. In terms of traditional threats, 91 percent of the respondents named North Korea or in an attempt to be more politically correct the interviewee would simply say, "The Korean Peninsula."[26] China or a China-Taiwan conflict was second, with 57 percent. This response was followed by Russia and United States abandonment, at 26 and 24 percent respectively. As expected, in terms of comprehensive security, many different potential threats were named. Some were surprising, and some were not so surprising. For a full examination of the responses given, refer to Figure 6.1. The opinions of the Japanese foreign-policy elites are reflected, but to a lesser extent, in a 1997 *Yomiuri Shimbun* poll, which asked, "Which of the following countries or regions do you think could become a military threat to Japan?" In response, 69 percent named the Korean peninsula, 32 percent named China-Taiwan, 23 percent named Russia, and the Middle East and the United States were both named 15 percent of the time.[27] The following section will examine the possibility that Japan might be abandoned by the United States or that it might be forced, through domestic political interests, to sever its relationship with the United States.

Abandonment

Any astute student of American domestic politics realizes that there is some (though not a probable) risk that the United States might abandon its security commitments to Northeast Asia. As Grieco writes, "For realists, a state will focus both on its *absolute and relative gains* from cooperation, and a state that is satisfied with a partner's compliance in a joint arrangement might nevertheless exit from it because the partner is achieving relatively greater gains."[28] Trade friction between the United States and Japan continues to present potential for a major United States-Japan rift.[29] Some critics of Japan, such as Chalmers Johnson and E. B. Keehn, have long argued that the United States should use the alliance (and thus, Japanese fears of abandonment) as a "tool" for American trade policy with Japan.[30] In an era where economics drives public opinion, popular opinion in the United States can easily drive American foreign policy. In the 1999 Chicago Council on Foreign Relations poll, the defense of America's allies was listed as "very important" by only 44 percent of the American public, as opposed to 61 percent in 1990.[31] By way of contrast, in a *Yomiuri Shimbun* poll that asked Japanese voters, "Do you think the United States would or would not help Japan militarily if Japan were attacked?" 68 percent felt that the United States would help. Only 22 percent felt that the United States would not help, and 10 percent had no opinion.[32] As Kang argues:

> There is a real danger that the United States might withdraw from or fundamentally rethink its security commitments in Northeast Asia. It must be kept in mind that not only "isolationists" but also prominent establishment figures such as Henry Kissinger think that the United States can, if necessary, play a "mediating" role between Japan and China. According to Kissinger, what the United States must do is to "help Japan and China coexist despite their suspicions of each other." Although he does not argue for an off-shore balancing strategy or disengagement for the United States in Northeast Asia, the logical implications of this view should be troubling to America's Asian allies and argues for a "community building" strategy that keeps democratic America actively engaged in a security community of Asian democracies.[33]

Japan needs the United States to be involved in the Northeast Asian secu- rity complex, not just for its own security, but also for regional stability. It is for this reason that the United States-Japan Security Treaty not only serves as a bilateral alliance for Japan, but also fills multilateral needs by reassuring East Asia that Japan is peaceful and by keeping potential regional hegemo- nies in check. The problem is that the importance of the United States-Japan Security Treaty has never been as appreciated as much in the United States as it has in Japan.[34] According to polls taken in 1996 and again in 1997, by the *Nihon Keizai Shimbun*, 56 percent of Japanese in each poll responded to the question, "What do you think of the Japan-US Security Treaty?" that it should be maintained, 33 percent felt that it should be abolished, and 11 percent had no opinion.[35] On the other hand, most Americans do not even know or are hardly aware of the treaty's existence.

Another potential event that might spell the end of the United States- Japan Security Treaty would be the collapse of North Korea and an ensu- ing reunification of the Korean peninsula. Without North Korea as the principal threat facing Japan, the need for the continuing existence of the United States-Japan alliance could be questioned by the people in both countries. The obvious response—that China still remains a threat—may be politically impossible to express.[36] In all probability, China would also feel threatened by the loss of the buffer zone of North Korea and would likely campaign loudly for the abolition of both the United States-Japan Security Treaty and the United States-Korea Security Treaty, along with the withdrawal of U.S. forces from the region. This is one possible sce- nario in which the United States-Japan Security Treaty could be abandoned, thus forcing Japan to go it alone.

Given the unspoken (and spoken) potential threat from China, Sino-Japanese relations are very critical for Japanese national security. There is a high level of awareness of this importance on the part of Japanese elites. It is very interesting to note that while the United States-Japan relationship is often called "the most important bilateral relationship in the world,"[37] when asked in interviews to name the top three priorities for Japanese foreign policy, Japanese elites named Japan's relationship with China just as frequently as that with the United States.[38] It is also significant that when Japanese were asked in a *Jiji Press* survey, "Which of the following countries or regions do you think will become more important for Japan to form closer relationships with? (choose up to three)," China polled 59 percent, just behind the United States at 60 percent. Southeast Asia was a distant third, at 39 percent.[39] How- ever, the prominence of the United States-Japan relationship was reinforced by a *Yomiuri Shimbun* poll, which asked, "Regarding political relations, do you think the United States or China will be more important in Japan's future?" As many as 50 percent chose the United States, 25 percent named China, and 21 percent felt that both were equally important.[40]

Many have begun to talk about a trilateral relationship between the United States, Japan, and China.[41] A noted Japanese foreign-policy expert, Reinhard Drifte, writes, "Without a doubt, the US-Japan-China security triangle is becoming the determining security relationship on which will depend the maintenance of peace and security of a region ranging from Southeast Asia to Northeast Asia."[42] Several of those interviewed expressed the need for Japan to push for a triangular relationship among the United States, Japan, and China in order for each side to play off the other's fears. They felt that if Japan did not do so, it would become a victim of *Japan passing* and be deemed irrelevant, at worst. In light of President Clinton's perceived slight of Japan in July 1998, Japan is feeling the need to aggressively cultivate its relations with both the United States and China in order to protect its status and power (security) in the region (something China is making increasingly difficult for Japan).[43]

A further area of concern for the United States-Japan relationship is the current budget debate over who should pay for the basing of U.S. troops in Japan. Japan wants the United States to pay, and the United States is adamant that Japan continue to pay. This is principally because if Japan were to stop paying for the stationing of United States troops in Japan, the U.S. Congress would likely balk at asking the American taxpayer to pay and call for the troops to be based back home in the United States. If this were to happen, the result would likely be the end of the United States-Japan Security Treaty in its present form. Japan would probably continue to have some kind of security guarantee from the United States, but not a strong one, on which it could depend in a crisis. Japan would be on its own to find new security guarantees. The following section will examine Japan's major security options within its security complex one by one.

Japan's Options*

As previously mentioned, the United States-Japan relationship is seen as the number-one bilateral relationship in the world, but Japan sees a need to work toward stronger relations with Asia in general.[44] According to former Foreign and Defense Minister Yukihiko Ikeda, "The end of the Cold War increased the number of players in Japanese foreign policy."[45] The problem for Japan is expanding its foreign policy to fit the post-Cold War realities that it faces.

When looking at Japan's foreign and security policy options, there is a need to consider Japan's limitation and goals. As discussed above, the greatest lim-

---

*This section is meant to be a *general* overview of Japan's options rather than a thorough treatment of them. A thorough and exhaustive treatment would be a text in and of itself.

iting factor for Japanese foreign policy is Article Nine. A major constitutional question of whether Japan can participate in bilateral or multilateral alliances would likely be revisited if Japan needs to consider formal alternatives to the United States in order to provide a security guarantee for itself.[46]

Furthermore, Japan is limited by the current weakness of its economy as Japan faces the hard fiscal reality of its domestic economic situation. The current weakness of the economy limits Japan's options internationally, in that it can not afford to contribute as much as it did in the past. As Aurelia George Mulgan wrote, "Japan's contributions to international organizations, humanitarian activities, and socio-economic development have undoubtedly been squeezed by the country's long-standing strategy of securing its position in the international community through financial means."[47]

As mentioned previously, the current ongoing economic crisis has also prompted the Japanese government to request that the United States pay for the basing of American troops in Japan.[48] This is something that the United States has been strongly resisting, because of congressional opposition and the ongoing trade friction between the two countries over access to Japanese markets.[49]

The United States continues to view Japan as an economic giant, and rightly so. Japan is the second-largest economy in the world and has been a major beneficiary of the post-Cold War world of the *Pax Americana* and such advantages as international free trade that go with it, but it has largely failed to adapt both its domestic and foreign economic policies to the opportunity presented by the end of the Cold War. Japan has stumbled each time that it was presented with an opportunity, and it has spent the last ten years failing to capitalize on the possibilities of the post-Cold War world, because of domestic political concerns, the principal concern being the political need to protect its domestic economy from foreign trade and Japanese markets from imported foreign goods.

Japan's domestic economy is the antithesis of its international economy. Domestically, Japan's economy is bloated and extremely inefficient; internationally it is lean and extremely efficient.[50] Agriculture is a major area of Japanese economic weakness, but it is an unduly powerful sector of Japanese politics. Politically prudent protectionist acts by the Japanese government have created a lot of ill will between the United States and Japan. What the United States might have overlooked during the Cold War is now the focus of large-scale trade disputes. Japan is stuck in a delicate balance between domestic politics and its international priorities.

So far, these concerns have held Japan back from exercising new foreign-policy options. The principal option lay in the circumstance that the end of the Cold War permitted it the possibility of moving outside the alliance with the United States (or in conjunction with it). The problem for Japan is that options that did not make the United States the central feature were anathema to Japan under the Yoshida Doctrine. It has been very hard for Japanese elites, especially those in MOFA, to think beyond an alliance with the United States. According to Masafumi Iishi, director of the Foreign Policy Planning Division of MOFA, "[Japanese] bureaucrats must think about the unthinkable: the loss of the U.S. alliance!"[51]

The principal security reason that Japan needs the United States is its nuclear umbrella, according to one senior Diet member. If Japan were abandoned, it would need to find an alternative way to deter nuclear attack upon itself.[52] Thus, the question centers on the options Japan can consider if it loses, or can no longer depend on, the United States for its security guarantee. And how can it develop relationships to hedge against a loss of the U.S. security guarantee? What choices does Japan have beside the United States? What relationships should Japan be cultivating in order to hedge its bets for the future? The next several subsections will briefly examine the strengths and weaknesses of Japan's major alternative allies to the United States. These are: China, Russia, ASEAN, South Korea, and/or North Korea.[53]

Option #1: China

In choosing alternative allies to the United States in East Asia, China is the first nation to come to mind in any discussion, because it is the third part of the Northeast Asian security triangle. As mentioned previously, many scholars see a United States-Japan-China security triangle, in which three powers balance against each other. Japan has large economic interests and investments in China. China desires these investments of capital and technology to continue and thus wants to have good relations with Japan. China is a major military power and a nuclear power, complete with intercontinental ballistic missiles (ICBMs). It is also a permanent member of the U.N. Security Council. At first glance, this combination of political power, size, and military strength could make China an attractive alternative to the United States for Japan. The problems are China's potential hegemonic ambitions and Japan's history in East Asia, particularly with China, during World War II.

In many ways China is an aspiring regional hegemon, which the nations of the region must recognize.[54] China wants to be *the* leader in Asia.[55] Some in Japan even believe that China wants to be a modern nineteenth-century-style expansive colonial power.[56] Thus, Japan would be the junior partner in any alliance with China. China would have it no other way. Japanese atrocities against China and the Chinese people during World War II would make it politically impossible for China to truly accept Japan on equal terms. Japan would be in a subservient role, more so than its present relationship with the United States. This change would represent a political loss for Japan and would be seen as a desperate move by an abandoned Japan to ally formally with China. It would also require Japan to come to terms with its actions during World War II.

Coming to terms with Japanese actions in China during World War II is problematic and a proverbial political hot potato in Japan. Many of Japan's senior-level officials are still in denial over Japan's role in the Pacific War. One senior MOFA official went so far as to describe China's anger at Japan as a " misunderstanding that frustrates the Japanese people [because of China's lack of understanding as to what Japan's real intentions were]."[57] Once, when former Japanese Prime Minister Morihiro Hosokawa mentioned at a press conference that he thought that Japan had made "mistakes" during World War II, there were calls on the floor of the Diet by former ministers of cabinet rank for him to be put to death. Japan is not ready to apologize to China for its actions in any meaningful way. This reluctance has bred suspicion in China over Japanese intentions in East Asia. It is also one of the reasons that China quietly accepts the United States-Japan Security Treaty, in that the treaty "keeps the Japanese genie in the bottle."

It is important to note the difference between Japan and Germany over the issue of atrocities by both nations during World War II. Because of its apology and remorse for its actions during World War II, Germany is seen as having repented. Thus, neo-Nazi groups within Germany are seen as extremists, atypical of the nation. In Japan, on the other hand, right-wing groups are often interpreted as representing the nation and the opinions of the nation, because Japan has failed to adequately apologize and show remorse for its actions. Japan lacks the social capital with its neighbors that Germany enjoys with its neighbors. The primary historical reason for this situation is explained very well by Grieco:

> The Cold War, in a word, required Franco-German reconciliation and the development of trust between those two countries, and this set the stage and even served as the motor for a wider institutionalization of state relationships in Western Europe. In East Asia the Soviet and Chinese threat was met by an American network of bilateral defense treaties. By consequence, the countries in the region that received American protection did not have a need to reconcile with Japan. Moreover, when China joined the American-led coalition of Pacific Rim states against the USSR in the 1970s, its joining was based on an informal entente with the United States and not a formal regional arrangement involving other regional states. Thus, while the Cold War induced cooperation and reconciliation in Western Europe, and set the stage for the formation of institutions and social capital able to

withstand the shocks of 1989–1990, it left Asia without either a habit of institutionalized cooperation or a reservoir of mutual trust able to contain or channel growing Chinese power.[58]

Japan does not enjoy reconciliation with its East Asian neighbors. It needs to forget about the propaganda of World War II that claimed Japan was liberating Asia from the West and face the fact that it was colonizing East Asia and behaving in a manner just as bad, if not worse, than any of the Western colonizers.[59]

Japan wants an interdependent relationship with China.[60] To have any hope of achieving this goal, Japan must deal honestly and forthrightly with its past. It also needs to engage in confidence-building measures with China.[61] Japan fears China's hegemonic aspirations almost as much as China fears a militarily independent Japan that once again is held in the sway of Japanese nationalism.

Japan also fears a close Sino-American relationship that would leave Japan on the outside looking in. China's actions in overly protesting the accidental bombing of its embassy in Belgrade by the United States during the Kosovo campaign, and the April 1, 2001, collision between a U.S. Navy EP-3 Aries electronic surveillance aircraft and a Chinese F-8 played into the hands of those who prefer to see stress or tension in the Sino-American relationship, such as Japan (Russia and India too). China's holding of the EP-3 crew and demands for an apology from the U.S. government rankled the administration of George W. Bush and heightened tensions that did not ease until the events of September 11, 2001. It is important to note that good relations between powerful rivals are not always welcomed by other nations when there are allies that fear abandonment if the relationship were to get too cozy (Japan).

Japan wants each side to depend on it to some extent. It prefers to keep its alliance with the United States, but it knows that it must and should hedge its bets by improving relations with China. While Japan may better its relations with China, China does not make a good ally for Japan. Japan would have to pay a huge political cost both at home and in pride to ally with China. Its best bet is to work with China to reduce tension in the China-United States-Japan triangle.

Option #2: Russia

Russia is considered the "sick man" of Northeast Asia, but it is a very strong "sick man." Russia is still the single biggest threat to Japan in terms of overall capabilities. A Japanese alliance with Russia would represent a

Photo 6.1 **U.S. Navy EP-3 Aries** (*Source:* U.S. Navy photo. www.chinfo.navy.mil)

Photo 6.2 **EP-3 on Hainan Island, China, Being Disassembled for Transport**
(*Source:* U.S. Navy photo. www.chinfo.navy.mil)

Photo 6.3 **Prime Minister Koizumi Speaks to a Political Rally on the Northern Territories (Kuril Islands)** (*Source:* Photo courtesy of the Office of the Cabinet Public Relations, Cabinet Secretariat, Japan)

direct threat to China's (possible) regional hegemonic aspirations. However, for Japan, an alliance with Russia is currently problematic, because Japan and Russia have never signed a peace treaty formally ending World War II.[62] A dispute exists over the Japanese claim to four small islands called the Kuril Islands, which are off the northeast coast of Hokkaido and have been occupied by Russia since August 1945. As one high-level MOFA official put it, "These four islands shouldn't determine Japanese policy toward Russia, but the principle is [the] issue."[63] Japan needs to solve this island issue as soon as possible.[64]

An alliance with Russia has one great advantage, which is Russia's nuclear capability.[65] A Russian nuclear umbrella over Japan could replace the United States nuclear umbrella, without Japan's being forced to develop its own independent nuclear deterrent. Whether Russia would be likely to offer nuclear protection to Japan is questionable, at best. A Russo-Japanese alliance would raise tensions in Northeast Asia and be a cause of great concern to China. Improving relations with Russia and solving the territorial disputes would be advantageous to Japan, but given the shaky political and economic state of Russia today, Russia would not likely make a good ally in the near future. Any alliance between Russia and Japan is likely to end up with Japan as a "cash cow" for Russia, and given the state of Japan's economy, such an outcome would be difficult to achieve.[66]

Option #3: Multilateral Options, including ASEAN/ARF

In general, Japan has had a very favorable attitude toward most of the East Asian multilateral initiatives, though it has approached most of these from a purely bilateral perspective.[67] Given this viewpoint, Japan has two major East Asian multilateral foreign and security policy options. The first is the existing ASEAN/ARF structure, which now includes most of the nations of East, Southeast, and Southern Asia. The second is any future Northeast Asian Security forum in which Japan chooses to participate. The great benefit of multilateral efforts for Japanese foreign policy is that not even the Japan Communist Party (JCP) opposes multilateralism. Representative Mitsuo Higashinaka, the JCP's leading foreign-policy expert, went so far as to say that multilateral efforts should be a priority of Japanese foreign policy, provided the forums are neutral, as ASEAN and ARF are.[68] In interviews with foreign policy makers in Japan, an overwhelming 83 percent favored Japanese multilateral efforts; only 5 percent opposed Japan's having a role in multilateral forums; 5 percent supported Japan's taking only a financial role; and 7 percent had no opinion or did not know.[69]

In the absence of a security crisis or a threat (such as an aggressor China or a China-Taiwan conflict that spills over into Southeast Asia or the SLOCs) that draws Japan and ASEAN together, an alliance is unlikely to occur. ASEAN is interested in Japan *economically,* not militarily. ARF, on the other hand, offers Japan a chance to raise the level of its security dialog with the rest of the region and to work for regional stability through confidence-building measures.

Northeast Asia lacks anything like Southeast Asia's ASEAN or ARF. The closest thing is the now defunct KEDO (Korean [Peninsula] Energy Development Organization). It is in Japan's interest to foster cooperation among Northeast Asian nations, but the dynamic is different in Northeast Asia than it is in Southeast Asia. Southeast Asia lacks a major power, while Northeast Asia has several. The Northeast Asian nations are more confident in their own power, whereas Southeast Asian states seek to shore up their own security (insecurities) through multilateral efforts. Additionally, the United States-Japan Security Treaty and the United States-Korea Security Treaty make, in many ways, Japan, South Korea, and the United States a de facto alliance because of the United States bilateral security commitments to both nations.[70] The United States-Japan Security Treaty also serves as a way to keep the United States closely tied to the region. As Professor Shin'ichi Ogawa of the National Institute for Defense Studies stated during an interview, "The United States-Japan alliance has many merits for Japan and compliments any [potential] regional security alliances."[71] For a nation that worries that the United States will abandon it, the pursuit of a Northeast Asian regional security forum that includes the United States would seem an excellent way to keep the United States engaged and lessen the likelihood that the United States will totally abandon Japan.[72]

Option #4: South Korea

South Korea is Japan's most natural ally in the region. Both nations have complimentary security needs. As Sheldon Simon, a noted expert on East Asian security, writes, "Both [Japan and South Korea] Asian states are dependent on the sea lanes of communications along the Pacific Rim for energy and general international commerce."[73] The greatest evidence that Japan is hedging its bets, against an unsought abandonment by the United States, are its efforts to repair relations with South Korea. Japan has apologized for its colonial occupation of Korea in a way that the South Korean government has chosen to accept.[74] In October 1998, Japanese Prime Minister Keizo Obuchi offered an unprecedented written apology that expressed regret for the suffering and harm that Japan inflicted as a colonial power on the Korean people.[75] In the interviews I conducted, Korea was ranked third as the most frequently mentioned foreign-policy priority for Japan (behind the United States and China) by Japanese foreign-policy makers.[76]

The stability of the Korean peninsula is critical to Japanese national security. The threat posed by North Korea gives the United States-Japan Security Treaty its unspoken raison d'être for Japan. North Korea represents the greatest single threat to Japanese national security. For this reason alone, Japan needs to advance its security relations with South Korea. Over 90 percent (n = 154) of the foreign and security experts interviewed in Japan listed either North Korea or the Korean peninsula as one of the top three concerns for Japanese national security; 61 percent listed it as the number-one threat to Japan. This

Photo 6.4 (and at right) **Schoolchildren's Artwork on Public Display in South Korea** (*Source:* Photos by GORD, used with permission. http://aog.2y.net/forums/index.php?s=1b087b1e170979978f8af314d0e010b1&showtopic=1550&st=0)

finding is in comparison to China, which, at 57 percent, was the second most frequently named threat to Japan; less than 10 percent listed China as the number-one threat to Japan (for more detail, see Figure 6.1 above).[77] It is for this reason that Japan's relationship with South Korea can be seen as indispensable to its national security. In any renewed Korean conflict, Japan and Korea would need to work closely together. While South Korea would probably never permit Japanese SDF troops on its soil, it would probably welcome Japanese naval and air power efforts against the North and Japan's assistance as a staging area for U.S. forces.[78]

South Korea's potential as an ally has been often understated or overlooked. Korea has frequently been described as " a shrimp swimming among whales."[79] The days during the Korean War when Korean troops were the first to flee in combat are in the past. Decades of staring at their Northern enemy across the DMZ (Demilitarized Zone) and training to face them have hardened South Korea forces into a potent military force. Even as far back as the Vietnam War, South Korean forces earned the respect of their American allies for their professionalism and valor. A removal of the North Korean threat for whatever reason would free up the tremendous military reserve of the South Korean

Picture 6.4.1: **"Fire"**

Picture 6.4.2: **"Standing on the Flag"**

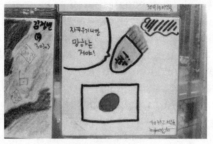

Picture 6.4.3: **"Bombing Japan"**

Picture 6.4.4: **"Japan You Suck"**   Picture 6.4.5: **"Bombs Away"**

(*Source:* GORD, used with permission. http://aog.2y.net/forums/index.php?s=1b087b1e
170979978f8af314d0e010b1&showtopic=1550&st=0)

army. Implicit in this possibility is the threat it would pose to China, even
without the presence of U.S. forces in Korea. A Japan-unified Korea alliance
would be a strong hedge against potential Chinese aggression in the region.

It is also in Korea's interest to reconcile its differences with Japan. One
can better understand this when one looks at Korea's potential alternatives.
Japan is South Korea's only potential regional ally. South Korea will try to
build relationships with the other powers in the region, especially China, but
it is Japan, with its similar democratic values and capitalist economy, that
makes Japan the better potential ally.[80] It is for this reason that the South
Korean government has been willing to reconcile with Japan.[81] As Zbigniew

Brzezinski argues, "[A] true Japanese-Korean reconciliation would contribute significantly to a stable setting for Korea's eventual reunification, mitigating the international complications that could ensue from the end of the country's division. . . . A comprehensive and regionally stabilizing Japanese-Korean partnership might in turn facilitate a continuing American presence in the Far East after Korea's unification."[82]

South Korea needs peace and stability in Northeast Asia if it is ever going to successfully unify with the North. The economic costs alone would require the sum total of ROK resources and economic aid from the United States and Japan. A solid and amiable relationship with Japan would make this reunification much easier.[83]

The problem is that this relationship may not be possible as anti-Japanese feeling is rising in South Korea over continued visits by Japanese leaders to Yasukuni Shrine, a monument to Japan's war dead, including "class A" war criminals. Japanese prime ministers and other leaders, including the current prime minister, Junichiro Koizumi, who has visited the shrine on multiple occasions including an October 7, 2005, visit, refuse to accept the reality that these visits do great harm to Japan's relations with its neighbors. A recent display of South Korean elementary-school art work in a subway station illustrates the problem for Japan. In these pictures, Japan is seen as the enemy to be attacked, not as an ally to befriend.

While one display of school art does not speak for the whole nation, the fact of its public display does indicate that there is strong popular anti-Japanese sentiment within South Korea.

Option #5: North Korea

North Korean-Japanese relations are strange at best. On one hand, the Korean community living in Japan is Pyongyang's number-one source of hard currency, which flows from Japan to North Korea, with Tokyo for the most part (historically) turning a blind eye to its transfer. On the other hand, North Korea's nuclear and missile programs are Japan's number-one traditional security threat. According to Professor Takesada of the Japanese National Institute for Defense Studies, an expert on Korea, Japan is the nation most threatened by North Korean nuclear weapons, because it is unlikely that the North would use nuclear weapons on the Korean Peninsula itself unless forced to do so.[84] The same is not true for Japan, whose history in Korea makes it a politically low-cost target for the North Koreans, and it is unlikely that it would cause strong resentment in South Korea either.[85] Again, Japan's history works against that situation.

North Korea is not really a true or practical option for Japan, except if

Japan were to be abandoned by the United States and the United States military presence were to be removed. In that eventuality, Japan might choose to
rid itself of its greatest threat by signing a nonaggression pact with North
Korea and agree not to be a staging area for the United States in any renewed
Korean conflict.[86] This scenario would possibly permit Japan to sit out a
Northeast Asian conflict, but it would likely result in hard feelings all around
by Japan's former allies and would be no real guarantee that the conflict
would not spill over to Japan anyway.

Option #6: Unilateral Options or Go It Alone

Japanese unilateral options may sound like an oxymoron. "There are so many
obstacles to unilateral action by Japan," according to Kiichi Fujiwara of the
Institute of Social Science at Tokyo University.[87] The number-one obstacle for
unilateral action by Japan is Article Nine. The most likely unilateral action by
Japan would be to choose to acquire nuclear weapons. Japan could pursue this
course at tremendous political cost, but it is not likely to do so, given the nearly
universal condemnation such a course would face at home and abroad.[88]

There is an option for Japan to go it alone as an independent and neutral
nation. This option carries benefits with it, in that it is the most consistent
with the current interpretation of the constitution. Japan would be allowed to
defend itself from an external attack, and it is well able to repulse any attack
on its home islands. Neutrality would reduce the risk of Japan's being brought
into a Korean conflict with the United States. North Korea would be less
likely to attack a neutral Japan with missiles than it would if the United
States were using Japan as a staging area for a Korean campaign.

The drawbacks of being a neutral nation would be the loss of prestige
brought by the alliance with the current hegemon, the United States. Japanese neutrality would also likely cede regional hegemony to China. In order
to make up for the loss of the American nuclear umbrella, and to secure
Japan from nuclear blackmail, Japan would likely have to develop its own
independent nuclear deterrent if it were faced with a threat, such as Chinese
hegemony or a nuclear-armed North Korea.[89] Japan's unique status as the
only nation that has been the victim of atomic weapons, would make it very
hard for Japanese leaders to convince the Japanese public to accept Japan as
a nuclear power.

The United Nations

One final option that Japan might pursue, if it goes it alone, is to step up its
U.N. diplomacy and rely on the United Nations and the goodwill of its mem-

bers for protection. This choice would be quite acceptable to the pacifist elements in Japan, which have always favored a United Nations-centered foreign and security policy. Since joining the United Nations, Japan has pursued a United Nation-centric foreign policy as its only alternative to the United States as an ally. The peaceful goals of the United Nations and Japan's pacifist constitution work well together. The problem is that Japan cannot depend on the United Nations while China, one of its major potential threats, sits on the Security Council as a permanent member with veto power. Russia, another potential threat, has the same advantage and potential to neutralize the United Nations as a protector of Japan.

Conclusion

Japan's options for alternatives to its alliance with the United States have many pluses and minuses. Figure 6.2 illustrates this fact. Clearly, a continued relationship with the United States is Japan's best option. Also, better relations with South Korea would help Japan in many ways and permit Japan to solidify the triangular relationship with the region's most logical allies— Japan, South Korea, and the United States, even if no alliance is ever formalized among the three. Japan should also continue to work on its relationship with China, to preserve peace and stability in East Asia.

Japan should also work toward the creation of a Northeast Asian security regime, although such an effort will be an uphill battle, at best, for all those involved. As Henry Kissinger wrote, "Wilsonianism has few disciples in Asia. There is no pretense of collective security or that cooperation should be based on shared domestic values, even on the part of the few existing democracies. The emphasis is all on equilibrium and national interest."[90] In the absence of a clear threat to regional security (for example, an aggressor China) the greatest argument for such a regime would be the necessity to keep the United States engaged in the region. This will not be easy. If Japan and Korea wish to have a strong security alliance with the United States, similar to the American relationship with Europe, they must appeal to the sector in the American foreign-policy community that believes that the United States must have close relations with the democratic capitalist nations of the world.[91] It is much easier to sell the American electorate on "value-based diplomacy" than on geopolitics.[92]

The logic of this idea would imply a trilateral relationship among the United States, Japan, and South Korea. How far or how formal such a relationship would or should go depends on the threat, or lack thereof, posed by China. It is an essential element of both deterrence theory and strategic theory that one does not provoke one's adversary into aggressive behavior. Even hardcore

Figure 6.2 **Japan's Options: Pluses and Minuses**

Potential Ally	Pluses	Minuses
USA	—High return —Nuclear umbrella —Alliance with the reigning hegemon —Stability	—Lack of independence —Loss of some sovereignty —Potential to be dragged into conflict unwillingly
China	—Good return —No competitors in East Asia	—Junior Partner —Lack of independence —Must apologize for WW II
South Korea	—Equal match —Balance against China —North Korea —Shared democratic and capitalist values	—Must deal with WW II issues —North Korea
ASEAN/ARF	—Hedge against regional Chinese hegemony —ARF confidence building measures would add to regional stability	—Not militarily practical —ASEAN not formally an alliance; very little security benefit
Russia	—Nuclear umbrella —Strong hedge against China	—Loss of North Islands —Instability of Russia —Possibly an undependable ally —Financial drain
North Korea	—Nonaggression pact might protect it from a Korean conflict spillover	—Allied with a rogue state —No status —No potential to protect Japan from other threats —Financial drain
United Nations	—Constitutional —Acceptable to the Pacifist elements in Japan	—Both Russia and China can neutralize the U.N.'s ability to protect Japan.
Go It Alone	—True Independence and neutrality —Free to pursue U.N. centered diplomacy as a neutral nation —Constitutional (without power projection capabilities)	—No allies —Potential Loss of Influence —Need for Military Buildup —Loss of Nuclear Umbrella or the need to develop nuclear weapons itself —China gets regional hegemony

realists would acknowledge that an alliance that precipitates aggression or hostilities on the part of an adversary is not helping one's national security (self-help). As E.H. Carr points out, "the most serious wars are fought to make one's own country stronger, or, *more often,* to prevent another from becoming militarily stronger."[93] Fear of one's adversary (or adversaries) is often a motive for aggression. As R. G. Hawtrey wrote, "the principal cause of war is war itself."[94] *If* China were provoked into a more openly hostile or aggressive foreign and/or military policy in Northeast Asia by a formal trilateral alliance among the United States, Japan, and South Korea, then the national security of all three nations would not have been well served. The flip side of this consideration is that if Chinese actions *cause* the formation of a three-way alliance, then the national security of all three nations is served by the formation of an alliance.[95] Fortunately or unfortunately for Japan, the current interpretation of the constitution holds collective defense to be unconstitutional, and the Japanese public supports this view.[96]

A better scenario would be one that included China (*and* South Korea and Russia) in any security arrangement or forums in order to remove the potential "threat" posed by a formal alliance among the United States, Japan, and South Korea that might be resented by a state left out.[97] Japanese-Korean cooperation will be needed for any security scenario to work in enhancing Japan's national security. While many see a triangular relationship in East Asia, among the United States, Japan, and China, considering the significance of South Korea and the potential of a unified Korea should the North collapse, and the still formidable capabilities and power of Russia, it might be better to view Northeast Asian security as a pentagon. This view of Northeast Asian security is closer to a multilateral forum in Northeast Asian that is similar to the ARF for Southeast Asia. Such a multilateral forum could lead to the confidence-building measures that will be needed to ease regional tensions and provide for a strong and safe security environment for Japan. This concept is illustrated in Figure 6.3.

If the United States-centered alliance should ever fall apart, South Korea is Japan's best alternative in the region. History aside, Korea shares Japan's democratic values and capitalist system. Both countries are strong nations with modern militaries that complement each other well. It behooves Japan to continue to work to strengthen this relationship on the off-chance that Japan is abandoned. Such a consideration is also in Japan's interest, even if the United States does not abandon its security commitments in the Pacific. With the exception of a possible China-Taiwan shooting match, Korea is the powder keg of East Asia. If conflict arises in Korea, Japan will be dragged in, one way or another. Japan needs to be prepared for this eventuality should it ever occur.

Any security relationship for Japan will be difficult. Its relations with other nations, for the most part, cannot be as equals. As Barry Buzan et al. argue, "This relationship among subjects is not equal or symmetrical, and the possibility for successful securitization will vary dramatically with the position

Figure 6.3   **How Should We Perceive East Asian Security?**

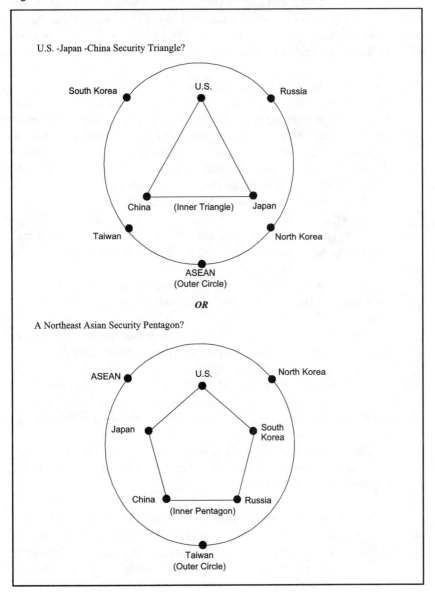

U.S.-Japan-China Security Triangle?

South Korea   U.S.   Russia

China   (Inner Triangle)   Japan

Taiwan   North Korea

ASEAN
(Outer Circle)

OR

A Northeast Asian Security Pentagon?

ASEAN   U.S.   North Korea

Japan   South
Korea

China   Russia
(Inner Pentagon)

Taiwan
(Outer Circle)

held by the actor."[98] Additionally, in thinking about Japan's future options in
East Asia, there is always "the problem of memory." This is true whether one
is talking about Japanese relations with China or with Korea. Nicholas D.
Kristof, a Pulitzer Prize-winning journalist, former Beijing and Tokyo bu-

reau chief, and current columnist for the *New York Times,* sheds a remarkable and disturbing light on the attitudes toward Japan in East Asia. Kristof recounts this incredible and shocking story from his days in Beijing shortly after the Tiananmen Square Massacre:

> The memory of a brief conversation nags me whenever I think about Asia's future. The conversation took place shortly after the Tiananmen Square crackdown, during a secret meeting with a leader of China's underground democracy movement. We met in a quiet corner of a Beijing restaurant, where he tapped the table suspiciously to see if it was bugged. This was a man whose vision I admired, so I listened intently when the waitress stepped away and he leaned forward to disclose his plans for promoting human rights.
>
> "We are going to kill Japanese," he said brightly.
>
> "What?"
>
> "We're going to kill Japanese businessmen. That'll scare them so they won't invest here. And the government will really be screwed!"
>
> "You're not serious?"
>
> "Of course we're serious. We can't demonstrate these days and we can't publish. The only thing we can do for democracy is kill Japanese businessmen."
>
> I protested that it seemed odd to promote human rights by murdering innocent businessmen. But he just smiled at my narrow-mindedness, with a "you-will-never-understand-Asia" grin.
>
> "They're Japanese," my friend said dismissively. "Japanese devils."
>
> He never did kill anyone. But the vitriol in his voice underscored Asia's historical tensions, which are especially intractable because they exist between peoples, not governments.
>
> While Asia has seemed remarkably peaceful since the end of the Vietnam War the peace is a fragile one, concealing dormant antagonisms and disputes that could still erupt.[99]

Nicholas Kristof's story is not unique. I personally have had several experiences, as a professor, with Chinese students both in the United States and outside the United States, where otherwise smart and enlightened students have made similar comments about the Japanese even though they knew that my wife was Japanese. It is important to note that my wife and I have also had warm relations with many Chinese where political attitudes toward each others nations were inconsequential. These stories, combined with the pictures by South Korean schoolchildren shown earlier, illustrate that even the most enlightened of people can be victims of culture and history. Japan is limiting its foreign-policy options by its refusal to deal with the past effectively. Japan needs the trust of its neighbors in East Asia. This trust will not come without a sincere show of remorse and contrition for Japan's history in East Asia. The conservative right wing in Japan is in denial as to Japan's situation vis-à-vis the rest of the world and Asia in particular. Its steadfast opposition to apologies in general and China specifically for actions taken during World War II has led to an ongoing mistrust of Japan and its intentions.

A valuable lesson could be learned from the positive results of Japan's apology to South Korea. Japan has the potential to develop strong relations within East Asia, and it needs to do so sooner rather than later. If Japan cannot do so, it will continue to find itself very lonely in a region where allies are important. The following chapter will look at what Japan is doing and its perspective on the world. It will also look at the all-important influence of *gaiatsu* on Japanese foreign-policy making.

7

The "Myth" of *Gaiatsu*

How Japan Views Its Place in the World

*There is no sadder sight in the world than to see a
beautiful theory killed by a brutal fact.*
—Thomas H. Huxley[1]

It is very difficult to argue that the U.S. military presence in East Asia has not
been the major factor in the stabilization of the region in the post-World War
II era. Japan's geostrategic position in East Asia has been the foundation of
the American presence in Asia. The United States-Japan Security Treaty and
the United States-South Korean Security Treaty have been the cornerstones of
the U.S. military presence in the region, especially since the closing of the
Philippine bases. In the post-Cold War era, the United States presence has
been both a blessing and a curse for Japan. Japan has benefited greatly from
the U.S. presence in the region. The region's peace and stability have permitted Japan to grow and flourish under the Yoshida Doctrine. At the same time,
Japan's potential for regional leadership remains weak in light of the larger
U.S. presence. To many, both inside and outside Japan, the presence of U.S.
forces based in Japan is an infringement on Japanese sovereignty.[2] They see
Japan as still occupied by the United States, and they feel that Japan must find
a way to assert itself in world affairs, independent of the United States.

The problem for Japan is that, head-to-head conflicts with the United
States aside, most of Japan's international needs and interests coincide with
the United States' needs and interests. As the world's second-largest economic power, Japan profits just as much as the United States, if not more,
from the *Pax Americana* that the world currently enjoys. Peace and stability
are good for Japan and Japanese business interests. National sovereignty
issues aside, Japan has a stake in supporting continued American hegemony.[3]
The question for Japan is how to support U.S. hegemony while at the same
time independently asserting itself. This chapter will examine Japan's foreign policy. It will also look at the concept of *gaiatsu,* which is often given
as the reason that Japan does many of the things it does.

Adjusting to the Post-Cold War World

The end of the Cold War brought about an unexpected independence from the United States, for which Japan was not prepared. The sudden demise of the Soviet empire made Japan's role as ally much less necessary for the United States. It was no longer as geostrategically important to the United States as it had been during the Cold War. Japan was not prepared for this reversal when the Persian Gulf War broke out. Tokyo struggled in the face of vocal condemnation on the part of its allies for not sending its men and women into combat when it had no real choice to do so under Article Nine. From the world's point of view, Japan had the third-largest defense budget (in dollar terms) in the world. A nation spending so much on defense should be able to contribute to the protection of commerce and freedom (and oil). The concept of a nation with a constitutional ban on armed force having such a large defense budget just did not compute.

From Japan's point of view, Article Nine of the constitution and internal politics were hard enough to explain or comprehend domestically, much less to the world at large. The leadership in Japan realized that a new interpretation of the constitution was the best way for Japan to deal with this issue in a way that was constitutionally acceptable.[4] From this consideration the PKO Law was born, as described in chapter 2.

Looking to the United Nations for an answer to its problem was a natural thing for Japan to do. Since the end of the U.S. occupation, Japan has made the United Nations a central focus of its foreign policy. The U.N. charter, with its commitment to the peaceful resolution of conflict, reflects Japan's constitution's pacifist nature. The Japanese people are some of the most pro-United Nations people on Earth. U.N. clubs and UNESCO chapters exist all over the country. That Japan should look to the United Nations to get itself out of its post-Cold War predicament is no surprise. Nevertheless, there are limits to its United Nations-based foreign policy. These limits are forcing Japan into areas of foreign policy that it has traditionally avoided because of constitutional limitations under Article Nine.

The problem for Japan is that, except for its United Nations-based pacifist foreign policy, the only principle it has as a guide is MOFA's unofficial creed, "the safety and prosperity of the nation." As one Diet member, who asked to remain anonymous, told me, "Japan has no firm principle guiding its foreign policy."[5] Another senior government official felt that foreign policy is not, and should not be, goal-oriented; it is, rather, a day-to-day business of avoiding conflicts.[6] Japanese foreign policy has therefore become a crisis-to-crisis policy. It is very well prepared to deal with the *last* crisis, not the next one.

One important aspect of foreign policy is how to set the nation's priorities. During my field research, the foreign-policy elites were asked to name what they thought to be the top three foreign-policy concerns for Japan. Many of the responses were predictable, but the number and variety were a testimony to the lack of focus in Japanese foreign policy. China and the U.S. alliance were predictable top vote getters, with 43 percent of the respondents naming them as a foreign-policy priority. Some showed remarkable foresight by recognizing the need to keep up with high technology and the information revolution,[7] the need to search for alternative allies should the United States abandon Japan, or the need to support other democracies. What was surprising was that only 4 percent named Japan's acknowledged and high-profile quest for a permanent seat on the U.N. Security Council as a foreign-policy priority. Other surprises included the fact that Russia was the third most often listed threat to Japan (see chapter 4), but only 11 percent of the interviewees listed Russia as a foreign-policy priority![8] The responses fanned out all over the spectrum. For a complete list of responses, see Figure 7.1.

Another example of the lack of foreign-policy focus and awareness came from an interview I conducted with the former defense minister and upper house councillor, Hideo Usui. After hearing the first few questions Councillor Usui ran out of time and had to go to an important meeting. On his way out, he instructed his secretary to schedule a second interview and to make sure that we would have at least ninety minutes. At the conclusion of this second interview, Councillor Usui asked if he could schedule appointments with other colleagues in the Diet and the defense and security community for me to interview, because he wanted them to be thinking about the questions I was asking. He stated that he had been trying to get his colleagues to think about these matters, and being interviewed would demonstrate the need to be thinking about the direction of Japanese foreign policy. The idea behind Usui's request was that, if foreigners were asking these questions about Japan, surely the Japanese should be asking the same questions of themselves. He proceeded to personally call and schedule appointments with five senior Japanese Diet members and ministry officials.[9]

The significance of this incident is that it demonstrates the lack of serious thinking (by the foreign-policy community as a whole) about the major foreign-policy questions that face Japan today by the very people who are responsible for making these decisions. The national debate on foreign policy seemed to be very much muted. In a small way, the research interviews were influencing the direction and thought of the foreign-policy debate in Japan; they did so by creating it and helping it open up. A further example of this lack of solid debate was an interview with Councillor Ichita Yamamoto. Councillor Yamamoto initially granted an interview only as a favor (obliga-

Figure 7.1   **Top Foreign-Policy Concerns as Named by Foreign Policy Elites**

Threat	Countries	No. of Times Mentioned	Percent of Respondents Listing in Top Three
1	China	22	
	MFN for China	1	
	Total:	23	43%
1	U.S./Japan Alliance	23	43%
3	Korea	14	26%
4	Nuclear Proliferation*	11	20%
5	Economic Integration/Trade	10	19%
5	Multilateral Institutions (support of)	10	19%
6	Russia	6	11%
7	Environment	5	9%
8	Southeast Asia	4	7%
8	U.S./Japan/China Trilateral Relationship	4	7%
8	Defense/Security Policy	4	7%
11	Middle East	3	6%
12	Apology for WW II	2	4%
12	Pursuit of High Technology	2	4%
12	U.N. Security Council Seat	2	4%

Also listed: Improving U.S./China Relations, Food Sources, Japan/Europe Relations, PKO, Taiwan, Search for New Allies, Democratization (support of). Total responses: 130 (N = 54).

*There is a possible time bias here in that both India and Pakistan tested nuclear weapons during the period (May–June 1998) that the interviews were conducted. Under normal circumstances it might not have been this high. It is also very interesting to note that considering the time bias only 20 percent of the respondents listed it as a top three foreign policy concern and only 24 percent listed it as a security threat.

Note: Totals do not add up to 162 (54 x 3) as some respondents refused to answer or could/would not name more than one or two. Two respondents refused to answer the question. Most respondents took their answers off the record.

tion, in Japan) to a colleague. The interview was rescheduled six times before he finally granted a short twenty-minute meeting. He figured that an interview with a foreign academic was a waste of his time. Upon hearing the questions, he became much more interested, and when I offered to end the interview after twenty minutes, he extended the meeting another twenty-five minutes into his next appointment. At the end of the interview, he got on the phone (without being asked) to schedule another appointment for me with another Diet member, because he thought that the questions being asked were important for Japan to be thinking about.[10]

Internal substantive debate would seem to be lacking in the higher circles of both the elected and career foreign-policy establishment. Very little thought, it would seem, is given to long-range goals. Part of this lack can be ascribed to the fact that the Japanese public has even less interest in foreign policy than do Diet members.[11] What matters is what interests one's constituents. If one's constituents believe a subject is important, then it is important. Image is everything. One of the reasons that foreign policy takes such a backseat is the influence of *gaiatsu* and its impact on Japanese political life. The following section will look at the concept of *gaiatsu* and how it influences the formulation of Japanese foreign policy.

Gaiatsu

It is important to note the role of the United States in the process of the formation of the SDF and Japanese foreign policy. U.S. pressure is an issue that runs throughout the formation of Japanese defense and security policy. Japanese politicians have been able to explain many of their bolder actions regarding the SDF by referring to pressure from the United States.[12] This "American Pressure" is called *gaiatsu,* which can literally be translated as "pressure from the outside" and is a common term in any newspaper reporting on foreign policy or security-related matters. The official Japanese explanation for many of the nation's defense and security policy decisions is essentially that "the Americans made us do it."[13]

This reasoning makes the concept of *gaiatsu* akin to the argument that "the devil made me do it." It denies personal or national responsibility and choice for Japan's actions, when in reality Japan is making choices in a given set of circumstances or situation. Furthermore, the concept denies Japan's sovereignty as a nation by giving the impression, both at home and abroad, that it is incapable of making its own decisions and, worse, is a possible puppet of the United States. *Gaiatsu* is part of the situation and part of the decision. All nations, including such hegemons as the United States, face foreign pressure. The question is how they react to pressure from abroad. Japan is not unique in facing foreign pressure. The ability to deal with foreign pressure depends on one's position vis-à-vis the pressure. In the scheme of Hermann's model, the role of external or foreign pressure should be represented as part of the decision-making process. Figure 7.2 illustrates this scheme.

Reinhard Drifte supports this argument in his book, *Japan's Foreign Policy for the 21st Century: From Economic Superpower to What Power?* In it he argues that Japan's continual trade conflicts with America are the true sign that it is a world power.[14] A "poor little Japan" argument is not valid when one considers the scope and breadth of Japanese power. As Drifte argues,

Figure 7.2   **Hermann's Model Plus External Pressure**

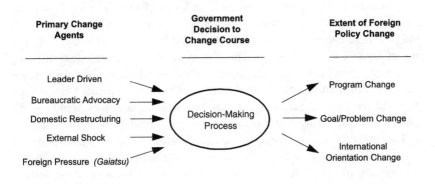

The question of Japanese power has implications for the policies of other countries which, for example, expect Japan to contribute to the international system in a way commensurate with its economic power. They exert strong influence (commonly referred to in Japan as "*gaiatsu*") on Japan to this effect. As a result, it is most opportune to appreciate in a more systematic way what sort of power Japan has, how and if at all this power is exerted, whether the demand for "commensurate contribution" is compatible with the internal and external conditions that Japan is facing, and whether those making these requests are conscious of the implications. It is obvious, but often not fully realized, that such contributions imply the exertion of power, and this has important implications for the world system, including for the relative power of the other countries. There are even Japanese who have to ask themselves whether the outside world really wants to face these consequences.[15]

In fact, Japan makes its own decisions because of its own needs and desires, *not* just in response to *gaiatsu*.

The "Myth" of *Gaiatsu*

As the strain of the Cold War grew, Americans were "making Japan do" more and more in terms of its own defense. Even with the 1 percent GDP limitation, by 1990, the size of the Japanese economy raised the Japanese defense budget to the third-largest in the world, behind the United States and the former Soviet Union.[16]

As mentioned previously, image is everything in the eyes of the electorate. The United States' image has taken a beating in recent years in Japan.

The United States comes across as a bully to many in Japan. Professor Osamu Iishi of the University of Tokyo illustrates this change by recounting that every year he asks his incoming students to name Japan's top three allies and top three enemies. Until 1990, the United States was always listed as one of Japan's top three allies. Then, in 1991, America started showing up as one of Japan's top three opponents. When asked about their answer, the students would say that the United States is a bully and cite the Persian Gulf War and the United States' trade disputes with Japan as examples of the United States ordering and forcing weaker nations to do what it wants.

This attitude was reinforced by a conversation I had with a woman at a sushi bar in Tokyo. She had asked why I was in Japan, and after explaining the purpose of my visit, she started to talk about her opinions on foreign policy. She felt that the United States, as the most powerful nation on earth, could not be trusted to protect Japan, because to do so was not in the United States' interest. The United States only used Japan to do its bidding (she used the term *gaiatsu*) and saw Japan only as a tool of its foreign policy.

These illustrations of the changing perception of the United States can in many ways be traced back to the increased use of *gaiatsu* by Japanese leaders to convince the public that Japan needs to do something that the United States wants it to do. It is also important to note that in spite of these hostile feelings, most Japanese still want to remain allied with the United States in the future. In a 1997 *Yomiuri Shimbun* poll, national voters were asked, "Do you want the United States to be an ally in the 21st century, or not?" In response, 68 percent of the respondents replied, "Yes, I do." Only 23 percent responded, "No, I don't"; 9 percent had no response.[17] Most Japanese also feel that United States-Japan Security Treaty, in conjunction with the SDF, is the best way to "maintain the peace and safety of Japan." In a poll by the Prime Minister's Office, 68 percent wanted to maintain the current treaty and SDF.[18]

During two months of interviews with Japanese foreign-policy elites in Japan, I heard only two interviewees out of fifty-six mention *gaiatsu* as a reason that a Japanese foreign-policy choice was made. One was a member of the JCP, and the other was an academic.[19] Japanese foreign-policy choices were always discussed in the context of Japanese sovereignty and what was best for Japan. This consideration was very surprising in that *gaiatsu* is a very common term in the literature on Japanese foreign policy.[20] In his paper, "Diplomacy and Domestic Politics: The Logic of Two-level Games," Robert Putnam describes an occurrence of *gaiatsu* in Japan:

> [I]n Japan a coalition of business interests, the ministry of Trade and Industry (MITI), the Economic Planning Agency, and some expansion-minded

politicians within the Liberal Democratic Party pushed for additional domestic stimulus, using U.S. pressure as one of their prime arguments against the stubborn resistance of the Ministry of Finance (MOF). Without internal divisions in Tokyo, it is unlikely that the foreign demands would have been met, but with external pressure, it is even more unlikely that the expansionists could have overridden the powerful MOF. "Seventy percent foreign pressure, 30 percent internal politics," was the disgruntled judgment of one MOF insider. "Fifty-fifty," guessed an official from MITI.[21]

The nearly total lack of allusion to *gaiatsu* by Japanese foreign-policy elites caused me to question whether *gaiatsu* was truly the factor in Japanese foreign policy that it is alleged to be. However, when one reads cases such as the one cited above by Putnam, it is easy to see that it is a factor in some form or another. Putnam further notes that, without the political divisions within the Japanese government, *gaiatsu* would not have been a factor.[22] Foreign pressure is clearly an agent of change that belongs in Hermann's model.

The more that the concept of *gaiatsu* is examined, the clearer it is that *gaiatsu* is related to the implementation of Japanese foreign policy choices, rather than being only a cause of Japanese foreign-policy choices. Putnam describes the "two-level games" that nations and leaders play to get what they want.[23] He cites the example of Helmut Schmidt's playing this "game" at a summit in Bonn: "Publicly, Helmut Schmidt posed as reluctant to the end. Only his closest advisors suspected the truth: that the chancellor 'let himself be pushed' into a policy that he privately favored, but would have found costly and perhaps impossible to enact without the summit's package deal."[24]

In the case of Japan, it seems that there is a two-level game at work. For example, the United States wants Japan to do something that is in Japan's overall or long-term interest, such as sending forces to contribute to international peace and stability. Japanese leaders want the same outcome, as they are trying to make Japan a "normal nation," but without violating the constitution, which inhibits Japan's normalization. Because the public and even political interests within the ruling party (or parties) are not likely to support it, Japanese leaders will use the excuse of foreign pressure as a way of convincing internal interests, both in government and in the public at large, that Japan is being forced to pass the PKO Law and that Japan cannot afford to say no to the foreign interests (the United States). This ploy sells the idea to an unwilling public, because "America is big and powerful and 'little' Japan cannot say 'no' to America."[25]

In this way, *gaiatsu* becomes the lightning rod for unpopular decisions that Japanese leaders want to make. The United States or other foreign countries take the heat. Often foreign pressure does exist, but it is pressure to do something that internal leadership already has decided to do. The first draft of the PKO Law was written in the early 1980s. Japanese leaders were just looking for a chance to implement it.[26] A perfect example of the role that *gaiatsu* plays in internal Japanese politics is an account given by a retired American foreign-service officer with over thirty years' experience in Japan. He said:

> In Japan, I've had this case where bureaucrats from MITI would come and say, "Would you write a letter to so-and-so in the Ministry of Finance in support of this particular position because we can't do it. That particular activity is under the Ministry of Construction." But, if you give them some *gaiatsu*—foreign pressure—saying you support this, then the budget process might be smoother.[27]

The "myth" of *gaiatsu* is that it is the sole explanation for why Japan does so many things in foreign policy that are unpopular. The reality is that, as Putnam describes, without some internal support or division (such as cited by the foreign-service official), foreign pressure has no chance.[28] In a comment to the Japan Forum of the National Bureau of Asian Research (NBR), Tom Fish stated that

> *Gaiatsu* has seldom been effective without a proponent on the "inside" also applying *naiatsu* (internal pressure). In my dealings with Japanese officialdom, both on the staff of the U.S. Army, Japan and as an assistant attaché, I was often asked by a Japanese counterpart to arrange some *gaiatsu* to help a proposal become "unstuck." U.S. pressure often gave "Mr. Inside" political cover to argue a position not favored by the bureaucracy.[29]

Gaiatsu, it would seem, is just a form of leverage within Japanese politics, rather than a primary explanatory source why Japan makes the choices that it does.

All nations make their own choices. National sovereignty can be defined as a nation's ability to make its own choices or decisions in the absence of controlling foreign interests. This is to say that a nation incapable of making its own choices is not sovereign.[30] An example of absence of sovereignty would be a nation that is militarily occupied by another nation, as Japan was after World War II. Japan has been a sovereign nation since the allied occupation ended in 1952. The United States is a powerful ally and therefore has great influence on Japan, but there are plenty of examples of Japan's publicly defying U.S. wishes. The problem for Japan is that with the end of the Cold War, the United States is more vocal about its disagreements with Japanese policy. This circumstance, combined with the overuse of *gaiatsu*, is contributing to the image of America as a bully.

All nations, no matter what their size or power, face external pressure. Foreign pressure is a norm in foreign-policy making. Thus, Japan is not unique in facing foreign pressure. Internal needs dictate what foreign pressures will make a nation acquiesce to external stimuli. An example is the United States during the Cold War. The United States often sacrificed its economic priorities for national-security concerns. It often chose to ignore unfair economic advantages taken by allies, such as Japan, or simply gave in to them. When I interviewed Ryozo Kato, then director general of the Foreign Policy Bureau of MOFA, he expressed the view, which seemed to speak for MOFA as well, that Japan has always given in 100 percent of the time to the United States and would like to have the United States give in sometimes, in order to be fair.[31] This begs the question: Does Japan give in to the U.S. 100 percent of the time? Absolutely not; Japan often refuses American requests. During the Cold War, the United States permitted or let Japan build up its economy (under the Yoshida Doctrine) at what was often the United States' expense, because the American priority was security. With the waning and end of the Cold War, the United States became more permissive with Japan on security issues and more demanding economically. The Japanese response has not always, or even most of the time, been positive from the American point of view.

Many in Japan feel that Japan has given in to the United States too many times. They look for ways to "show" Japan's independence by disagreeing with the United States.[32] What they ignore is that for most of the Cold War it was the United States that looked the other way. Former Director General Ryozo Kato described Japan as suffering from "interdependent fatigue syndrome" and related it to the Anglo-American relationship, in which the United States and Britain often have identical foreign policies on most issues.[33] Britain, however, does not seem to suffer from this "interdependent fatigue syndrome" as Japan does. Britain is confident; Japan is not. The trouble for Japan in this case is that what is good for the United States is often good for Japan, too.

This may be one reason why Japan is so heavily influenced by American pressure. Another possible reason that Japan is susceptible to American pressure is that U.S. foreign policy is largely based on power politics, whereas Japan's foreign policy is based on goodwill, particularly U.S. goodwill. Japan needs U.S. goodwill because of its constitutional limitations under Article Nine. There is a need for Japan to realize that it cannot always depend on goodwill.[34] It needs to chart its own course. However, the course that it is currently following (the U.S. course) is a course of its own choosing.

According to Councillor Keizo Takemi, the real pressure for change in Japanese foreign policy is coming from business and from the younger generation.[35] The pressure is from the inside rather than the outside. The outside (the United States) is encouraging change, but it is the needs of business and the generational shift in power that is causing Japan to move forward with change. With this in mind, we also have to remember that the main reason for almost any political action by a politician is to gain support for the next general election. If the public does not feel that it is in Japan's best interest, no amount of *gaiatsu* will ever be effective at persuading elected political leaders to take an action that is against their own political interests. The concept of *gaiatsu,* at its core and the way it is used in Japan in the public arena, implies that Japan is not an independent nation. It postulates that foreign powers control its policy-making apparatus or that these powers at least have a veto power. This is the "myth" of *gaiatsu.*

In arguing that *gaiatsu* is a myth, I am not claiming that *gaiatsu* does not exist. Rather, it is argued that external pressure exists, as it does for every other nation, and that Japan is no exception. Reality is that Japanese leaders make a cost-benefit analysis and implement decisions on that basis. What is interesting is how *gaiatsu* is used domestically in Japan. *Gaiatsu* is an excuse or cover for a national need (see quotes above by Tom Fish and the retired American foreign-service officer). A senior member of MOFA described *gaiatsu* as a politically easy out for Japanese leaders.[36] The frequent use of *gaiatsu* reflects a need by Japan's foreign-policy leadership to often sell publicly unpopular choices that are in Japan's long-term interests by scapegoating the United States for actions that could cause adverse political consequences.

Japanese elites want Japan to be a normal nation. Article Nine prevents this outcome. *Gaiatsu* is a tool for normalizing Japan without risking public displeasure over the rejection of Japan's pacifist constitution. Japanese elites are using foreign pressure to their own ends. *Gaiatsu* has permitted Japan to develop the second-largest defense budget in the world. It has given Japan a modern fighting force. While many in Japan still do not accept the legitimacy of the SDF and the Defense Agency, they are a source of pride to others.

Military might is a source of pride for the peoples of many nations, and Japan is no exception. When I was living in Japan on the north island of Hokkaido, a Japanese Maritime SDF vessel (Aegis class) made a port call at the city of Otaru. The ship was opened to visitors and their families to come aboard. While the tours emphasized the role of the vessel in search-and-rescue operations and maritime safety, the highlight of the tour for most was the weapons system. Many questions were asked about how the system worked, and there was a clear pride in the fact that this was a Japanese *warship*. At an air show in Chitose, Hokkaido, a similar scenario played out in that there was noticeably greater interest in the military aircraft over the civilian aircraft.

The images and attitudes of the people were remarkably similar to events that I had attended in Europe and the United States. There was a noticeable awe and sense of pride that Japan can protect itself. This sentiment demonstrates that the Japanese people's attitudes toward the tools and symbols of modern warfare are changing. In spite of the pacifist leanings of the majority in Japan, the Japanese see the SDF as a source of pride and an example of what Japan can do. This pride helps Japan down the path to normalization. The clear desire on the part of Japan's foreign-policy makers to see Japan behave as a normal nation is reflected in their willingness to give in to *gaiatsu*.

What Is Japan Doing?

Japanese security depends on the United States-Japan Security Treaty, but given Japanese fears of abandonment, Japan needs to be considering its options. As Sheldon Simon, an expert on East Asian security writes, "For Japan, security still depends primarily on the U.S.-Japan Defense Treaty, but in the post-Cold War era, Japanese leaders realize that reliance exclusively on the United States is insufficient.[37] Japan's constitutional limitations under Article Nine limits what it can do. Its history in East Asia further constrains it. As Hendrik Spruyt writes:

> Ever since the Second World War, Japan has emphatically distinguished itself from its previous expansionist policies. Institutional and ideological constraints on the level of military spending and the prohibition on the deployment of troops abroad have made Japan a distinctly atypical great power. Such restraints have been augmented with substantial foreign aid and foreign policy declarations that aim to allay any fears of renewed Japanese might.[38]

Because of the limitations imposed on Japan, Japanese foreign policy is, for all intents and purposes, very narrow in its primary focus: the United Nations, China, the Koreas, the United States, and more recently, multilateral efforts. Japanese nationalists desire Japan to have an independent foreign policy toward all of these nations.[39] The next several sections will be an overview of what Japan is doing to foster better relations with these nations.

China

China represents the most powerful threat to any possible Japanese aspirations of regional hegemony. Shin'ichi Ogawa of the National Institute for Defense Studies has stated: "[There is a need to] manage the relationship with China carefully or conflict will be inevitable."[40] China and Korea are the unnamed foci of the "areas surrounding Japan" statement in the 1997 revisions to the United States-Japan Security Treaty Guidelines. Neither Japan nor the United States wishes to see China upset the regional status quo. The key to China's containment, as seen by many in MOFA, is for the United States to have the ability to establish a good working relationship with China (without abandoning Japan).[41] Japan is also working to establish better military ties with China. Both China and Japan are attempting to upgrade a bilateral security forum between the two to the deputy-ministerial level.[42]

The political problem with deterring China is that, as one senior MOFA official stated, "The Socialists fear that deterrence will make peace disappear."[43] There is an attitude that peace will stay if everything is left alone. Japan prefers an interdependent relationship with China. The problem with this is that there is no word in Chinese for interdependence.[44] Japan wants something from China that China has no concept of in its own language.

Multilateral Efforts

Multilateralism in the Asia-Pacific region is still in its infancy. The problem for East Asian multilateralism is that the distances are so vast that what may be a security threat to one country may not be a concern to others in the region.[45] However as Simon writes,

> Great distances among regional actors have been reduced as factors, favoring protection by increases in naval and air power projection as well as the proliferation of missile technology. The resultant higher levels of security interdependence provide incentives for greater security cooperation.[46]

When one considers the issue of Japan and multilateralism, the question that invariably comes up is "why?" Hendrik Spruyt put it succinctly:

> Given Japan's ability to build a reasonably strong, and modern, self-defense force, and given the U.S. security guarantee, it is perhaps not obvious why Tokyo would choose to upgrade its multilateral commitments rather than rely on more conventional means of managing its security environment specifically through internal balancing and alliances.[47]

Given Japan's fear of abandonment, which was discussed in previous chapters, it becomes obvious that Japan is seeking to hedge its bets because with or without the United States alliance, it is still constrained by its limitations. Some (particularly those on the political left) would say that Japan's multilateral efforts are an alternative to the bilateral relationship with the United States, but, as Professor Osamu Iishi argues, Japan needs to be developing both bilateral and multilateral relationships. He stated that the bilateral relationship with the United States was more important to Japan than multilateral relationships, but that multilateral relationships could not and should not be ignored by Japan.[48] Japan's economic power gives it tremendous potential for regional leadership in the creation of multilateral forums.[49]

Japan needs to cooperate with other nations if it is to achieve its primary foreign-policy goal of national security.[50] There is the legitimate worry that if nations do not cooperate, the result will be a loss of stability and order. Fear could lead to arms races throughout the region. As C. S. Kang argues,

> Realists worry that contemporary economic and political developments in East Asia are leading to uneven rates of growth among nations, impacting differential growth power. Even liberals worry that, compared to post-cold war Europe, East Asia suffers from a "thinness" of multilateral organizations as well as democracy, institutions they believe mitigate the instability of multipolarity.[51]

Of the elites that were interviewed in Japan, an overwhelming 83 percent strongly favored Japanese multilateral efforts. Only 5 percent opposed Japan's having a role in multilateral forums. Another 5 percent supported Japan's playing only a financial role, and 7 percent had no opinion or did not know.[52]

There seems to be almost universal support for Japanese multilateral efforts. This support crosses party lines from the right to the left. As Simon states, "Broad support for multilateralism in Japan stems from diverse expectations about its potential benefits."[53] Those on the conservative right in Japanese politics see a way for Japan to be active in collective security—something the constitution has forbidden up until now. For those on the left wing of Japanese politics, multilateralism provides an opportunity to free Japan from its United States-centric security policy. Those on the political left perceive multilateralism as cooperative security, rather than seeing it as collective security.[54]

Japanese elites see multilateral participation on the part of Japan as the direction for the future. Limited by its inability to engage in collective defense, Japan is throwing itself into the next-best option: multilateralism. Again, Spruyt wrote, "the reason why Japan will gravitate to Multilateral fora such as the UN (*and ARF*), in addition to its other policy options, resides in its (still) artificially constrained repertoire of choice."[55] Simon notes two major reasons why Japan is pursuing multilateralism in East Asia. They are:

> The first concerns the country's evolution toward a normal state with security interests independent of—though not incompatible with—its American ally. The second reason coincides with the concerns of most other Asian actors: how best to cope with a rising China.[56]

The problem is that Japan does not seem to have been able to develop a long-term multilateral policy. As Professor Akihiko Tanaka argues, "Japan has yet to produce a coherent policy or strategy on regional cooperation. Part of the reasons seem to be that Japan is not sure about its long-term regional orientation especially in relation to its very close relations with the United States."[57] The problem seems to be in how Japan should adapt itself to Asian multilateralism while at the same time balancing its relations with the United States. Again Professor Tanaka wrote,

> Since the first diplomatic bluebook published in 1957 posited three elements of Japan's foreign policy—the importance of the ties with the free world, the affinity with Asia, and the importance of the United Nations, the Japanese have been struggling to find out the appropriate priority between the ties with the U.S. and the relations with Asia.[58]

This effort is increasingly financial, with over $42 billion spent by Japan to help Asia.[59] Economics continues to be Japan's best tool for its foreign policy. As Japan develops its multilateral foreign policy, Japanese investment and Official Development Assistance (ODA) are opening new doors for Japan. Japan is increasingly trying to create goodwill for itself through checkbook diplomacy. In spite of the setback caused by the Gulf War, Japan is increasingly proud of its record of giving. In many interviews, the interviewee noted that Japan's aid was greater than that provided by the United States and that Japan is paid up in full on its U.N. dues, while the United States is not. Money buys a lot of friends, but the real question for Japan should be, does it buy security?

The United Nations

As noted earlier, the United Nations has long been the focus of Japanese foreign policy beyond its relationship with the United States. One foreign-policy goal for Japan that was clearly expressed by Ryozo Kato, former director general of Foreign Policy Planning at MOFA, was to strengthen the

United Nations and its various functions as an international governing body. Japan would like to see reform of the Security Council (with Japan being given a permanent seat on the Security Council), but it recognizes that whatever reform takes place it will be gradual.[60] While Security Council reform is a governmental priority, it draws a surprisingly lukewarm response from the public, with only 50 percent supporting it in a mixed way (only 14 percent support Japan's bid for a seat), while a solid 30 percent oppose Japan's reform agenda.[61]

Japan's efforts to make a personnel contribution through the United Nations Peacekeeping Operations (UNPKO) are growing. The PKO mission served the political purpose of selling the Japanese people on greater SDF deployment outside of Japan. As Ogawa noted, "PKO is not a military mission, it is a political mission."[62] Each successful mission strengthens future use of the SDF in more and more dangerous missions. Many in Japan would like to see Japan's contribution be enlarged to include peacekeeping forces (PKF) missions. While this is not likely in the near future, because of domestic politics, it is likely that Japan will expand its current contributions under the existing PKO Law. Of the foreign-policy makers who were interviewed, 80 percent supported the expansion of Japan's responsibilities under the current PKO Law.[63] The Japanese public also tends to support Japan's PKO role. In a poll sponsored by the Prime Minister's Office, Japanese adults were asked, "Do you think Japan should continue participating in PKO activities, or not?" Of the respondents, 24 percent felt that Japan should be a more active participant, while 46 percent felt that Japan should maintain the current level of participation. Only 19 percent felt that Japan should reduce its participation, and 4 percent felt that Japan should not participate at all; 7 percent did not know.[64] The following year, a *Yomiuri Shimbun* poll asked, "Do you approve or disapprove of the Self-Defense Forces participating in United Nations Peace-Keeping Operations throughout the world?" A whopping 74 percent approved, while only 17 percent disapproved.[65] All of this public support should be encouraging to Japan's U.N. diplomacy, but as any astute politician would tell you, public opinion can be fickle and, moreover, can change overnight. If Japan overreaches too quickly with the SDF, and if a current PKO or future PKF mission goes badly, public support could dry up. However, public opinion may not be as fickle as it might seem at first glance. People support Japan's taking on a greater role in the world; the question is about the kind of role, and this question must be answered in the political arena. Most of the major political parties recognize Japan's need to do something. Japan and the SDF should be able to work *under U.N. command* on PKO and PKF missions without violating the constitution, but this is a minority view.[66]

The United States

As one partner in what is often called the most important bilateral relationship in the world, the United States is and will remain the true center of Japanese diplomacy. Indicative of the priority given the United States in Japanese politics is the fact that two of the highest posts in MOFA are the ambassadorships to the United States and to the United Nations. Japan is doing what it needs to do to keep its relationship with the United States strong. The September 1997 revision to the Guidelines marked a watershed event in United States-Japan relations. Prime Minister Junichiro Koizumi's personal relationship with President George W. Bush has taken Japanese-American relations to their highest level in recent memory. Under Koizumi's leadership, Japan is attempting to make itself a worthy ally in a crisis for the United States.

For the first time, Japan is trying to legitimize and legalize what it would have probably done anyway in a crisis. As Kiichi Fujiwara, of the Institute of Social Science at Tokyo University, said in an interview, "The Guidelines just give legitimacy to what Japan would have done anyway. They have no effect on foreign policy."[67] But they do have an effect on the perception of Japanese foreign and security policy. Japan appears more normal. It is a nation that is sending its men and women in uniform overseas for the good of international order. The limitations placed on the SDF by the Japanese government do little to destroy the perception that Japan is doing something. The Catch-22 is that, if a shooting conflict erupts on a PKO mission, the withdrawal of SDF would be devastating to Japan's image, especially among the nations whose troops stayed behind to fight.

The revised Guidelines are seen by some as favoring the United States but not resulting in real change for Japan.[68] In reality, however, while the United States gains from a more able ally, because Japan has a clearer definition of its role within the alliance, the revised guidelines have moderately strengthened Japan's role in the alliance.[69] Japan's primary motivation for revising the Guidelines was to preserve the United States' commitment to Japan. Japan primarily wants and needs the United States to be engaged in the region. *Gaiatsu* played a part in selling the revisions, but Japan's leadership wanted these revisions and used American pressure to get the Guidelines past their detractors. United States and Japanese detractors aside, Japan can and will do all it can to keep America allied with it. As it had often done before, it disguised its desires in order to sell the changes to its public under the auspices of *gaiatsu*. Furthermore, the changes made in the Guidelines, for Japan, were made "on its own terms."[70] The problem for Japan here is that, while the Guidelines give Japan more direction in its security policy, it also restricts its foreign-policy options. As Mulgan writes,

Moreover, even though Japan desires more freedom of diplomatic action in the United States-Japan security relationship, the guidelines may mean it ends up with considerably less. Keeping an appropriate diplomatic distance from the United States on regional issues will become more problematic in the same way that insulating Japan's strategic options will.[71]

Japan will face increasingly tougher choices than it did before the Guidelines. In a China-Taiwan crisis in which the United States chooses to involve itself, Japan could be faced with choosing between its ally and its pacifism.[72]

When one looks at public opinion in general, there is strong support for a continued U.S. role in Japanese security. In a national survey by the *Nihon Keizai Shimbun,* 70 percent of the Japanese electorate think that the current level of U.S. support for Japan's national defense is fine; 27 percent thought that it should be increased.[73] In the same poll, a surprisingly large plurality felt that Japan's laws should be changed to back the United States in a conflict in the Far East.[74] Among the Japanese, 63 percent felt that the United States-Japan Security Treaty is useful in providing the Asia-Pacific Region with security.[75]

The Koreas

"The areas surrounding Japan" that are mentioned in the Guidelines probably include, but do not specifically name, the Korean Peninsula. Before, and particularly since, the North Koreans sent missiles over Japan, the Japanese government has increasingly been focusing on improving relations with South Korea and studying ways to deal with North Korea.[76] The North Korean threat has served as a unifying factor for Japan, South Korea, and the United States. The three countries warned and worked jointly to persuade North Korea to halt future missile tests.[77]

Japan's apology to South Korea has gone a long way toward healing government-to-government relations. The two nations are cooperating more closely with each other. They are conducting joint naval exercises and are working to solve their territorial disputes peaceably.

The North Korean situation is causing Japan to rethink it definition of self-defense. Japan is now pondering the idea that it can be considered self-defense to destroy missile sites in foreign countries if they threaten Japan. To this end, the Japanese government has submitted bills to the Diet requesting funding for refueling aircraft in order to permit Japanese strike aircraft to destroy targets in Korea and elsewhere if necessary. Furthermore, Japan is already sending air crews to the United States for training on midair refueling.

Photo 7.1 **A Japanese ASDF Pilot Prepares to Fly a Midair Refueling Training Mission with a USAF Pilot** (*Source:* U.S. Air Force Photo. www.af.mil)

This marks a dramatic change in Japanese defense policy. For the first time, the SDF will have power projection capability. This is a long way from the SDF that once believed that the very possession of jet fighters was unconstitutional.[78]

Conclusion

It is important to note what Japan is not prepared to do in its foreign policy. Like many nations, Japan is not prepared to take on primary or great-power responsibility for the maintenance of world order.[79] The principal reason is constitutional limitations, but second, there is a strong feeling among Japanese elites that Japan cannot or will not take on the costs of maintaining world order as the United States does. Among those I interviewed, 78 percent felt that Japan could not pay the price to be a true leader or would be willing to do so, but that it could not pay the price of world leadership. No one felt that Japan was able to be a true world leader, and 22 percent felt that they did not know whether Japan was or was not able to achieve world leadership. Most, however, expressed the idea that Japan would be willing to take on that role if it was able.[80] Polls of the Japanese public indicate the same thing. When asked during an *Asahi Shimbun* survey, "If Japan was asked to cooperate in solving international conflicts, do you think it would be able to play its role adequately under the current constitution?" only 24 percent felt Japan would do an adequate job; 60 percent felt that Japan would do an inadequate job.[81] Part of this response is the fact that economics cannot be separated from defense and foreign policy.[82] Japan's fifteen-year economic recession that began in 1991 and from which it is only now emerging, leaves it in a weak position to take up world leadership. It much prefers to follow U.S. leadership. Another reason that may be causing Japan to feel inadequate is that 67 percent of Japanese voters feel that Japan is not respected by other countries,[83] while 53 percent feel that raising the level of its foreign diplomacy is the best way to increase respect for Japan.[84]

It appears that, in spite of right-wing rhetoric to the contrary, Japan is not pursuing global leadership. It has too much to lose if it does. There also seems to be a realization that Japan is limited in what it can do by itself. In concert with other great powers, Japan can do much, but alone it sees its own weaknesses and is not willing to risk its position in the world in pursuit of greater power.

One thing that is clear for Japan is that its people do not want war again. The peoples of most nations would express the same sentiments, but in Japan it can be said that the aversion to war is stronger than most national interests that force could be used to protect.[85] Professor Fujiwara stated that "Japan is addicted to pacifism like an alcoholic is to alcohol."[86]

On the other hand, Japan wants the respect of its fellow nations. As Professor Akihiko Tanaka of Tokyo University's Institute of Oriental Culture stated, "Japan felt it was a loser in the Gulf War, and it wants to avoid the same situation in future."[87] The problem is that Japan is better at reacting than at acting. Toshiya Hoshino, of the Osaka School of International Policy, Osaka University, noted that "It is harder to be active than reactive."[88] As Professor Ogawa asserted, "Japan has been a reactive state since the nineteenth century."[89] What Japan seems to be lacking is firm goals and policies for the actions it takes. Professor Hoshino feels that "Japan is not good at the 'vision thing.'"[90] Professor Tanaka confirmed this belief when he contended that "Japan has no real long-term goals. It is a status-quo power, in realist terms."[91]

Japan still needs to further mature politically. Japan still operates under too many constraints to be a "normal state." If Japan wants normalization in the eyes of its own people, the concept of *gaiatsu* must be abandoned. Japan must stand independent and take credit for its own actions, for better or worse. If Japan is sovereign, then *gaiatsu* is irrelevant. Is Japan a sovereign nation? Of course it is. Japan, then, needs to stop complaining how the world perceives its actions and start playing the game. This attitude must be held even when Japan is siding with the United States. Professor Tanaka affirmed that "Japan prefers to be bashed rather than passed."[92] Japan needs to have strong priorities if it wants to avoid being passed over. It must formulate its own direction and priorities for its foreign policy. Professor Seiichi Kubota, formerly of the *Asahi Shimbun,* already has one: "It should be a foreign policy priority to find more friends in Asia."[93] Whether Japan chooses this priority or another, Japan must make its own choices with respect to its interests.

8

Triangulating Politics

America, China, and Japan

*The purpose of foreign policy is not to provide an
outlet for our own sentiments of hope or indignation;
it is to shape real events in a real world.*
—John Fitzgerald Kennedy

As described in chapter 3, Japan sits in the Northeast Asian security complex. This complex has six principal members: China, Japan, the Koreas, and Russia, as well as the United States as the global hegemonic power with substantial interests in the region, including forward-deployed troops in South Korea and Japan. Sitting on the edge of this complex are Taiwan and ASEAN as outsiders looking in.[1] However, the three most important members of this complex are Japan, China, and the United States. Figure 8.1 illustrates this relationship. Alternately the United States-Japan relationship and the Sino-United States relationship are called the most important bilateral relationships in the world. It is important to note that the Sino-Japan relationship is never mentioned as being important for either China or Japan. Presently, Chinese-Japanese relations can easily be said to be at their worst since the end of World War II. China's recent, quasi-official media campaign to demonize Japan among its citizens is working very well, with the unintended consequence of strengthening nationalism in Japan. The problem here is that if the region is to be peaceful, then these two major powers need to work out their differences. The problem is, thus, how Japan and its ally, the United States, deal with the challenge of China to their foreign and security policies.

It is essential to remember that security and foreign policy go hand in hand. To paraphrase Carl von Clausewitz, diplomacy is war by other means. In essence, Clausewitz was saying that when the shooting stops, diplomacy begins (and conversely when diplomacy fails or ends, the shooting begins): however, the conflict does not end when the shooting stops, it simply moves to the negotiating table. Both war and diplomacy

Figure 8.1   **China-U.S.-Japan in the Northeast Asian Security Complex**

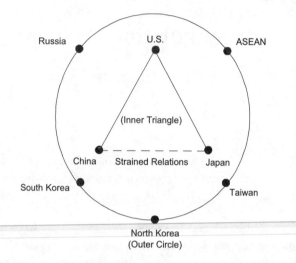

are forms of conflict. One is violent the other is not. It is important to understand that two nations having diplomatic relations is conflict management even if they are not negotiating anything. The two nations are managing potential and existing conflict by communicating. The lack of diplomatic relations still signifies conflict even if it has not become violent. The United States and Iran are perfect examples of this. They have no direct diplomatic relations but do have relations through the good offices of the Swiss who help manage the conflict between the two to keep it from becoming violent.

In *Politics Among Nations,* Hans J. Morgenthau argued that the quality of a nation's diplomacy was an element of its national power and was thus linked to its security.[2] For Japan, like any other nation, foreign policy revolves around and emanates from the security needs. In the previous chapter, we looked at Japan's security options. In this chapter we will examine Japan's security predicament.

Japan's global foreign-policy agenda is dictated by its security needs within its security complex. That is to say, most of what Japan is doing globally has relevance for its security needs within Northeast Asia. A clear example of this circumstance is the way Prime Minister Junichiro Koizumi "sold" to the Japanese public the need for Japan to help the United States in rebuilding Iraq by sending the SDF. Essentially, Koizumi argued that if we do not help out our ally, the United States, in Iraq, why would the

United States help us out if we are threatened by North Korea? While sending the SDF to Iraq certainly had other political benefits (and costs), the overriding need was stated in terms of Japanese security in Northeast Asia. However, in spite of the threat posed by a nuclear armed North Korea, the number-one concern within Japan's security complex is China. In the following pages, we will look at the challenge of China and North Korea and Japan's response to them in relation to Japan's security relationship with the United States.

The China Question

The "million dollar question" of Northeast Asian security (and of global security in general) is about China's true intentions. Is China a growing hegemon, which will return the world to a bipolar system, as an aggressor nation against American hyperpower, and thus is to be seen as a threat to Japan as America's principal ally in the region? Or is it simply, as it claims, a developing nation that is simply peacefully expanding its power base to protect its own interests? For Japanese foreign and security policy, there is currently no question that needs a more urgent answer. Prudence and realism dictate that Japan prepare for an aggressor China. Idealism indicates that Japan should work with China and try to engage China politically and economically, in order to encourage the peaceful growth of China politically, militarily, and economically. So what is Japan doing? In many ways it is choosing both courses, but it is prioritizing the more prudent and cautious realist hard line.

Strategically Speaking

Strategic theory dictates that a nation never wants to put itself in a position of making itself a tempting target for an aggressor state. There are two ways to make a state a tempting target. The first and more obvious one is to unilaterally disarm to the point of weakness. An aggressor state would see the weak state as a tempting target for expansion or domination. The second way a state can make itself a target of aggression is to grow its military capabilities to a level that make it a potential threat to the larger state, thus potentially causing the more powerful state to preemptively attack it out of its own security concerns. Examples of this possibility currently are China and North Korea, with Japan and the United States being the more powerful states. The status quo is currently acceptable to the United States and to Japan. However, the military buildup in China and the North Korean pursuit of nuclear weapons change the balance of power and will cause Japan and the United States to pursue a more aggressive policy toward these two nations, the possible result being the possibility of conventional or (worst case) nuclear conflict.

It can be convincingly argued that, in many ways, China is counting on American greed for cheap products to avoid a new Cold War while it builds the People's Liberation Army (PLA) into a modern military force that can compete with the U.S. military, at least regionally, if not, eventually, globally. The Chinese are hoping to build up militarily to the point of advantage or parity with the United States, while continuing to trade with the United States at a large surplus. They hope to put the United States in a position where it cannot afford, militarily or economically, to defend Taiwan, Japan, or any other imperial aspirations it has in East Asia or what it believes to be "Greater China."

The United States, on the other hand, is hoping to keep China engaged economically to the point at which it is too economically dependent on the Western markets to risk invading Taiwan or any other state in Asia because of the threat of sanctions and the resulting collapse of its economy. In many ways, the United States is counting on China's greed for more profits to keep it from becoming more aggressive. However, this being said, China would appear to be crossing the line to being a true threat to both America and Japan, and both nations are seeing China as a growing threat. The reason is that China seems to be announcing to the world through its actions (not words) that it is planning to go to war with the United States in the future. Maybe not in the near future, but someday in the future, China plans to be America's enemy and is preparing its military for that day. As former CIA director R. James Woolsey put it, "China is pursuing a national strategy of domination of the energy markets and strategic dominance of the western Pacific."[3] In an editorial for the *Houston Chronicle,* Cragg Hines put it this way, "It's the 'notion of tectonic plates shifting' the geopolitics of the region and the world, said Randy Schriver, who until recently was deputy assistant secretary of State for East Asia and Pacific affairs. We are in danger of a steady but discernible drift into a strategic rivalry."[4]

China's military modernization is not a recent phenomenon. The Chinese military and political establishments were truly shocked by the First Gulf War, when the United States so quickly and easily defeated Sadaam Hussein's veteran Iraqi army, including the Republican Guard. Only after the war did China come to recognize that the most recent Revolution in Military Affairs (RMA) had occurred. The technology and in particular the equipment used to fight war by the United States would force a change in the way war would be fought in the future if a nation had any hope of standing up to the American army. An example of a past RMA that required a change in military tactics was what the machine gun did to the mass charge in World War I. In the case of the most recent RMA, China saw the need for its own military modernization. Previously, China had counted on its own sheer numerical superiority in manpower to challenge and intimidate the United States from taking any hostile action, including defending Taiwan. The Persian Gulf War taught China that numerical superiority would not tip the balance against the U.S. military. Only technological equality or superiority and numerical advantage would make China a true challenger to American hegemony.

Challenging America

Since the end of the Gulf War in the early 1990s, China has embarked on a rapid military modernization and overall numerical downsizing program, with the U.S. armed forces in mind as the potential enemy. The downsizing of China's army is seen as a practical necessity in order to free up resources for a more professional and better-trained army. This restructuring of China's military continues to this day and is an ongoing process. The *Xinhua News* reported on 13 July 2005 in a headline that reads: "Chinese Military to be Restructured." The article stated that (paraphrased by me):

> According to a statement issued by the Headquarters of the General Staff of the PRC People's Liberation Army [PLA], the PLA is expected to shift its traditional structure by adding new battle units and cutting outdated ones in an effort to create new combat effectiveness. The PLA program is attempting to change the structure of the PLA by cutting its divisions and increasing brigades, reported *Liberation Army Daily,* the traditional mouthpiece of the Chinese armed forces.[5]

In order to modernize quickly, China has purchased as much of the latest weaponry and technology from Russia, Israel,[6] and the European Union[7] as it has been able to acquire. It has also begun to build up its own technological military-industrial complex in order to be less dependent on foreign sources of arms. An example is the Chinese J-10 all-weather fighter plane, which can be seen in Photos 8.1 and 8.2.

The J-10 is very similar to the now-canceled Israeli *Lavi* program and is thought to be based on technology purchased from Israel, given the similarities between the two aircraft. For comparison, the *Lavi* can be seen in Photo 8.3.

A further example of China's military buildup is its pursuit of cruise-

Photos 8.1 and 8.2 **Chinese J-10 During a Test Flight** (*Source:* Used with permission of Niels Hillebrand of MILAVIA Military Aviation. http://www.milavia.net/aircraft/j-10/j-10.htm)

missile technology in order to offset the power of the U.S. Navy and its growing antiballistic missile systems. China is particularly interested in obtaining supersonic cruise-missile technology in order to force the American carrier battle groups to stay further out to sea in order to protect the asset.[8]

China is also intent on demonstrating its technological advancements through its space program. On 15 October 2003, China became just the third nation to independently send a man into space and return him successfully to earth when Lt. Col. Yang Liwei became China's first astronaut. Almost two years later, on 12 October 2005, China repeated the feat by sending two men into space for almost a week. The Chinese have had a space program since the 1970s; however, much of its recent success is due to a close working relationship with the Russian space program, an association that permitted them to leapfrog over many technological hurdles that otherwise might have delayed their independent space program. China has a stated goal of putting a man on the moon by the year 2020, something only the United States has done previously (and currently is trying to repeat by 2018). Time will tell if China can do it too.

The United States is not oblivious to China's military buildup. The Voice of America reports that on a visit to China, Admiral William Fallon, commander of U.S. forces in the Pacific, suggested that the PRC's ongoing military buildup might be too extensive for a country not facing any outside threats. He stated, "I'm not about to sit here and determine what percentage of GDP or how many Yuan or whatever ought to be devoted, but my sense is that I don't see a particular threat to China, so military capabilities expansion, [it] seems to me, ought to be commensurate with the growth and development of a country."[9]

The point Admiral Fallon was making was that the United States is not a threat to China and that China is wasting money on military development that could be better used to help develop China. The admiral has a point. If the United States were planning to attack China (for whatever reason), it would have done so already, when China was in a much weaker position. In addition, China's "city buster" nuclear deterrent is more than adequate reason for the United States to keep conflicts with China under control, includ-

Photo 8.3 **Israeli Lavi Jet Fighter Which is Very Similar in Design to the Chinese J-10 (leading some military experts to conclude that it is based on Israeli technology).** (*Source:* Used with permission of Niels Hillebrand of MILAVIA Military Aviation. www.milavia.net/aircraft/j-10/j-10.htm)

ing any efforts by Taiwan to declare independence.[10] A conventional conflict with China is not in the United States' or China's interests.

However, in spite of statements to the contrary, China does seem to be keeping the option of a "first use" policy on the table. On 14 July 2005, the *Financial Times* reported from Beijing that a senior Chinese military official had stated that China is prepared to use nuclear weapons against the United States if it is attacked by Washington during a confrontation over Taiwan.[11] The official is quoted as saying:

> "If the Americans draw their missiles and position-guided ammunition on to the target zone on China's territory, I think we will have to respond with nuclear weapons," Zhu Chenghu, a major general in the People's Liberation Army, said at an official briefing. Zhu, who is also a professor at China's National Defense University, was speaking at a function for foreign journalists organized, in part, by the Chinese government. He added that China's definition of its territory includes warships and aircraft.[12]

A *Wall Street Journal* reporter is quoted as saying:

> [T]hat recent warnings about Beijing's military buildup took on a very real significance, when Chinese Maj. Gen. Zhu Chenghu of the People's Liberation Army warned last week that U.S. military "interference" in a conflict over Taiwan could lead to a Chinese nuclear attack on the U.S., and he reinforced every worst fear of a "China threat." According to the

writer, "it was clear to those of us who witnessed last Thursday's warning that *it was no accidental outburst.*"[13]

China seems confident and willing to play a game of potential nuclear brinkmanship with the United States. This attitude is of concern, not only to the United States, but also to her main ally in the region, Japan. For the first time in several hundred years, China feels confident enough to challenge a global power such as the United States.

Much of this newfound confidence is reflected, not only in its surging economy—which in purchasing power parity (PPP) terms has already passed Japan, making China the second-largest economy in the world—but in a general perception that the current hegemon, the United States, is in decline. While many scholars may lament (or rejoice) in the seeming decline of American power, I would argue that there is no conclusive empirical evidence of American decline. The only evidence is anecdotal. Rather, the empirical evidence would indicate that American power is still in overall ascendancy. To illustrate this situation in terms of economic growth, if China were to continue it rapid growth of 8–9 percent annually, and increase it to, say, 15 percent annually (almost an impossible number to maintain), and the United States were simply to *maintain* its current 3–4 percent growth rate, it would be several hundred years before China could catch up with the United States in terms of economic power based on the size of the economy. This is not to say that there could not be currently unknown intervening variables that would change this equation, it is merely to emphasize the sheer size of the gap between American and Chinese economic power.

Furthermore, unlike the leadership of France and Germany among others within the European Union who believe American is in decline, it would seem that American ascendancy is widely recognized within Asian capitals. Japan in particular seems to recognize this fact in its choice to continue its alliance with the United States. In a December 2004 Japanese Defense Agency White Paper, China has been declared Japan's greatest security concern. As a rising world power in Asia, China represents a very potent foe for Japan without its alliance with the United States. Nevertheless, China is preparing for a long and drawn-out challenge to American power that will likely be over a hundred years in the making (again, in the absence of currently unknown intervening variables).

Challenging Japan

This brings us to our next area of inquiry, China's challenge to Japan. China's expansionism and hegemonism, begun by Jiang Zemin, is now continued by Hu Jintao. More than anything else except the threat of North Korea, the threat of China is propelling Japan forward in its efforts to alter its constitution. China has been called a sleeping dragon, but in reality, Japan is the real sleeping dragon, which China may be taunting recklessly. In fact, Deng Xiaoping is said to have warned his successors about Japan by telling them to let sleeping dogs lie, but they have been loath, or unable, to follow his advice. Article Nine has truly limited Japan in its military development and its ability to project power. If the threat of China ever causes Japan to abandon Article Nine, China might regret its bullying of Japan. An example of such an eventuality occurred on 9 September 2005, just two days before national elections in Japan. In what appeared to be an effort to intimidate Japanese voters the same way it intimidates voters in Taiwan, China sent warships to patrol an area surrounding disputed islands and natural gas fields in the East China Sea. If this maneuver was meant to intimidate Japanese voters, then it had the opposite effect when the right wing and more nationalistic Junichiro Koizumi and the LDP won reelection over a more pacifist opposition in a major landslide victory.

This is not an isolated incident. In recent years and months, China has grown bolder about fomenting anti-Japanese nationalism within China. This new boldness includes riots and street demonstrations outside of Japanese consulates and business assets within China. Many of these protests are triggered by Japanese actions, such as visits to Yasukuni Shrine (where several "class A" war criminals are enshrined) by Japanese leaders and the publication of revisionist textbooks approved by the Japanese Ministry of Education that whitewash Japanese atrocities during World War II. In the past, these event have sparked official protests by China (and Korea), but what is different now is that the Chinese government and Communist Party seem to have given sanction to the street protests.[14] However, the Chinese street protests have had the unintended result of awakening the average Japanese citizen to the challenge and potential threat that China is to Japan.

The problem for China is that, having awakened large-scale anti-Japanese sentiment among its general population, it may find it politically impossible in the future to repair relations with Japan if it needs to. This dilemma can lead to generational hatreds of the kind the world witnessed in the former Yugoslavia. However, the current state of relations is not solely China's fault in that Japan could have done more in the last sixty years to heal the Sino-Japanese relationship by demonstrating greater sensitivity to Chinese suffering under its rule and offering a more sincere apology for its actions, one that China could accept. Nevertheless, the current state of relations between the two great powers in Asia does not bode well for the future.

Historically, since World War II, Japan has been very circumspect about naming threats to Japan. The 1997 Guidelines simply referred to the "areas surrounding Japan" as the threat. However, Japan is beginning to openly voice its concerns about China's growing military power. In its annual 2004 Defense White Paper, it noted China's increasingly bold maritime ambitions. The defense paper—which echoes concerns expressed in the U.S. Defense Department about China's military buildup—stated that Japan's public was "exceedingly concerned" about the intrusion of Chinese vessels, including a nuclear submarine, into Japanese waters. "Regarding the pick-up in China's maritime activity, the trends need to be watched," it read. "It has been pointed out that the Chinese navy is aiming to become a so-called 'blue-water navy,'" the paper added, referring to development of a deep-water fleet.[15] This trend continued in 2005, with a new defense white paper that argued that Japan needed to start to respond to Chinese military spending.[16] This attitude could mark the beginnings of an arms race in East Asia and pull Japan further away from Article Nine and toward constitutional revision and normalcy.

It is important to note that China really has nothing to fear from Japan. Japan no longer has the imperial capability (or desire) that it once had, as a result of a declining population and a changed world. Each nation has the capacity to harass the other, but neither can really invade or conquer the other. This current status quo should be good enough to allay any Chinese fears about a resurgent imperial Japan, but China is not satisfied with the status quo. On the other hand, China's internal anti-Japan message has been very successful at raising a generation of anti-Japanese Chinese, with the unintended consequence of a growing nationalism within Japan as well. Faced with growing and potent hostility from China, the Japanese have become more patriotic and open to a militarily stronger and more assertive Japan.

China's Achilles' Heel

China's newfound assertiveness is not without risks to itself. China's new economy is energy-dependent. Energy—or rather, the lack of adequate energy reserves to fuel its industrial appetite—is China's great weakness. China is not like the United States, which has greater oil reserves than Saudi Arabia (the problem for the United States is the cost of extracting the oil, which is prohibitive, even at $70 a barrel, but not technically or fiscally impossible). China needs new energy sources to feed its new industries and provide continuing access to its current imports. Brownouts are frequent and common in some major cities of China. Many Chinese factories need to keep generators on standby, just to keep the factories running. Evidence of China's energy problem can be seen in this Associated Press report of 19 July 2005:

BEIJING POWER CRUNCH PROMPTS SHUT DOWN (2005–07–19)

[It was] reported that workers at thousands of Beijing companies are about to get an unscheduled vacation thanks to the scorching summer heat. Beginning this week, 4,689 businesses will take mandatory weeklong breaks on rotation to cut down on energy use in the PRC capital and avoid pushing up already rapidly climbing power prices, the official *Xinhua News Agency* said Tuesday.[17]

It is important to note that China is still a developing economy and that its energy needs are growing. China is rushing to develop hydroelectric power, at the cost of massive environmental upheaval and population displacement. The Three Gorges Dam on the Yangtze River is but one example of this effort.

China has also lobbied furiously with Russia for a pipeline from the Siberian oilfields to Manchuria. Japan, on the other hand, lobbied just as furiously for the pipeline to be built to the east coast of Siberian (also known as the Russian Far East Coast) as not to be dependent on China for the free flow of oil. Both nations got part of what they wanted, in that the pipeline will split and go to both Manchuria and the east coast of Siberian, as Russia wants China to be a major market for its oil but does not want to be dependent on China's control of the spigot to market its oil to international customers. The problem will now be to build this new pipeline in a politically and economically volatile Russia.

While Japan and China share the common need for a secure energy supply, Japan is approaching the issue from a much different perspective. Japan sees the United States as an ally that it can depend on, so it works with the United States to secure its energy needs. China, on the other hand, sees the United States as a potential rival and does not like its dependence on the U.S. Navy's 7th Fleet for securing safe passage for its energy supplies to its coastal ports in southeastern China. It is interesting that both China and Japan share an interest in dependency on oil, and it would seem that cooperation between the two would be helpful to both. There seems to be some evidence of this cooperation, as evidenced by this news report from *Xinhua News:*

CHINA SHARING COMMON INTEREST WITH JAPAN IN OIL, ENERGY FIELD, BFA OFFICIAL (2005–08–25)

The PRC and Japan ride on the same boat in the area of oil and energy, so the two nations should seek more common grounds in economic and trade relations, Long Yongtu, secretary-general of the Bo'ao Forum for Asia (BFA) was quoted as saying by the China News Service. At a seminar held by the China Daily and Beijing University here on Wednesday, Long said, as two major oil importers in the world, the PRC and Japan share

many common interest [sic]. He expressed his wish for better cooperation
between the two nations with regard to the energy problem.[18]

China's energy needs have risen as spectacularly as its economy. China
has gone from a net exporter of oil in 1992 to the world's second-largest
importer of oil behind the United States. China is very aware of its oil
problem and is doing everything it can to secure energy resources on the
open market. Its recent attempt to buy the American oil giant Unocal, and
its August 2005 purchase of PetroKazakhstan, are evidence of this growth.
If China were ever to attack Taiwan, it would likely loose its access to oil
through maritime interdiction from the U.S. Navy's 7th Fleet, MSDF, the
Australian navy, and possibly the Indian navy, and Russian sanctions. Such
a state of affairs could force China to attempt to militarily seize the Russian oil fields, bringing Russia into a war with China (which could go
nuclear), which would force China into a two-front war, of which its prob-
abilities of success would be almost zero. China could use its nuclear weapons only to ensure that there are no winners, only losers. China's
dependence on energy in the form of Middle East oil is the Achilles' heel
of its military ambitions in East Asia.

Energy is not China's only Achilles' heel. The environment in China is
also an important threat to Chinese power. China's virtually unregulated
industrial expansion has produced an environmental disaster of biblical pro-
portions. Reports of untreated toxic waste flowing freely into rivers, workers and children growing up with near-toxic levels of air pollution, and a
near-total breakdown in preventive public-health services, as evidenced by
the growth of "snail fever"[19] and the SARS outbreak of 2004 have led to
almost daily reports of riots in rural China by peasants demanding that the
government protect them. The government in China is doing very little to
curb or control polluters, and in absence of government control, the peasants are taking the law into their own hands and shutting the offenders down
(at least temporarily).[20] The cost of cleanup will be prohibitive when China
is finally forced to deal with the problem.

This situation leads us to China's third Achilles' heel: its newfound
wealth—or, in reality, the lack thereof. China is accumulating wealth at an
unprecedented rate as the result of its trade surpluses with the United States
and Europe. However, China is hoarding this wealth rather than investing it
in its own country. While it is spending (almost recklessly) on the PLA, it is
neglecting its own infrastructure, people, the environment, and future stability. China's current domestic policy resembles the actions of a person
who takes a cash advance from a credit card, puts the money in the bank,
and declares himself rich. The problem is that the interest and payments will

eventually destroy him. China is in the same situation: by investing in its military and by neglecting its people and domestic needs, it will eventually pay a price that it does not want to pay.

This consideration leads us to a fourth and final Achilles' heel of China: China's position in the world system. China represents an opportunity for the world economy, but it is not an essential element. China produces goods cheaply, but the goods that it produces are not essential commodities for the West. This is why in a conflict over Taiwan, the United States and its allies could embargo oil going into China and not be threatened by the loss of Chinese goods being exported. There is nothing that China currently produces that cannot be produced elsewhere if necessary. There would be a temporary loss of supply, but the long-term result would be the relocation of the industries. The world basically does not depend on China, China depends on the world. It is for this reason that the world and the United States are willing to continue engagement of China, while being aware of the military threat China poses to the region. Other nations see China as the eventual loser of any conflict, because the world can turn its back on China, but China cannot turn its back on the world.

The Question of North Korea

The next question we will study in our examination of Japan's foreign policy situation is the question of North Korea. North Korea's recent (and past) actions have done more to push forward normalization in Japanese foreign policy than anything since the end of the Cold War and the shock of the Gulf War. Japanese Prime Minister Koizumi was hoping to normalize and repair Japanese relations with North Korea when he negotiated the return of Japanese nationals abducted from Japan over twenty-five years earlier by North Korean agents. What he got was the law of unintended consequences. The return of the abductees on 16 October 2002 sent Japanese relations with North Korea to their lowest level since the end of the Korean War.[21] The return from North Korea forced the hand of Japanese elites, and the Japanese public, in an unusual move, dictated a foreign-policy agenda. To put it simply, the public was outraged that any nation would be so bold as to abduct the youth of another nation, taking them off of the streets and forcing them to work for the foreign regime. The actions of North Korea in committing these abductions bring into question one of the fundamental responsibilities of the state, which is to protect its citizens. For Japan, the abduction issue, and the ongoing questions as to the fate of abducted Japanese nationals still alive and deceased in North Korea, is of paramount importance to the Japanese public, and thus to the government, at any summit with North

Korea. The fact that Japan continues to raise this issue is lending further strain to the already strained relationship with the DPRK. Japan continues to make the abduction issue part of the Six-Party Talks in Beijing (the Six-Party talks will be dealt with shortly).

It is a testimony to the pacifism in Japan that the Japanese did not react more strongly. One could only imagine what would happen if it were to be discovered that something similar (hypothetically) had happen to American youth. War by the popular demand of the American people would likely be inevitable. In the case of Japan, those who were not aware of the threat posed by North Korea after the 1998 missile tests over Japan were now made aware of the true nature of Kim Jong Il's regime by the abduction issue. Japanese officials within MOFA and in the Prime Minister's Office expressed both frustration and understanding at the public's reaction. The public wanted to punish North Korea, and the government had to obey the will of its people, but the government tempered its response, in line with Japan's foreign-policy needs and maintaining international goodwill. Japan's dilemma can be seen in this *Kyodo News* report:

UN Cautions Japan Against Sanctions on N Korea (2005–03–07)

UN officials asked Japan on Monday not to impose sanctions against the DPRK over the issue of abductions of Japanese citizens by the DPRK as a reduction of aid would hurt vulnerable women and children. Japan should be "careful" with any sanctions so they do not hurt people who need food, said Pierette Vu Thi, the UN Children's Fund representative in the DPRK. "If they're not targeted very carefully, then it does tend to hurt the most vulnerable parts of the population," the representative said at a press conference in Beijing to discuss a 2004 UN nutritional survey.[22]

The Nuclear Debate

As important as the abduction issue is to Japan, the real security issue is North Korea's nuclear-weapons program and the threat it poses to regional stability. In 1994, it was discovered that North Korea was pursuing a nuclear-arms program. The United States, under President Bill Clinton, was preparing for a renewed Korean War when former American President Jimmy Carter flew to Pyongyang and engaged in direct talks with the North Korea leader Kim Il Sung, the father of current DPRK president, Kim Jong Il. The result of the these negotiations was the Agreed Framework, in which the United States, along with Japan, South Korea, and others, agreed to help North Korea build two light-water nuclear reactors in exchange for the DPRK's freezing its nuclear program and eventually dismantling it. The United States agreed to do four main things in return for the freezing and dismantlement of the DPRK nuclear program. They are:

1. Finance and construct in the DPRK two light-water reactors (LWR) of the Korean Standard Nuclear Power Plant model; and, in so doing,
2. Provide the DPRK with an alternative source of energy in the form of 500,000 metric tons of heavy fuel oil each year for heating and electricity production, until the first of those reactors is completed;
3. Conduct its activities in a manner that meets or exceeds international standards of nuclear safety and environmental protection; and
4. Provide for the implementation of any other measures deemed necessary to accomplish the foregoing or otherwise to carry out the objective of the Agreed Framework.[23]

Based on this agreement, the Korean (Peninsula) Energy Development Organization (KEDO) was established to build the two reactors. Until the new light-water reactors were built, KEDO would supply fuel oil to replace the graphite-moderated reactor that was to be shut down. For more on the full history of KEDO and the Agreed Framework, go to www.kedo.org.

By the beginning of George W. Bush's presidency in 2001, it had become obvious to the outgoing Clinton administration and the incoming Bush administration that North Korea was cheating on the Agreed Framework and had restarted its nuclear program. In November 2002, KEDO suspended fuel-oil shipments to the DPRK. Several diplomatic initiatives were started. The most notable was the Six-Party Talks, involving China, Japan, South Korea, Russia, North Korea, and the United States. North Korea has long insisted that this issue is a bilateral issue between it and the United States, but the Bush administration has steadfastly insisted that it will only negotiate in the Six-Party framework. The reason is that the Bush administration feels that North Korea will be less likely to break an agreement with all of its neighbors than an agreement made just with the United States, as it did the first time. As U.S. Secretary of State Condoleezza Rice stated on 13 July 2005: "We've been very clear that this is not a bilateral issue between the United States and North Korea. The North Korean programs are a problem for all of its neighbors, and that's why the Six-Party framework is the appropriate framework. We cannot let the North try and turn this into a bilateral negotiation with the United States."[24] In the meantime, North Korea has declared that it has several nuclear bombs, but it has not tested them as of yet. Kim Jong Il delayed North Korea's return to the Six-Party Talks until after the 2004 presidential election, in hopes that Senator John Kerry would win and engage in bilateral talks with North Korea as he had promised on the campaign trail. After George W. Bush's victory, the DPRK reluctantly returned to the talks in Beijing.

For Japan, a nuclear North Korea is a very scary thought. Japan would be the primary target. With Japan's history in Korea, U.S. bases throughout Japan, and the fact that North Korean missiles can easily reach Japan, any renewed Korean conflict could threaten Japan with a nuclear attack. It is in Japan's extreme interest to see North Korea give up its nuclear weapons and program. This goal will not be easy to achieve, as North Korea sees its nuclear program as giving it the ability to be noticed rather than ignored. It also sees it as preserving the dream of Korean unity, the regime, and the Kim dynasty. *Yonhap News* reported on May 24, 2005:

> N.K. SAYS ITS NUCLEAR POWER GUARANTEES PEACE IN ASIA
> The DPRK claimed on Tuesday that its nuclear capability serves as a deterrent and a fundamental guarantor of peace and stability in Northeast Asia, including the Korean Peninsula. "Our possession of nuclear weapons is the best option to safeguard our sovereignty and dignity from the escalating U.S. nuclear manoeuvre [sic] to crush the Republic and realize a nuclear-free Korean Peninsula," the DPRK said in a commentary carried by the KCNA.[25]

For Japan, North Korea's program represents a need to consider what was previously unthinkable, a nuclear-armed Japan. The problem (and solution?) is that a nuclear Japan as a counterweight to a nuclear North Korea is exactly what China would not want to see. A nuclear Japan would be seen as China's equal globally, and a deterrent to its ambitions within Asia. This situation could force China into twisting North Korea's arm into giving up its nuclear weapons. If North Korea refuses and tests a nuclear device, thus announcing to the world that it is a nuclear power, the big loser could be China if Japan does the same in response. China, it seems, is counting on Japan's pacifist constitution and its nuclear taboo, given the attacks on Hiroshima and Nagasaki in 1945, to keep Japan from becoming a nuclear power, too. If Japan were to indicate its willingness to acquire nuclear weapons, and if North Korea does want to test a nuclear weapon, it would be in China's interest to keep North Korea's nuclear ambitions in check. It has long been recognized that Japan has the technology and the know-how to "go nuclear" on very short notice (six months, maximum). Japan currently is the only nonmember of the nuclear club to be permitted to operate all types of nuclear fuel reprocessing facilities.[26]

The only barrier to Japan's nuclear capabilities is internal and domestic opposition. This obstacle is unsurprising, given Japan's status as the only nation to have had atomic warfare waged against it. Public opposition to Japan's becoming a member of the nuclear club would be tremendous. It would take a clear threat to convince the majority of Japanese that a nuclear armed Japan was necessary for Japanese national security. North Korea potentially provides this threat to national security in a very clear way, thus North Korean policy of pursuing nuclear weapons is helping those in Japan who would advocate a nuclear armed Japan to overcome a nearly insurmountable public opinion barrier to Japan being nuclear armed. The long-held argument that Japan holds greater moral status in the world community because it is not a nuclear (weapons) power has been steadily losing ground as Japan takes a more active role on the world stage. Currently, there is little evidence that Japan gains anything by not being an independent nuclear power like Great Britain or France. This is not to say that Japan definitely would choose to develop nuclear weapons, but merely to note the opportunity to make the choice if North Korea does become a nuclear power.

Japanese Policy: Action and Reaction

Given Japan's situation in Asia, the question can be asked about what Japan is doing and how is it reacting to the situation within its complex. Has Japan pushed North Korea into the balancer role by its failure to acknowledge past crimes? Repeated visits by Japanese prime ministers to Yasukuni Shrine have hurt Japan's ability to work with South Korea—its natural ally in the region. Japan's emperors, both Showa and Heisei, stopped going to Yasukuni after the "class A" war criminals were enshrined there, but why have the politicians not been more sensitive by doing the same? Japan has been aggressively working to shore up its legal claims to disputed islands and atolls. Its aggression has been matched by China, which has continued to probe Japanese territorial waters with its submarines. North Korea has also been pushing the limits with spy ships. There is the potential for violent confrontation if either side wants to cross the line.

Strategic Action

So what is Japan doing to defend itself and balance the threats that it faces? Japan knows that nuclear weapons are important to its security. It may not possess them, but it knows it depends on the American "nuclear umbrella" to keep other nuclear states from threatening it. If North Korea becomes a member of the "nuclear club," the only thing that will keep Japan from going nuclear is the credibility of the U.S. nuclear security guarantee. If the United States is seen as wavering in its commitment to defend Japan with nuclear weapons,

Japan is likely to try to acquire them. How strong is the United States' nuclear commitment Japan? If American bases in Japan were attacked or threatened with nuclear weapons, then the United States would almost certainly respond in kind. The former secretary of state Colin Powell is said to have reminded those who would question American nuclear resolve that the United States is the only nation to use nuclear weapons in anger. However, the United States is not likely to try to save a Japanese city if an American city might be lost. The first and foremost loyalty is to one's own citizens.

A second reason for Japan to consider joining the nuclear club as an independent member would be a decline in its relationship with the United States or a decline in the credibility of the United States' nuclear umbrella over Japan. Japan's nuclear restraint is basically self-imposed. Only the political will (to join the nuclear club) stands in the way of Japan's becoming a nuclear power. If Japan ever acquires its own nuclear weapons, it will be to deter nuclear war with its Asian neighbors, not to encourage it, and Japan is feeling the heat of hatred from its neighbors. This hatred is beginning to be reciprocated in the halls of power in Japan. The *Kyodo News Agency* reported on 11 June 2005 that a "'hate-China' sentiment is gradually spreading among top officials at Japan's foreign ministry, according to ministry sources. The Koizumi administration's emphasis on U.S. relations has also diluted diplomatic efforts toward China, ministry sources stated."[27]

So, in this atmosphere of hostility, is the question remains of whether China is a threat to Japan. Former U.S. secretary of state Henry Kissinger, does not think so. On 22 June 2005 he wrote in the *Washington Post* that a

> China containment policy won't work. Concerning Japan and Chinese military threat he said, "But even at its highest estimate, the Chinese military budget is less than 20 percent of America's; it is barely, if at all, ahead of that of Japan and, of course, much less than the combined military budgets of Japan, India and Russia, all bordering China—not to speak of Taiwan's military modernization supported by American decisions made in 2001. Russia and India possess nuclear weapons. In a crisis threatening its survival, Japan could quickly acquire them and might do so formally if the North Korean nuclear problem is not solved. When China affirms its cooperative intentions and denies a military challenge, it expresses less a preference than the strategic realities. The challenge China poses for the medium-term future will, in all likelihood, be political and economic, not military.[28]

Japan is still not sure. It made the mistake of attacking a militarily more powerful nation in World War II and lost. It knows that others (China or North Korea) could make the same mistake. To protect itself, Japan is investing heavily with its American ally in Ballistic Missile Defense (BMD). Lt. Gen. Henry A. Obering III, USAF, director, Missile Defense Agency, in testimony before Congress on 15 March 2005 had this to say about Japanese BMD:

> The Government of Japan is proceeding with the acquisition of a multilayered BMD system, basing its initial capability on upgrades of its Aegis destroyers and acquisition of the Aegis SM-3 missile. We have worked closely with Japan since 1999 to design and develop advanced components for the SM-3 missile. This project will culminate in flight tests in 2005 and 2006. In addition, Japan and other allied nations are upgrading their Patriot fire units with PAC-3 missiles and improved ground support equipment. This past December we signed a BMD framework Memorandum of Understanding with Japan to expand our cooperative missile defense activities.[29]

Japan is preparing for hostile acts against it. It is important to note that these acts are all within the realm of self-defense. BMD does not give Japan power projection capability, something the United States would like to see Japan acquire. Japan is not likely to acquire this capability, as it still faces the issue of Article Nine of its constitution. Prime Minister Koizumi recognized this when, on 2 February 2005, he stated, "No matter what it is called, whether it's a self-defense capability or an organization to defend Japan, the Self-Defense Force should have a solid foundation in the Constitution to eliminate any argument branding it as contrary to the nation's fundamental law."[30]

Constitutional limitations aside, Japan does not want to be seen as a pushover and is standing up for itself and what it believes belongs to Japan. This stance is encouraging to its American ally and should be watched very closely by its rivals. Agence France Presse reported on 10 February 2005 that

> MORE ASSERTIVE JAPAN BECOMING "NORMAL NATION"
> . . . the growing assertiveness of Japan, which has just entered a new row with PRC over a disputed island, shows it is becoming a "normal nation," a senior US official said. "I think Japan in the course of its own internal domestic political discussions is moving in the direction of what a number of Japanese politicians and commentators call the idea of a normal nation," said John Bolton, US undersecretary of state for arms control and international security.[31]

Japan is also aggressively pursuing its international economic future. Energy security is a driving issue in Japanese foreign and security policy. Japan imports over 90 percent of its oil from the Middle East; its interest lies in developing alternative and diversified sources of oil. It is for this reason that it has so aggressively pursued the Siberian oil pipeline to the Pacific coast with Russia. Because Japan knows it cannot totally depend on the United States, it is working to do what it can under Article Nine. One of these things is to build international goodwill.

Building Goodwill

As discussed in chapter 4, Japan is working to build goodwill, but it wants status to be the reward of its goodwill. Aiding the tsunami victims in Southeast Asia has been part of its overall goodwill efforts at nation building. Japan wants to be seen as a nation that is doing good. Ambassador Kenzo Ohshima, Permanent Representative of Japan to the United Nations, stated on 26 May 2005,

> One of the priority issues in my country's international assistance policy is its support for "consolidation of peace and nation-building" in countries emerging from conflict. Japan has long stressed the need for seamless assistance in the comprehensive settlement of conflicts. In particular, my government believes in the importance of peace-building right from the earliest stages of conflict settlement. As a result, Japan has supported peace-building activities in Timor-Leste, Afghanistan, Iraq and various conflict areas in Africa.[32]

The status that Japan wants as part of its global efforts at goodwill is a permanent seat on the U.N. Security Council. The permanent members (P5) of the U.N. Security Council are loath to give up their status by permitting others to join. Japan is working hard to broker a deal that would permit itself and the others of the so-called G4, who are all seeking permanent status. Agence France-Presse reported on 26 June 2005 that

> JAPAN STILL BACKS WIDER EXPANSION OF UN SECURITY COUNCIL AFTER U.S. NOD
> Japan says it continues to support wider expansion of the UN Security Council after the U.S. threw its weight only behind Tokyo for an enlargement limited to two countries. "America made a proposal but Japan cannot go along with it," Prime Minister Junichiro Koizumi, one of U.S. President George W. Bush's closest international allies, told reporters. He said Japan was determined not to break up a joint bid with Brazil, Germany and India, dubbed the Group of Four or G4, which are seeking permanent seats on the powerful UN organ. "We cannot say 'that's right' and jump on to the U.S. proposal as we have been in the G4 campaign," said Foreign Minister Nobutaka Machimura.[33]

Japan will do what it takes to achieve its goals, even if it means criticizing its primary ally.

Relations with the United States

Japan and the United States have had an up-and-down relationship since the 1970s. In the 1980s, Japan was seen as the United States' challenger. In the 1990s, Japan was trying to rescue its economy, while much of the world was booming. However, Japan has no real friends in East Asia or in its security complex except the United States. South Korea, its natural ally in the region, has the same problem with Japan as China does. Japan is seen as historically an imperial power that conquered them and is unwilling to fully admit its past crimes. It is thus a simple fact that Japan has no friends, only rivals, in Northeast Asia.

It is this lack of friendship that makes its alliance with the United States so important to it. Japan needs the United States and is willing to work with the United States to achieve its goals. Both Japan and the United States clearly see China as a potential adversary. The ultimate goal of the renewed Japan-American alliance is not just to contain China, but to contain Chinese *militarism,* so that China can eventually become integrated into the global economic and democratic community.

As China and Japan become more aware of the potential security threat of each other within the Asia-Pacific region, Japan is finding itself as a more and more willing and active member of the United States alliance. This is exactly what those who aspire to Japanese foreign-policy normalcy desire, even if they do not aspire to a conflict or face-off with China.

Japan is betting on the United States as a long-term hyperpower, and as the evidence indicates, the United States is a global power in ascendance, not decline. China is and will remain Japan's rival in Asia. China currently is the United States' only true rival for power, and it is currently only a regional rival for power, not a global one. However, this makes the Japan-United States alliance a logical continuing choice for the national security for both nations. The old adage, "my enemy's enemy is my friend" thus still holds true.

Japan is also dealing with its own isolation within the region. It has never officially settled World War II with the Russians, Korea has not forgiven Japan for its occupation and, more recently, its publishing of textbooks whitewashing its crimes during the occupation of Korea. The same is true for China as it is for Korea: Japan is not to be forgiven until it makes a meaningful apology and compensates the victims. This leaves Taiwan; while occupied by Japan the longest, Taiwan was administered by the Japanese navy,

Photo 8.4 **Prime Minister Koizumi greets U.S. Secretary of State Condoleezza Rice in Tokyo 12 July 2005** (*Source:* Photo courtesy of the Office of the Cabinet Public Relations, Cabinet Secretariat, Japan)

which was more "enlightened" than the Japanese Army was in Manchuria. Taiwan's own diplomatic isolation also plays a role in its pragmatism. An isolated Japan has few options outside of the United States-Japan alliance. If Japan could deal with its history in East Asia in a meaningful way, it might have more options; however, currently the United States is the only choice for Japan, and it is one that it has already made under the leadership of Prime Minister Junichiro Koizumi.

The problem for Japan is burden sharing in Japan. U.S. bases in Japan cause some hardship on the communities where they are located, especially Okinawa, which supports the lion's share of American forward-deployed forces within the region. The United States is working with Japan to ease the burden of large numbers of young Americans serving in Japan. At the same time, America is asking for understanding about the role it is playing and a realization that the burden is carried in both directions. In a 20 July 2005 speech, the U.S. ambassador to Japan, Thomas Schieffer, stated:

Right now, we are in discussions on the posture of our military forces in Japan. We hope you understand that we are looking at those discussions from a strategic point of view. Those forces have an importance to the United States and Japan that must not be overlooked. While the Cold War has gone away, traditional threats and terrorism have not. American forces in Japan the last 60 years have guaranteed the peace of Japan and contributed to the stability of the region. While we understand that those forces are a burden on the people of Japan, we hope the people of Japan understand that they are a burden on us as well. As lovely as Japan is, the young Americans stationed here would just as soon serve their country by staying in America. And despite the Host Nation Support that Japan contributes to their success, it would still be cheaper for America to keep those troops at home. The reason we are willing to bear the burden of having those troops overseas is the same reason you are willing to bear the burden of having them stationed here in Japan—their presence keeps the peace. We must both keep that in mind as we negotiate their status.[34]

Currently, United States-Japanese relations are at the strongest that they have been in recent memory. Part of this friendship is due to Japan's security needs, but part of it is also Prime Minister Koizumi's strong relationship with American president George W. Bush. Koizumi has been one of Bush's strongest supporters, at a time when many other world leaders would not support Bush or were openly critical of him. Japan has taken a lot of political heat and lost a lot of goodwill by supporting Bush. The importance of personal relationships between leaders cannot be underestimated. Bush and Koizumi have a very good working relationship, but the reasons for Koizumi and Japan's support of Bush's American foreign policy go deeper.

Japan did not have a positive experience with the last American Democratic president, Bill Clinton. This situation was partly because there were eight Japanese prime ministers during Clinton's eight years in office. None of them were able to establish a working relationship with Clinton or vice versa. Koizumi has been able to establish a working relationship with Bush, because of the relative stability of the prime ministership in Japan these last few years. This relationship could continue (if Koizumi decides to stay on as prime minister) for the remainder of Bush's presidency, since Koizumi won reelection on 11 September 2005 for the next five years in a landslide. The other reason for the lack of positive relations with Japan during the Clinton years is the fact that Clinton's policies were perceived as favoring China over Japan.

A second argument for why Koizumi and Japan prefer Bush might be the general preference among Asian leadership for dealing with Republican presidents. China, in particular, seems to prefer Republicans historically because, in my opinion, they understand the strategic thinking (realist thinking) of Republicans better than the mindset of Democrats. Republican presidents tend to act in similar ways to the way Asian leaders would when faced with similar situations. Thus, Republican policies are more predictable and understandable than those of the Republicans' Democratic counterparts. Leaders tend to prefer stability and predictability over the unknown, even if the unknown results in the potential for a more positive outcome. European leaders, on the other hand seem—again, in my opinion—seem to prefer Democratic presidents in the United States for the same reasons. They understand Democratic strategic thinking better, as it is more like their own.

As much as Koizumi has strengthened relations with the United States through his relationship with President Bush, it is important to remember that the 11 September 2005 election could have gone the other way if the "experts" had been right. During the election campaign, the DPJ had promised to bring the SDF home, and if that party had won, a radical shift in Japanese policy toward America might have ensued. As Agence France-Presse reported on 25 August 2005:

JAPAN OPPOSITION LEADER READY TO MEET BUSH, PULL IRAQ TROOPS
The leader of Japan's main opposition party has said a victory in next month's election means Japanese troops out of Iraq—and he wants to meet George W. Bush to tell him so. Katsuya Okada, president of the Democratic Party of Japan, railed against Prime Minister Junichiro Koizumi's decision to extend the historic deployment of Japanese forces.[35]

Conclusion

We have seen how strategic theory teaches us that nations that build up their militaries face two potential threats. The first threat is the more obvious one, of a nation's failing to militarize and thus becoming a tempting target for an aggressor state. The second threat is a less obvious one of making the state a danger to another state that, under normal circumstances, would have kept the status quo. China is in the process of making itself into the United States' strategic threat, rather than rival. The question is whether China will be a threat. China may or may not be a future threat. In spite of the challenge and potential rival that it is making itself to be to America and Japan, China is an even greater threat to itself. Whether it becomes incorporated over time into the world community or becomes a threat to regional stability is anyone's guess at this point in time. Only China's leaders know for sure, and even they may not know where fate will lead them.

North Korea presents a second threat within the region for Japan. How the threat resolves itself depends on the results of the Six-Party Talks, China's willingness to lean on Kim Jong Il, and the unknowns of international politics. Should Japan be unleashed from Article Nine to be a major power in the traditional sense? It can only become unleashed, and will do so, when China and North Korea dictate that action by becoming a threat that Japan can no longer ignore.

Japan's relationship with the United States is a key relationship for both nations. One cannot underestimate how critical this relationship is. Both nations need each other in order to support their global position. As Admiral Walter F. Doran, commander of the U.S. Pacific Fleet, stated on 11 June 2005, "The relationship between the United States and Japan, particularly between the Japanese Maritime Self-Defense Force and the U.S. Navy, is key critical to our ability to have a persistent presence in the Western Pacific."[36] There is a strategic advantage to the United States' having its forces forward-deployed in Asia. Both nations gain from their relationship. However, Japan has more to lose if it abandons the United States. This fact is because Japan has far more to *fear* if it leaves the United States-Japan alliance than if it stays. The benefits of the United States-Japan alliance outweigh any "burden" on Japan from having the American military forward deployed in Japan. In fact, it would be cheaper for the United States to base its forces within the United States rather than keeping them stationed in Japan, as Ambassador Thomas Schieffer pointed out.

Japan has made its choice under the current leadership of Prime Minister Koizumi. For the time being, it is going to stick with the United States. Its alternative choices are bleak. Japan has much more to gain from working with the United States than working against it.

9

Where Is Japan Going?

*Japan is an example of a nation working very
hard not to be a great power.*
—Kenneth Waltz[1]

The post-Cold War world of *Pax Americana* has experienced wars and uprisings on all fronts. For Japan, the simple world it knew during the Cold
War became complex. Choices for Japan are no longer clear. Decisions are
difficult. This final chapter will look at the sources of Japanese foreign policy,
including the growing role of the Diet in future foreign-policy making. It
will also examine the prospect of Japanese hegemony and possible world
leadership. The role of the SDF in Japanese foreign policy will also be examined, and recommendations will be made for the continued normalization of Japanese foreign policy. Finally, we will conclude by revisiting
Hermann's model and the theoretical foundations of this text.

The "Wide" View of Japanese Security

The events of 9/11 and the emergence of the North Korean threat in the minds
of the Japanese public have encouraged Japan to embark on its most radical
foreign-policy and security-policy changes since the end of the Cold War. The
SDF supported Operation Enduring Freedom and is now serving as part of the
reconstruction effort in Iraq. Japan has come a long way from being the nation
that until the end of the Cold War was content to sit on the sidelines of international conflict. As Japan increases its role globally, however, its regional security complex is growing increasingly complicated and worrisome.

In order to deal with its own security complex, Japan must first securitize
its domestic economy. Currently, Japan's status as a major world power is
based entirely on the size and strength of its economy. In the late 1980s,
Japan was on top of the world. It was seen as the up-and-coming challenger
to the reigning hegemon, the United States. Its economy was the second-
largest in the world behind the United States. The Japanese yen was strong
and stable. People around the world were studying Japanese as the "it" language for movers and shakers who wanted to succeed. At the same time,

trouble was brewing for Japan. Land speculation had led the Tokyo metropolitan area to achieve a paper value greater than that of the forty-eight contiguous United States. Then, the Japanese economic bubble burst. Soon after, the rest of the Japanese economy started to decline. This decline continued throughout the 1990s. So, while the United States and most of the world boomed during the decade, Japan sank deeper into recession and is currently attempting to pull out of a deflationary spiral.

The major blame for the continued stagnation of the Japanese economy has been placed on Japan's unwillingness to implement meaningful economic or political structural reform. The Japanese government has continued to prop up bankrupt firms and financially insolvent banks, while implementing stimulus package after stimulus package that never work. Currently, the political leadership in Japan is fighting an uphill battle against cultural and political norms to implement structural reforms needed to bolster its sagging economy. A series of prime ministers, culminating with Prime Minister Junichiro Koizumi, have all promised structural change but have failed to muster the political capital needed to break down the existing structures. With Koizumi's landslide victory on 11 September 2005, he should finally be able to pass his Postal Reform Bill, along with many other much-needed reforms. Failure to do so would signal that Japan is not ready to be a great power.

The recognition of the need for Japan to securitize its economy has been very slow in coming, but the recent economic rise of China has caused Japan to move forward more aggressively than in the past to spell out the terms of its security needs in the global context. Japan's 28 November 2002 executive report to the prime minister on strategies for the twenty-first century highlights this need. It states:

> Japan will be more directly influenced by Chinese economic development than any other country and has a responsibility to articulate a national economic vision under this new paradigm. *The essential first steps will be to quickly dispose of non performing loans and at the same time reform the economic structure itself.*
>
> The promotion of science and technology will be an absolute prerequisite to achieving this. *Nor can regulatory reform be avoided.* Japan must rectify high-cost structures, enhance educational facilities, and accept more foreign students, with the ultimate aim of attracting direct investment from overseas in high value-added areas such as high technology industries and research and development.
>
> Structural reforms in the agricultural sector are also essential. Japan must study mechanisms to mitigate the impact on domestic agriculture and to ensure food security.[2]

This acknowledgment of the need to reform its economy in light of the challenge from China is remarkable, in view Japan's recent economic problems and its slowness in dealing with its structural problems.

During the last round of General Agreement on Tariffs and Trade (GATT), Japan (along with South Korea) attempted to negotiate an exemption for rice as a staple food in which Japan felt the need to remain self-sufficient. Successive crop failures in the early 1990s destroyed the myth that Japan could ever be self-sufficient in rice. However, the political need to protect domestic agriculture remained. Japan is a nation that cannot feed its population without food imports. Japan imports over 40 percent of its domestic food consumption. Much of the 60 percent it does not import comes from the seas surrounding Japan, particularly the Sea of Japan. It is for this reason that environmental issues in the Sea of Japan should be among Japan's highest priorities. However, Japan has largely failed to prioritize the Sea of Japan as an essential issue. Instead, it has chosen to focus on the recently ratified Kyoto Protocols, though without the participation of China, the United States, and India—the three largest polluters—the treaty seems meaningless. While the Kyoto Protocol focuses on greenhouse gases, the Sea of Japan faces the twin threats of growing Chinese industry and the resulting pollution and the nuclear waste disposed of by the Soviet navy during the Cold War.

Japan's strategies for the twenty-first century include a focus on the creation of an international framework that would include the establishment of "environmental rules in Asia, particularly for Chinese companies," which it sees as potentially the largest polluters.[3] Notably absent from the list is any mention of Russia. This omission may in part be due to the continuing dispute over the Kuril Islands and the economic need for diversified oil resources. Over 90 percent of Japanese oil currently comes from the Middle East. Japan is looking to Russian oil as an alternative to Japanese dependency on the Middle East. To this end, the Japanese have lobbied strenuously, and seemingly successfully, for an oil pipeline to be built from the Siberian oil fields to the Siberian coast of Russia, rather than having the pipeline go only through China and Manchuria, which is the more economical route. Japan does not want to trade dependency on the Middle East for dependency on China, a potential rival within its security complex.

A second area of securitization for Japan that is of interest to those studying alternative security is the area of culture. Japan imports massive amounts of Western culture, and for the most part, it is like the United Kingdom and the Scandinavian countries in permitting the foreign culture to be absorbed without hindrance. The issue of whaling is different, however. Time and time again, Japan has stood up in international forums to support a dying and economically nonessential and unneeded industry. It claims the necessity of preserving the traditional culture of whaling in Japan. This reasoning is basically false, in that the whaling that is being fought for today is the product of Japan's post-World War II need to feed its population.[4] However, as Yoichiro Sato argues, Japan's willingness to fight for continued whaling is primarily for political, rather than economic, reasons. First, Japan is looking for ways to prove to the world that it can stand up to international pressure and not give in. Second, it wants to demonstrate that it can have a foreign policy independent of the United States. Third, Japan worries that if it gives in on the whaling issue, other Japanese sea-based industries might begin to face international pressure to shut down.[5] It wants to draw "a line in the water," if you will, to protect its dependence on the sea for much of its national food supply.

Japan is willing to spend international goodwill in order to protect what it considers a vital area for its security: its food supply. At the same time, it feels that it needs a more internationally assertive foreign policy, in order to boost its standing in the world. This need can be likened to the previously used illustration of a new kid in school picking a fight with the biggest guy in school. The object is not to win, but to gain the respect of his peers by demonstrating his toughness. Japan is trying to demonstrate its willingness to stand virtually alone on an international issue. The issue is high-profile, but in the long term, the consequences are not strategic.[6]

A third area of alternative security is international goodwill, augmented by the assets of the SDF. The 26 December 2004 tsunami, also called the Boxing Day Tsunami, that struck the Indian Ocean provided Japan with an opportunity to demonstrate its abilities to be a major player in disaster relief, through the use of the SDF as well as its famous "checkbook diplomacy" of aid.

On 1 January 2005, Prime Minister Koizumi pledged a half-billion dollars in aid to the disaster area. Much of the aid, however, was targeted at Indonesia, which, while being the hardest-hit nation, is also the nation within the region that Japan most wishes to build stronger relations with. More significantly, however, is the fact that Japan was able to quickly deploy over a thousand SDF personnel to the region, along with multiple Maritime SDF ships, which were soon followed by helicopters. The incredible abilities of the MSDF and other naval forces (most notably, those of the United States) to render aid and assistance quickly and efficiently shocked traditional relief workers. The two greatest needs were emergency transport to and from remote areas and fresh drinking water. These needs were quickly met by the naval forces deployed to the region, as most naval ships contain onboard desalinization plants. Sea-based helicopters provided transportation of workers and supplies to areas where local land-based transportation could no longer go.

Through its efforts to alleviate the suffering from the Boxing Day Tsunami, Japan was able to securitize its goodwill efforts. Japan had a need to demonstrate its abilities as a nation, so that it could be taken more seriously in international forums. To use an old adage of the late President Theodore Roosevelt, Japan wants to speak softly but carry a big stick, the "big stick" being its ability to show that it has the capabilities that most nations lack when it comes to rendering aid. Japan's efforts are in marked contrast to its regional rival China, which in spite of its now being the world's second-largest economy (in PPP terms) was able to give only a paltry sum in aid (in comparison to others) and virtually no military rendered assistance, because of its lack of a blue-water navy. Japan is looking to build up goodwill internationally as a world power that deserves to be recognized. Japan's quest for a permanent seat on the U.N. Security Council is using this goodwill to boost support for its bid; nevertheless, it is threatening the use of the "stick" of its financial commitments to the United Nations as leverage.

The current five members of the Security Council were, in many ways, chosen because they were thought capable of policing the world. Japan's case for its UNSC seat is based on economic power, not military contribution. Under Article Nine, Japan cannot contribute military power at the level that the current five members can raise, a situation that is problematic for Japan's aspirations. However, if funding U.N. Security Council actions is enough, then Japan's case is made. A permanent seat on the U.N. Security Council brings with it, not only prestige, but also the security of always having a voice in times of international crisis.[7] Furthermore, other states would need to consult and work with Japan to achieve international goals. Japan would thus have the added security of being able to prioritize its security needs vis-à-vis potential threats.

In previous chapters, we have looked at the meaning of alternative security and what it means to securitize (or not to securitize) an issue. Additionally, we have looked at Japan's security limitations imposed by Article Nine and the effects of these limitations, constricting its ability to act to make *gains* in traditional ways. It is because of these limitations that Japan has explored alternative security issues as part of its overall security strategy. In terms of alternative security, Japan is just beginning to examine its options and to prioritize them. Domestic economic issues are, rightly, at the forefront, with whaling close behind. Japan is nothing without its economy. If it can securitize and then fix its domestic economic problems, Japan has the potential to be a player of consequence in the twenty-first century. The world already recognizes Japan's economy as essential to Japan's security and is waiting for Japan to take the needed actions in order to fix the problems that have lost it a decade of international progress. The risks of doing nothing are great for Japan, considering China's rising economic and military power.

The issue of Japan's only partially securitizing its environment presents a second great challenge for Japan, in light of alternative security issues. Pollution in the seas around Japan will continue to grow unless Japan, the nation most affected by the pollution, creates a securitized awareness within the Northeast Asian security complex. There are competing interests that Japan must weigh in light of the dynamic nature of East Asian security in the coming years. However, in spite of its limitations, Japan is moving forward to deal with its future and its role in the world community.

Future Sources of Foreign Policy: The Diet

Most previous studies of Japan have looked at the Prime Minister's Office or MOFA as the primary sources of Japanese foreign policy. While not denying the great and continuing influence of these two entities, I see change in the wind. In Japan, there seems to be a growing influence of the Diet on foreign policy, at the expense of MOFA's power. In the future, the prime minister's office will more likely be providing leadership while the Diet provides direction, with MOFA reduced to a moderating role; MOFA will be in charge of implementation of foreign policy, rather than making it. The reason for this change comes from the changes within the Diet, which give it a greater voice.

At the same time, MOFA is losing its influence because of stagnation within its organization. The decline of MOFA's power can be seen in the effort to raise the JDA to ministry status. With the JDA as a full and legitimate ministry, MOFA will no longer hold a monopoly on the bureaucratic side of foreign and security policy. Another reason for the decline of MOFA's power is its bureaucratic rigidity. While serious thinking occurs in the ministry, it seems to suffer from a group mindset. Very little dissenting opinion from the official ministry line was found in the interviews. Within the organization, open policy debate is frowned upon. Original thinking and genuine policy debate seem to be suppressed, from the top down. Midlevel bureaucrats within the ministry are not used to their full potential. MOFA does not normally tolerate dissent from ministry policy. Senior-level bureaucrats seem to be the only ones who have the freedom to speak out and debate issues.[8]

Overall, there seems to be an effort within Japan to decentralize political systems, so as to bring more power into the Diet and away from the bureaucracies. The bureaucracies in Japan will no doubt resist this effort, but given that the constitution legally places policy-making power in the Diet, there is little the bureaucrats can do if the Diet chooses to exercise its prerogative. Foreign policy will be no exception to this decentralization of the policy-making apparatus. MOFA will still wield tremendous influence, but the direction of foreign policy will be governed more generally by politics rather than by foreign-policy elites. Japan's foreign policy under Diet control will be less stable and predictable, but it will be more democratic and reflective of the nation as a whole.

Traditionally, the Diet has not intervened in foreign-policy making. The reason for this attitude has been that foreign policy does not get Diet members elected. This relationship is changing, according to a member of the upper house, Ichita Yamamoto, who stated, "People are becoming more aware of foreign policy."[9] Traditionally, Japanese politicians have been fearful of public reaction and constitutional limits, but public opinion is changing. As Japanese foreign policy becomes more high-profile, people are paying more attention to it. There is a growing awareness of how the world is interlinked and that national interests can not be secured only from domestic sources.

There is also a growing popular pride in Japanese contributions to the international community. As one Diet member proudly commented, "[Japanese] ODA [Official Development Assistance] is the pillar of Japanese foreign policy, and Japan is number one in the world."[10] The support of the Japanese public of ongoing SDF participation in PKO missions is further evidence of what Councillor Yamamoto is arguing. Yamamoto disclosed further that the upper house of the Diet is taking a particular interest in ODA and has formed a subcommittee on ODA because ODA is Japan's "most important [foreign policy] card."[11] Kuniko Nakajima, former MOFA official and now a researcher with the Okazaki Institute, concurs with Yamamoto in believing that there is a shift in public opinion toward foreign policy. She feels that the Gulf War marked a turning point in Japanese foreign policy and that the PKO Law and the support of the Japanese people for PKO missions was a sign that attitudes are changing with respect to Japan's responsibility for sending its own personnel on international peace missions.[12] Nakajima's and Yamamoto's opinions are supported by polling data. It seems that attitudes toward overseas missions for the SDF are changing. The Japanese public now supports what would have been unthinkable before 1990: sending the SDF overseas to handle natural disasters, as happened after the Boxing Day Tsunami in Southeast Asia. (Note: This excursion was independent of U.N. PKO missions; Japanese troops were under the sole command of Japanese officers and ultimately of politicians in Tokyo.[13])

In a poll commissioned by the Prime Minister's Office, 78 percent of

Japanese "agreed" or "somewhat agreed" with the "idea of sending the Self-Defense Forces overseas to handle natural disasters in foreign countries." Only 12 percent "disagreed" or "somewhat disagreed" with the idea.[14] The Japanese public has also warmed to the idea of SDF participation in exchange programs that are part of multilateral confidence-building measures. In the same survey by the Prime Minister's Office, 67 percent "approved" or "somewhat approved" of the SDF participation in exchange programs. Only 7 percent disapproved in any way.[15] It has been said that some nations live by the sword and perish by the sword. In Japan's case, since World War II, it has lived by the dove, and now it seems to be choosing not to let its role in the world be limited by a self-imposed pacifism. Rather, it is taking up a military role for the SDF in the name of international peace and stability and risking the consequences of such a role.

In the future, if the Diet exerts some control over the reins of foreign policy, Japan is less likely to behave in a highly risk-averse way. Ideologues who do not let their ideology stop at the water's edge may be a new element in Japan's foreign policy, which is likely to contain a broader array of interests than it currently does.

Constitutional Reform: Potential for Revision

Some would say that the Japanese people have no power over Japanese foreign policy.[16] But in many ways, they have the ultimate power over Japanese foreign policy, in the sense that they must approve any changes to the constitution, and thus, to Article Nine. Article Nine controls Japanese foreign policy through its power to limit Japanese military efforts. The constitution gives the people the ultimate right to amend the constitution. Article Ninety-six of the constitution describes how the constitutional amendment process works. It reads as follows:

> Amendments to this Constitution shall be initiated by the Diet, through a concurring vote of two-thirds or more of all the members of each House and shall thereupon be submitted to the people for ratification, which shall require the affirmative vote of the majority of all votes cast thereon, at a special referendum or at such election as the Diet shall specify.[17]

The final power over foreign policy is in the hands of the people. There will be no changes to the constitution without the people's consent. Article Ninety-six thus gives the power to amend the constitution to the people. Most of those interviewed from the LDP supported the first paragraph of Article Nine, which states: "Aspiring sincerely to an international peace based on justice and order, the Japanese people forever renounce war as a sovereign right of the nation and the threat or use of force as a means of settling international disputes."[18] It is the second paragraph that many conservatives in Japan find inconsistent with Japan's status as a leader in the world. It states: "In order to accomplish the aim of the preceding paragraph, land, sea, and air forces, as well as other war potential, will never be maintained. The right of belligerency of the state will not be recognized."[19]

This second paragraph is, in reality, inconsistent with the very existence of the SDF. Many in the Japanese Diet (68 percent of those interviewed) feel that the rewording or revision of this second paragraph would go a long way to establishing Japan as a normal nation. The problem is that, politically, it may be possible to change this part of the constitution only if the constitution undergoes a total revision in the context of a constitutional convention. Of those in government interviewed during the field research phase, 62 percent favored revising/deleting all or part of Article Nine, while 36 percent felt that Article Nine should be left alone, and 2 percent had no opinion.[20] By way of contrast, those outside of government favored keeping Article Nine as is by 56 percent to 44 percent.[21] Overall, Japanese elites favored revising Article Nine in some way, by 58 percent to 40 percent, with 2 percent having no opinion.[22]

In 1955, the LDP's founding charter set a goal of establishing a Japanese constitution written by the Japanese themselves. This goal has never been realized due to the popularity of the constitution written by the American occupation forces after World War II. It is very important to keep in mind that the enduring legacy of the efforts of MacArthur's staff in writing the constitution is that Japan is a democracy with power resting in the hands of the people. Any changes in the constitution will be governed by the people's will, not the desires of the politicians, according to one senior MOFA official.[23] Public attitudes will govern the extent to which Japan can go in its interpretation of the constitution, and whether any changes can or will ever be made. Of those who favored revising the constitution, 50 percent were very pessimistic that any changes would happen in the near future.[24]

Those who support Article Nine believe that Japan's leadership can come from peaceful relations with the world through the example of its "Peace Constitution." Mitsuo Higashinaka, of the JCP, argued that Japan should be encouraging other nations to renounce war.[25] The public in general seems to reflect this same opinion. In a poll conducted by the *Asahi Shimbun* in April 1997, Japanese voters were asked, "Do you think the renunciation of war [article] in the constitution will help attain world peace in the future, or not?" Of those responding, 73 percent felt that it "will help."[26]

Despite the efforts by the LDP and other conservatives in Japan to jump-start a constitutional revision process; for the first time, these attempts have the potential for success. The 11 September 2005 lower-house election gave the LDP and its political partner, *Komeito*, a two-thirds majority; enough to pass a constitutional amendment and, with consent from the upper house, refer it to the people. Now, with the election of Seiji Maehara as the leader of the main opposition party, the Democratic Party of Japan, this two-thirds upper house consent is possible. Maehara has openly expressed a desire to see the constitution revised. Agence France-Presse reported that "Japan's new opposition leader sought to revise the nation's pacifist constitution and lift restrictions on Japanese troops' use of weapons overseas. Seiji Maehara, fresh from his slim victory in the Democratic Party of Japan's leadership election on Saturday, said Japan should stipulate its right of self-defense in the U.S.-imposed constitution."[27]

The greatest hurdle for constitutional reformers is now public support for revision. However, the same pacifist attitude that MacArthur and his staff tapped into during the occupation is still strong today, and some would say that Japan needs Article Nine. Japan has the second-largest defense budget in the world. Article Nine keeps Japan in check by exerting moral pressure on the country.[28] The current interpretation of Article Nine may make it seem a worthless scrap of paper, but it does make Japan think about its actions, and it gives those actions principles to guide them. However, as Professor Jun Morikawa said in an interview, "When Japanese say they have principles, there are always exceptions."[29] Depending on the way and the political environment in which it is presented, there may be a chance for Japan to release itself from the limitations imposed by Article Nine.

The SDF in Japanese Foreign Policy

With the passage of the PKO Law, for the first time, the SDF became an official part of Japanese foreign policy. Japan now has the ability to make a human contribution to international order and stability. Japanese foreign policy can be more than just checkbook diplomacy. As discussed earlier, the SDF is becoming a source of pride for the Japanese people, but it is also a worry for Japan's neighbors, because of Japan's history in the region. Initial Japanese PKO missions were met with harsh criticism within the region. Nonetheless, the peaceful nature of PKO missions in which Japan has participated have muted even the most vocal opponents, such as China.

Another aspect of the growing influence of the SDF is its expanding capability, which is mostly directed at North Korea. If Japan continues to modernize and upgrade the SDF's capabilities, it might provoke or give North Korea an excuse to continue or resume missile testing. This situation can become a proverbial Catch-22 for Japan. If it fails to develop adequate defenses to prepare for a missile attack or deter a possible attack, it may find itself in an untenable position. It could find its cities and population vulnerable to attack and its foreign policy subject to blackmail. On the other hand, if it does develop a missile defense system, it may invite the very kind of threat that it seeks to avoid.

Under the revised guidelines, the SDF has a much clearer mission than before, while at the same time the Guidelines strengthen the United States-Japan Security Treaty, which had been under attack as having lost its significance in the post-Cold War world. The greatest current threat to the continuation of the United States-Japan Security Treaty is the possibility that the North Korean threat would disappear. Without the threat of North Korea, the only true remaining threat to Japan is China, and until recently, it was a political impossibility for either nation to name China as the reason for the treaty's existence.

However, for the first time, the February 2005 United States-Japan accord labeled Taiwan "a mutual security concern." While China's rising military power is not explicitly mentioned, the inclusion of Taiwan, which China regards as its sovereign territory, marks a turning point in East Asian relations. Japan and the United States have signaled China that they are concerned and are ready to adopt a more assertive stance toward China.

There is one major problem for Japan if the United States-Japan Security Treaty is ever abandoned: Japan would lose its nuclear umbrella. As Professor Masashi Nishihara of the National Defense Academy noted, "If there is no alliance [with the United States], then Japan must consider the nuclear option if there is a threat that justifies it."[30] The loss of the U.S. alliance would push Japan down a dangerous road, one that may give strength and credibility to nationalist-militaristic elements in Japanese society, and such a situation is likely to cause further alarm to Japan's neighbors.

The role of the SDF in Japanese foreign policy is likely to grow. There is a role for the SDF to balance Chinese power, and possibly Russia and India in the future. There is also a need to initiate confidence-building measures in East Asia to ensure the peace and stability of the region.[31] But first, a new legal foundation for the SDF to take on this increased role must be laid.[32] Geoffrey Smith reported in the *Washington Times* that

> U.S. experts said that Japan appears ready to assume a greater defense role to promote stability in East Asia. Joseph Nye, Dean of the Kennedy School of Government at Harvard University, said that trends over the past 10 years that show Japan to be increasing its security role in the world are expected to continue and probably even accelerate in the years ahead.

Nye said at a conference on US-Japan relations at the Center for Strategic and International Studies (CSIS) last week that "Japan is doing drastically more in the world than it was 10 years ago." Defense Attache Major General Noboru Yamaguchi said in a speech last week at Johns Hopkins University's School for Advanced International Studies that "new types" of threats have appeared in the region. Yamaguchi specifically cited the August 1998 DPRK launch of a Taepodong missile and increased tensions over Taiwan. Yamaguchi said, "Japanese sea lines go through and around Taiwan, so Japan also is going to lose [if there is a war]. My personal feeling is that if something happens over the Taiwan Strait, everyone is going to lose." William Breer, who holds the Japan chair for CSIS, said that the US seems mixed in its reaction to Japan's efforts to build a stronger military. Breer said, "I think most thinking Americans would say that if [a stronger Japanese military] happens through Japan's revisional process, then it's OK." Breer said that efforts were under way to amend the constitution in Japan "to bring the constitution in line with the current reality" but not to "remilitarization a la the 1930s."[33]

Clearly, the United States has no problem with Japan's rearming and trusts it to do so. The problem is that Japan must deal with this issue domestically as well as internationally, in order to find a larger role for the SDF.

Japan must also continue to modernize its laws for dealing with the SDF. The lack of laws governing crisis and emergency situations is a critical problem for the SDF. Until recently, Japanese tanks have been required to stop at traffic lights when they were involved in a battle situation. This restriction represents a silly, but consistent, oversight in the development of law concerning the actions that may or may not be taken by the SDF within Japan.

World Leadership

Japan is not ready to become a global leader. According to Kenjiro Monji of the Cabinet office of the Prime Minister, "[Japan] couldn't send people when most needed [the Gulf War]. Economic strength is not enough to be respected. Some power is needed to have some 'teeth.'"[34] According to one senior Japanese official, "Japan needs to be prepared to spill [its own] blood."[35] These are the lessons that Japan learned from the Gulf War, and hence, the push for passage of the PKO Law and the search for new ways to use the SDF. There is also the fear (unjustified) that if Japan takes on a more active role in the world, the result will be militarism on the part of Japan.[36] Until Japan deals with its history, this issue will continue to haunt Japan.

One of the major problems with Japan as a world leader is that the country has become more inward-looking as its economy struggles to recover from a decade-long recession. Japan has lost its confidence. Most of its people do not see Japan as a world power, and furthermore, they do not see Japan in a world crisis that would require Tokyo's leadership.[37] As one senior MOFA official put it, "There is a general feeling that Japan should be like [the] United States, but I disagree. Japan should play [the] foreign policy [game] based on its abilities [not on its aspirations]."[38] The idea expressed here is that capable nations work from their strengths. This official went on to say that "Japan's military contribution could never be more than a minor one."[39] Japan's people will need a very good reason to make a *major* contribution to a multinational military effort. The Japanese people do not seem eager to play a major military role. In this sense, the legacy of the disaster of World War II lives on. According to this MOFA official, the majority of Japanese do not believe in the PKO solution because they see it as nonessential for Japan. However, they do see it as a significant and acceptable contribution for Japan to make, even if they feel that it is unnecessary for Japan.[40] In this sense, the Japanese public is becoming more accepting of Japan's responsibilities in the world, but with reservations or limits on these responsibilities.

According to Ryozo Kato, the former director general of Foreign Policy Planning at MOFA, and currently ambassador to the United States, Japan's unwillingness to take risks is a risk in and of itself.[41] Japan risks world condemnation for its inaction and the possibility of being ignored and passed-by by the rest of the world if it fails to take leadership where genuine risk is involved.

Japan must cooperate with nations other than the United States if it is to achieve its primary foreign-policy goal of national security.[42] The problem is Japanese pacifism. The Japanese people hold Japan's pacifism as an example for other nations. They do not want to give up Article Nine.[43] This faith in pacifism represents a great stumbling block for Japan in its quest to make itself a normal nation. Lower-house representative Hideo Usui stated that Japan needs to "remove the barriers" to making "Japan an ordinary nation as soon as possible."[44] Article Nine represents a fundamental barrier that may be insurmountable in the near term. The revision or removal of Article Nine from the constitution is not likely to happen without a crisis to motivate the Japanese people to change attitudes. The Japanese people do not want to talk about the possibility of Japan's being attacked. They see Japan as a nation without an enemy, and they ask, "So why would any nation attack Japan?"[45] The Japanese leadership tends to take a very realist view of the world, while the Japanese people take an idealist view of the world, a situation that is the frustration of Japanese policy makers. The reality that Japan has no friends in East Asia has not been recognized by the Japanese public.

Japan's Limitations

As stated previously, the primary obstacle to the normalization of Japan's foreign policy is Article Nine. As noted above, the quest to revise the constitution is in the hands of the people. As one senior MOFA official said, "[T]he behavior of the Japanese people is not limited by the constitution but by the people's feelings [toward the constitution]."[46] Japan needs to play the foreign-policy game based on its limitations and it abilities rather than its potential.[47] According to Diet member Shigeru Ishiba, "Unless Article Nine is changed, Japan cannot be a leader in the world."[48]

According to Professor Ogawa Akira of the Okazaki Research Institute in Tokyo, the greatest failure of the present generation of leadership in the Diet is the fact that these people have not trained the next generation to lead Japan.[49] The political leadership of Japan is heavy with old men who will not step aside and let a new generation take control. Neither is this older generation grooming the next generation to succeed them. This failure will hurt the potential for Japanese world leadership in the future, as the current younger generation, which is biding its time until it can seize the reins of power, will not be prepared for leadership in the international arena.

Japanese Hegemony?

There is a general feeling among the foreign-policy elite in Japan that Japan needs the United States. Japan will not be a hegemon if it is dependent on the United States. Thus, it can safely be said that Japan has no hegemonic aspirations for the next ten or fifteen years.[50] However, it does want to be seen as a major power, like Britain and France, playing a major supportive role. Given this desire to be a significant support, and the limitations placed on Japan by Article Nine, the United Nations is likely to be the focus of Japan's non-United States foreign policy in the future. Japanese leaders want to feel the pride again of being a major international player, while at the same time clinging to pacifism. This schizophrenia is reflected in public attitudes toward Japanese foreign-policy initiatives abroad. Japan may dispatch forces abroad as long as there are no significant casualties to the SDF.[51]

The fact that, in general, the Japanese public has traditionally shown little interest in foreign affairs, and that Japan's elected leadership in the Diet has similarly shown little interest, is a strong indication, in and of itself, that Japan is not seeking hegemonic status. The reality of Japan's decade-old economic crisis is that Tokyo is more concerned with matters at home than with things abroad. Professor Toshiya Hoshino of the Osaka School of International Policy, Osaka University, notes that "Without a healthy economy, it is hard to pursue an international role."[52] Witness Japan's desire to cut funding for U.S. bases in Japan. Japan does not feel that it has the financial capability to support its international commitments. However, this attitude may change if Japan's economy continues to improve.

America's slow withdrawal from a forward deployment in the Philippines and elsewhere in Asia is often cited as evidence that America is a declining hegemon. In the 1980s, Japan was touted as a rising hegemon, which would supplant the United States' hegemonic status.[53] This assertion raises the question of whether Japan's economic troubles and inability to make a significant international commitment are signs that it was a potential or rising hegemon now in decline, or whether these signs are merely indications that Japan was never a candidate for hegemony. According to Professor Akihiko Tanaka of the Institute of Oriental Culture at Tokyo University, "Japan has no tradition of missionary zeal [to help the world]. It has only the memory of bad mistakes [World War II]. Japan needs ulterior motives."[54] Furthermore, "economic conditions limit future [options]."[55]

It is a combination of Japan's role in World War II and Article Nine that prevents Japan's foreign-policy normalization. While Japan's foreign policy is slowly maturing, its normalization is held back by the country's history and its inability to seem sincere. Sincerity is at the heart of the issue. Many in Japan feel that China is just using Japan's history in East Asia as a tool of its foreign policy.[56] Yet if Korea and China use Japan's history for political purposes, it is Japan's lack of sincerity that gives resonance to the issue with the peoples of East Asia. Germany is seen as sincere—its actions in monetary terms and in education testify to this effect. Japan's efforts to sweep these issues under the rug or to bury them as already dealt with hurt Japan. Japan must show that it understands the suffering it caused by waging war in East Asia in the first place. The government of Japan may not have approved all the actions (crimes by the Imperial Army), but the government created the conditions for the atrocities to be committed. Japan must deal with this legacy before becoming a normal nation.

One way that Japan could begin to deal with its past is to begin by apologizing to its citizens for World War II. It was the Japanese people, along with the other peoples of Asia, that suffered under the imperialism of Japan's military and political leadership. The Japanese government could begin by asking the emperor, "as the symbol of the nation," to apologize for the destruction, suffering, and pain caused by the war waged in his father's name. The Japanese people had built Japan from a feudal society into an empire capable of going toe to toe with the great powers in the world including the United States, only to see it all destroyed by a war of conquest. Japan needs to admit to its own people that its leaders betrayed the nation by taking it down the path of imperialism. Once Japan recognizes this crime, committed by its leaders, against itself then it can more easily recognize and sincerely admit to the crimes against other nations, like China and Korea, committed by Imperial Japan.

Until Japan takes care of the issue of its past, it will not be ready to take on a leadership role comparable to that of the United States. One of the most surprising findings during the field interviews was the answer given to the question, "Countries that are seen as world leaders are seen as willing to bear the costs of world order. (For example, the United States keeping forces in East Asia and Europe.) Is Japan prepared to undertake a world leadership role, and what cost would it be willing to pay in order to take on that role? (Or, to put it another way, is Japan willing to sacrifice for the good of the world?) Not a single respondent believed that Japan could undertake a "world leadership role." The majority—78 percent—said that Japan could not do so, and 22 percent responded that they "did not know." However, 48 percent claimed that Japan would be willing to assume a leadership role if only it could.[57]

It is for this reason that Japan is continuing its pursuit of a United Nations-centered foreign policy. The United Nations is critical to Japanese foreign policy, in that its peaceful ideals reflected in the U.N. Charter conform to the pacifist sentiments in Japan and its constitution. It is for these reasons that the United Nations is likely to remain the focus of Japanese foreign-policy efforts outside of its bilateral relations with the United States. This is a constitutionally valid aspiration on the part of Japan, in that it is in line with both the Japanese constitution's preamble and the current interpretation of Article Nine that permit action by the SDF under United Nations auspices.

Japan's foreign-policy elite are searching for a more prominent global role for Japan. But, at the same time, Japan is a pacifist nation that cannot independently flex its military strength abroad. Its twentieth-century history argues against a more prominent role, but its history is not a defining factor when one studies the attitudes of the Japanese today. Pacifism is more important than past aggression in understanding Japanese attitudes toward foreign policy today. Japan has no intention of repeating its World War II mistakes. Rather, it seeks to be a positive influence and part of the world community by making a contribution to international and regional peace and stability as a pacifist nation, unless forced to do otherwise by threats to the nation.

To make that contribution, Japan must walk a fine line internationally and domestically. Japan has the desire to be a normal nation, but is it willing to bear the costs? Can Japan take casualties in support of international and regional peace and stability? Perhaps Japan can, but only after facing a few more criticisms for inaction, such as those it incurred in connection with its decisions during the Gulf War, or if Japan finds itself truly threatened.

Japan's Future

During the Cold War, Japan was part of the Western alliance against Communism, an alliance that made its foreign-policy formulation straight forward and easy. Since the end of the Cold War, the task has been much more difficult. Japan needs a new role in international affairs.[58] Japan definitely wants to be seen as the leader in Asia. It already represents Asia by being the only Asian nation in the G8, but it wants its global standing to mature, so that it can be Asia's bridge to the West.[59] Japan has often found itself caught between Asia and the West; it is now seeking to use this position to its advantage by being both East and West. The problem lies in China's opposition to Japanese leadership. China believes that it should represent Asia, and that Japan should subordinate its ambitions to China's. China uses Japan's history in China to undermine Japan's ambitions.

Japan has it in its power to rid itself of this problem of history, if it is willing. The greatest hindrance to Japan's future is its unwillingness to deal with its past. If Japan fails to deal with its past, it is likely to remain isolated (as a security player) in East Asia, with continued dependence on the United States. As the noted East Asian security expert Sheldon Simon argues, Japan needs "to accept responsibility and sincerely apologize for past misdeeds. It may still take years before Japan can earn the confidence of potential security partners."[60] In a world that is integrating more quickly every day, Japan may also lose its potential for regional leadership because no one in East Asia will be willing to fully trust it. Japan should fully apologize for its actions during the Pacific War. Given Japan's muddled history of insincere and half expressions of remorse by various prime ministers, the emperor, as "the symbol of the nation," should be the one to make the apology. The government's official position on this proposal is that such an action would be an unconstitutional exercise of power by the emperor.[61] However, many of those interviewed outside of government felt this belief to be untrue and that only the emperor could truly apologize for the nation, since he is the symbol of the nation and the war was waged in his father's name.[62]

In dealing with Japan's past, there also seems to be a generation gap among Japanese elites. Of the young Japanese elites I interviewed, 96 percent favored an honest look at Japanese history and the issuing of a sincere formal apology to those whom Japan has harmed. On the other hand, older interviewees opposed an honest look at Japanese history during World War II, and they rejected any apology, by 72 percent to 28 percent. Overall, the elites of all ages favored an honest look at the past by a margin of 61 percent in favor to 39 percent opposed.[63]

Japanese participation in peacekeeping forces (PKF)[64] is the next step for Japan. Japanese participation in PKF under U.N. auspices would move the SDF toward a more normal military force, something that has heretofore been absent in Japan. It will also raise the prestige and visibility of Japan in international crises.[65] The ground SDF is the most resistant to expanding its PKO role; "but Japan has to sweat," according to Colonel Noboru Yamaguchi of the SDF.[66] The important fact here is that Japanese forces serve under U.N. command rather than under the Japanese chain of command, thus denying Japan and the SDF a chance to truly prove that they are responsible and willing to sacrifice. Until such a time when the SDF operates under Japanese command overseas, the SDF would be "borrowed" by the United Nations. This tactic could remove the possible constitutional obstacle to the SDF's being used in combat. However, the public would have to be sold on the idea that it was necessary for Japan to send the SDF into harm's way (under United Nations command) for the good of international order.

The younger generation in Japan desperately wants Japan to be normal. According to Nobuto Hosaka, "Young Diet members want Japan to be a ordinary, a normal nation. There is a need to get rid of the image of a Japan that just sells and [replace it with] one that gives."[67] Naoko Saiki of MOFA noted, "Internationalization or Mass Culture is taking away Japanese identity. Youth want to be identified with the world not as Japanese. Japan embarrasses them."[68] Japan needs normalization in order to have its own youth respect its international efforts and foreign policy.

Suggestions for Foreign-Policy Normalization

Here are some important points to consider for Japan to normalize its foreign policy:

1. The generation gap in Japanese politics must be overcome if Japan is to move forward.[69] The younger generation is realist and pragmatic and very internationalized. These young people want a Japan that they can respect.
2. If Japan is ever to achieve normal status as a nation, Article Nine must be revised. Article Nine takes away a basic and useful tool of foreign policy: the threat of force. Japan's quest for normalcy will

hinge on the future of Article Nine. However, the desires of the LDP and others on the right in Japanese politics to see a constitutional revision is likely to remain an uphill battle for the time being, but one that can be won if waged carefully. It would take a crisis that threatens Japan or something Japan holds dear for Japan to fully abandon Article Nine outside of a drawn-out political process.

3. Japan needs new thinking if it is to flourish in the post-Cold War world. However, many feel that the current Japanese leadership (MOFA and the Prime Minister's Office) is too cautious to innovate.[70] Nevertheless, one of Japan's greatest problems is the lack of vision and leadership by the governing elites concerning the future direction of Japanese foreign policy. Tokyo governor Shintaro Ishihara is a vocal critic of Japan's governing elite. He believes that "Japan has no worthy political leadership, no real intellectual or political debate and, worst of all, *no direction*."[71] This circumstance will make aggressive new thinking unlikely in the near term.

4. Japan should offer a sincere apology and show of remorse in the next few years before the last of the World War II generation dies off. Issues such as the legalization of a national anthem and flag are good for restoring national pride, but they hurt efforts to show that attitudes have changed toward Japan's East Asian neighbors. Japanese politicians must also stop visiting Yasukuni Shrine, where Japan's war dead are enshrined along with "class A" war criminals. Japan's war dead can be memorialized, but they should be memorialized in a secular memorial that does not include those convicted of war crimes.

5. Change is not likely to occur unless there is a crisis that forces Japan to change. Japan needs to plan for the next crisis, not the last one.

6. Japan has to prove its value to the United States while at the same time becoming more independent from the United States. It needs a strong United States-Japan Security Treaty as well as a strong constructive relationship with China.[72]

Japan is likely to be a much more activist nation in its foreign policy in the future.[73] Given the uncertainties of the post-Cold War and post-9/11 world, Japan must have a greater voice in its own security. The problem for Japan will be one of vision and direction. It needs to chart its course rather than sail blindly from crisis to crisis. Japan may also be forced to take sides in a conflict, such as a Taiwan-China clash or a renewed Korean conflict, in order to keep the United States as an ally. As Mulgan writes, "Japan runs the risk of becoming a mere pawn in American strategy because it is now more locked into this strategy than ever before. . . . Japan may be forced to take sides even when reluctant to do so."[74] Japan must also recognize that it may be in its interest to take sides, even as it is forced to do so.

Japan must alter the free-rider attitude that developed under the Yoshida Doctrine. This attitude, held by many Japanese toward foreign affairs, has resulted in Japan's general inability to act as a major world player. Japan did as little as possible for the world community until the end of the Cold War. "The problem is that Japan is having to do something more, and Japan needs principles to guide its foreign policy, currently it has none in foreign policy," according to Representative Shozo Azuma.[75]

The biggest obstacle to the development of principles and reform in Japanese foreign policy will be the bureaucracy. The legislature may attempt reform, but MOFA may fight it. Just as T. J. Pempel argued in the arena of economic reform, I argue in foreign policy. Institutional change is difficult without a crisis.[76] A crisis, such as the Gulf War and the end of the Cold War, gave Japan the push to make changes. PKO enlargement primarily depends on conflict or crisis in order to justify Japan's increasing the role of the SDF.[77] Shin'ichi Ogawa of the National Institute for Defense Studies in Tokyo argues that "[the Japanese] people need a big event, crisis, or shock to be woken up."[78] However, Japan must wake up before the crisis hits and look toward the future and its role beyond its borders. The following sections will examine what we have gained theoretically from our study of Japanese foreign policy in the post-Cold War period and conclude with a summary of Japan's position for the future.

Implications for Hermann's Model:
What Have We Learned?

Hermann's model helps to clarify much of what we see in Japanese foreign policy in the post-Cold War era. It teaches us that the formation and restructuring of Japanese foreign policy do not differ from those of any other nation. Hermann's model describes what happens when a government sees a need to change or restructure a foreign policy that it has implemented and turn it in for a new one that better reflects its current needs. In Japan's case, this is exactly what has happened; however, there is one dynamic that Hermann's model fails to account for. This oversight is the generational shift in attitudes toward foreign policy within the Diet.

To some extent, Hermann's model assumes a relatively constant influence by the Primary Change Agents (see Figure 9.1).

It does not take into account the possibility of major shifts in the change agents. In the case of Japan, it was initially true that there were no major shifts in the change agents but as I observed during field interviews, there

Figure 9.1   **Hermann's Model with Foreign Pressure and Intervening Variables (a)**

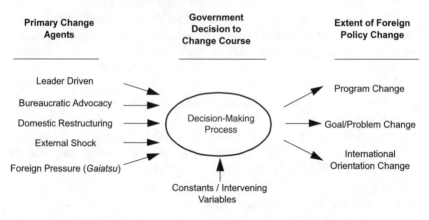

seems to be a shift in power from MOFA (bureaucratic advocacy) to the Diet (leader driven). This internal shift requires no political reorientation; rather, it requires only a change in sources of influence on the part of foreign-policy elites. In Japan's case, the generational shift in Diet representation seems to be giving more power to the Diet in foreign-policy decisions at the expense of MOFA. MOFA will continue to be a strong and dominant influence on Japanese foreign policy, but it will be on a more equal footing with the Diet, and the Diet will be taking greater leadership and supply more input. This change is illustrated in Figures 9.2 and 9.3.

One of the primary omissions in Herman's model is its failure to include foreign pressure as a change agent. All nations face foreign pressure, or in Japan's case, *gaiatsu*. The addition of foreign pressure to the list of "change agents" helps us to understand why some nations choose to redirect their foreign policies. Foreign pressure can be a key reason for nations to change the direction of their foreign policy, especially if that pressure comes from a particularly important ally. Such pressure is an external source of foreign-policy change, and it can be part of an equation in which nations choose to redirect their foreign policy. Nations normally choose foreign policies that represent their best interests despite foreign pressure. However, in the case of Japan, foreign pressure will often move Japan in a direction that it might not have chosen without *gaiatsu*. At the same time, this pressure may conform to the Japanese leadership's own preferences. Foreign pressure becomes a device to justify an apparently unpopular policy.

Additionally, we have learned that *gaiatsu* is often used as a two-level game in selling unpopular foreign-policy choices. Japanese leaders, like all political leaders, struggle to point policy in the direction that they desire it

Figure 9.2 **Hermann's Model with Foreign Pressure and Intervening Variables (b)**

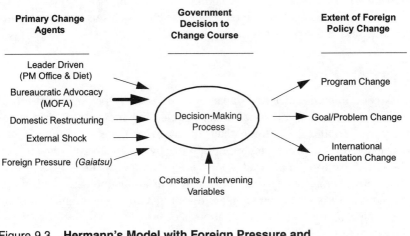

Figure 9.3 **Hermann's Model with Foreign Pressure and Intervening Variables (c)**

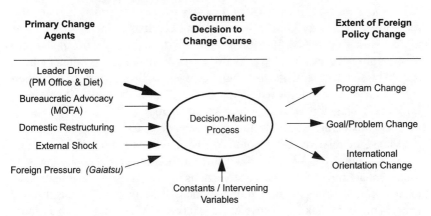

to go. In the face of public opposition, many leaders will drop these policies. In Japan, political leaders frequently blame a powerful foreign power—that is, the United States—and thus justify an unpopular policy at little political cost to themselves. This is the "myth" of *gaiatsu*, in that political leaders purport that it is foreign pressure that is solely responsible for an unpopular policy, when in fact, it is often the case that many in the leadership desire the same policy as the foreign entity does.

The addition of constants or intervening variables to Hermann's model helps us to understand how the situational dynamics may play out when decisions are made. These constants, such as Article Nine in the case of

Japan, have the potential to change over time, but usually they are relatively stable over time in the decision-making "matrix" (process). Understanding the influence of constants or intervening variables helps us to better predict the outcome of the decision-making process.

Pragmatic Realism

As argued in earlier chapters, Japan is fundamentally practicing a form of realism, but Japan's limitations under Article Nine prevent it from practicing power politics *à la* Morgenthau. Recognizing these limitations, Japan has adapted its approach to foreign policy by pragmatically pursuing an institutionalist foreign policy. Grieco[79] argued, and I concur, that states may cooperate internationally (institutionalism) in an anarchical world, while the motives for such cooperation are realist in nature. The premise guiding this perspective is that realism dominates or influences all calculations going into relations between nations. States want relative gains, but with the survival of the state as the primary goal of a nation's foreign policy, a state will choose *absolute gains* over a net loss in *relative gains*. It is for this reason that we can see both realism and neoliberalism or idealism occurring in East Asia, as noted by Sheldon Simon.[80] To talk about the triumph of this neoliberalism or idealism over realism is a to make a false statement; it should be said that realism has triumphed over idealism. Many of the adherents of idealism do so for realist reasons. This premise makes it very easy for them to abandon idealism when it suits them.

This consideration adds to the debate between Grieco and Powell over the nature of relative and absolute gains in international-relations theory because it notes the simultaneous nature of relative and absolute gains by Japan. Japan may desire pure relative gains in security and economics in an ideal world, but given its limitations, Japan will continue to pursue absolute gains in hopes of making relative gains in terms of intangibles, such as goodwill and influence, particularly vis-à-vis its relations with the United States.

This pursuit of absolute gains over relative gains is demonstrated by the fact that Japan has maintained a United Nations-centric foreign policy while relying on the United States for its security guarantee. This choice is made necessary because of Japan's constitutional limitations. As demonstrated in chapters 3 and 4, the end of the Cold War has weakened the security guarantee of the United States. (The United States does not need Japan as much now as it did during the Cold War.) Japan is now faced with seeking other options while dealing with the same existing limitations. Japan needs to be more independent, vis-à-vis the United States in its foreign policy and more active in both regional and international affairs. Multilateralism offers the best hope for absolute gains, at the same time making relative gains in terms of goodwill and influence, but Japan's steadfast refusal to deal with its history in East Asia limits its ability to gain the trust that is needed for multilateralism to work in Northeast Asia.

The questions that were asked in chapter 1 are: "What is Japan's new role in the world?" "What accounts for the gradual change in the role of the SDF?" "What are the driving forces domestically behind these changes?" and "What is Japan's long-term foreign-policy agenda?" This book has endeavored to answer these questions. Japan's role in the world is increasing through U.N. PKO missions and its growing participation in multilateral forums. The gradual increase in the role of the SDF comes from a desire on the part of Japan to make a contribution toward international peace and stability. Additionally, there is a desire on the part of some Japanese elites to continue the process of Japan's normalization through the reinterpretation of Article Nine. This process is being implemented by giving the SDF greater responsibilities and duties overseas in order to normalize it as a military force.

Driving Forces

The driving forces behind the changes in Japanese foreign policy are primarily two. One force is the change agent of foreign pressure (*gaiatsu*), pressuring Japan to contribute to the international community at a level commensurate with its economic strength. The second is the generational shift in Japan that is redirecting the source of foreign policy from MOFA to the Diet. While the World War II generation is content with the status quo under Article Nine, the younger generation wants Japan to be a normal nation.

Japan's long-term foreign policy agenda is still in the making. Japan, like all nations, wants to guarantee its peace and safety. However, there seems to be no agenda for discussion or real debate over the question of where Japan should direct its foreign policy in the next five to ten years.

Concluding Observations

The stated goal of this text was to explore the inner workings of Japanese foreign policy making and the direction of Japanese foreign and security policy. The central thesis was a challenge to the conventional wisdom in the existing literature that believes that Japan is not really changing. I have observed, and continue to observe change in the Japanese foreign policy-making community to an extent greater than was thought possible a few years ago. The drafting and the passage of the PKO Law in reaction to the Gulf War, as

Photo 9.1 **The 100th Meeting of the Japanese Security Council** (*Source:* Photo courtesy of the Office of the Cabinet Public Relations, Cabinet Secretariat, Japan)

described in chapter 3, marked the beginning of this change process, which is adapting Japanese foreign policy to the realities of the post-Cold War world.

Chapter 4 challenged the belief that Japan is merely pursuing an institutionalist foreign policy by noting that under Article Nine Japan does not have the choice of pursuing relative gains but is pursuing absolute gains for realist reasons, in hopes of making intangible relative gains. Chapter 5 described the application of Hermann's model to Japanese foreign policy and noted the omission of foreign pressure as an agent of change. Also noted was the need to include constants, such as Article Nine, and cultural norms, such as Japanese pacifism, as intervening variables in the foreign-policy/decision-making process. The decision-making matrix is influenced both internally by cultural norms and externally by foreign pressure. These variables are part of the process by which foreign-policy changes occur, and they should be considered in any study of foreign policy change.

The research interviews conducted to supplement the textual analysis of this book provided insight into the making of Japanese foreign policy and yielded two important findings. The first was a surprise: that much of Japanese foreign policy is made on an emergency basis. There seemed to be few planned-response scenarios for the government to fall back on when a major foreign or security policy event took place.

Considering what an important event the nuclear tests conducted by India and Pakistan were for Asian security, it was surprising to observe at first hand that the Japanese foreign-policy community was very unprepared to react to these events. The lack of contingency planning on the part of the government of Japan that was evidenced by the slow government response to the Kobe earthquake or the lack of emergency laws (tanks having to stop at traffic lights) governing the SDF and U.S. forces in Japan seems to pervade the foreign-policy community as well. While no nation can plan for every eventuality, Japan does not seem to plan at all for very many. With the exception of the new policies put in place by the September 1997 revised Guidelines (which are intentionally vague in many areas), Japanese foreign and security policy is ill prepared for future crises. However, it should be noted that Japan is making slow but steady progress to improve this situation. The Japanese Security Council was meeting to deal with a typhoon that struck Japan when the attack of 9/11 occurred in the United States. Japan was the first nation to respond and offer help and condolences to the United States and President Bush.

Excluding its general capitalist, democratic, and pacifist tendencies, Japan does not seem to have a particular ideology or philosophy to guide its strategic planning. This means that Japan has been very slow to react to an international security event in a timely and appropriate manner.

The second major finding was the power shift that is moving major foreign policy issues from the more cautious MOFA to the more volatile Diet largely because of the generational shifts taking place in Japan. The Diet as the source of foreign policy offers many new and interesting considerations to the Japanese foreign-policy community and the scholars studying it.

Chapter 4 also delved into the concept of security and Japan's security options in a changing environment. Japan's original innovative comprehensive security concept may have to be modified and revert to more traditional security concerns. The more normal Japanese foreign policy becomes, the more Japan must think in traditional terms. Thus, absolute and relative gains both become important for Japanese foreign policy.

Many in Japan continue to believe in Japan's exceptionalism or uniqueness. We found that Japan is not unique, in that it experiences the same situations and events that the rest of the world faces. What makes Japan different is Article Nine. It is because of the limitations imposed by Article Nine that Japan needs to better plan its responses to world events so that it can respond in a timely and appropriate manner. Japan needs to build the internal structures to deal with crises. These structures are best built in conjunction with the United States, so that Japan's responses, particularly in East Asia, are coordinated with its only ally.

Chapter 6 looked at the ways the Japanese view themselves in the world; it did so through the use of existing survey data and my research interviews.

Japan's desire to be an active member of the world community, commensurate with its economic status, was noted. It was further seen that both the Japanese people and the foreign-policy elite recognize Japan's limitations and that Japan has no interest in East Asian hegemony, despite its economic strength. It is also important to note that Japan has just as strong an interest in seeing that no other nation in the region becomes a regional hegemon. Japan's efforts to raise its world standing through the United Nations and other multilateral organizations represent its alternative to hegemony. Continued pursuit of multilateral options offers Japan a way of ensuring its security along with continued efforts to improve relations with South Korea. The research found that multilateral efforts have broad support across the political spectrum.

One of the most important contributions of this book to the understanding of the making of Japanese foreign policy is the description, offered in chapter 7, of *gaiatsu* as a two-level game. Japanese foreign-policy elites will use *gaiatsu* to force an issue that they desire to see approved, for that purpose shifting the onus to the United States for "making" Japan do something. This use of *gaiatsu* runs counter to the existing literature, which for the most part, fails to note the use of *gaiatsu* as a two-level game or to acknowledge the questions that *gaiatsu* raises about Japanese sovereignty if a two-level game does not exist.

The problem of Japan's unwillingness to deal with its history in East Asia was noted throughout the book. Contrary to the conventional wisdom among the ruling elite, Japan will never gain its full stature as a nation until it deals with its historical responsibilities in a forthright and honest way. The documentation of an obvious generation gap regarding the issue of an apology for World War II was another major finding. Japan's quest for normalcy in its foreign relations in East Asia will be obstructed until it adequately addresses this issue.

In conclusion, the world is a nasty place, and the militaries of the world's great powers should serve the purpose of preventing the worst of the worst from wreaking havoc. However, they also serve the humanitarian purpose of relief in times of crisis. They represent a well-trained, versatile, well-equipped, and virtually self-sustaining force, capable of going to the farthest reaches of the earth and giving aid. The Southeast Asian Boxing Day Tsunami is evidence of this ability, particularly in the cases of the United States and, notably, Japan. The United States and its allies were able, to some extent, to reverse perceptions of military power in a hostile region by its quick and professional response to the crisis.[81] Through judicious use of the SDF, Japan has the potential to create goodwill in a politically tense region of great interest to Japan, especially vis-à-vis China, which lacks the capability to extend goodwill very far beyond its own shores.

However, operations in Iraq show that the goodwill operations are potentially a double-edged sword that can cut both ways. The goodwill Japan is attempting can and may be perceived as kowtowing to United States policy and serving as part of an occupation force. The problem for Japan is that to be seen as a world power, it must be willing to take the good and the bad together and in stride. Japanese foreign-policy makers who are pushing this policy recognize that they are walking a fine line between traditional Japanese pacifism and historical Japanese militarism. Failure in one direction or the other could spell disaster for Japan's foreign-policy aspirations of global respect.

This being said, Japanese foreign policy can be considered to have matured in the post-Cold War world (helped along by 9/11). Japan has grown up and is working with the United States (the father; to use the illustration from chapter 4) in a partnership of master and journeyman. Still constrained by Article Nine, Japan is ever moving forward. The choice has been made, and under Prime Minister Koizumi, Japan is placing its bets on America and continued American hegemony. However, choices can change and Japan is a democracy. The conservative LDP may not always be in power, and neither will Prime Minister Koizumi. The political entity that replaces the LDP is unlikely to have free reign on foreign policy and security policy. The conservative bureaucracy and the public, constrained by fear of North Korea, will limit any change in policy.

Further research and study is needed on the sources of change in Japanese foreign policy. The differences between the older and younger generation of elites in Japan over an apology by the emperor for World War II will be a defining event in Japanese history and of great interest to scholars of the decision-making process and Japanese politics in general. The slowness of Japan to react in a crisis is symptomatic of a larger problem within Japan as a whole, but the power shifts that are now under way offer the best hope for a more responsive foreign policy, one that will serve and protect Japan throughout the twenty-first century.

Appendix A
Partial List of Elites Interviewed

Ministry of Foreign Afffairs:

Vice Minister Shunji Yanai
Ministry of Foreign Affairs

Director General Ukeru Magosaki
Intelligence and
  Analysis Bureau
Ministry of Foreign Affairs

Director General Ryozo Kato
Foreign Policy Bureau
Ministry of Foreign Affairs

Director Naoko Saiki
International Peace Cooperation
  Division
Ministry of Foreign Affairs

Director Masafumi Iishi
Foreign Policy Planning
  Division
Ministry of Foreign Affairs

Tadahiko Yamaguchi, Official
General Coordination Division,
  Minister's Secretariat
Ministry of Foreign Affairs

Director Jiro Kodera
First International Economic
  Affairs Division
Ministry of Foreign Affairs

Deputy Director Tomiko Ichikawa
Northeast Asia Division
Ministry of Foreign Affairs

Director Toshio Kaitani
Human Rights and Refugee
  Division
Ministry of Foreign Affairs

Japan Defense Agency:

Vice Minister Masahiro Akiyama
Japan Defense Agency

Mr. Kiyoshi Serizawa
Assistant Director
Defense Policy Division
Japan Defense Agency

Col. Noboru Yamaguchi
Deputy Chief, Defense
  Planning Division
Ground Staff Office
Japan Defense Agency

Major Takashi Motomatsu
Planning Section
Plans & Operations Dept. GSO
Japan Defense Agency

Director Hideshi Tokuchi
Operations Division
Operations Bureau
Japan Defense Agency

House of Councillors (Upper):

Councillor Tomoharu Yoda (LDP)

Councillor Yoshimasa Hayashi
(LDP)

Councillor Keizo Takemi (LDP)

Councillor Kei Hata (LDP)

Councillor Ichita Yamamoto (LDP)

Councillor Hideki Tamura (LDP)

Representative Mitsuo Higashinaka
(CP)

Representative Hajime Funada
(LDP)

Representative Eisuke Mori
(LDP)

Representative/Pastor Ryuichi Doi
(DPJ)

Representative Shozo Azuma
(Liberal Party)

House of Representatives (Lower):

Representative Hideo Usui (LDP)

Representative Tomoko Nakagawa
(SDP)

Representative Yoshinori Suematsu
(DPJ)

Representative Shingo Nishimura
(DPJ)

Representative Eiichi Nakao (LDP)

Representative Masaharu
Nakagawa (DPJ)

Representative Shigeru Ishiba
(Liberal Party)

Representative Yukihiko Ikeda
(LDP)

Representative Hosaka Nobuto
(SDP)

Prime Minister's Office:

Director Teruaki Nagasaki
Secretariat of the International
    Peace Cooperation Headquarters

Mr. Nobushige Takamizawa,
Cabinet Councillor
Cabinet National Security Affairs
    Office

Mr. Kenjiro Monji
Cabinet Councillor
Cabinet Councillors' Office
    on External Affairs

Mr. Hiroshi Shigeta
Executive Secretary
International Peace Cooperation
    Headquarters

**Government-Employed
Researchers:**

Professor Masashi Nishihara
National Defense Academy

Professor Shin'ichi Ogawa
National Institute for Defense Studies

Professor (Col.)Yoshihisa Nakamura
The National Institute for Defense
    Studies

Professor Yuzuru Kaneko
The National Institute for Defense
    Studies

Professor Takesada
The National Institute for Defense
    Studies

Academics & Others:

Professor Akihiko Tanaka
Institute of Oriental Culture
Tokyo University

Professor Hideo Sato
United Nations University

Professor Kazuo Ota, Dean
Rakuno Gakuen University

Professor Hajime Oshitani
Rakuno Gakuen University

Professor Akira Ogawa, Jr.
The Okazaki Institute

Professor Kenichi Nakamura, Dean
Faculty of Law
Hokkaido University

Professor Jun Morikawa
Rakuno Gakuen University

Professor Seiichi Kubota
Faculty of Modern Culture
(former journalist with *Asahi
    Shimbun*)

Professor Osamu Iishi
Institute of Oriental Culture
Tokyo University

Professor Takeshi Igarashi
Faculty of Law
(co-author of LDP Foreign Policy
    Platform)

Professor Toshiya Hoshino
Osaka School of International
Public Policy
Osaka University

Professor Kiichi Fujiwara
Institute of Social Science
Tokyo University

Ms. Kuniko Nakajima
The Okazaki Institute
(former official with Foreign
    Ministry)

Professor Yoshihide Soeya
Faculty of Law
Keio University
(co-author of LDP Foreign Policy
    Platform)

Mr. Kenichi Mizuno
(LDP official and son and adopted
    son of two very senior party
    officials)

Appendix B
The Constitution of Japan,
3 November 1946

Preface

We, the Japanese people, acting through our duly elected representatives in the National Diet, determined that we shall secure for ourselves and our posterity the fruits of peaceful cooperation with all nations and the blessings of liberty throughout this land, and resolved that never again shall we be visited with the horrors of war through the action of government, do proclaim that sovereign power resides with the people and do firmly establish this Constitution. Government is a sacred trust of the people, the authority for which is derived from the people, the powers of which are exercised by the representatives of the people, and the benefits of which are enjoyed by the people. This is a universal principle of mankind upon which this Constitution is founded. We reject and revoke all constitutions, laws, ordinances, and rescripts in conflict herewith.

We, the Japanese people, desire peace for all time and are deeply conscious of the high ideals controlling human relationship and we have determined to preserve our security and existence, trusting in the justice and faith of the peace-loving peoples of the world. We desire to occupy an honored place in an international society striving for the preservation of peace, and the banishment of tyranny and slavery, oppression, and intolerance for all time from the earth. We recognize that all peoples of the world have the right to live in peace, free from fear and want.

We believe that no nation is responsible to itself alone, but that laws of political morality are universal; and that obedience to such laws is incumbent upon all nations who would sustain their own sovereignty and justify their sovereign relationship with other nations.

We, the Japanese people, pledge our national honor to accomplish these high ideals and purposes with all our resources.

Chapter I: The Emperor

Article 1:
The Emperor shall be the symbol of the State and the unity of the people, deriving his position from the will of the people with whom resides sovereign power.

Article 2:
The Imperial Throne shall be dynastic and succeeded to in accordance with the Imperial House Law passed by the Diet.

Article 3:
The advice and approval of the Emperor in matters of state, and the Cabinet shall be responsible therefor.

Article 4:
(1) The Emperor shall perform only such acts in matters of state as are provided for in this Constitution and he shall not have powers related to government.
(2) The Emperor may delegate the performance of his acts in matters of state as may be provided for by law.

Article 5:
When, in accordance with the Imperial House Law, a Regency is established, the Regent shall perform his acts in matters of state in the Emperor's name. In this case, paragraph one of the preceding Article will be applicable.

Article 6:
The Emperor shall appoint the Prime Minister as designated by the Diet. The Emperor shall appoint the Chief Judge of the Supreme Court as designated by the Cabinet.

Article 7:
The Emperor shall, with the advice and approval of the Cabinet, perform the following acts in matters of state on behalf of the people:

(1) Promulgation of amendments of the constitution, laws, cabinet orders, and treaties.
(2) Convocation of the Diet.
(3) Dissolution of the House of Representatives.
(4) Proclamation of general election of members of the Diet.

(5) Attestation of the appointment and dismissal of Ministers of State and other officials as provided for by law, and of full powers and credentials of Ambassadors and Ministers.
(6) Attestation of general and special amnesty, commutation of punishment, reprieve, and restoration of rights.
(7) Awarding of honors.
(8) Attestation of instruments of ratification and other diplomatic documents as provided for by law.
(9) Receiving foreign ambassadors and ministers.
(10) Performance of ceremonial functions.

Article 8:
No property can be given to, or received by, the Imperial House, nor can any gifts be made therefrom, without the authorization of the Diet.

Chapter II: Renunciation of War

Article 9:
(1) Aspiring sincerely to an international peace based on justice and order, the Japanese people forever renounce war as a sovereign right of the nation and the threat or use of force as means of settling international disputes.
(2) In order to accomplish the aim of the preceding paragraph, land, sea, and air forces, as well as other war potential, will never be maintained. The right of belligerency of the state will not be recognized.

Chapter III: Rights and Duties of the People

Article 10:
The conditions necessary for being a Japanese national shall be determined by law.

Article 11:
The people shall not be prevented from enjoying any of the fundamental human rights. These fundamental human rights guaranteed to the people by this Constitution shall be conferred upon the people of this and future generations as eternal and inviolate rights.

Article 12:
The freedoms and rights guaranteed to the people by this Constitution shall be maintained by the constant endeavor of the people, who shall refrain

from any abuse of these freedoms and rights and shall always be responsible for utilizing them for the public welfare.

Article 13:

All of the people shall be respected as individuals. Their right to life, liberty, and the pursuit of happiness shall, to the extent that it does not interfere with the public welfare, be the supreme consideration in legislation and in other governmental affairs.

Article 14:

(1) All of the people are equal under the law and there shall be no discrimination in political, economic, or social relations because of race, creed, sex, social status, or family origin.
(2) Peers and peerage shall not be recognized.
(3) No privilege shall accompany any award of honor, decoration, or any distinction, nor shall any such award be valid beyond the lifetime of the individual who now holds or hereafter may receive it.

Article 15:

(1) The people have the inalienable right to choose their public officials and to dismiss them.
(2) All public officials are servants of the whole community and not of any group thereof.
(3) Universal adult suffrage is guaranteed with regard to the election of public officials.
(4) In all elections, secrecy of the ballot shall not be violated. A voter shall not be answerable, publicly or privately, for the choice he has made.

Article 16:

Every person shall have the right of peaceful petition for the redress of damage, for the removal of public officials, for the enactment, repeal, or amendment of laws, ordinances, or regulations and for other matters; nor shall any person be in any way discriminated against for sponsoring such a petition.

Article 17:

Every person may sue for redress as provided by law from the State or a public entity, in case he has suffered damage through illegal act of any public official.

Article 18:

No person shall be held in bondage of any kind. Involuntary servitude, except as punishment for crime, is prohibited.

Article 19:

Freedom of thought and conscience shall not be violated.

Article 20:

(1) Freedom of religion is guaranteed to all. No religious organization shall receive any privileges from the State, nor exercise any political authority.
(2) No person shall be compelled to take part in any religious acts, celebration, rite, or practice.
(3) The State and its organs shall refrain from religious education or any other religious activity.

Article 21:

(1) Freedom of assembly and association as well as speech, press, and all other forms of expression are guaranteed.
(2) No censorship shall be maintained, nor shall the secrecy of any means of communication be violated.

Article 22:

(1) Every person shall have freedom to choose and change his residence and to choose his occupation to the extent that it does not interfere with the public welfare.
(2) Freedom of all persons to move to a foreign country and to divest themselves of their nationality shall be inviolate.

Article 23:

Academic freedom is guaranteed.

Article 24:

(1) Marriage shall be based only on the mutual consent of both sexes and it shall be maintained through mutual cooperation with the equal rights of husband and wife as a basis.
(2) With regard to choice of spouse, property rights, inheritance, choice of domicile, divorce, and other matters pertaining to marriage and the family, laws shall be enacted from the standpoint of individual dignity and the essential equality of the sexes.

Article 25:

(1) All people shall have the right to maintain the minimum standards of wholesome and cultured living.
(2) In all spheres of life, the State shall use its endeavors for the promotion and extension of social welfare and security, and of public health.

Article 26:

(1) All people shall have the right to receive an equal education correspondent to their ability, as provided for by law.

(2) All people shall be obligated to have all boys and girls under their protection receive ordinary education as provided for by law. Such compulsory education shall be free.

Article 27:

(1) All people shall have the right and the obligation to work.

(2) Standards for wages, hours, rest, and other working conditions shall be fixed by law.

(3) Children shall not be exploited.

Article 28:

The right of workers to organize and to bargain and act collectively is guaranteed.

Article 29:

(1) The right to own or to hold property is inviolable.

(2) Property rights shall be defined by law, in conformity with the public welfare.

(3) Private property may be taken for public use upon just compensation therefor.

Article 30:

The people shall be liable to taxation as provided for by law.

Article 31:

No person shall be deprived of life or liberty, nor shall any other criminal penalty be imposed, except according to procedure established by law.

Article 32:

No person shall be denied the right of access to the courts.

Article 33:

No person shall be apprehended except upon warrant issued by a competent judicial officer which specifies the offense with which the person is charged, unless he is apprehended, the offense being committed.

Article 34:

No person shall be arrested or detained without being at once informed of the charges against him or without the immediate privilege of counsel; nor shall he be detained without adequate cause; and upon demand of any person such cause must be immediately shown in open court in his presence and the presence of his counsel.

Article 35:

(1) The right of all persons to be secure in their homes, papers, and effects against entries, searches, and seizures shall not be impaired except upon warrant issued for adequate cause and particularly describing the place to be searched and things to be seized, or except as provided by Article 33.
(2) Each search or seizure shall be made upon separate warrant issued by a competent judicial officer.

Article 36:

The infliction of torture by any public officer and cruel punishments are absolutely forbidden.

Article 37:

(1) In all criminal cases the accused shall enjoy the right to a speedy and public trial by an impartial tribunal.
(2) He shall be permitted full opportunity to examine all witnesses, and he shall have the right of compulsory process for obtaining witnesses on his behalf at public expense.
(3) At all times the accused shall have the assistance of competent counsel who shall, if the accused is unable to secure the same by his own efforts, be assigned to his use by the State.

Article 38:

(1) No person shall be compelled to testify against himself.
(2) Confession made under compulsion, torture, or threat, or after prolonged arrest or detention, shall not be admitted in evidence.
(3) No person shall be convicted or punished in cases where the only proof against him is his own confession.

Article 39:

No person shall be held criminally liable for an act which was lawful at the time it was committed, or of which he had been acquitted, nor shall he be placed in double jeopardy.

Article 40:

Any person may, in case he is acquitted after he has been arrested or detained, sue the State for redress as provided for by law.

Chapter IV: The Diet

Article 41:
The Diet shall be the highest organ of the state power, and shall be the sole law-making organ of the State.

Article 42:
The Diet shall consist of two Houses, namely the House of Representatives and the House of Councillors.

Article 43:
(1) Both Houses shall consist of elected members, representative of all the people.
(2) The number of the members of each House shall be fixed by law.

Article 44:
The qualifications of members of both Houses and their electors shall be fixed by law. However, there shall be no discrimination because of race, creed, sex, social status, family origin, education, property, or income.

Article 45:
The term of office of members of the House of Representatives shall be four years. However, the term shall be terminated before the full term is up in case the House of Representatives is dissolved.

Article 46:
The term of office of members of the House of Councillors shall be six years, and election for half the members shall take place every three years.

Article 47:
Electoral districts, method of voting, and other matters pertaining to the method of election of members of both Houses shall be fixed by law.

Article 48:
No person shall be permitted to be a member of both Houses simultaneously.

Article 49:
Members of both Houses shall receive appropriate annual payment from the national treasury in accordance with law.

Article 50:
Except in cases as provided for by law, members of both Houses shall be exempt from apprehension while the Diet is in session, and any members apprehended before the opening of the session shall be freed during the term of the session upon demand of the House.

Article 51:
Members of both Houses shall not be held liable outside the House for speeches, debates, or votes cast inside the House.

Article 52:
An ordinary session of the Diet shall be convoked once per year.

Article 53:
The Cabinet may determine to convoke extraordinary sessions of the Diet. When a quarter or more of the total members of either House makes the demand, the Cabinet must determine on such convocation.

Article 54:
(1) When the House of Representatives is dissolved, there must be a general election of members of the House of Representatives within forty (40) days from the date of dissolution, and the Diet must be convoked within thirty (30) days from the date of the election.
(2) When the House of Representatives is dissolved, the House of Councillors is closed at the same time. However, the Cabinet may, in time of national emergency, convoke the House of Councillors in emergency session.
(3) Measures taken at such session as mentioned in the proviso of the preceding paragraph shall be provisional and shall become null and void unless agreed to by the House of Representatives within a period of ten (10) days after the opening of the next session of the Diet.

Article 55:
Each House shall judge disputes related to qualifications of its members. However, in order to deny a seat to any member, it is necessary to pass a resolution by a majority of two-thirds or more of the members present.

Article 56:
(1) Business cannot be transacted in either House unless one-third or more of total membership is present.
(2) All matters shall be decided, in each House, by a majority of those

present, except as elsewhere provided for in the Constitution, and in case of a tie, the presiding officer shall decide the issue.

Article 57:

(1) Deliberation in each House shall be public. However, a secret meeting may be held where a majority of two-thirds or more of those members present passes a resolution therefore.
(2) Each House shall keep a record of proceedings. This record shall be published and given general circulation, excepting such parts of proceedings of secret session as may be deemed to require secrecy.
(3) Upon demand of one-fifth or more of the members present, votes of the members on any matter shall be recorded in the minutes.

Article 58:

(1) Each House shall select its own president and other officials.
(2) Each House shall establish its rules pertaining to meetings, proceedings, and internal discipline, and may punish members for disorderly conduct. However, in order to expel a member, a majority of two-thirds or more of those members present must pass a resolution thereon.

Article 59:

(1) A bill becomes a law on passage by both Houses, except as otherwise provided for by the Constitution.
(2) A bill, which is passed by the House of Representatives, and upon which the House of Councillors makes a decision different from that of the House of Representatives, becomes a law when passed a second time by the House of Representatives by a majority of two-thirds or more of the members present.
(3) The provision of the preceding paragraph does not preclude the House of Representatives from calling for the meeting of a joint committee of both Houses, provided for by law.
(4) Failure by the House of Councillors to take final action within sixty (60) days after receipt of a bill passed by the House of Representatives, time in recess excepted, may be determined by the House of Representatives to constitute a rejection of the said bill by the House of Councillors.

Article 60:

(1) The budget must first be submitted to the House of Representatives.
(2) Upon consideration of the budget, when the House of Councillors makes a decision different from that of the House of Representatives, and when

no agreement can be reached even through a joint committee of both Houses, provided for by law, or in the case of failure by the House of Councillors to take final action within thirty (30) days, the period of recess excluded, after the receipt of the budget passed by the House of Representatives, the decision of the House of Representatives shall be the decision of the Diet.

Article 61:

The second paragraph of the preceding Article applies also to the Diet approval required for the conclusion of treaties.

Article 62:

Each House may conduct investigations in relation to government, and may demand the presence and testimony of witnesses, and the production of records.

Article 63:

The Prime Minister and other Ministers of State may, at any time, appear in either House for the purpose of speaking on bills, regardless of whether they are members of the House or not. They must appear when their presence is required in order to give answers or explanations.

Article 64:

(1) The Diet shall set up an impeachment court from among the members of both Houses for the purposes of trying those judges against whom removal proceedings have been instituted.

(2) Matters relating to impeachment shall be provided for by law.

Chapter V: The Cabinet

Article 65:

Executive power shall be vested in the Cabinet.

Article 66:

(1) The Cabinet shall consist of the Prime Minister, who shall be its head, and other Ministers of State, as provided for by law.

(2) The Prime Minister and other Ministers of State must be civilians.

(3) The Cabinet shall, in the exercise of executive power, be collectively responsible to the Diet.

Article 67:

(1) The Prime Minister shall be designated from among the members of the

Diet by a resolution of the Diet. This designation shall precede all other business.

(2) If the House of Representatives and the House of Councillors disagree and if no agreement can be reached even through a joint committee of both Houses, provided for by law, or the House of Councillors fails to make designation within ten (10) days, exclusive of the period of recess, after the House of Representatives has made designation, the decision of the House of Representatives shall be the decision of the Diet.

Article 68:

(1) The Prime Minister shall appoint the Ministers of State. However, a majority of their number must be chosen from among the members of the Diet.
(2) The Prime Minister may remove the Ministers of State as he chooses.

Article 69:

If the House of Representatives passes a non-confidence resolution, or rejects a confidence resolution, the Cabinet shall resign en masse, unless the House of Representatives is dissolved within ten (10) days.

Article 70:

When there is a vacancy in the post of Prime Minister, or upon the first convocation of the Diet after a general election of members of the House of Representatives, the Cabinet shall resign en masse.

Article 71:

In the cases mentioned in the two preceding Articles, the Cabinet shall continue its functions until the time when a new Prime Minister is appointed.

Article 72:

The Prime Minister, representing the Cabinet, submits bills, reports on general national affairs and foreign relations to the Diet, and exercises control and supervision over various administrative branches.

Article 73:

The Cabinet shall, in addition to other general administrative functions, perform the following functions:

(1) Administer the law faithfully; conduct affairs of state.
(2) Manage foreign affairs.
(3) Conclude treaties. However, it shall obtain prior or, depending on circumstances, subsequent approval of the Diet.

(4) Administer the civil service, in accordance with standards established by law.
(5) Prepare the budget, and present it to the Diet.
(6) Enact cabinet orders in order to execute the provisions of this Constitution and of the law.
(7) However, it cannot include penal provisions in such cabinet orders unless authorized by such law.
(8) Decide on general amnesty, special amnesty, commutation of punishment, reprieve, and restoration of rights.

Article 74:

All laws and cabinet orders shall be signed by the competent Minister of State and countersigned by the Prime Minister.

Article 75:

The Ministers of State shall not, during their tenure of office, be subject to legal action without the consent of the Prime Minister. However, the right to take that action is not impaired hereby.

Chapter VI: Judiciary

Article 76:

(1) The whole judicial power is vested in a Supreme Court and in such inferior courts as are established by law.
(2) No extraordinary tribunal shall be established, nor shall any organ or agency of the Executive be given final judicial power.
(3) All judges shall be independent in the exercise of their conscience and shall be bound only by this Constitution and the laws.

Article 77:

(1) The Supreme Court is vested with the rule-making power under which it determines the rules of procedure and of practice, and of matters relating to attorneys, the internal discipline of the courts, and the administration of judicial affairs.
(2) Public procurators shall be subject to the rule-making power of the Supreme Court.
(3) The Supreme Court may delegate the power to make rules for inferior courts to such courts.

Article 78:

Judges shall not be removed except by public impeachment unless judicially declared mentally or physically incompetent to perform official duties. No disciplinary action against judges shall be administered by any executive organ or agency.

Article 79:

(1) The Supreme Court shall consist of a Chief Judge and such number of judges as may be determined by law; all such judges excepting the Chief Judge shall be appointed by the Cabinet.

(2) The appointment of the judges of the Supreme Court shall be reviewed by the people at the first general election of members of the House of Representatives following their appointment, and shall be reviewed again at the first general election of members of the House of Representatives after a lapse of ten (10) years, and in the same manner thereafter.

(3) In cases mentioned in the foregoing paragraph, when the majority of the voters favors the dismissal of a judge, he shall be dismissed.

(4) Matters pertaining to review shall be prescribed by law.

(5) The judges of the Supreme Court shall be retired upon the attainment of the age as fixed by law.

(6) All such judges shall receive, at regular stated intervals, adequate compensation which shall not be decreased during their terms of office.

Article 80:

(1) The judges of the inferior courts shall be appointed by the Cabinet from a list of persons nominated by the Supreme Court. All such judges shall hold office for a term of ten (10) years with privilege of reappointment, provided that they shall be retired upon the attainment of the age as fixed by law.

(2) The judges of the inferior courts shall receive, at regular stated intervals, adequate compensation which shall not be decreased during their terms of office.

Article 81:

The Supreme Court is the court of last resort with power to determine the constitutionality of any law, order, regulation, or official act.

Article 82:

(1) Trials shall be conducted and judgement declared publicly. Where a court unanimously determines publicity to be dangerous to public order or morals, a trial may be conducted privately, but trials of political offenses, offenses involving the press, or cases wherein the rights of people

as guaranteed in Chapter III of this Constitution are in question shall always be conducted publicly.

Chapter VII: Finance

Article 83:
The power to administer national finances shall be exercised as the Diet shall determine.

Article 84:
No new taxes shall be imposed or existing ones modified except by law or under such conditions as law may prescribe.

Article 85:
No money shall be expended, nor shall the State obligate itself, except as authorized by the Diet.

Article 86:
The Cabinet shall prepare and submit to the Diet for its consideration and decision a budget for each fiscal year.

Article 87:
In order to provide for unforeseen deficiencies in the budget, a reserve fund may be authorized by the Diet to be expended upon the responsibility of the Cabinet. The Cabinet must get subsequent approval of the Diet for all payments from the reserve fund.

Article 88:
All property of the Imperial Household shall belong to the State. All expenses of the Imperial Household shall be appropriated by the Diet in the budget.

Article 89:
No public money or other property shall be expended or appropriated for the use, benefit, or maintenance of any religious institution or association, or for any charitable, educational, or benevolent enterprises not under the control of public authority.

Article 90:
(1) Final accounts of the expenditures and revenues of the State shall be audited annually by a Board of Audit and submitted by the Diet, to-

gether with the statement of audit, during the fiscal year immediately following the period covered.

(2) The organization and competency of the Board of Audit shall be determined by law.

Article 91:

At regular intervals and at least annually the Cabinet shall report to the Diet and the people on the state of national finances.

Chapter VIII: Local Self-Government

Article 92:

Regulations concerning organization and operations of local public entities shall be fixed by law in accordance with the principle of local autonomy.

Article 93:

(1) The local public entities shall establish assemblies as their deliberative organs, in accordance with law.

(2) The chief executive officers of all local public entities, the members of their assemblies, and such other local officials as may be determined by law shall be elected by direct popular vote within their several communities.

Article 94:

Local public entities shall have the right to manage their property, affairs, and administration and to enact their own regulations within law.

Article 95:

A special law, applicable only to one local public entity, cannot be enacted by the Diet without the consent of the majority of the voters of the local public entity concerned, obtained in accordance with law.

Chapter IX: Amendments

Article 96:

(1) Amendments to this Constitution shall be initiated by the Diet, through a concurring vote of two-thirds or more of all the members of each House and shall thereupon be submitted to the people for ratification, which shall require the affirmative vote of a majority of all votes cast thereon, at a special referendum or at such election as the Diet shall specify.

(2) Amendments when so ratified shall immediately be promulgated by the Emperor in the name of the people, as an integral part of this Constitution.

Chapter X: Supreme Law

Article 97:
The fundamental human rights by this Constitution guaranteed to the people of Japan are fruits of the age-old struggle of man to be free; they have survived the many exacting tests for durability and are conferred upon this and future generations in trust, to be held for all time inviolate.

Article 98:
(1) This Constitution shall be the supreme law of the nation and no law, ordinance, imperial rescript, or other act of government, or part thereof, contrary to the provisions hereof, shall have legal force or validity.
(2) The treaties concluded by Japan and established laws of nations shall be faithfully observed.

Article 99:
The Emperor or the Regent as well as Ministers of State, members of the Diet, judges, and all other public officials have the obligation to respect and uphold this Constitution.

Chapter XI: Supplementary Provisions

Article 100:
(1) This Constitution shall be enforced as from the day when the period of six months will have elapsed counting from the day of its promulgation.
(2) The enactment of laws necessary for the enforcement of this Constitution, the election of members of the House of Councillors, and the procedure for the convocation of the Diet and other preparatory procedures necessary for the enforcement of this Constitution may be executed before the day prescribed in the preceding paragraph.

Article 101:
If the House of Councillors is not constituted before the effective date of this Constitution, the House of Representatives shall function as the Diet until such time as the House of Councillors shall be constituted.

Article 102:
The term of office for half the members of the House of Councillors serving in the first term under this Constitution shall be three years. Members falling under this category shall be determined in accordance with law.

Article 103:
The Ministers of State, members of the House of Representatives, and judges in office on the effective date of this Constitution, and all other public officials who occupy positions corresponding to such positions as are recognized by this Constitution, shall not forfeit their positions automatically on account of the enforcement of this Constitution unless otherwise specified by law. When, however, successors are elected or appointed under the provisions of this Constitution, they shall forfeit their positions as a matter of course.

Date of promulgation: 3 November 1946
Date of enforcement: 3 May 1947

THE CONSTITUTION OF JAPAN (3 November 1946)

I rejoice that the foundation for the construction of a new Japan has been laid according to the will of the Japanese people, and hereby sanction and promulgate the amendments of the Imperial Japanese Constitution effected following the consultation with the Privy Council and the decision of the Imperial Diet made in accordance with Article 73 of the said Constitution.

Signed:

HIROHITO, Seal of the Emperor, This third day of the eleventh month of the twenty-first year of Showa (3 November 1946).

Countersigned:

Prime Minister and concurrently and concurrently Minister for Foreign
    Affairs: YOSHIDA Shigeru
Minister of State: Baron SHIDEHARA Kijuro
Minister of Justice: KIMURA Tokutaro
Minister for Home Affairs: OMURA Seiichi
Minister of Education: TANAKA Kotaro
Minister of Agriculture and Forestry: WADA Hiroo
Minister of State: SAITO Takao

Minister of Communication: HITOTSUMATSU Sadayoshi
Minister of Commerce and Industry: HOSHIJIMA Jiro
Minister of Welfare: KAWAI Yoshinari
Minister of State: UEHARA Etsujiro
Minister of Transportation: HIRATSUKA Tsunejiro
Minister of Finance: ISHIBASHI Tanzan
Minister of State: KANAMORI Tokujiro
Minister of State: ZEN Keinosuke

Discussion Questions

Chapter 1

1. Does Japan, due to the size of its economy, have a global responsibility to provide a "human" contribution to United Nations and to global peacekeeping? Why?
2. Does Japan desire to be a hegemon regionally or globally?
3. Does Japan want to raise its stature in the world?
4. Can Japan be content in the shadow of the United States as the "Tonto" to the American "Lone Ranger" or the "Robin" to the American "Batman?"

Chapter 2

1. Was Japan right in reinterpreting Article Nine to permit defensive capabilities?
2. Are the Self-Defense Force (SDF) a legal entity under the Japanese constitution? Why, or why not?
3. Should Japan be considered a virtual nuclear power? Could Japan acquire nuclear weapons for "defensive" purposes? (Are nuclear weapons capable of being defensive weapons only?)
4. Where is Japan, as a nation, headed in relation to its role in the world?
5. How will its U.N. role be perceived by its neighbors?
6. Does Japan wish to be a great power again?
7. Can Japanese foreign policy swing to domestic demands even if it swings in a pacifist direction? How important should domestic concerns be to the formation of Japanese foreign policy?
8. Was it "right" for the victorious allies to impose democracy on Japan over the objections of the ruling elites? Was it "right" for MacArthur's staff to write the draft of the constitution given to Japan?
9. Do you agree with the author's argument that the evidence indicates that Article Nine is of Japanese origin?

10. Does Article Nine violate Japan's sovereignty?
11. Has Japan truly been living in the spirit of Article Nine since 1946?
12. Is peace simply the absence of war, as many Japanese seem to feel?
13. How great a role has fear played in the foreign policies of Japan?

Chapter 3

1. What can and should Japan do in maintaining international order and stability? What is its responsibility toward these issues?
2. Why do you think the Socialists gave up their traditional opposition to the existence of the SDF when they came to power?
3. Should Japan have been better prepared for the end of the Cold War and the demise of the Yoshida Doctrine?
4. Given Japan's large oil imports from the Middle East, should Japan have made a military or "human" contribution to the Gulf War?
5. Are the fears of a rearmed Japan justified? Why, or why not?
6. Is SDF participation needed on the international stage? Why, or why not?
7. Does Japan deserve a permanent seat on the U.N. Security Council, given its past history, but also considering its economic clout and the fact that it is the second-largest supporter (after the United States) of the United Nations? Why, or why not?
8. Has Japan learned from the results of World War II, and what has it learned? Can Japan be trusted to act as a civilized nation rather than resorting to militarism again?
9. Does Japan still need to apologize to its neighbors in East Asia in a meaningful way? What way would be meaningful and acceptable to nations such as Korea and China? Will China and Korea ever accept an apology from Japan?
10. Is Japan currently a great power? If it is a great power, what is the source of its power?

Chapter 4

1. How significant are Japan's limitations as a result of Article Nine?
2. What are the implications to Japan as a nation and a society of its shrinking population?
3. How important are long-term goals and plans for states in general? For Japanese foreign policy?
4. What does alternative security provide for Japan?

5. Who are Japan's "friends" within the Northeast Asian security complex?
6. Can Japan politically restructure its foreign policy? And if it can, what form will such a policy take?
7. How important are relative and absolute gains to Japanese foreign policy?
8. Is the author correct in subjugating all other theories of state behavior to realism? Why or why not?
9. How much of an impact do you think that Japanese efforts at obtaining international goodwill are making on its position in the world?

Chapter 5

1. Is Japan really restructuring its foreign policy?
2. Why is it so hard politically to amend the Japanese constitution?
3. Hermann's investigation of foreign-policy change finds that the "decision-making process itself can obstruct or facilitate change." Do you agree?
4. Can the study of foreign policy and the study of foreign-policy restructuring be one and the same?
5. Under what circumstances do foreign-policy changes occur in which an existing (Japanese) government recognizes that its current course is seriously inadequate, mistaken, or no longer applicable?
6. Why do you believe that Japan felt it necessary to pass the PKO Law?
7. What do you believe are the long-term goals of Japanese foreign policy? (Or, where do you feel that Japan is going in the future with its foreign policy?)
   a. Do you feel these are the right long-term goals?
   b. Why, or why not? If not, where would you like to see it go in the future?
8. What role, if any, should Japan seek in international security forums (such as ARF and KEDO)?
9. What are Japan's top three security threats or concerns? Top three foreign-policy concerns?
10. What should be the role of the SDF in Japanese foreign policy?
11. What limits, if any, should be placed on the SDF?
12. How should Japan deal with its history in East Asia if it does take on a larger role in world affairs?

13. What, in your opinion, should the goals of Japanese security and foreign policy be?
    a. What are the international and domestic obstacles to these goals?
    b. How do domestic politics affect these foreign-policy goals?
    c. How should Japan deal with these domestic political obstacles?
    d. How do these choices fit with Article Nine?

Chapter 6

1. Should Japan be considering security options outside of the framework of the United States-Japan alliance, as the author asserts?
2. Are the United States-Japan alliance and relationship, in fact, as strong as they have ever been?
3. Should Japan be doing more to cultivate friendships in its security complex?
4. Is Japan prepared for abandonment if that eventuality should ever come to pass? Does Japan have a so-called plan B?
5. Does Japan need to cultivate better relations with China? Could it cultivate better relations in the current climate within China of anti-Japanese sentiment?
6. Do the United States and other nations tend to take Japan for granted and pass over Japan?
7. Is Japan's need for more foreign labor a threat to its racial homogeneity? What might the long-term consequences for Japanese society be?
8. Is Japan's greatest Achilles' heel its economic vulnerability, as the author contends? Is Japan doing what it needs to do to protect itself from this vulnerability? Could it be doing more, and if so, what?
9. Would the United States defend Japan if Japan or its territory were to be attacked by a foreign opponent?
10. What are Japan's security options outside of its relationship with the United States? What options can Japan pursue if it loses or can no longer depend on the United States for its security guarantee?
11. How can Japan develop relationships to hedge against a loss of the U.S. security guarantee? What relationships should Japan be cultivating in order to hedge its bets for the future?
12. Is it in Japan's interest to see tensions in the Sino-American relationship?
13. Should Japanese political leaders stop their visits to Yasukuni Shrine in order to ease tensions within East Asia?

14. Can Japan depend on the United Nations for a security guarantee?
15. How can Japan effectively deal with its history in East Asia?

Chapter 7

1. Is the concept of *gaiatsu* more of a myth (or legend), as the author purports, or is it a reality of Japanese foreign policy that makes it different from the foreign pressure all nations face? Does the concept of *gaiatsu* strip Japan of its sovereignty?
2. Do all nations face foreign pressure in the same way Japan does? Do they deal with it in the same way?
3. Has Japan given in to the United States too much in the past? Is the relationship a one-way relationship, with Japan being the submissive partner, as Ryozo Kato alleges?
4. Does Japan need to show its independence from the United States, or is it independent already?
5. Is what is good for America often what is good for Japan as well?
6. Can Japan play the role of a great power? Should it take on the responsibility of a great power in the maintenance of world order?
7. Should Japan have a permanent seat on the U.N. Security Council? If it does, should it have veto power as the current permanent five members do?
8. Does Japan need more friends in Asia?

Chapter 8

1. The author argues that all foreign policy is security-based in some way or another. Do you agree, and why?
2. How should Japan deal with China?
3. What are China's intentions regionally and globally?
4. What is keeping Japan from becoming a nuclear power?
5. Is the United States a declining power, and is Japan right to continue its alliance with the United States, or as the author argues, is U.S. power still in the ascendant?
6. If Taiwan declared itself independent, would the United States come to its aid if China went to war to stop Taiwan's independence? Would Japan assist the United States?
7. Why and to what purpose is China restructuring and building its military to challenge the United States?
8. What can and should America and Japan do about the Chinese military buildup?

9. Will China ever forgive Japan for its "crimes" during its occupation of China?

10. Is the author correct in his analysis that Asian leaders prefer Republican presidents in the White House over Democrats because they are more predictable? Why might this be so?

11. Does Japan have more to gain by working with the United States than against it?

12. Can Japan depend on the United States' "nuclear umbrella" of extended deterrence?

Chapter Nine

1. Where is Japan going as a nation? Is it a team player in world affairs, or is it a nation seeking power and the ability to dominate?

2. Is Japan's inability to implement structural reform an indication of its inability to take on a global leadership role?

3. Is constitutional revision likely to occur in Japan in the near future? Would such revision be a good thing if it included revision of Article Nine?

4. Should Japan apologize to its people for the nation's actions in World War II, as the author suggests? Could such an apology help to start the process of repairing the harm done by Japanese imperialism?

5. Japan has the desire to be a normal nation, but is it willing to bear the costs?

6. Can Japan politically accept casualties in support of international and regional peace and stability?

7. The author makes six suggestions for normalization of Japanese foreign policy. How practical and valid are these suggestion? Would you recommend any additions to this list?

8. Returning to the questions asked in chapter 1: "What is Japan's new role in the world?" "What accounts for the gradual change in the role of the SDF?" "What are the domestic driving forces behind these changes?" and "What is Japan's long-term foreign-policy agenda?"

9. What will be MOFA's response to the Diet's more assertive role in the foreign-policy decision-making process? How will MOFA adjust to a reduced role in the decision-making process if the Diet assumes a stronger leadership?

10. Has Japanese foreign policy matured in the post-Cold War and post-9/11 world, as the author concludes?

Notes

Notes to Chapter 1

1. James N. Rosenau, *The Study of Political Adaptation: Essays on the Analysis of World Politics,* pp. 1–2.

2. For students interested in more information and news accounts of the hostage crisis at the time, a simple Google search of the terms "1997 Peruvian hostage crisis" will provide the desired information. However, given the controversial nature of former Peruvian President Fujimori, the student would be advised to weigh carefully differing accounts and perspectives of the crisis.

3. The Diet is the legislative body in Japan. It has both an upper house, the House of Counselors (*Sangin*), and a lower house, the House of Representatives (*Shugin*). The lower house is primary in that it may override a vote of the upper house by a two-thirds majority. The prime minister and the cabinet usually come from the lower house, but they may come from either.

4. Japan's pacifist constitution was externally imposed on it during the occupation by General MacArthur and the allies at the end of World War II, but as will be argued in chapter 2, the Japanese people have adopted it as their own, and the constitution reflects the democratic will of the people.

5. The term "uniqueness" is used here in the sense that all nations have unique foreign policies. In no way should it be construed to mean that I subscribe to the argument or theory of "Japanese uniqueness" that has been put forth by many conservative revisionists in Japan, some of which have gone so far as to argue that the Japanese people are a unique evolutionary subset of the human race and different from their fellow humans. An example of this was the Japanese Diet member who argued during a trade dispute over the importation of American beef that Japanese could not eat American beef because they were unique in having longer intestines than Americans.

6. "The Constitution of Japan," *Law and Contemporary Problems,* Spring 1990, pp. 200–14.

7. For the purposes of this text, all Japanese names will be written in the Western style of given name followed by the family name, rather than the Japanese style, which requires the family name to be listed first.

8. Takashi Inoguchi, "Japan's Response to the Gulf Crisis: An Analytic Overview," p. 257.

9. Jiro Yamaguchi, "The Gulf War and the Transformation of Japanese Constitutional Politics," p. 155.

10. The concept of the levels of analysis was introduced to international-relations theory by Kenneth N. Waltz in *Man, the State, and War: A Theoretical Analysis.*

11. I do not intend to introduce the concept of regionalism here as a level of analy-

sis. Japan tends to deal with the individual ASEAN member states in the same way a major state would deal with a minor state, but it deals with the unit of ASEAN as it would a "major" state in the international system.

12. Holsti defines foreign-policy restructuring as "the dramatic, wholesale alteration of a nation's pattern of external relations." Kal J. Holsti, ed., *Why Nations Realign: Foreign Policy Restructuring in the Postwar World*, p. ix.

13. Rosenau, *The Study of Political Adaptation*, pp. 1–2.

14. Holsti, *Why Nations Realign*, pp. 4–7.

15. Kjell Goldmann, *Change and Stability in Foreign Policy: The Problems and Possibilities of Détente*, pp. 3–4.

16. Charles F. Hermann, "Changing Course: When Governments Choose to Redirect Foreign Policy," pp. 34, 3.

17. Ibid., p. 13.

18. Ibid., p. 4.

19. Ibid., p. 5.

20. Ibid., p. 7.

21. Ibid., pp. 10–11.

22. Ibid., p. 11.

23. As a measure of the significance of this book, the Japanese edition of van Wolferen's book was effectively banned by the Japanese government (bureaucracy) as being too revealing for the general Japanese public.

24. Reinhard Drifte, *Japan's Foreign Policy for the 21st Century: From Economic Superpower to What Power?* pp. 1–2.

25. Ibid., p. 14.

26. A partial list of those interviewed is provided in Appendix A.

27. An important point here is that politicians will change their opinions like the wind when there is a popular need for such a change. It has long been argued that if Japanese troops were to receive significant casualties while on a PKO mission, support for the PKO in the general populace could evaporate, and thus the politicians would stop supporting the PKO. The reaction to the first death of a Japanese soldier overseas since World War II will set the tone of Japanese foreign policy for years to come.

28. *Gaijin* is most often translated as "foreigner," but literally means "outsider"; it carries a connotation that can at times be considered derogatory.

29. The rationale for this belief stems from Japanese attitudes toward their language. The Japanese view their language as being very difficult (and rightly so), especially for foreigners. They thus tend to be more frank in English or when talking to a foreigner because they can always claim to have been misquoted or translated if their comments come back to haunt them.

30. For more on this view that Japan is an up-and-coming hegemon, see Paul Kennedy, *The Rise and Fall of the Great Powers: Economic Change and Military Conflict from 1500 to 2000.*

Notes to Chapter 2

1. "The Constitution of Japan," *Law and Contemporary Problems,* Spring 1990, pp. 200–14 (emphasis added).

2. Ibid.

3. The Liberal Democratic Party (LDP), a center-right-wing party ruled Japan continuously from 1958 until July of 1993, when it was temporarily ousted for eleven months by a center-left coalition. The uninterrupted reign of the LDP permitted the SDF to exist and grow throughout the Cold War period. Only since July 1993, when the largest of the center-left-wing parties, the Socialists (SDP), joined in a center-left-coalition government, and later, when they defected to join the center-right-wing LDP in another coalition government, have the Socialists accepted the legitimacy of the SDF. Several of the Socialists whom I interviewed expressed strong displeasure at their party's willingness, in order to gain power, to accept the SDF as legitimate under the constitution. At the same time, they demonstrated a realization that the SDF is here to stay. However, the Communist Party of Japan (CPJ) continues to view the SDF as illegitimate.

4. Martin W. Sampson III and Stephen G. Walker, "Cultural Norms and National Roles: A Comparison of Japan and France," in Stephen G. Walker, ed., *Role Theory and Foreign Policy Analysis,* chapter 7, pp. 105–22.

5. Ibid. p. 109.

6. The Diet is the legislative body in Japan. It has both an upper house, the House of Counselors (*Sangin*), and a lower house, the House of Representatives (*Shugin*). The lower house is primary in that it may override a vote of the upper house by a two-thirds majority. The prime minister and the cabinet usually come from the lower house, but they may come from either.

7. The SDP used "ox walk" tactics (similar to a filibuster but considerably less elegant) tactics to slow down the inevitable and succeeded in dragging out the final vote for several days. However, the SDP's tactics backfired with the Japanese public in general and proved to be a national source of embarrassment when the debate was broadcast internationally. The "ox walk" led to the perception that the SDP was outdated and out of touch with reality. The July 1993 elections resulted in severe losses at the polls for the SDP. The SDP's acceptance of the SDF in order to gain share power with the LDP helped to accelerate its demise as the number-two party in Japan as its supports abandoned it.

8. Robert W. Tucker, *The Inequality of Nations,* p. 88.

9. Some have begun to question Japan's status as a "virtual" nuclear power in light of the October 1999 nuclear accident and the disclosures of gross neglect within the Japanese nuclear power industry. The feeling is that Japan would have to undertake a large and long-lasting Manhattan Project-style project with a questionable prognosis for success, especially in face of large-scale public opposition to the idea of Japan "going" nuclear. I disagree with this assessment for two principal reasons. First, it assumes that Japan does not already have plans for nuclear weapons in blueprint or another advanced form (with South Africa as an example). Second, it assumes that a public facing a clear potential threat would not support a government attempting to protect it from this threat. An extensive discussion of Japan's nuclear potential took place on the Internet list ssj-forum@iss.u-tokyo.ac.jp during the late fall of 1999, following Japan's nuclear accident in October 1999.

10. *New York Times,* "Japan Discovers Defense," 26 August 1999, Internet edition www.nytimes.com/yr/mo/day/editorial/26thu1.html.

11. Kazuo Ota, dean, Rakuno Gakuen University, interview by author, 6 June 1998, Tokyo, tape recording, in author's personal possession.

12. These foreign-policy norms being the tendency of democratic states to set

foreign policy based on perceived needs rather than on agendas. The idea is that nations are merely reacting and taking action as opportunities and problems present themselves rather than pressing forward with agendas or "master plans" that would guide the nation's foreign policies.

13. Mutsuyoshi Nishimura, "Peace-keeping Operations: Setting the Record Straight,"p. 51.

14. Ibid., p. 55.

15. *New York Times,* "Japan Discovers Defense."

16. Charles L. Kades, "The American Role in Revising Japan's Imperial Constitution," p. 217.

17. Proclamation by Heads of Governments, United States, United Kingdom, and China, Part I (a) and (b), PR 423 as quoted by Kades, "The American Role," p. 217 (emphasis added). It is important that these directives did *not* call for the renunciation of war or for outlawing the maintenance of military forces by the Japanese as contained in Article Nine of the Japanese constitution.

18. Sandra Madsen, "The Japanese Constitution and Self-Defense Forces: Prospects for a New Japanese Military Role," p. 553.

19. James E. Auer, "Article Nine of Japan's Constitution: from Renunciation of Armed Force 'Forever' to the Third Largest Defense Budget in the World," p. 173. Under the feudal Meiji constitution, the imperial army and navy were cabinet ministries, and their ministers were required by law to be active-duty officers, not elected officials.

20. Kades, "The American Role," p. 218. The Meiji Era was named after the period of the reign of the Emperor Meiji (1868–1912), and the constitution of that era was in effect until the end of World War II. It centered the power structure in Japan around the upper feudal lords and the military.

21. The awareness in political science that democracies do not tend to fight each other predates the Democratic Peace Theory by several decades and demonstrates an awareness by the occupation government that true democracy (whatever that may be), with power in the hands of the people, was desirable and necessary to the maintenance of peace with Japan.

22. John Mensing, commenting on Japan's way of embracing defeat, 13 October 1999, H-Net/KIAPS List for United States and Japanese Relations, H-US-Japan@H-Net.msu.edu.

23. Kades, "The American Role," pp. 219–22.

24. Kendrick F. Royer, "The Demise of the World's First Pacifist Constitution: Japanese Constitutional Interpretation and the Growth of Executive Power to Make War," p. 777.

25. Robert B. Funk, "Japan's Constitution and U.N. Obligations in the Persian Gulf War: A Case for Non-Military Participation in U.N. Enforcement Actions," p. 369.

26. See Royer, "The Demise of the World's First Pacifist Constitution," pp. 782–84.

27. As cited by Funk, "Japan's Constitution and U.N. Obligations in the Persian Gulf War," p. 371, and Auer, "Article Nine of Japan's Constitution," p. 174.

28. Kades, "The American Role," p. 224. Kades gets the idea that the emperor was the origin of Article Nine from the Imperial Prescript of January 1946 denying his divinity. The emperor proclaimed that "we will construct a new Japan through thoroughly being pacific." Comment: This seems to be a reasonable deduction, based on the fact that at the time, the paramount desire of many leaders was to preserve the imperial system and that this origin might give them a strong case for its preservation.

This idea is also noted by Funk, "Japan's Constitution and U.N. Obligations," p. 371, note 45.

29. Major General Frank Sackton, United States Army (Ret.) and former aid to General Douglas MacArthur during the occupation of Japan. Interviews by the author, 19 and 24 September 1997, tape recording in the author's personal possession. General Sackton is currently professor emeritus in the School of Public Affairs at Arizona State University.

30. Sackton interview.

31. American interests were often not well defined during the occupation, leading the Americans to undercut their own democratic policies and institutions through which they had attempted to place power in the hands of the people (and take it out of the hands of the elite). The Japanese leaders reacted better to indecision on the part of the American occupation authorities and were able to play elements (New Dealers versus anti-Communists) within SCAP off against each other (Sackton interview). For more information on this, see Alex Gibney, *The Pacific Century: Reinventing Japan (#5)*.

32. For more information on MacArthur's personality, see the PBS video series, *MacArthur: An American Caesar.*

33. Professor Keichi Fujiwara, Institute of Social Science, Tokyo University, interview by the author, 11 June 1998. Under Japanese law, citizens, if attacked, do not have the right to defend themselves without risking being found guilty of assaulting their attacker themselves.

34. Kades, "The American Role," p. 224, and Sackton interview.

35. Ibid., pp. 229–30 (emphasis added).

36. Ibid., p. 230.

37. Toshihiro Yamauchi, "Gunning for Japan's Peace Constitution," p. 160.

38. Funk, "Japan's Constitution and U.N. Obligations," p. 372.

39. As cited by Kades, "The American Role," p. 243.

40. The democratization of Japan after World War II was unique (distinct from most democratization struggles) in that the Japanese constitution was democracy given by a foreign occupier against the desires of Japanese elites who had no desire for real democratic reform. SCAP captured the democratic desires of the Japanese people. For an alternative look at the democratization process more typical of struggles for democratization, see: Peter McDonough, Samuel H. Barnes, and Antonio López Pina, *The Cultural Dynamics of Democratization in Spain.*

41. Funk, "Japan's Constitution and U.N. Obligations," p. 372.

42. Kades, "The American Role," p. 242.

43. The new *kenpou* was finally passed out of the Diet, with only five members dissenting (only a simple majority was required for passage). It should be noted, however, that the Japanese elite have never been happy with the way the constitution was forced upon them. Witness former Prime Minister Yasuhiro Nakasone's comments in Gibney, *The Pacific Century: Reinventing Japan* (#5), where he asserts that it was a wrong done to Japan.

44. Funk, "Japan's Constitution and U.N. Obligations," pp. 373–75.

45. Ibid., p. 376, and Kades, "The American Role," p. 237. "In support of Yoshida's concern about the misuse of self-defense wars, Kades notes that General Tojo, who was both prime minister and army minister during World War II, testified that Japanese wartime efforts, including the bombing of Pearl Harbor, were not aggressive acts but acts of self-defense." Funk, "Japan's Constitution and U.N. Obligations, p. 376, note 86. The phrase Yoshida used, "War of Greater

East Asia," is the Japanese term for what we call the Pacific theater of World War II.

46. Percy R. Luney, Jr. and Kazuyuki Takahashi, eds., *Japanese Constitutional Law*, pp. 72–74.

47. Auer, "Article Nine of Japan's Constitution," p. 176, and Kades, "The American Role," pp. 225–36.

48. Auer, "Article Nine of Japan's Constitution," p. 177.

49. Royer, "The Demise of the World's First Pacifist Constitution," p. 782.

50. Cited by Royer, "The Demise of the World's First Pacifist Constitution," p. 782, note 149 (emphasis added).

51. Jiro Kodera, Director First International Economic Affairs Division of the Japanese Ministry of Foreign Affairs, interview by author, 20 May 1998, Tokyo, tape recording in author's personal possession.

52. Auer, "Article Nine of Japan's Constitution," p. 177.

53. Ibid.

54. It is important to note that this is not a law or a constitutional provision but merely a policy statement that was subscribed to in 1967 by the government of the time. It has never been put into or given the status of law. Auer, "Article Nine of Japan's Constitution," p. 178, note 31.

55. Auer, "Article Nine of Japan's Constitution," pp. 178–79, as cited from K. Masuhara, *Nihon no Boei* (Japan's Defense), 1961, at p. 59.

56. Ibid.

57. It is important to note that, unlike the United States, the majority of the Japanese supreme court is made up of nonlawyers who are political appointees.

58. Funk, "Japan's Constitution and U.N. Obligations," pp. 379–83, and Royer, "The Demise of the World's First Pacifist Constitution," p. 782.

59. For background on this and on the separation of executive and judicial powers, see Madsen, "The Japanese Constitution and Self-Defense Forces," especially Part III.

60. Madsen, "The Japanese Constitution and Self-Defense Forces," p. 561.

61. Karel van Wolferen, *The Enigma of Japanese Power*, p. 41.

62. This minimal level gradually increased as Japan's economic power grew and the burden of the Cold War increased for the United States. In the 1970s, defense spending was limited to less than 1 percent of GDP, but in the 1980s it broke the 1 percent barrier for the first time since the 1960s, though it has always remained around 1 percent. For a more complete analysis of this issue, see Auer, "Article Nine of Japan's Constitution," pp. 180–81.

63. Michael W. Chinworth, ed., *Inside Japan's Defense: Technology, Economics & Strategy*, pp. 26–27.

64. Auer, "Article Nine of Japan's Constitution," p. 184.

65. Chinworth, *Inside Japan's Defense*, p. 9.

66. The concept of *gaiatsu* will be extensively discussed and analyzed in chapter 5.

67. Chinworth, *Inside Japan's Defense*, p. 9.

68. For a complete analysis, see Auer, "Article Nine of Japan's Constitution,"

69. Royer, "The Demise of the World's First Pacifist Constitution," p. 787.

Notes to Chapter 3

1. Takashi Inoguchi, "Japan's Response to the Gulf Crisis: An Analytic Overview," p. 257.

2. Jiro Yamaguchi, "The Gulf War and the Transformation of Japanese Constitutional Politics," p. 155.

3. Inoguchi, "Japan's Response to the Gulf Crisis," pp. 257–58.

4. Ibid., p. 258.

5. Ibid.

6. Kendrik F. Royer, "The Demise of the World's First Pacifist Constitution," p. 790.

7. Shinichi Kitaoka, "A Green Light for Japanese Peace-keepers," p. 42.

8. As prime minister, Kaifu led both the Diet and the Cabinet (selected by the prime minister) in fulfilling executive functions. He was also the leader of the Liberal Democratic Party (LDP). Normally the leader of the LDP is a fairly strong politician, but Kaifu was not. Kaifu was elected head of the LDP and thus prime minister in August 1989, after a series of scandals toppled his immediate predecessors. Kaifu was a compromise candidate in that he was squeaky clean and not likely to be touched by scandal. His faction within the LDP was small and not very influential. He was seen as a nice man, but not really suited to the problems he would face as prime minister during the Gulf crisis. This inadequacy was especially evident during the debate on the first PKO Bill (to be discussed below).

9. Robert B. Funk, "Japan's Constitution and U.N. Obligations in the Persian Gulf War," p. 385. Bracketed statement added.

10. Ibid.

11. Ibid, pp. 387–88.

12. Lieutenant Colonel Andrew H. N. Kim, "Japan and Peace-keeping Operations," pp. 24–25.

13. The United Nations Charter, Article 1, Paragraph 1.

14. The United Nations Charter, Article 2, Paragraphs 5 and 25 (emphasis added).

15. Hirofumi Iseri, "Clearing the Mist from the Peace-keeping Debate," p. 45.

16. Reproduced from the unofficial translation provided by the Embassy of Japan in Washington, D. C. "Japan: Law Concerning Cooperation for United Nations Peace-keeping Operations and Other Operations," pp. 215–16 (3–35) as summarized by Shunji Yanai, "The Law Concerning Cooperation for United Nations Peace-Keeping Operations and Other Operations," p. 41.

17. Jiro Yamaguchi, "The Gulf War and the Transformation of Japanese Constitutional Politics," p. 167.

18. Shunji Yanai, "The Law Concerning Cooperation for United Nations Peace-Keeping Operations and Other Operations," p. 58.

19. Sandra Madsen, "The Japanese Constitution and Self-Defense Forces," pp. 574–77.

20. Iseri, "Clearing the Mist from the Peace-keeping Debate," p. 46.

21. Ibid. One of the strongest criticisms of Japan in the postwar years is in the way the Japanese refuse to educate their children on the mistakes of the past and World War II. An example of this failure is that of a Japanese junior-high history textbook that is used in northern Japan. It contains only four pages covering World War II. Many Japanese teachers avoid the issue of World War II altogether by simply not finishing the textbook before the end of the school year or stopping at the beginning of the twentieth century.

22. Ibid.

23. From news accounts of March 1992 in the *Japan Times* and the *Daily Yomiuri*.

24. As quoted by Yoshitaka Sasaki, "Japan's Undue International Contribution," p. 261.

25. Victor Fic, "The Japanese PKO Bill," p. 30.

26. Ibid., p. 31.

27. All four of the following are outlined in further detail by Atsushi Odawara, "The Kaifu Bungle," pp. 7–12.

28. Fic, "The Japanese PKO Bill," pp. 32–33.

29. While the public generally sympathized with the efforts to stop the PKO Bill, the "ox walk" tactic seemed to backfire and caused people to view it as childish and disgusting. It is considered one of the major reasons why the SDP (the largest opposition group that engineered the "ox walk") fared so badly in the next election.

30. Fic, "The Japanese PKO Bill," pp. 32–33.

31. Kim, "Japan and Peace-keeping Operations," pp. 22–33.

32. Interview by the author with one of the Golan Heights' commanders, 5 June 1998, in Tokyo, Japan.

33. Akiho Shibata, "Japanese Peacekeeping Legislation and Recent Developments in U.N. Operations," p. 346.

34. Jiro Yamaguchi, "The Gulf War and the Transformation of Japanese Constitutional Politics," p. 167.

35. Japan served on the Security Council during the years 1958–59, 1966–67, 1971–72, 1975–76, 1981–82, 1987–88, 1992–93, 1997–98, and 2005–6. See Sadako Ogata, "The Changing Role of Japan in the United Nations," p. 31, note 2. While Japan's public effort for a permanent seat on the Security Council has been only recent, its Ministry of Foreign Affairs has been making an ongoing effort since the 1960s to position Japan to gain a permanent seat.

36. J. A. A. Stockwin, *Japan: Divided Politics in a Growth Economy,* as cited by Inoguchi, "Japan's Response to the Gulf Crisis," p. 268.

37. Takashi Inoguchi, *Japan 1960–1980: Party Election Pledges,* as cited by Inoguchi, "Japan's Response to the Gulf Crisis," p. 268.

38. Fic, "The Japanese PKO Bill," p. 30. Ozawa and Ishihara differ in ways to bring this about.

39. Royer, "The Demise of the World's First Pacifist Constitution," pp. 800–801, note 247.

40. Sasaki, "Japan's Undue International Contribution," p. 264.

41. Japanese *manga* comics are read, not just by children, but also by adults from all walks of life.

42. David E. Sanger, "U.S. and Japanese Told to Resolve Dispute on Trade—Blunt Warning to Both—New World Trade Chief Calls Conflict a 'Delicate Matter'—Nationalism Is Cited," p. A1. Nationalism is cited as a primary reason for the intensity of this dispute.

43. Inoguchi, "Japan's Response to the Gulf Crisis," p. 261, and Kenji Urata, "The Peace and Security of Japan," pp. 75–86.

44. The sanctions imposed on Japan were due to Japan's war of aggression in China. Some revisionist historians in Japan have tried (in many ways successfully) to use the sanctions as an excuse to justify the surprise attack on Pearl Harbor. These historians claim that Japan's war in China was a war of liberation, intended to free China of colonial influences. The evidence of Japanese actions clearly shows this claim to be false. To this day, the Chinese harbor a hatred for the Japanese for the atrocities they committed in this "war of liberation." Japan's failure to recognize and

take responsibility for its actions is a source of deep resentment and suspicion for most Chinese, and many East Asians in general. This legacy continues to haunt Japanese foreign policy today as actions by Japan that would appear to be normal for any other nation are greeted with suspicion by East Asian nations and China in particular. For more on Japanese atrocities during World War II, see Iris Chang, *The Rape of Nanking: The Forgotten Holocaust of World War II.*

45. Nicholas D. Kristof, "A Big Exception for a Nation of Apologizers," pp. A1 and A4.

46. Some teachers do buck the system and teach World War II honestly, warts and all, but they risk the Japanese adage: "The nail that sticks up gets hammered down."

47. See the comment made by Chinese Communist Party General Secretary Jiang Zemin, page 43 of this chapter and note 22 on the same page.

48. As quoted by Fusakazu Izumura, "Should Japan Get a Permanent Seat on the U.N. Security Council?" p. 54.

49. Ryozo Kato, then director general, Foreign Policy Bureau of the Japanese Ministry of Foreign Affairs and current ambassador to the United States, interview by the author, 21 May 1998, tape recording in author's personal possession.

50. Tendencies discovered during field research interviews will be discussed at length in chapter 4.

51. Kei Hata, member of the House of Councillors of the Japanese Diet, interview by the author, 18 May 1998, Tokyo, tape recording in author's personal possession; Ichita Yamamoto, member of the House of Councillors of the Japanese Diet, interview by the author, 18 June 1998, Tokyo, tape recording in author's personal possession.

52. Nicholas D. Kristof, "Japan Expresses Regret of a Sort for the War," pp. A1, A11.

Notes to Chapter 4

1. Charles F. Hermann, "Changing Course: When Governments Choose to Redirect Foreign Policy," p. 3.

2. It should be noted that at the time of this writing, there is a strong movement, both within the LDP and without, to amend, revise, or completely rewrite the Japanese constitution. While the success of these efforts may still be a long while off, it does lend credence to the argument that Japan is on the path to normalization of its foreign policy.

3. Parts of a previous version of this chapter was published in "Alternative Visions of Japanese Security: The Role of Absolute and Relative Gains in the Making of Japanese Security Policy."

4. Some Japanese politicians, especially from the LDP, see the possibility of amending the constitution as possible if that process is done as a whole-scale revision rather than just simply targeting Article Nine. There also seem to be some efforts to couch the need for a rewriting of the constitution in nationalistic terms by emphasizing that the *constitution* was written largely by Americans and is not Japanese in origin (see former Prime Minister Nakasone's comments in the PBS video series by Alex Gibney, *The Pacific Century: Reinventing Japan*). As previously mentioned, the LDP has formed a constitutional committee to draft possible changes or amendments to the constitution as a whole. Some (mostly in the LDP) are hopeful, but many (mostly opposition members and members of the SDP) are openly skeptical. Interview with Kei Hata, member of the House of Councillors of the Japanese Diet, interview by the author, 18 May 1998, Tokyo, tape recording in author's personal possession.

5. For more on this concept see: Martin W. Sampson III and Stephen G. Walker, "Cultural Norms and National Roles: A Comparison of Japan and France," pp. 105–22.

6. My interviews with several members of the opposition parties and even with the Socialists (SDP), who were in a power-sharing coalition with the LDP at the time, confirm the need and desire for political consensus. Those interviewed expressed strong displeasure with the heavy-handedness that was occurring in Japanese politics. In other words, they felt that their views and concerns were being ignored by the party leaders, thus creating a loss of harmony.

7. The Social Democratic Party of Japan was the predecessor of the current SDP.

8. A direct contrast to this concern about balance and consensus would be the United States system, which is probably the most open to outside influences, including foreign ones. The majority in Congress over the last twenty-five years has demonstrated an increasing willingness to push or block legislation regardless of the views of the opposition. This trend has been largely attributed to loose American campaign-finance laws and the fallout of the Watergate scandal. Money buys influence in Washington, but Congress is limited to what constituents will *not* oppose at the polls. Based on Reinhard Drifte, "The U.S.-Japan-China Security Triangle and the Future of East Asian Security," in Laurent Goetschel, ed., *Security in a Globalized World: Risks and Opportunities,* p. 1, and a conversation with former Republican congressman and minority whip, John Rhodes of Arizona, at the University Club, Arizona State University, Tempe, Arizona, spring 1996, author's personal notes in author's personal possession.

9. In PPP (purchasing power parity) terms, China has already passed Japan in economic size; however, Japan has less than 10 percent of China's population.

10. Sheryl WuDunn and Nicholas D. Kristof, *New York Times,* 1 September 1999, Internet edition, www.nytimes.com/yr/mo/day/news/financial/japan-debt.html.

11. Some of these overseas jobs are designed to gain access to foreign markets and/or to escape high wages in Japan, but many are jobs that Japanese workers simply do not want to do anymore because they are menial or physically hard.

12. The figure is the ratio of the total working-age population to the retirement-age population (the actual ratio is probably lower when nonworkers from working-age groups, such as housewives, are factored in) and come from the (Japanese) National Institute of Population and Social Security Research. For more on Japan's aging population, see Milton Ezrati, "Japan's Aging Economics," pp. 96–104.

13. Ibid.

14. Interview taken from John W. Kennedy, "Tokyo: Indifferent to the Risen Son," p. 10.

15. Many couples cite the high cost of raising and educating children as the main reason for not having children or having only one child. Japanese municipal governments are so alarmed at this trend that they are offering financial incentives for couples to have more children, such as paying for the medical costs and the first year's worth of diapers and formula. These incentives are having little effect. Those couples that do have children are not willing to risk them in dangerous international conflicts. In several of my interviews with Japanese elites, the interviewee cited the need for the country to concentrate its resources at home, as Japan is facing tremendous domestic issues that require all its resources. The clear implication is that, while Japan is willing to do its part to protect its interests, it is unwilling to go the extra mile and place itself at risk for the interests of others (more on this below).

16. Ezrati, "Japan's Aging Economics," p. 101.

17. This "family" illustration is based on the United States-Japan relationship since World War II, when the United States wrote Japan's constitution and established many of its governmental institutions and norms. The "mother" in this scenario is the democratic values and economics that both nations share.

18. During the occupation, the United States broke up the *kiretsu* (cartels) that worked hand-in-hand with the government and gave legal legitimacy and independence to trade unions and others. This permitted Japan to develop a much more truly capitalist economic system than it had before the war and it laid the foundation for Japan's post-war prosperity and economic boom.

19. Nicholas D. Kristof, "Seeking To Be Tokyo's Governor, Politician Attacks U.S. Presence," p. A12.

20. MOFA officials interviewed almost unanimously and in rote form stated that the "goals" of Japanese foreign policy were "[t]he safety and prosperity of the nation." When probed for specifics, these officials had difficulty giving any, and they tended to repeat the same mantra, "The safety and prosperity of the nation." This "goal" of the nation seems to be drilled into bureaucrats working for MOFA from day one as their raison d' être. While this seems a good statement of purpose for MOFA, it does not specify tangible goals for the nation as a whole.

21. Councillor Takemi has worked to create greater awareness of foreign-policy issues by championing the creation of subcommittees in the Diet and having them hold hearings and issue policy statements rather than rely on MOFA, as has been done traditionally. He was also instrumental in the formation and adaptation of LDP's foreign policy platform independent of MOFA.

22. Ukeru Magosaki, "New Diplomatic Challenges in East Asia."

23. Barry Buzan, Ole Wæver, and Jaap de Wilde, *Security: A New Framework for Analysis*, pp. 2–5 and 239.

24. Ibid., p. 1.

25. Hans J. Morgenthau, *Politics Among Nations.*

26. Buzan et al., *Security*, p. 25.

27. Ibid., pp. 4–5.

28. Ibid., pp. 28–31.

29. Ibid., p. 11.

30. Ibid. The rise of global terrorism may change this situation eventually; however, it is important to note that even terrorism (in its current form) does not travel well. It is easier for groups like Al-Qaeda to operate in Iraq than in the United States. Culture, language, and even religion offer formable barriers to would-be terrorists.

31. Buzan et al., *Security*, pp. 11–12.

32. Ibid., p. 13.

33. Ichiro Ozawa, *Blueprint for a New Japan: The Rethinking of a Nation.*

34. Shintaro Ishihara, *The Japan That Can Say "No."*

35. An example of this lack of foresight and desire for petty gratification is a Diet member who expressed a desire to see the American economic "bubble" collapse as the Japanese "bubble economy" did in 1989, just for the chance to prove to America that Japan was not as dumb as America thought, and that such a collapse could happen to anyone. The member clearly had not thought through the impact that an American economic collapse would have on the already fragile Japanese economy, not to mention the disastrous impact on the rest of the world.

36. Upon completion of my interview with Representative Eisuke Mori, Representative Mori asked to interview me. He proceeded to ask a series of questions about Japan's international economic options. He was clearly looking for a solution to Japan's economic crisis that he could campaign on and possibly implement. Representative Mori clearly understood that if Japan was to have a larger role in the world, it needed to solve its economic problems first. The question for him was how to sell a workable solution to the electorate in a politically acceptable way that would not throw Japan into social turmoil at the same time. Eisuke Mori, member of the House of Representatives of the Japanese Diet, interview by the author, 22 May 1998, Tokyo, tape recording in author's personal possession.

37. Interview with a high-ranking MOFA official who asked that his comments not be attributed or quoted directly with his name attached. Interview by author, during May–June 1998, Tokyo, tape recording, in author's personal possession, emphasis added.

38. The Yoshida Doctrine is basically a doctrine of self-help. Japan was maximizing its situation given its limitations.

39. Joseph M. Grieco, "Anarchy and the Limits of Cooperation: A Realist Critique of the Newest Liberal Institutionalism," pp. 118–19.

40. Hans J. Morgenthau, *Politics Among Nations.*

41. For the purposes of this book, the terms "institutionalism" and "neoliberalism" are used interchangeably and are seen as synonymous.

42. I am indebted to my friend and colleague Tong Ge for introducing me to this concept of a realistic approach to institutionalism. In her master's thesis, Tong Ge argued that, in spite of a long-standing (and continuing) opposition to institutionalist approaches to foreign policy, China is now pursuing institutionalist foreign-policy options out of a realistic need for international legitimacy. That is to say, China sees a realist need to use institutions for its foreign-policy needs. In the same way, Japan seems to have used an institutionalist approach for realist purposes. For more on this concept, see Tong Ge, "Realism and Chinese Foreign Policy in East and Southeast Asia in the Post-Cold War Era."

43. Grieco, "Anarchy and the Limits of Cooperation," p. 117.

44. The United States-Japan Security Treaty is viewed by this author as a bilateral institution with multilateral implications rather than simply as a bilateral security arrangement between Japan and the United States. This view is because of the three-fold role that the treaty plays, providing Japan its security guarantee, promoting East Asian security, and psychologically benefiting other East Asian nations by "keeping the Japanese genie in the bottle." Japan is being very realist by depending on the Security Treaty, because it would find it very difficult, politically, to develop the SDF into the modern "military" that it is today without the political cover the treaty provided. Japan did the most realist thing it could do, given the hand that it was dealt after World War II.

45. Sheldon W. Simon, "International Relations Theory and Southeast Asian Security," p. 6.

46. I would disagree with the hypothesis that the United States is currently in decline. In fact, the opposite would seem to be occurring, in that American power is on the rise and that other nations are currently trying to ally themselves with the United States or to counterbalance the United States through other alliances.

47. Simon, "International Relations Theory and Southeast Asian Security," p. 7.

48. Grieco, "Anarchy and the Limits of Cooperation," p. 118. The idea of a partner's

exiting from a relationship is very significant for Japan in light of its fears of abandonment by the United States. Japan can easily be seen as profiting more than the United States from the relationship, and thus, according to Grieco, is a possible candidate for abandonment by the United States. As a nation that is fundamentally practicing realism, Japan realizes this imbalance; hence its fears of abandonment.

49. To be clear, a nation facing a *net* loss of, say, 100 points in *absolute* gains verses a *net* loss of 50 points in *relative* gains would be likely to choose the relative gains over the absolute gains in order to keep the "game" close, so that as the situation improves for them, they have less ground to recover. This is a delaying action, if you will. It is important to remember that in this scenario there are no gains only a choice of greater or smaller losses. Other authors (Robert Powell) have argued as to the types of *gains* that a state practicing realism might chose; this book, however, is arguing as to the choice a state facing two different levels of *losses* might make in order to position itself for the future. In other words, a state will choose to minimize losses and focus on the future.

50. This concept of "localized rationality" partially comes from comments by Paul Bracken and Ralph Cossa at the National Bureau of Asian Research's conference at Arizona State University, Tempe, Arizona, held on April 27, 2000 (the author's personal notes). This localized rationality reflects thinking from the perspective of those locally making the decision. It may not appear to be rational from an outsider's perspective, but it is very rational for those making the decision. Examples of this are Saddam Hussein's decision to invade Kuwait, in spite of the strong interdependent relationship between the two states, and Japan's decision to attack Pearl Harbor, in spite of the fact that it knew that it would most probably lose a war with the United States. Both of these cases led to disaster, but the same does not have to be the case. A "localized rationality" may be the best choice for a nation.

51. Grieco, "Anarchy and the Limits of Cooperation," pp. 116–40. Robert Powell, "Absolute and Relative Gains in International Relations Theory," pp. 1303–20, and "Anarchy in International Relations Theory: The Neorealist-Neoliberal Debate," pp. 313–44.

52. Grieco, "Anarchy and the Limits of Cooperation."

53. Powell, "Absolute and Relative Gains."

54. In addition to the listed benefits, Japan is still exempt, because of the treaty, from having to provide its own security. In many ways, part of the Yoshida Doctrine still works for Japan. It does not have to invest as much in its own defense as it would if the United States were not allied with it.

55. Off-the-record interview with a government researcher in the employ of the Japan Defense Agency (JDA), Tokyo, May–June 1998, tape recording in the personal possession of the author.

56. For more on Japan's role in regional forumsa, see Paul Midford, "From Reactive State to Cautious Leader: The Nakayama Proposal and Japan's Role in Promoting the Creation of the ASEAN Regional Forum (ARF)."

57. Gilles Paris, "Le Japonais Kochiro Matsuura da succeder a Federico Mayor a la tete de l'Unesco."

58. Task Force on Foreign Relations for the Prime Minister, *Basic Strategies for Japan's Foreign Policy in the 21st Century New Era, New Vision, New Diplomacy* (emphasis added).

59. Ibid.

60. Yoichiro Sato, "Modeling Japan's Foreign Economic Policy with the United States" in Akitoshi Miyashita and Yoichiro Sato, eds. *Japanese Foreign Policy in Asia and the Pacific,* p. 27.

61. Ibid., pp. 27–30.

62. Japan can always draw a new line if and when there is pressure to give up some of its fishing industry.

63. To truly understand the security benefit of a permanent seat (called the P5), on the Security Council, one must consider what current members' international standings would be like without their P5 status. Consider France; without P5 status, it would still be a nuclear power, but its voice would be reduced to that of a large European state, such as Germany (also a candidate for permanent status). The same would also be true for China; it would still be the world largest nation in terms of population, but its ability to dictate or moderate the actions of the other P5 members would be greatly reduced.

Notes to Chapter 5

1. World of Quotes, www.worldofquotes.com/author/George-F.-Kennan/1/index.html.

2. The inequalities in the Japanese electoral system resulted in a gap between rural votes and some city votes that amounted to 10 to 1 difference in favor of the rural districts. For more information, see Raymond V. Christensen and Paul E. Johnson, "Toward a Context-Rich Analysis of Electoral Systems: The Japanese Example," pp. 575–598.

3. Major Takashi Motomatsu of the Japanese Ground Self-Defense Forces and former commander of a SDF PKO mission to the Golan Heights, current station, Planning Section of the Plans and Operations Department, Japan Defense Agency. Interview by the author, 5 June 1998, Tokyo, author's notes in author's personal possession.

4. Charles F. Hermann, "Changing Course: When Governments Choose to Redirect Foreign Policy," p. 3.

5. Ibid.

6. Ibid., p. 13.

7. The idea here is that leaders or governments that implement a foreign policy can be faced with three possible results of that policy: (1) They may be faced with positive feedback and may thus choose to accelerate or enhance the existing policy. (2) The policy maker may choose to continue the foreign policy (the status quo) with incremental changes in the absence of either positive or negative feedback. Or (3) in the face of negative feedback from a foreign policy, the policy maker may choose to change the foreign policy or implement a new one. This last choice obviously reflects restructuring and is the case for Japan. The same policy maker that implemented the policy is making the change. The second choice can involve restructuring to a lesser extent. However, the first choice is foreign-policy change but not restructuring. All foreign-policy restructuring is foreign-policy change but not all foreign-policy change is restructuring. Foreign-policy restructuring is the result of negative feedback, causing the makers of the policy to redirect (restructure) their foreign policy.

8. Hermann, "Changing Course," p. 4.

9. Ibid., p. 5.

10. Off-the-record interview with a government researcher in the employ of the

Japan Defense Agency, Tokyo, May–June 1998, tape recording in the personal possession of the author.

11. Grieco, "Anarchy and the Limits of Cooperation," p. 118 (emphasis added).

12. Japan's quest for allies while still maintaining its ties with the United States will be discussed in detail in chapter 6.

13. Since the Korean War it is evident that the United States regrets allowing Article Nine to be part of the Japanese constitution, no matter who the author was.

14. Hermann, "Changing Course," pp. 10–11 (emphasis added).

15. The Cold War's end was the system change, but only the Persian Gulf War brought the realization that the Cold War was over and that the system had changed. In other words the Persian Gulf War constituted a wake-up call for Japan.

16. Hermann, "Changing Course," p. 6.

17. Ibid.

18. Ibid., p. 7.

19. "Cybernetics," *Oxford American Dictionary.*

20. Hermann, "Changing Course," p. 9.

21. Ibid., pp. 8–9.

22. Ibid., p. 10.

23. Ibid., pp. 10–11.

24. Ibid., p. 11.

25. Ibid.

26. Hermann, "Changing Course," p. 14.

27. Ibid.

28. This text is primarily interested in the decision-making process as a whole rather than its stages. The detail needed to discuss the impact of each of these stages in detail on the Japanese decision to pass the PKO Law is beyond the scope of this chapter and this book. Suffice it to say that the stages of Japanese decision making tend to closely follow the stages Hermann listed.

29. George F. Kennan, *Memoirs 1925–1950,* pp. 54–55. The author is very grateful to his friend and colleague Seng Tan, who introduced him to this quote.

30. Yukihiko Ikeda, former foreign minister and member of the House of Representatives of the Japanese Diet, interview by the author, 16 June 1998, Tokyo, tape recording in author's personal possession.

31. It was not felt that this subtle reminder would in any way bias the interviewee's answers, as it is the norm for change to take place around us and few notice it until it is pointed out to them. This subtle prompt was designed only to awaken the respondent to the issues; not to direct or prompt answers.

32. Eisuke Mori, member of the House of Representatives of the Japanese Diet. Interview by the author, 22 May 1998, Tokyo, tape recording in author's personal possession.

33. Off-the-record interview (the interviewee did not want to be cited by name) at interviewee's request at the Japanese Ministry of Foreign Affairs, Tokyo May–June 1998, tape recording in author's personal possession.

34. Kei Hata, member of the House of Councillors of the Japanese Diet, interview by the author, 18 May 1998, Tokyo, tape recording in author's personal possession.

35. This response is, in and of itself, very fascinating, in that it shows the low priority of foreign policy on the agenda of many of the elites that are responsible for making foreign policy decisions or are at least part of the process. Hideo Usui, mem-

ber of the House of Representatives of the Japanese Diet and former defense minister and vice Defense Agency minister (career ministry appointment), interviews by the author, 26 and 29 May 1998, Tokyo, tape recording in author's personal possession.

36. Based on my conversations with multiple people connected with the JDA, it seems to me that low-profile attitude may be changing. It seems that the success of the respective PKO missions has given the JDA confidence in advocating its own cause in the debate over its role in Japanese foreign policy.

37. I was continually impressed with the quality of the people working for MOFA, but at the same time it was disappointing to see such bright minds being locked into the organizational box, unable to freely explore and debate ideas. A part of this restriction is thought to be due to Japanese social and cultural norms, which govern every aspect of Japanese life.

38. Jiro Kodera, director, First International Economic Affairs Division of the Japanese Ministry of Foreign Affairs, interview by author, 20 May 1998, Tokyo, tape recording in author's personal possession.

39. T. J. Pempel, "Structural 'Gaitsu.'" For more on this topic, see also the August 1999 online discussion of this subject between T. J. Pempel and Richard Katz, ssj-forum@iss.u-tokyo.ac.jp.

40. *Daily Yomiuri,* "Defense Legislation Leaves Some Questions Unanswered," 27 May 1999, Internet edition, www.yomiuri.co.jp/newse/0527p017.htm.

41. Noboru Yamaguchi, colonel, Ground Self Defense Forces, Deputy Chief of Defense Planning Division, Ground Staff Office, Japan Defense Agency, interview by author 2 June 1998, Tokyo, Japan, tape recording in author's personal possession.

42. Ryozo Kato, director general, Foreign Policy Bureau of the Japanese Ministry of Foreign Affairs, interview by author, 21 May 1998, Tokyo, tape recording in author's personal possession.

43. Ibid.

44. Witness the spring 1999 Tokyo governor's race and the accusations by candidate Shintaro Ishihara in the *New York Times,* 26 March 1999, p. A12.

45. Interview with Ryozo Kato.

46. Yoko Takagi noted this in her paper that an independent foreign policy vis-à-vis the United States assumes conflict in areas that have no conflict. She was very surprised by Kato's attitude toward the United States. Yoko Takagi, "Japan's Foreign Policy: Japan's Decision Making of the Foreign Policy and the PKO Law [sic]" pp. 10–11.

47. A notable exception to this view was Professor Osomu Iishi of the Institute of Oriental Culture at Tokyo University. Professor Iishi expressed great dismay over this lack of discernment as to Japan's position and the benefits gained in the world as the United States' ally. Osamu Iishi, Professor Institute of Oriental Culture, Tokyo University, interview by author, 29 May 1998, Tokyo, tape recording in author's personal possession.

48. Only one younger person interviewed seemed to want to stay in the older established ways of doing things. He was the son of a senior LDP member and had previously unsuccessfully sought election to the Diet. Part of the reason for his lack of success in spite of excellent connections and a family name to go with them might be his old-fashioned style of politics, which is not in tune with the country as a whole. Many of the younger Diet members have young and hip campaign images (one even gave me a copy of a pop music CD he had cut). Many of their news clippings show them as men (or women) of the people. They are seen singing karaoke, drinking beer, and laughing with constituents. Old-style campaigning and paying one's dues to the party do not seem to matter so much any more.

49. It should be noted that my example, Hajime Funada lost his next election but this was largely due to an affair he had had that went public in the tabloid press.

50. *Interflux*—"being among a continuous succession of changes. From the prefix *inter,* meaning 'between or among,' and *flux* meaning a continuous succession of changes, *in a state of flux.*" *Oxford American Dictionary.*

51. Ryozo Kato made an observation (to be discussed in a later chapter)—to the effect that Japan needs only to wait until the World War II generation dies out, and all will be forgotten—as proof of this "head-in-the-ground" mentality. The longer Japan waits the harder it will be to forgive.

52. The movie *Pride* is a revisionist attempt to rewrite Japan's wartime prime minister's life so that he is an Asian hero who stood up to the United States and the West and was martyred for his efforts. For more on this subject, see Nicholas D. Kristof, "A Tojo Battles History, for Grandpa and for Japan," Setsuko Kamiya and Kanako Takahara, "Tojo Film Opens to Applause, Criticism," p. 2, and Ryuichiro Hosokawa, "Japanese Need a Good Dose of 'Pride,'" p. 18.

53. Ezra F. Vogel, *Japan as Number One: Lessons for America.*

54. *Yomiuri Shimbun,* 4 August 1999. www.yomiyuri.co.jp/ newse/0805s007.htm.

55. Howard W. French, "Two Wary Neighbors Unite to Confront North Korean Arms," pp. A1, A6.

Notes to Chapter 6

1. Donald Snow, *National Security: Defense Policy in a Changed International Order,* p. 24.

2. Hideo Usui, member of the House of Representatives of the Japanese Diet and former defense minister and vice Defense Agency minister (career ministry appointment), interview by the author, 26 and 29 May 1998, Tokyo, tape recording in author's personal possession.

3. Masashi Nishihara, "Japanese Defense Policy: Issues and Options," p. 4 (emphasis added).

4. Shigeru Ishiba, member of the House of Representatives of the Japanese Diet (LDP), interview by the author, 4 June 1998, Tokyo, tape recording in author's personal possession.

5. Pronounced in Japanese *katakana:* Ja-pa-nu pas-su-i-n-gu. This term was used in many interviews by the interviewees and even commented on by several academics as a major policy worry for Japan.

6. The Clinton administration told the Japanese government that Clinton wanted to be in the United States to spend the Fourth of July with U.S. troops, some of which were stationed in Hawaii. As a compromise, it was suggested that Clinton stop in Okinawa on the Fourth of July and visit the troops there. Japan's Prime Minister Ryutaro Hashimoto could then travel to Okinawa and be briefed by Clinton on his China visit. This compromise would have permitted all sides to save face, as Clinton could say he was visiting U.S. troops and thus in principle, complying with China's request, and Japan could feel that it was not passed over by the United States. The Clinton administration rejected this compromise, however, and Japan was left with the feeling that it was ignored by its only ally—the United States—even though Secretary of State Madeleine Albright did brief the prime minister in the end. Current U.S. Secretary of Defense Donald Rumsfeld recently passed over Japan on his October 2005 visit to China.

7. Ted Galen Carpenter, "Roiling Asia: U.S. Coziness with China Upsets the Neighbors," p. 2 (emphasis added). The closeness of the Clinton administration's relationship to China is especially ironic or interesting in that during the 1992 presidential season, the Clinton campaign continually hammered at President George H. W. Bush's policy of engaging China, claiming that coddling China too much in the wake of the 1989 Tiananmen Square massacre. In a 1 May 1998 speech at Arizona State University, former President George H. W. Bush sarcastically noted Clinton's change of heart by saying that "he [Clinton] had finally got it [Clinton's China policy of engagement] right." Author's personal notes.

8. Several of those I interviewed, both inside and outside of government, stated off the record that they were worried about the Clinton administration's being influenced by China. The recent strains in Sino-American relations—as the result of the bombing of the Chinese embassy in Belgrade, the Cox Report, the emergency landing of a U.S. Navy spy plane in China (after colliding with a Chinese fighter jet that killed the Chinese pilot), and the difficulty of getting WTO through Congress—are probably a relief in Japan. It is important to note that several other interviewees scoffed at the idea that the United States would abandon Japan in favor of China, but the reality is that many in Japan fear or at least wonder about the possibility of such an occurrence.

9. Masafumi Iishi, director, Foreign Policy Planning Division, MOFA, described abandonment as a "worst case" scenario, for which Japanese officials need to plan. Masafumi Iishi, interview by author, 1 June 1998, Tokyo, tape recording in author's personal possession.

10. Ken Yamada, "Searching for Ways to Coexist: Clinton's First Trip to China," *Mainichi Shimbun,* 25 June 1998 as cited by Carpenter, "Roiling Asia," p. 4.

11. Carpenter, "Roiling Asia," p. 5.

12. For more on the traditional definition of what constitutes national security, see Snow, *National Security,* and Barry Buzan, Ole Waever, and Jaap de Wilde, *Security: A New Framework for Analysis.*

13. In many ways, the greatest legacy left by General Douglas MacArthur is Japan's constitution. In spite of its flaws, the Japanese constitution is supported and respected by the Japanese people. The fact that it has never been amended is a testament to its durability as an institution in Japanese society.

14. Since the test firing of the Taepodong-1 by North Korea in August 1998, in response to this threat to the Japanese homeland, the Japanese government has sought appropriations for the purchase of midair refueling aircraft. If acquired, these planes would give Japan a limited power projection capability *if* Japan also acquired bomber capabilities for its fighter aircraft. The rationale behind the proposed purchase in light of the current interpretation of Article Nine is that it would be an act of "self-defense" to destroy missiles that threaten the Japanese homeland in time of war. For more information on this topic, see: *Yomiuri Shimbun,* "Appropriation Sought for Refueling Aircraft," 21 July 1999, Internet edition, www.yomiuri.co.jp/newse/ 0722p001.htm.

15. Snow, *National Security,* p. 30.

16. Ibid., p. 24.

17. For the purposes of this chapter, the terms *comprehensive* and *alternative* security will be treated as synonymous.

18. When asked about Japanese foreign-policy goals, every interviewee from

MOFA immediately said, "The security and prosperity of the nation." MOFA offi-cials had to be pushed to give specific responses of how to achieve this "security and prosperity of the nation." None of the other interviewees ever gave this re-sponse to the same question.

19. For more on the concept of *wa,* see Martin W. Sampson III and Stephen G. Walker, "Cultural Norms and National Roles: A Comparison of Japan and France."

20. Muthiah Alagappa, "Comprehensive Security: Interpretations in ASEAN Coun-tries," pp. 50–78; Alan Dupont, "Concepts of Security,"pp. 1–15. See also Seng Tan, "Constituting Asia-Pacific (In)Security: A Radical Constructivist Study in 'Track II' Security, Dialogues," pp. 144–45. I am very grateful to my friend and colleague Seng Tan of the Institute of Defence and Strategic Studies, Nanyang Technological Univer-sity in Singapore, for his help in talking through the concept of comprehensive or alternative security as it relates to Japan.

21. The Japanese government viewed Japanese self-sufficiency in the production of rice, the primary food product consumed by Japanese, as a national-security issue. The Japanese government had created a national myth around rice to the effect that it was a centuries-old staple food source for Japanese, when in reality, it became a staple food for the Japanese only early in the twentieth century, with the introduction of modern farming methods. The ban on imported rice was never complete, because in the postwar era, it was never possible for Japan to be totally self-sufficient where its rice needs are concerned. The whole concept of self-sufficiency collapsed in 1993 when the rice crop suffered a catastrophic failure and Japan was forced to import large quantities of rice from the United States, Australia, and Thailand.

22. The Japanese environmental record outside of its immediate interests has been very spotty, at best.

23. The illegal-immigration problem from Iran stems from a lax visa law for Ira-nian citizens (no advance visa is required) and the Japanese government's unwilling-ness to offend the government of Iran by clamping down in harshly.

24. The influx of illegal immigrants into Japan has led to a backlash against for-eigners in general, which is upsetting Japan's traditional welcoming but shy attitude toward foreigners. For more on this topic, see Howard W. French, "Japan's Cultural Bias against Foreigners Comes Under Attack"; Howard W. French, "Still Wary of Outsiders, Japan Expects Immigration Boom"; and Calvin Sims, "Tokyo Chief Starts New Furor on Immigrants."

25. The level of Japan's vulnerability without the United States would depend on the stability of the world system supported by U.S. hegemony. If, on the other hand, U.S. hegemony were to collapse, Japan, as a "free rider," would be in serious need of powerful allies in other areas of the world. If U.S. hegemony were to con-tinue, Japan would probably be able to continue to benefit from the stability brought about by U.S. hegemony.

26. The question was asked several months *before* the North Korean missile crisis occurred, and several years before the abduction issue came to light (more on this in subsequent chapters). Thus, the test firing of the missiles over Japan by North Korea did not influence the high response rate for North Korea.

27. *Yomiuri Shimbun* survey of 1,952 national voters, conducted 25–26 October 1997 by personal interview. Source: JPOLL, Roper Center for Public Opinion Re-search, University of Connecticut. (For required full disclaimer, please see the Bibli-ography.) http://roper1.ropercenter.uconn.edu.

28. Grieco, "Anarchy and the Limits of Cooperation," p. 118 (emphasis added). The prospect of a partner exiting from a relationship is very significant for Japan in light of its fears of abandonment by the United States. On the surface, Japan can easily be seen as getting more from the relationship than the United States, and thus, according to Grieco, it is a possible candidate for abandonment by the United States unless a strong case can be made that the United States cannot do without Japan. Japan is a nation that is fundamentally practicing realism, Japan understands this possibility, hence the fears of abandonment.

29. The current strength of the U.S. economy and the weakness of the Japanese economy are making trade frictions less of a concern, but the potential remains that if the U.S. economy enters into a recession, then trade conflicts might reemerge in the bilateral relationship.

30. Chalmers Johnson and E. B. Keehn, "The Pentagon's Ossified Strategy," pp. 103–114.

31. John E. Rielly, ed., *American Public Opinion and Foreign Policy 1999,* pp. 16, 38, as cited by C. S. Kang, "Korea and Japanese Security," p. 107.

32. *Yomiuri Shimbun* survey of 2,030 national voters, conducted 18–19 January 1997 by personal interview. Source: JPOLL, Roper Center for Public Opinion Research, University of Connecticut. (For required full disclaimer please see the Bibliography.) http://roper1.ropercenter.uconn.edu.

33. Kang, "Korea and Japanese Security," p. 108. Kissinger citation by Kang from Henry Kissinger, *Diplomacy,* p. 828.

34. Marc Gallicchio, "Japan in American Security Policy: A Problem in Perspective."

35. *Nihon Keizai Shimbun* survey of 1,774 national voters, conducted 25–27 April 1997 by telephone. *Nihon Keizai Shimbun* survey of 1,776 national voters. Conducted 19–21 April 1996 by telephone. Source: JPOLL, Roper Center for Public Opinion Research, University of Connecticut. (For required full disclaimer please see the Bibliography.) http://roper1.ropercenter.uconn.edu.

36. Current and growing tensions between the United States and China make it much more likely that "the China threat" could be expressed. China's military build-up seems to be directly aimed at the United States as a challenge to American hegemony. The administration of President George W. Bush is looking very warily at China's growing military and economic power.

37. Kang, "Korea and Japanese Security," p. 95.

38. China and the United States were both mentioned twenty-three times by elites when they were asked to name Japan's top three foreign-policy priorities. Field Research interviews conducted May–June 1998 in Japan. These views would undoubtedly change if the United States abandoned Japan or seemed about to do so. Also, given recent seemingly sanctioned anti-Japan protests in China, the answers might be different today.

39. *Jiji Press* survey of 1,430 national adults, conducted 1 May 1996 by personal interview. Source: JPOLL, Roper Center for Public Opinion Research, University of Connecticut. (For required full disclaimer please see the Bibliography.) http://roper1.ropercenter.uconn.edu.

40. *Yomiuri Shimbun* survey of 1,952 national voters, conducted 25–26 October 1997 by personal interview. Source: JPOLL, Roper Center for Public Opinion Research, University of Connecticut. (For required full disclaimer please see the Bibliography.) http://roper1.ropercenter.uconn.edu.

41. Examples of this perception of the United States-Japan-China relationship as a triangular one are: Reinhard Drifte, "The U.S.-Japan-China Security"; David Arase, "Japan Needs Alliance-Plus in Northeast Asia"; and Mark Berger, "Miracles of Modernization and Crisis of Capitalism: The United States-Japan-China Triangle and the Vicissitudes of the East Asian Model 1940s–1990s."

42. Drifte, "The U.S.-Japan-China Security," p. 1.

43. Professor Hideshi Takesada, National Institute for Defense Studies, interview by the author, 5 June 1998, Tokyo, tape recording in author's personal possession. It is important to note that even if the United States abandoned Japan, as the reigning hegemon the United States would still be an important factor in the East Asian and Japanese security equation.

44. This view of closer relations within East Asia was mentioned by Naoko Saiki, director, International Peace Cooperation Division, Ministry of Foreign Affairs, and others during interviews. Naoko Saiki, interview by author, 4 June 1998, Tokyo.

45. Yukihiko Ikeda, member of the House of Representatives of the Japanese Diet (LDP), former foreign and defense minister, interview by the author, 16 June 1998, Tokyo, tape recording in author's personal possession.

46. There was great debate as to the legality of Japan's participation in the United States-Japan Security Treaty, particularly when it came up for renewal in the late 1950s and early 1960s. The one-sided nature of the current treaty (the United States is pledged to defend Japan, and Japan is not expected to reciprocate) permitted the treaty to be interpreted as constitutional. Any future treaty with another nation is not likely to be as one-sided, thus raising the constitutionality question once again (if a country could be found that would want to ally itself with Japan).

47. Aurelia George Mulgan, "Strategic Update—Japan," p. 11.

48. The Japanese government has traditionally paid for the costs incurred by United States forces in Japan, such as labor, utilities, facilities (rent), maintenance, and training. This obligation cost Japan about 2.5 billion U.S. dollars annually.

49. For more on this topic, see Calvin Sims, "U.S. Resists Cut in Funds by Japan for G.I.'s."

50. As an example of how inefficient the Japanese domestic economy is, the average manufactured good travels through the hands of ten middlemen on its way from the manufacturer to the consumer. Much of this complexity is due to Japan's arcane distribution system, which relies heavily on the culturally imposed loyalty and obligation from one person to the next. Foreign companies have found it notoriously hard to get this distribution system to open up to their merchandise.

51. Masafumi Iishi, director, Foreign Policy Planning Division of the Japanese Ministry of Foreign Affairs, interview by author, 1 June 1998, Tokyo, tape recording in author's personal possession.

52. Off-the-record comment by a senior Diet member. Interview by the author, May–June 1998, Tokyo, Japan, tape recording in the personal possession of the author.

53. The following discussion in no way advocates that Japan seek other alliances. It merely examines all the possibilities that exist for Japan.

54. Takesada interview.

55. Hajime Funada, member of the House of Representatives of the Japanese Diet (LDP), chairman of the Sub-Committee on Asia and the Pacific, interview by the author, 28 May 1998, Tokyo, tape recording in author's personal possession.

56. Shingo Nishimura, member of the House of Representatives of the Japanese Diet (Liberal Party), interview by the author, 17 June 1998, Tokyo, tape recording in author's personal possession.

57. Off-the-record comment by a senior member of MOFA, interview by author, May–June 1998, Tokyo, tape recording in author's personal possession.

58. Joseph M. Grieco, "China, Japan, and Germany in the New World Polity," p. 163.

59. For more on the problem of Japan's history in East Asia and the problems it is causing for its foreign policy, see: Steven T. Benfell, "Profound Regrets: The Memory of World War II in Japan and International Relations in East Asia."

60. Many of those interviewed at MOFA said that Japan needed to work towards interdependence with China to hedge against China size vis-à-vis Japan.

61. Takesada interview.

62. At the last Russian-Japanese summit in Tokyo, both sides agreed to set a deadline for signing a formal peace treaty by the end of the year 2000. This deadline came and went with no progress on the issue. The sticking point is the Kuril Islands which are a political hot potato for the ruling LDP and a nationalist issue for Russian leaders. Boris Yelstin tried to return the islands to Japan in 1994, but nationalist interests in the Russian parliament forced him to abandon the idea.

63. Off-the-record comment by a high-level MOFA official. Interview by author, May–June 1998, Tokyo, tape recording in author's personal possession.

64. For more on the Kuril Islands dispute with Russia, see Yakov Zinberg, "In Search for Alternative National Interests: Russo–Japanese Territorial Disputes After the Cold War."

65. China also has nuclear capabilities, but these are currently limited in quantity and in sophistication. It is unlikely that China would be willing to extend its limited nuclear deterrent to ensure Japan's safety.

66. For more on Japan's relations with Russia please see: Tsuneo Akaha, "Japanese-Russian Relations: An Overview or Japanese Views of Russia: Through the Eyes of Others."

67. Akihiko Tanaka, "Japan and Regional Integration in Asia-Pacific."

68. Mitsuo Higashinaka, member of the House of Representatives of the Japanese Diet (JCP), interview by the author, 19 May 1998, Tokyo, tape recording in author's personal possession.

69. Field interviews conducted in Japan May–June 1998 (N = 41).

70. B. C. Koh, "U.S.-Japan Security Cooperation and the Two Koreas," p. 72.

71. Shin'ichi Ogawa, professor, National Institute for Defense Studies, interview by author, 11 June 1998, Tokyo, tape recording in author's personal possession.

72. For more on Japanese multilateral efforts and options, see the following three papers: Akihiko Tanaka, "Japan and Regional Integration in Asia-Pacific"; Takashi Terada, "The Origins of Japan's APEC Policy: Foreign Minister Takeo Miki's Asia-Pacific Policy and Current Implications"; and Paul Midford, "From Reactive State to Cautious Leader: The Nakayama Proposal and Japan's Role in Promoting the Creation of the ASEAN Regional Forum (ARF)."

73. Sheldon W. Simon, "Multilateralism and Japan's Security Policy," p. 91.

74. It is important to note that, while the South Korean government of Kim Dae Jung might have accepted Japan's apology, many Koreans did not. They feel that Japan has not been especially remorseful or frank in its apologies. There is also the lingering issue of compensation for Korean "comfort women." For more on Japan's

troubled "history" of apologizing for its actions during World War II, see Nicholas D. Kristof, "A Big Exception for a Nation of Apologizers."

75. The very fact that Prime Minister Keizo Obuchi was able politically to make this apology to South Korea, considering right-wing opposition within the LDP (Obuchi's party) to apologies on the part of Japan for *any* actions taken during World War II, may be testimony to the shock that Japan suffered when North Korea sent a ballistic missile over Japan on 31 August 1998. This test firing of the Taepodong-1 ballistic missile by the North Koreans awakened many in Japan to the fact that their safety and security was closely tied to South Korea's and the stability of the Korean Peninsula. Several Diet members whom I interviewed initiated personal contact by email to express their concern over the test firing. The political pressure of the moment may have permitted Prime Minister Obuchi to issue an apology to South Korea, when in other circumstances he never would have been able to do so. This may also be further evidence of the reactionary nature of Japanese foreign-policy making that was discussed in chapter 3.

76. Field research interviews conducted May–June 1998 in Japan, question number 6 or 7, depending on the questionnaire.

77. Field research interviews conducted May–June 1998 in Japan.

78. This conjecture assumes that the Republic of Korea would choose to resist an invasion from the North. Recent public opinion in the ROK has unexplainably turned in favor of the DPRK and against the United States and Japan. This shift holds particularly true in the case of the younger generation, who do not remember the Korean War.

79. Kang, "Korea and Japanese Security," p. 97.

80. South Korea's relationship with Japan has progressed to the point at which the two are now conducting joint naval exercises. For more on this subject, see Associated Press, "Japan, S. Korea Hold Naval Exercise."

81. Kang, "Korea and Japanese Security," p. 101.

82. Zbigniew Brzezinski, "A Geostrategy for Eurasia," pp. 62–63 as cited by Kang, "Korea and Japanese Security," p. 109.

83. For more on the relationship between Japan and Korea, see: Eunbong Choi, "Balancing the Past and the Future: A Korean View of the Korea-Japan Relationship."

84. Takesada interview.

85. By "low cost" is meant that North Korea would pay a lower cost (in relative terms) by attacking Japan with nuclear weapons than if it attacked South Korea, and if North Korea has developed the capability of reaching the United States, then there is the question if the United States would use nuclear weapons if it can be targeted with nuclear weapons. Even if the United States is safe from North Korean nuclear weapons, there is the question of whether they would be used on the Korean Peninsula over the likely objections of the ROK.

86. This potential loss of Japan as a staging area for the United States in a renewed Korean conflict is probably the greatest reason that the United States would choose not to abandon Japan. However, if the threat of a renewed Korean conflict were to be removed, the United States might feel confident in withdrawing from Japan. This scenario assumes that the United States and Japan are no longer allies for whatever reason.

87. Kiichi Fujiwara, professor, Institute of Social Science, Tokyo University, interview by author, 11 June 1998, Tokyo, tape recording in author's personal possession.

88. The only scenario in which Japan might choose the nuclear option is one in which Japan faces a direct threat that only a Japanese nuclear deterrent could potentially alleviate.

89. In the author's interview with Director Masafumi Iishi of MOFA's Foreign Policy Planning Division, Mr. Iishi, in talking about Japan's options, stated that nuclear weapons represented a cheap and feasible deterrent for Japan, but only in a "worst case" scenario, in which Japan has been abandoned by the United States. Masafumi Iishi, director Foreign Policy Planning Division of the Japanese Ministry of Foreign Affairs, Interview by author, 1 June 1998, Tokyo, tape recording in author's personal possession.

90. Kissinger, *Diplomacy*, p. 826.

91. The values of this sector of the American foreign-policy community are based on the democratic peace theory in political science, which claims that democracies do not fight each other. The Clinton administration made democratization an American foreign-policy goal, based on the assumed validity of this theory, and the second Bush doctrine furthers this theory with its focus on democratic nation building.

92. Kang, "Korea and Japanese Security," p. 108.

93. Edward Hallett Carr, *Twenty Years' Crisis, 1919–1939: An Introduction to the Study of International Relations*, p. 111.

94. R. G. Hawtrey, *Economic Aspects of Sovereignty*, p. 105 as cited by Carr, *Twenty Years' Crisis, 1919–1939*, p. 111.

95. How China views the United States-Japan/South Korea relationship is of critical importance. As Kang writes, "This view [the United States-Japan-South Korea relationship] was expressed to the author [Kang] by senior Chinese diplomats in Tokyo, December 1997. The author would like to note that in his ongoing informal survey of Chinese officials and scholars, he has observed that there appears to be a generational divide regarding the Chinese view of the Japan-United States and South Korea-United States alliances. The older Chinese appear more comfortable with the alliances, to the extent that they ensure limited Japanese armament, but the younger ones are prone to see them as tools for containing rising Chinese power." Kang, "Korea and Japanese Security," p. 114, note 14.

96. Kang, "Korea and Japanese Security," p. 111. The constitutional limitations imposed by Article Nine work in Japan's favor by reassuring China (and Korea) of Japan's benign intentions. A constitutional reinterpretation or the amendment of Article Nine would remove this reassurance. The United States-Japan Security Treaty is the U.S. guarantee of Japan's security and defense. It is not an alliance by Japan with the United States in which both sides have pledged to support the other in a conflict. It is because of this fact that the Japanese government can interpret the constitution to permit the treaty, on the grounds that it is not collective security because the United States is providing a one-way guarantee and Japan has only to provide for its own self-defense in cooperation with the United States.

97. North Korea might be better left out of any future Northeast Asian security forums, as it might prove too disruptive for the forums to be successful. However, the flip side of this consideration is that the inclusion of North Korea might bring North Korea into a more cooperative relationship with the United States and the other states in the region, thus diminishing the threat posed by the North Korean regime. The success of North Korea in the ARF, which it has been invited to join, might be a good indication of its potential in a Northeast Asian forum.

98. Barry Buzan, Ole Wæver, and Jaap de Wilde, *Security: A New Framework for Analysis*, p. 31.

99. Nicholas D. Kristof, "The Problem of Memory," pp. 37–38.

Notes to Chapter 7

1. As cited by Robert Markman, "A Whole Lot of Bull $*#%," p. 118.

2. Chalmers Johnson would be an example of a person who holds this view outside Japan, and the Communists (JCP) and the conservative far right of Japanese politics would be examples of those who oppose the U.S. presence on grounds that it violates and undermines Japanese sovereignty.

3. One of the strengths of U.S. hegemony is that so many other nations have an interest in seeing it continue. Japan is not alone in preferring U.S. hegemony to an unknown alternative.

4. The realization that a new interpretation of the constitution was indeed needed was confirmed by Vice Foreign Minister Shunji Yanai and former Foreign Minister Yukihiko Ikeda during my interviews with them. For more on the origins of the PKO Law and the political origins of the law, see Shunji Yanai, "Law Concerning Cooperation for United Nations Peace-Keeping Operations and Other Operations: the Japanese PKO Experience"; Shunji Yanai, interview by author, 20 May 1998, Tokyo, tape recording in author's personal possession; Yukihiko Ikeda, interview by the author, 16 June 1998, Tokyo, tape recording in author's personal possession.

5. Interview with a lower-house Diet member, who asked that his comments not be attributed to him or quoted directly, interview by author, during May–June 1998, Tokyo, tape recording in author's personal possession.

6. Interview with a senior government official who requested that the entire interview be off the record. Interview by author, during May–June 1998, Tokyo, tape recording in author's personal possession.

7. Councillor Kei Hata is an example of this attitude in her spearheading of the Diet drive to bring Japan into the information revolution. Her paper, "Urgent Recommendation Regarding Information Infrastructure Strategy," sets out what the goals of Japan should be in technology. Kei Hata, member of the House of Councillors of the Japanese Diet (LDP), interview by the author, 18 May 1998, Tokyo, tape recording; in author's personal possession; and Kei Hata, "Urgent Recommendation Regarding Information Infrastructure Strategy."

8. Research interviews conducted May–June 1998 in Japan.

9. Hideo Usui, member of the House of Representatives of the Japanese Diet and former defense minister and vice Defense Agency minister (career ministry appointment), interview by the author, 26 and 29 May 1998, Tokyo, tape recording in author's personal possession.

10. Ichiro Yamamoto, member of the House of Councillors of the Japanese Diet, interview by the author, 18 June 1998, Tokyo, tape recording in author's personal possession.

11. This is not to say that the public is not aware of foreign-policy issues; they are just not motivated to vote by them. In a 1994 *Asahi Shimbun* poll that asked, "How closely would you say you follow news about world affairs and foreign policy issues?" 75 percent of the respondents replied, "Very closely" or "Somewhat closely." *Asahi Shimbun* survey of 1,192 national adults. Conducted 5–6 March 1994 by personal interview. Source: JPOLL, Roper Center for Public Opinion Research, University of Connecticut. (For required full disclaimer, see the Bibliography.) http://roper1.ropercenter.uconn.edu.

12. Michael W. Chinworth, ed. *Inside Japan's Defense: Technology, Economics & Strategy*, p. 9.

13. Ibid.

14. Reinhard Drifte, *Japan's Foreign Policy for the 21st Century: From Economic Superpower to What Power?* pp. 1–14.

15. Ibid., p. 3.

16. For a complete analysis, see James E. Auer, "Article Nine of Japan's Constitution: from Renunciation of Armed Force 'Forever' to the Third Largest Defense Budget in the World," pp. 171–87.

17. *Yomiuri Shimbun* survey of 1,952 national voters, conducted 25–26 October 1997 by personal interview. Source: JPOLL, Roper Center for Public Opinion Research, University of Connecticut. (For required full disclaimer, see the Bibliography.) http://roper1.ropercenter.uconn.edu.

18. Prime Minister's Office survey of 2,114 national voters, conducted 6–16 February 1997 by personal interview. Source: JPOLL, Roper Center for Public Opinion Research, University of Connecticut. (For required full disclaimer, see the Bibliography.) http://roper1.ropercenter.uconn.edu.

19. One reason that so many Japanese did not mention *gaiatsu* in the interviews is that they may have been embarrassed to do so. *Gaiatsu* implies a lack of sovereignty, and many Japanese could be embarrassed to tell a foreigner that foreign pressure is a major part of foreign-policy formation in Japan. The two outspoken respondents were Mitsuo Higashinaka, member of the House of Representatives of the Japanese Diet (JCP), interview by the author, 19 May 1998, Tokyo, tape recording in author's personal possession; and an academic researcher who asked that all his comments be off the record.

20. For example, Leonard J. Schoppa, "Two Level Games and Bargaining Outcomes: Why 'Gaiatsu' Succeeds in Japan in Some Cases but Not in Others."

21. Robert Putnam, "Diplomacy and Domestic Politics: The Logic of Two-Level Games," p. 429.

22. Ibid.

23. Ibid., pp. 427–60.

24. Ibid., p. 429.

25. The PKO Law is just an illustration of how this form of *gaiatsu* might be applied, but evidence (from field-interview questions) indicates that this process seems to be what happened.

26. Yanai interview.

27. Quote provided by Ed McDaniel, Ph.D., tape recording in the possession of Ed McDaniel, San Diego, California.

28. Putnam, "Diplomacy and Domestic Politics," p. 429.

29. Tom Fish, NBR Forum, 17 January 2001. www.nbr.org.

30. This is my own definition of sovereignty, based on my study of the literature over the years.

31. Ryozo Kato, director general, Foreign Policy Bureau of the Japanese Ministry of Foreign Affairs, interview by author, 21 May 1998, Tokyo, tape recording in author's personal possession.

32. Witness the spring 1999 Tokyo governor's race and the accusations by candidate Shintaro Ishihara, *New York Times,* 26 March 1999, p. A12.

33. Kato interview.

34. Colonel Yoshihisa Nakamura, professor at the National Institute for Defense Studies, Japan Defense Agency, interview by the author, 28 May 1998, Tokyo, tape

recording in author's personal possession.

35. Keizo Takemi, member of the House of Councillors of the Japanese Diet, current Cabinet vice foreign minister and past House of Councillors Chair of Foreign Relations Committee and founding chair of the subcommittee on Pacific Affairs, interview by the author, 25 May 1998, Tokyo, tape recording in author's personal possession.

36. Jiro Kodera, director, First International Economic Affairs Division of the Japanese Ministry of Foreign Affairs, interview by author, 20 May 1998, Tokyo, tape recording in author's personal possession.

37. Sheldon W. Simon, "Multilateralism and Japan's Security Policy," p. 79.

38. Hendrik Spruyt, "A New Architecture for Peace? Reconfiguring Japan Among the Great Powers," p. 367.

39. Kodera interview.

40. Shin'ichi Ogawa, professor, National Institute for Defense Studies, interview by author, 11 June 1998, Tokyo, tape recording in author's personal possession.

41. Kodera interview.

42. Hisane Masaki, "Japan, China Consider Upgrading Security Forum."

43. Off-the-record comment by a senior official in MOFA.

44. Kato interview.

45. Simon, "Multilateralism and Japan's Security Policy," p. 80.

46. Ibid.

47. Spruyt, "A New Architecture for Peace?" p. 370.

48. Osamu Iishi, professor, Institute of Oriental Culture, Tokyo University, interview by author, 29 May 1998, Tokyo, tape recording, in author's personal possession.

49. Simon, "Multilateralism and Japan's Security Policy," p. 80.

50. Usui interview.

51. C. S. Kang, "Korea and Japanese Security," p. 101.

52. Field research interviews conducted in Japan May–June 1998 (N = 41).

53. Simon, "Multilateralism and Japan's Security Policy," p. 82.

54. Ibid.

55. Spruyt, "A New Architecture for Peace?" p. 371, "(and ARF)" added.

56. Simon, "Multilateralism and Japan's Security Policy," p. 94.

57. Akihiko Tanaka, "Japan and Regional Integration in Asia-Pacific," p. 11.

58. Ibid., pp. 11–12.

59. Yanai interview.

60. Kato interview.

61. *Yomiuri Shimbun* survey of 2,030 national voters, conducted 18–19 January 1997 by personal interview. Source: JPOLL, Roper Center for Public Opinion Research, University of Connecticut. (For required full disclaimer, see the Bibliography.) http://roper1.ropercenter.uconn.edu.

62. Ogawa interview.

63. Field research interviews. When asked about whether or not they would like to see the current PKO Law expanded, 80 percent of respondents said, "Yes," 20 percent said, "No" (N = 35).

64. Prime Minister's Office survey of 2,015 national adults, conducted 3–13 October 1996 by personal interview. Source: JPOLL, Roper Center for Public Opinion Research, University of Connecticut. (For required full disclaimer, please see the Bibliography.) http://roper1.ropercenter.uconn.edu.

65. *Yomiuri Shimbun* survey of 2,031 national voters, conducted 30–31 August 1997 by personal interview. Source: JPOLL, Roper Center for Public Opinion Research, University of Connecticut. (For required full disclaimer, see the Bibliography.) http://roper1.ropercenter.uconn.edu.

66. Kenjiro Monji, Cabinet Office of Prime Minister, Office on External Affairs, interview by author, 11 June 1998, Tokyo, tape recording in author's personal possession.

67. Kiichi Fujiwara, professor, Institute of Social Science, Tokyo University, interview by author, 11 June 1998, Tokyo, tape recording in author's personal possession.

68. Kodera interview.

69. Aurelia George Mulgan, "Strategic Update—Japan," p. 10.

70. Ibid., 9.

71. Ibid., 15.

72. This may be the very position that some Japanese leaders would like Japan to be in order to force the Japanese public to give up its pacifism.

73. *Nihon Keizai Shimbun* survey of 1,776 national voters, conducted 19–21 April 1996 by telephone. Source: JPOLL, Roper Center for Public Opinion Research, University of Connecticut. (For required full disclaimer, see the Bibliography.) http://roper1.ropercenter.uconn.edu.

74. Ibid.

75. *Asahi Shimbun* survey of 2,307 national voters, conducted 16–17 September 1996 by personal interview. Source: JPOLL, Roper Center for Public Opinion Research, University of Connecticut. (For required full disclaimer, see the Bibliography.) http://roper1.ropercenter.uconn.edu.

76. *Asahi News,* "North Korea Focus of Defense White Paper."

77. Miyuki Hokugo, "Japan, S. Korea, U.S. Warn N. Korea Against Missile Test."

78. See chapter 2 for more on the evolution of the SDF.

79. Former defense minister Hideo Usui made this point abundantly clear. Japan is willing to help, but its role should be one of support rather than leadership. Usui interview.

80. During field research in May–June 1998, fifty-six Japanese elites were asked, "Countries that are seen as world leaders are seen as willing to bear the costs of world order. (For example, the United States' keeping forces in East Asia and Europe.) Is Japan prepared to undertake a world leadership role and what cost would it be willing to pay in order to take on that role? (Or to put it another way is Japan willing to sacrifice for the good of the world?)" I coded the answers into three categories: Can, Cannot/only under U.S. leadership, and Don't Know.

81. *Asahi Shimbun* survey of 2,251 national voters, conducted 20–21 April 1997 by personal interview. Source: JPOLL, Roper Center for Public Opinion Research, University of Connecticut. (For required full disclaimer, see the Bibliography.) http://roper1.ropercenter.uconn.edu.

82. Usui interview.

83. *Nihon Keizai Shimbun* survey of 1,725 national voters, conducted 15–17 December 1995 by telephone interview. Source: JPOLL, Roper Center for Public Opinion Research, University of Connecticut. (For required full disclaimer, see the Bibliography.) http://roper1.ropercenter.uconn.edu.

84. Ibid.

85. Repeatedly during the field research interviews, the interviewees expressed

concern over the foreign-policy "problem" of the Japanese people's aversion to war and military conflict. Japanese pacifism is strong and represents a problem for policy makers when they consider the entire scope of foreign-policy options.

86. Fujiwara interview.

87. Akihiko Tanaka, professor, Institute of Oriental Culture, Tokyo University, interview by author, 16 June 1998, Tokyo, tape recording in author's personal possession.

88. Toshiya Hoshino, professor, Osaka School of International Policy, Osaka University, interview by author, 10 June 1998, Tokyo, tape recording in author's personal possession.

89. Ogawa interview.

90. Hoshino interview.

91. Tanaka Interview.

92. The terms "Japan passing" and "Japan bashing" sound almost the same in Japanese and are sometimes used together as a pun.

93. Seiichi Kubota, professor, Faculty of Modern Culture, Tokyo Junshin Women's College (former journalist with the *Asahi Shimbun*) interview by the author, 1 June 1998, Tokyo, tape recording in author's personal possession.

Notes to Chapter 8

1. Taiwan is included as a quasi-independent state and ASEAN as a region in which all members of the complex have substantial political and economic interests.

2. Hans J. Morgenthau, *Politics Among Nations,* pp. 158–62.

3. Steve Lohr, Andrew Ross Sorkin, and Jad Mouawad, "Unocal Bid Denounced At Hearing," *New York Times,* Section C , p. 1, col. 5, available at www.nytimes.com, and *The China Daily,* 14 July 2005, available at http://www.chinadaily.com.cn/english/doc/2005–07/14/content_460173.htm.

4. Cragg Hines, "Why Hu Needs the Ranch Instead of the South Lawn," *Houston Chronicle,* 7 September 2005, available at http://www.chron.com/cs/CDA/ssistory.mpl/editorial/outlook/3342368.

5. Compiled from *NAPSnet Daily Report,* 13 July 2005, and www.chinadaily.com.cn/english/doc/2005–07/13/content_459875.htm.

6. Under U.S. diplomatic pressure, Israel has currently stopped publicly selling weapons to China but is thought to be quietly still selling some weapons and technology to that country.

7. The European Union currently will not sell advanced weapons to China because of China's human-rights record. The EU was contemplating dropping the arms-sales ban in the spring of 2005, when China passed the antisuccession law against Taiwan. The passage of this law made it politically unpalatable to resume arms sales.

8. Supersonic cruise missile technology escaped the Soviets' technological abilities and to this day no nation has been able to overcome the technological hurdles. If the hurdles are overcome and China obtains the technology and the weapons, there will be a dramatic shift in the balance of power in East Asia unless the United States develops effective counter measures to defend its aircraft carriers.

9. Voice of America, 9 July 2005, as reported by *NAPSnet Daily Report,* 9 July 2005.

10. China's "city buster" deterrent is not based on Mutual Assured Destruction (MAD) of the kind the United States and the Soviet Union observed during the Cold

War. China's deterrent is based on that country's ability to inflict the loss of twenty or more major cities on the United States—too high a price to pay for aggression against China. The U.S. nuclear arsenal would be able to destroy China several times over, but at the price of the United States' losing its largest cities.

11. *Financial Times,* 14 July 2005, available at http://news.ft.com/cms/s/28cfe55a-f4a7–11d9–9dd1–00000e2511c8.html.

12. Ibid.

13. As quoted by *ViewPoints,* 14 July 2005, US Forces Japan (USFJ), available at www.usfj.mil. From http://ebird.afis.mil/ (emphasis added).

14. It is interesting to note that when Prime Minister Koizumi made his promised post election visit to Yasukuni Shrine in October 2005, China reverted back to making only official protests rather than permitting street demonstrations. The leadership in China had perhaps recognized that the nation's policy was having undesired consequences.

15. 2004 Defense of Japan White Paper. http://www.jda.go.jp/e/pab/wp2004/.

16. 2005 Defense White Paper summary, available at www.fpcj.jp/e/mres/japanbrief/jb_560.html.

17. As quoted by *NAPSnet Daily Report,* 19 July 2005.

18. As quoted by *NAPSnet Daily Report,* 25 August 2005.

19. Jim Yardley, "A Deadly Fever, Once Defeated, Lurks in a Chinese Lake," *New York Times,* 22 February 2005, p. A1.

20. Edward Cody, "China's Rising Tide of Protest Sweeping Up Party Officials; Village Chiefs Share Anger Over Pollution," *Washington Post Foreign Service,* 12 September 2005, p. A01.

21. Charles Scanlon, "Brief Return for Japanese Abductees," BBC, 16 October 2002, available at: http://news.bbc.co.uk/2/hi/asia-pacific/2331447.stm.

22. As quoted by *NAPSnet Daily Report,* 7 March 2005.

23. See Korean Peninsula Energy Development Corporation, available at www.kedo.org.

24. U.S. Department of State, available at http://usinfo.state.gov/xarchives/.

25. As quoted by *NAPSnet Daily Report,* 24 May 2005.

26. USFJ Public Affairs, *ViewPoints,* 10 May 2005, p. 2.

27. As quoted by USFJ, *ViewPoints,* 11 June 2005, and www.japantimes.co.jp/cgi-bin/getarticle.p15?nn20050611f2.htm.

28. As quoted by USFJ, *ViewPoints,* 24 June 2005, available at www.washingtonpost.com/wpdyn/content/article/2005/06/12/AR2005061201533.html.

29. Lieutenant General Henry A. Obering III, USAF, director, Missile Defense Agency, Missile Defense Program, Fiscal Year 2006 Budget testimony before the Strategic Forces Subcommittee House Armed Services Committee, 15 March 2005.

30. Available at http://www.japantimes.co.jp/cgi-bin/getarticle.p15?nn20050204a4.htm.

31. As quoted by *NAPSnet Daily Report,* 10 February 2005.

32. As quoted in USFJ, *ViewPoints,* 16 June 2005, available at www.mofa.go.jp/announce/speech/un2005/un0505–3.html.

33. As quoted by *NAPSnet Daily Report,* 20 June 2005.

34. As quoted in USFJ, *ViewPoints,* 20 July 2005, available at http://tokyo.usembassy.gov/e/p/tp-20050720–70.html.

35. As quoted by *NAPSnet Daily Report,* 25 August 2005.

36. As quoted in USFJ, *ViewPoints,* 15 June 15, 2005.

Notes to Chapter 9

1. Kenneth Waltz, conference comment January 1999, Scottsdale, Arizona, author's personal notes, in the author's personal possession, January 1999.

2. Task Force on Foreign Relations for the Prime Minister, "Basic Strategies for Japan's Foreign Policy in the 21st Century: New Era, New Vision, New Diplomacy," 28 November 2002, Executive Summary, unofficial translation (emphasis added). Available at www.kantei.go.jp/foreign/policy/2002/1128tf_e.html.

3. Ibid.

4. Yoichiro Sato, "Modeling Japan's Foreign and Economic Policy with the United States," in Akitoshi Miyashita and Yoichiro Sato, eds., *Japanese Foreign Policy in Asia and the Pacific*, p. 27.

5. Ibid., pp. 27–30.

6. Japan can always draw a new line if and when there is pressure to give up some of its fishing industry.

7. The security benefit of a permanent seat on the Security Council is substantial. One must consider what the P5's international standings would be like without their veto power. Consider Britain: without P5 status, it would still be a nuclear power, but its voice would be reduced to that of any large European state. The same would be true for China; it would still be the world largest nation in terms of population, but its ability to influence global politics would be greatly reduced.

8. During interviews with various mid-level members of MOFA, a sense of paranoia seemed to be evident on the part of interviewees. While they seemed grateful to be able to express their own views, they appeared to behave as if the walls had ears. They were very careful to take anything that diverged from the official line off the record. Senior-level directors seemed to express the opposite sense, and they were much more relaxed and willing to offer differing opinions.

9. Ichita Yamamoto, member of the House of Councillors of the Japanese Diet, interview by the author, 18 June 1998, Tokyo, tape recording in author's personal possession.

10. Ibid.

11. Ibid.

12. Kuniko Nakajima, former career diplomat with the Japanese Ministry of Foreign Affairs and currently a researcher with the Okazaki Institute, interview by the author, 18 June 1998, Tokyo, tape recording in author's personal possession.

13. This is a marked change in future policy, in that the chain of command in the field would be exclusively Japanese. One of the strongest arguments for the constitutionality of the PKO Law is that the SDF troops are on loan to the United Nations and are commanded by U.N. commanders. Thus, the SDF troops are not being commanded by Tokyo except for being ordered to and from the field with conditions on what they can and cannot do. The authorization for the potential future use of SDF troops in natural disasters quietly steps over the line by permitting Tokyo to command troops on overseas missions.

14. Prime Minister's Office survey of 2,114 national adults, conducted 6–16 February 1997 by personal interview. Source: JPOLL, Roper Center for Public Opinion Research, University of Connecticut. (For required full disclaimer please see the Bibliography.), available at http://roper1.ropercenter.uconn.edu

15. Ibid.

16. Several Diet members stated, off the record, that the people have no real voice in foreign policy. What they were alluding to is the control of foreign policy by MOFA, and not by the people's representatives in the Diet. Other Diet members, particularly younger ones, stated that the Diet was taking a stronger hands-on approach to foreign policy and that MOFA was not the ultimate source of foreign policy.

17. Article Ninety-six of the Japanese Constitution, as cited by *Yomiuri Shimbun*, "Law on Constitutional Poll Needed," 9 August 1999, Internet edition, www.yomiuri.co.jp/newse/0809ed16.htm.

18. "The Constitution of Japan." *Law and Contemporary Problems*, Spring 1990, pp. 200–14.

19. Ibid.

20. Field research interviews conducted with both elected and career government foreign policy elites in Japan, May–June 1998 (N = 39).

21. Field research interviews conducted with academics in Japan, May–June 1998 (N = 9).

22. Field research interviews conducted in Japan, May–June 1998 (N = 48).

23. An off-the-record comment by a senior MOFA official. Interview by the author, May–June 1998, Tokyo, tape recording in author's personal possession.

24. Field research interviews conducted in Japan May–June 1998. Of the twenty-four government elites answering in favor of revising Article Nine, twelve felt that such a revision would not happen (N = 48).

25. Mitsuo Higashinaka, member of the House of Representatives of the Japanese Diet (JCP), interview by the author, 19 May 1998, Tokyo, tape recording in author's personal possession.

26. *Asahi Shimbun* survey of 2,251 national voters, conducted 20–21 April 1997 by personal interview. Source: JPOLL, Roper Center for Public Opinion Research, University of Connecticut. (For required full disclaimer please see the Bibliography.)

27. As cited by the Northeast Asia Peace and Security Network Daily Report for 19 September 2005 from Berkeley, California, available at NAPSNet@nautilus.org.

28. Kenichi Nakamura, dean of law, Hokkaido University (top Japanese Researcher on the PKO Law), interview by author, 20 June 1998, Tokyo, tape recording in author's personal possession.

29. Jun Morikawa, professor, Rakuno Gakuen University, interview by author, 22 June 1998, Tokyo, tape recording in author's personal possession.

30. Masashi Nishhara, professor at the National Defense Academy, Japan Defense Agency, interview by the author, 31 May 1998, Tokyo, tape recording in author's personal possession.

31. Ibid.

32. Aurelia George Mulgan, "Strategic Update—Japan," p. 3.

33. Geoffrey Smith, "Japan Expanding Defense Role," available at NAPSNet @nautilus.org (NAPSNet).

34. Kenjiro Monji, Cabinet Office of the Prime Minister, Office on External Affairs, interview by the author, 11 June 1998, Tokyo, tape recording in author's personal possession.

35. Off-the-record interview by the author, May–June 1998, Tokyo, tape recording in author's personal possession.

36. Yamamoto interview.

37. Jiro Kodera, director, First International Economic Affairs Division of the Japa-

nese Ministry of Foreign Affairs, interview by author, 20 May 1998, Tokyo, tape recording in author's personal possession.

38. An off-the-record comment by a senior MOFA official. Interview by the author, May–June 1998, Tokyo, tape recording in author's personal possession.

39. Ibid.

40. Ibid. These feelings may seem contradictory on the surface, but given that public opinion often contains such contradictions, the Japanese public is not being totally hypocritical. For example, most Americans supported President Clinton's actions in Kosovo, while at the same time they expressed the feeling that the United States did not belong there. The situation in Japan is much the same. Most Japanese support the SDF and see the need for the PKO missions, while simultaneously preferring the SDF's not being deployed overseas.

41. Ryozo Kato, director general, Foreign Policy Bureau of the Japanese Ministry of Foreign Affairs, interview by author, 21 May 1998, Tokyo, tape recording in author's personal possession.

42. Hideo Usui, member of the House of Representatives of the Japanese Diet and former Defense Minister and Vice Minister, Defense Agency (career ministry appointment), interview by the author, 26 and 29 May 1998, Tokyo, tape recording in author's personal possession.

43. Repeatedly during the field research interviews, the interviewees would express concern over the foreign policy "problem" of the Japanese people's aversion to war and military conflict. Japanese pacifism is strong and represents a problem for policy makers when they consider the entire scope of foreign-policy options.

44. Usui interview.

45. Ibid.

46. Off-the-record statement by a senior member of MOFA, interview by the author, May–June 1998, Tokyo, Japan, tape recording in the personal possession of the author.

47. Ibid.

48. Shigeru Ishiba, member of the House of Representatives of the Japanese Diet (LDP), interview by the author, 4 June 1998, Tokyo, tape recording in author's personal possession.

49. Akira Ogawa, professor, Okazaki Research Institute, Tokyo, Japan, interview by author, 18 June 1998, Tokyo, tape recording in author's personal possession.

50. Nishihara interview.

51. What would qualify as significant is anybody's guess. It could be one death or as many as a hundred casualties (deaths and injuries). It would depend on the situation or the mission.

52. Toshiya Hoshino, professor, Osaka School of International Policy, Osaka University, interview by author, 10 June 1998, Tokyo, tape recording in author's personal possession.

53. An example of this belief is expressed in Paul Kennedy, *The Rise and Fall of the Great Powers: Economic Change and Military Conflict From 1500 to 2000.*

54. Akihiko Tanaka, professor, Institute of Oriental Culture, Tokyo University, interview by author, 16 June 1998, Tokyo, tape recording in author's personal possession.

55. Ibid,

56. One interviewee felt that Japan was hiding behind the issue of World War II in

order to avoid contributing to world order. Hajime Oshitani, professor at Rakuno Gakuen University, interview by author, 25 June 1998, Tokyo, tape recording in author's personal possession.

57. Field research interviews conducted in Japan May–June 1998 (N = 50).

58. Kato interview.

59. Kei Hata, member of the House of Councillors of the Japanese Diet (LDP), interview by the author, 18 May 1998, Tokyo, tape recording, in author's personal possession; Usui interview; Kodera interview.

60. Sheldon W. Simon, "Multilateralism and Japan's Security Policy," p. 81.

61. This view was very explicitly expressed by Director General Ryozo Kato; Kato interview.

62. Two examples of academics who expressed this opinion are Kazuo Ota and Keichi Fujiwara. Several LDP Diet members also expressed this view off the record, along with Tomoko Nakagawa and Hosaka Nobuto of the Socialist Party. Kazuo Ota, dean, Rakuno Gakuen University, interview by author, 6 June 1998, Tokyo, tape recording in author's personal possession; Keichi Fujiwara, professor, Institute of Social Science Tokyo University, interview by author, 11 June 1998, Tokyo, tape recording in author's personal possession; Tomoko Nakagawa, member of the House of Representatives of the Japanese Diet (SDP), interview by the author, 16 June 1998, Tokyo, tape recording in author's personal possession; Hosaka Nobuto, member of the House of Representatives of the Japanese Diet (SDP), interview by the author, 16 June 1998, Tokyo, tape recording in author's personal possession.

63. Field research interviews conducted May–June 1998 in Tokyo. Interviewees were asked to "How should Japan deal with its history in East Asia?" (N = 49). The "young" and "old" were classified according to those older or younger than fifty years old. Diet members were classified the same way, except anyone who had been in the Diet for more than fifteen years was classified as old. Alternately, if they were between fifty and fifty-five and had served less than five years in the Diet, they were classified with the younger generation (for the young, N = 24; for the old, N = 25).

64. The Japanese government is very aware of the problems of distinguishing between PKO missions and PKF missions. The primary difference is that a PKF mission would require SDF involvement in the *enforcement* of a United Nations-brokered peace and a PKO mission requires the SDF to *support* a United Nations-brokered peace. Under U.N. command on a PKF mission, the SDF would potentially be required to take not only defensive action, but also offensive action to support the United Nations-brokered peace. Part of this discussion on the differences between the PKO and the PKF comes from an off-the-record interview with a government-sponsored researcher working for the Japanese Defense Agency.

65. Colonel Yoshihisa Nakamura, professor, the National Institute for Defense Studies, Japan Defense Agency, interview by the author, 28 May 1998, Tokyo, tape recording in author's personal possession.

66. Colonel Noburo Yamaguchi, colonel, Ground Self-Defense Forces, interview by the author, 2 June 1998, Tokyo, tape recording in author's personal possession.

67. Nobuto Hosaka interview.

68. Naoko Saiki, director, International Peace Cooperation Division, Ministry of Foreign Affairs, interview by author, 4 June 1998, Tokyo, tape recording in author's personal possession.

69. Keizo Takemi, member of the House of Councillors of the Japanese Diet, current Cabinet vice foreign minister and past House of Councillors chair of Foreign Relations Committee and founding chair of the subcommittee on Pacific Affairs. Interview by the author, 25 May 1998, Tokyo, tape recording in author's personal possession.

70. Nakajima interview.

71. Howard W. French, "An Upstart Governor Takes on Japan's Mandarins."

72. Ishiba interview.

73. Hendrik Spruyt, "A New Architecture for Peace? Reconfiguring Japan Among the Great Powers, " p. 380.

74. Mulgan, "Strategic Update—Japan," p. 14.

75. Shozo Azuma, member of the House of Representatives of the Japanese Diet (Liberal Party), interview by the author, 6 June 1998, Tokyo, tape recording in author's personal possession.

76. T. J. Pempel, "Structural 'Gaiatsu': International Finance and Political Change in Japan," pp. 907–32.

77. Kiichi Fujiwara, professor, Institute of Social Science, Tokyo University, interview by author, 11 June 1998, Tokyo, tape recording in author's personal possession.

78. Shin'ichi Ogawa, professor, National Institute for Defense Studies, interview by author, 11 June 1998, Tokyo, tape recording in author's personal possession.

79. Joseph M. Grieco, "Anarchy and the Limits of Cooperation: A Realist Critique of the Newest Liberal Institutionalism."

80. Sheldon W. Simon, "International Relations Theory and Southeast Asian Security," pp. 5–24.

81. This positive goodwill within Southeast Asia may not have worked throughout the Muslim world, as various Middle Eastern media and newspapers made the patently false assertion that it was the United States and Indian governments who caused the earthquake that caused the tsunami. To the extent that this belief is held within the Middle East, it will determine the long-term effectiveness of U.S. policy.

Bibliography

Aikawa, Takaaki, and Lynn Leavenworth. *The Mind of Japan: A Christian Perspective.* Valley Forge, PA: The Judson Press, 1967.

Akaha, Tsuneo. "Japan's Security Agenda in the Post-Cold War Era." *The Pacific Review* 8, no. 1 (1995): 45–76.

_____. "The Russian Far East as a Factor in Northeast Asia." *Peace Forum* 25 (Winter 1997): 91–108.

_____. *New Guidelines for U.S.-Japan Defense Cooperation: Its Background and Implications.* Monterey, CA: Monterey Institute of International Studies, 1997.

_____. "The Impact of Foreign Governments: The Case of Japan." Paper presented at the International Studies Association Annual Conference, Minneapolis, MN, 17–21 March 1998.

_____. "Japanese-Russian Relations: An Overview or Japanese Views of Russia: Through the Eyes of Others." Paper presented at the International Symposium on Japan and Its Neighbors in the Global Village: Current and Emergent Issues, Nanzan University, Nagoya, Japan, 16–17 October 1999.

Akaha, Tsuneo, and Frank Langdon, eds. *Japan in the Posthegemonic World.* Boulder, CO: Lynne Rienner, 1993.

Alagappa, Muthiah. "Comprehensive Security: Interpretations in ASEAN Countries." In *Asian Security Issues: Regional and Global,* ed. R.A. Scalapino, S. Sato, J. Wanandi, and S.-J. Han, pp. 50–78. Berkeley: Institute of East Asian Studies, University of California-Berkeley Press, 1989.

Alexander, Arthur J. *In the Shadow of the Miracle: The Japanese Economy Since the End of High-Speed Growth.* Lanham, MD: Lexington Books, 2002.

Allinson, Gary D., and Yasunori Sone, eds. *Political Dynamics in Contemporary Japan.* Ithaca, NY: Cornell University Press, 1993.

Arase, David. "Japan Needs Alliance-Plus in Northeast Asia." Editorial from the *Nichibei Shimbun.* Internet edition, 20 March 1999. Available at www.nichibei.org/je/arasemarch.html.

Asada, Sadao. *Japan and the World 1853–1952: A Bibliographic Guide to Japanese Scholarship in Foreign Relations.* New York: Columbia University Press, 1989.

Asahi News, "North Korea Focus of Defense White Paper." Internet edition, 27 July 1999. Available at www.asahi.com/english/enews.enews.html.

Associated Press, "Japan, S. Korea Hold Naval Exercise." *New York Times.* Internet edition, 4 August 1999. Available at www.nytimes.com/apoline/i/AP-Koreas-Japan-Military.

Auer, James E. "Article Nine of Japan's Constitution: from Renunciation of Armed Force 'Forever' to the Third Largest Defense Budget in the World." *Law and Contemporary Problems,* Spring 1990: 171–87.

Azuma, Shozo. Member of the House of Representatives of the Japanese Diet (Liberal Party). Interview by the author, 6 June 1998, Tokyo. Tape recording in author's personal possession.

Bamba, Nobuya, and John F. Howes, eds. *Pacifism in Japan: The Christian and Socialist Tradition.* Vancouver, British Columbia: University of British Columbia Press, 1978.

Bandow, Doug. "Old Wine in New Bottles: The Pentagon's East Asia Security Strategy Report." *International Journal of Korean Studies* III, no. 1 (Spring/Summer 1999): 60–93.

Barnhart, Michael A. *Japan and the World Since 1868.* New York: Edward Arnold, 1995.

Beauchamp, Edward, ed. *East Asia: History, Politics, Sociology, and Culture.* New York: Routledge, 2002.

Becker, Jasper. *The Chinese: An Insider's Look at the Issues which Affect and Shape China Today.* New York: Oxford University Press, 2000.

Benedict, Ruth. *The Chrysanthemum and the Sword: Patterns of Japanese Culture.* Boston: Houghton Mifflin, 1989.

Benfell, Steven T. "Profound Regrets: The Memory of World War II in Japan and International Relations in East Asia." Paper presented at the 40th Annual Conference of the International Studies Association, Washington, DC, 17 February 1999.

Berger, Mark. "Miracles of Modernization and Crisis of Capitalism: The United States-Japan-China Triangle and the Vicissitudes of the East Asian Model 1940s–1990s." Paper presented at the International Symposium on Japan and Its Neighbors in the Global Village: Current and Emergent Issues. Nanzan University, Nagoya, Japan, 16–17 October 1999.

Bessho, Koro. *Identities and Security in East Asia.* New York: Oxford University Press, 1999.

Bowen, Roger W. *Japan's Dysfunctional Democracy: The Liberal Democratic Party and Structural Corruption.* Armonk, NY: M.E. Sharpe, 2003.

Brooks, Stephen G. "Dueling Realisms." *International Organization* 52, no. 3 (Summer 1997): 445–77.

Brzezinski, Zbigniew. "A Geostrategy for Eurasia." *Foreign Affairs* 76, no. 5 (September/October 1997): 62–63.

Bullens, Hendrik, and Seiitsu Tachibana, eds. *Restructuring Security Concepts, Postures and Industrial Base.* Mosbach, Germany: Afes Press, 1997.

Buzan, Barry. "Japan's Defence Problematique." *The Pacific Review* 8, no. 1 (1995): 25–43.

Buzan, Barry, Ole Wæver, and Jaap de Wilde. *Security: A New Framework for Analysis.* Boulder, CO: Lynne Rienner, 1998.

Carlsnaes, Walter. "The Agency-Structure Problem in Foreign Policy Analysis." *International Studies Quarterly* 36 (1992): 245–70.

Carpenter,Ted Galen. "Roiling Asia: U.S. Coziness with China Upsets the Neighbors." *Foreign Affairs* 77, no. 6 (November/December 1998): 2–6.

Carpenter, William M., and David G. Wiencek, eds. *Asian Security Handbook: Terrorism and the New Security Environment.* Armonk, NY: M.E. Sharpe, 2005.

Carr, Edward Hallett. *Twenty Years' Crisis, 1919–1939: An Introduction to the Study of International Relations.* New York: Harper & Row, 1939.

Chai, Sun-Ki. "Entrenching the Yoshida Defense Doctrine: Three Techniques for Institutionalization." *International Organization* 51, no. 3 (Summer 1997): 389–412.

Chan, Steve. "Asia Pacific Regionalism: Tentative Thoughts on Conceptual Basis and Empirical Linkages." Paper presented at the International Studies Association Conference, Washington, DC, 16–20 February 1999.

Chang, Iris. *The Rape of Nanking: The Forgotten Holocaust of World War II.* New York: Penguin Putnam, 1997.

Charlton, Sue Ellen M. *Comparing Asian Politics: India, China, and Japan,* 2nd ed. Boulder, CO: Westview Press, 2004.

Chinworth, Michael W., ed. *Inside Japan's Defense: Technology, Economics & Strategy.* Dulles, VA: Brassey's (US), 1992.

_____. "Defense-Economic Linkages in U.S.-Japan Relations: An Overview of Policy Positions and Objectives." Working paper, 14 April 1999. Available at www.seas .gwu.edu/ nsarchive/japan/chinworth_wp.htm.

Choi, Eunbong. "Balancing the Past and the Future: A Korean View of the Korea-Japan Relationship." Paper presented at the International Symposium on Japan and Its Neighbors in the Global Village: Current and Emergent Issues, Nanzan University, Nagoya, Japan, 16–17 October 1999.

Christensen, Raymond V., and Paul E. Johnson. "Toward a Context-Rich Analysis of Electoral Systems: The Japanese Example." *American Journal of Political Science* 39, no. 3 (August 1995): 575–98.

Clausewitz, Carl von. *On War.* Trans. Anatol Rapoport. Baltimore, MD: Penguin, 1968.

Clesse, Armand, Takashi Inoguchi, E. B. Keehn, and J. A. A. Stockwin, eds. *The Vitality of Japan: Sources of National Strength and Weakness.* New York: St. Martin's Press, 1997.

Cody, Edward. "China's Rising Tide of Protest Sweeping Up Party Officials; Village Chiefs Share Anger Over Pollution," *Washington Post Foreign Service,* 12 September 2005, p. A01.

"Constitution of Japan, The." *Law and Contemporary Problems,* Spring 1990: 200–214.

Collinwood, Dean W. *Japan and the Pacific Rim,* 5th ed. Guilford, CT: Dushkin, 1999.

Cooney, Kevin J. "Alternative Visions of Japanese Security: The Role of Absolute and Relative Gains in the Making of Japanese Security Policy," *Asian Perspective* 29, no. 3 (2005).

Cossa, Ralph A. ed. *Restructuring the U.S.-Japan Alliance: Toward a More Equal Partnership.* Washington, DC: Center for Strategic and International Studies, 1997.

_____. "Prospects for Northeast Asian Multilateral Security Cooperation." *International Journal of Korean Studies* III, no. 1 (Spring/Summer 1999): 35–59.

Cowhey, Peter F. "Domestic Institutions and the Credibility of International Commitments: Japan and the United States." *International Organization* 47, no. 2 (Spring 1993): 299–326.

Cullen, L. M. *A History of Japan, 1582–1941.* New York: Cambridge University Press, 2003.

Curtis, Gerald L., ed. *Japan's Foreign Policy After the Cold War: Coping with Change.* New York: M.E. Sharpe, 1993.

_____. *The Japanese Way of Politics.* New York: Columbia University Press, 1988.

_____. *The Logic of Japanese Politics: Leaders, Institutions, and the Limits of Change.* New York: Columbia University Press, 1999.

_____. ed. *The United States, Japan, and Asia.* New York: W.W. Norton, 1994.

Daily Yomiuri. "Defense Legislation Leaves Some Questions Unanswered," Internet edition, 27 May 1999. Available at www.yomiuri.co.jp/newse/0527p017.htm.

de Kieffer, Donald. "Exercise of Force by the Japanese Self-Defense Force." *North Carolina Journal of International Law & Commercial Regulation* 16 (Winter 1991): 69–77.

Dong, Wonmo, ed. *The Two Koreas and the United States: Issues of Peace, Security, and Economic Cooperation.* Armonk, NY: M.E. Sharpe, 2000.

Dori, John T., and Richard D. Fisher, Jr. *U.S. and Asia Statistical Handbook 1998–1999 Edition.* Washington, DC: The Heritage Foundation, 1998.

Drifte, Reinhard. *Japan's Foreign Policy.* New York: Council on Foreign Relations Press, 1990.

_____. *Japan's Foreign Policy for the 21st Century: From Economic Superpower to What Power?* Oxford: St. Antony's Press, 1998.

_____. "The U.S.-Japan-China Security Triangle and the Future of East Asian Security." In *Security in a Globalized World: Risks and Opportunities,* ed. Laurent Goetschel. Baden-Baden: Nomos Verlag, 1999.

Dupont, Alan. "Concepts of Security." In *Unresolved Futures: Comprehensive Security in the Asia Pacific,* ed. J. Rolfe, pp. 1–15. Wellington: Center for Strategic Studies.

Eberstadt, Nicholas, and Richard J. Ellings, eds. *Korea's Future and the Great Powers.* Seattle, WA: University of Seattle Press, 2001.

Edström, Bert. "Japan's Quest for a Role in the World: Roles Ascribed to Japan Nationally and Internationally 1969–1982." Ph.D. diss., Institute of Oriental Languages, University of Stockholm, 1988.

Ellings, Richard J., and Aaron L. Friedberg, eds. *Strategic Asia: Purpose and Power 2001–2002.* Seattle, WA: National Bureau of Asian Research, 2001.

Embassy of Japan in Washington, D. C. (Reproduced from the unofficial translation provided by). "Japan: Law Concerning Cooperation for United Nations Peacekeeping Operations and Other Operations." *International-Legal Materials* 32: 3–35, 215–216.

Ezrati, Milton. "Japan's Aging Economics," *Foreign Affairs* 76, no. 3 (May/June 1997): 96–104.

Feldman, Ofer. "The Political Personality of Japan: An Inquiry into the Belief Systems of Diet Members." *Political Psychology* 17, no. 4 (1996): 657–82.

Fic, Victor. "The Japanese PKO Bill." *Asian Defense Journal,* Nov. 1992: 28–33.

_____. "Geopolitical Implications of Japan's PKO Law." *Asian Defense Journal* (January 1993): 126–31.

Foreign Affairs. *The Rise of China.* New York: W.W. Norton, 2002.

French, Howard W. "Japan's Cultural Bias Against Foreigners Comes Under Attack," *New York Times,* Internet edition, 15 November 1999. Available at www.nytimes.com/library/ world/asia/111599japan-discriminate.html.

_____. "Two Wary Neighbors Unite to Confront North Korean Arms." *New York Times,* 4 August 1999.

_____. "Still Wary of Outsiders, Japan Expects Immigration Boom," *New York Times,* Internet edition, 14 March 2000. Available at www.nytimes.com/library/world/asia/031400japan-immigration.html.

_____. "An Upstart Governor Takes on Japan's Mandarins." *New York Times.* Internet edition, 30 March 2000. Available at www.nytimes.com/library/world/asia/033000japan-ishihara.html.

Friedman, Edward. *The Politics of Democratization: Generalizing East Asian Experiences.* Boulder, CO: Westview Press, 1994.

Friedman, Edward, and Barrett L. McCormick, eds. *What If China Doesn't Democratize: Implications for War and Peace.* Armonk, NY: M.E. Sharpe, 2000.

Friedman, George, and Meredith LeBard. *The Coming War with Japan.* New York: St. Martin's Press, 1991.

Fujiwara, Kiichi. Professor, Institute of Social Science, Tokyo University. Interview by author, 11 June 1998, Tokyo. Tape recording in author's personal possession.

Fukui, Haruhiro. "Japan in the East Asian Regional Order: An Historical Retrospective." *Peace Forum,* no. 25 (Winter 1997): 59–70.

Funabashi, Yoichi, ed. *Japan's International Agenda.* New York: New York University Press, 1994.

Funada, Hajime. Member of the House of Representatives of the Japanese Diet (LDP), Chairman of the Sub-committee on Asia and the Pacific. Interview by the author, 28 May 1998, Tokyo. Tape recording in author's personal possession.

Funk, Robert B. "Japan's Constitution and U. N. Obligations in the Persian Gulf War: A Case for Non-Military Participation in U.N. Enforcement Actions." *Cornell International Law Journal* 25 (1992): 363–99.

Gaenslen, Fritz. "Decision Making Groups." In *Political Psychology and Foreign Policy,* ed. E. Singer and V. M. Hudson, pp. 165–194. Boulder, CO: Westview Press, 1992.

Gallicchio, Marc. "Japan in American Security Policy: A Problem in Perspective." Working Paper #10. Available at www.seas.gwu.edu/nsaarchive/japan/gallicciowp.htm, downloaded April 14, 1999.

Ge, Tong. "Realism and Chinese Foreign Policy in East and Southeast Asia in the Post-Cold War Era." Master's thesis, Arizona State University, Department of Political Science, 1999.

George, Alexander L. *Bridging the Gap: Theory and Practice in Foreign Policy.* Washington, DC: United States Institute of Peace Press, 1993.

Gibney, Alex. *The Pacific Century: Reinventing Japan (#5).* Produced by the Pacific Basin Institute in association with KCTS/Seattle. 60 min. Jigsaw Productions, 1992. Videocassette.

———. *The Pacific Century.* Produced by the Pacific Basin Institute in association with KCTS/Seattle. Tapes 1–6. Jigsaw Productions, 1992. Videocassette.

Goldmann, Kjell. *Change and Stability in Foreign Policy: The Problems and Possibilities of Détente.* Princeton: Princeton University Press, 1988.

Goodman, Roger, and Kirsten Refsing, eds. *Ideology and Practice in Modern Japan.* New York: Routledge, 1992.

Gorden, Raymond L. *Interviewing: Strategy, Techniques and Tactics.* Homewood, IL: The Dorsey Press, 1969.

Gourevitch, Peter, Takashi Inoguchi, and Courtney Purrington, eds. *United States-Japan Relations and International Institutions After the Cold War.* San Diego, CA: Graduate School of International Relations and Pacific Studies, University of California, 1995.

Grieco, Joseph M. "Anarchy and the Limits of Cooperation: A Realist Critique of the Newest Liberal Institutionalism." In *Neorealism and Neoliberalism: The Contemporary Debate,* ed. David A Baldwin, pp. 116–40. New York: Columbia University Press, 1993.

_____. "China, Japan, and Germany in the New World Polity." In *Peace, Prosperity, and Politics,* ed. John Mueller, chapter 8. Boulder, CO: Westview Press, 2001.

Guertner, Gary L. *Collective Security in Europe and Asia.* Carlisle Barracks, PA: Strategic Studies Institute, 1992.

Hata, Kei. "Urgent Recommendation Regarding Information Infrastructure Strategy." Paper presented to Prime Minister Hashimoto, 8 December 1997 (English version, April 1998). Downloaded from: www.k-hata.or.jp/itproe.

_____. Member of the House of Councillors of the Japanese Diet (LDP). Interview by the author, 18 May 1998, Tokyo. Tape recording in author's personal possession.

Hayao, Kenji. *The Japanese Prime Minister and Public Policy.* Pittsburgh, PA: University of Pittsburgh Press, 1993.

Hayes, Louis D. *Introduction to Japanese Politics,* 4th ed. Armonk, NY: M.E. Sharpe, 2004.

Heinrich, William L. Jr., and Akiho Shibata and Yoshihide Soeya. *United Nations Peace-keeping Operations: A Guide to Japanese Policies.* New York: United Nations University Press, 1999.

Hermann, Charles F. "Changing Course: When Governments Choose to Redirect Foreign Policy." *International Studies Quarterly* 34 (1990): 3–21.

Hermann, Margaret G., and Charles F. Hermann. "Who Makes Foreign Policy Decisions and How: An Empirical Inquiry." *International Studies Quarterly* 33 (1989): 361–87.

Higashinaka, Mitsuo. Member of the House of Representatives of the Japanese Diet (JCP). Interview by the author, 19 May 1998, Tokyo. Tape recording in author's personal possession.

Hines, Cragg. "Why Hu Needs the Ranch Instead of the South Lawn," *Houston Chronicle,* 7 September 2005, available at www.chron.com/cs/CDA/ssistory.mpl/editorial/outlook/3342368.

Hokugo, Miyuki. "Japan, S. Korea, U.S. Warn N. Korea Against Missile Test," *Asahi News.* Internet edition, 27 July 1999. Available at www.asahi.com/english/enews.enews.html.

Holsti, Kal J., ed. *Why Nations Realign: Foreign Policy Restructuring in the Postwar World.* London: George Allen and Unwin, 1982.

Hosaka, Nobuto. Member of the House of Representatives of the Japanese Diet (SDP). Interview by the author, 16 June 1998, Tokyo. Tape recording in author's personal possession.

Hoshino, Toshiya. Professor, Osaka School of International Policy, Osaka University. Interview by author, 10 June 1998, Tokyo. Tape recording in author's personal possession.

Hosokawa, Ryuichiro. "Japanese Need a Good Dose of 'Pride,'" *Japan Times,* 2 June 1998, p. 18.

Hoye, Timothy. *Japanese Politics: Fixed and Floating Worlds.* Upper Saddle River, NJ: Prentice Hall, 1999.

Hughes, Christopher W. "Japanese Policy and the North Korean 'Soft Landing.'" *The Pacific Review* 11, no. 3 (1998): 389–415.

_____. *Japan's Security Agenda: Military, Economic, and Environmental Dimensions.* Boulder, CO: Lynne Rienner, 2004.

Hunsberger, Warren, ed. *Japan's Quest: The Search for International Role, Recognition, and Respect.* Armonk, NY: M.E. Sharpe, 1997.

Igarashi, Takeshi. "Circumventing Japan-U. S. Conflict." *Japan Quarterly* (January–March 1991): 15–22.

Iishi, Masafumi. Director Foreign Policy Planning Division of the Japanese Ministry of Foreign Affairs. Interview by author, 1 June 1998, Tokyo. Tape recording in author's personal possession.

Iishi, Osamu. Professor, Institute of Oriental Culture, Tokyo University. Interview by author, 29 May 1998, Tokyo. Tape recording in author's personal possession.

Ike, Nobutaka. *The Beginnings of Political Democracy in Japan.* Baltimore, MD: The Johns Hopkins University Press, 1952.

_____. *Japanese Politics: Patron-Client Democracy,* 2nd ed. New York: Alfred A. Knopf, 1972.

Ikeda, Yukihiko. Member of the House of Representatives of the Japanese Diet (LDP), Former Foreign and Defense Minister. Interview by the author. 16 June 1998, Tokyo. Tape recording in author's personal possession.

Inoguchi, Takashi. *Japan's International Relations.* London: Pinter Publishers, 1990.

_____. "Japan's Response to the Gulf Crisis: An Analytic Overview," *Journal of Japanese Studies* 17, no. 2 (1991) 257–90.

Iseri, Hirofumi. "Clearing the Mist from the Peace-Keeping Debate." *Japan Echo* XIX, no. 3 (Autumn 1992): 44–49.

Ishiba, Shigeru. Member of the House of Representatives of the Japanese Diet (LDP). Interview by the author, 4 June 1998, Tokyo. Tape recording in author's personal possession.

Ishihara, Shintaro. *The Japan That Can Say "No"* (*No to Ieru Nihon*). Trans. and ed. Frank Baldwin. New York: Simon and Schuster, 1991.

Ito, Mayumi. *Globalization of Japan: Japanese "Sakoku" Mentality and U.S. Efforts to Open Japan.* New York: St. Martin's Press, 1998.

Izumura, Fusakazu. "Should Japan Get a Permanent Seat on the U. N. Security Council?" *Tokyo Business Today* (March 1993): 54.

Johnson, Chalmers. *Japan: Who Governs?* New York: W.W. Norton, 1995.

Johnson, Chalmers, and E. B. Keehn. "The Pentagon's Ossified Strategy," *Foreign Affairs* 74, no. 4 (July/August 1995): 103–14.

JPOLL, Roper Center for Public Opinion Research, University of Connecticut. The data used in this book were originally collected by the *Asahi Shimbun, Jiji Press, Yomiuri Shimbun, Nihon Keizai Shimbun,* and the Prime Minister's Office. The data were obtained from the Japan Public Opinion Location Library, JPOLL, Roper Center for Public Opinion Research, University of Connecticut. Neither the original collectors of the data, nor the Roper Center, bear any responsibility for the analysis or interpretations presented here. Available at http://roper1.ropercenter.uconn.edu.

Kades, Charles L. "The American Role in Revising Japan's Imperial Constitution." *Political Science Quarterly* 104, no. 2 (1989): 217.

Kamiya, Setsuko, and Kanako Takahara. "Tojo Film Opens to Applause, Criticism." *Japan Times,* 24 May 1998, p. 2.

Kang, C. S. "Korea and Japanese Security." *International Journal of Korean Studies* III, no. 1 (Spring/Summer 1999): 94–115.

Karan, Pradyumna P. *Japan in the 21st Century: Environment, Economy, and Society.* Lexington: The University of Kentucky Press, 2005.

Kataoka, Tetsuya. *The Price of a Constitution: The Origin of Japan's Postwar Politics.* New York: Crane Russak, 1991.

Kato, Ryozo. Director General, Foreign Policy Bureau of the Japanese Ministry of Foreign Affairs. Interview by author, 21 May 1998, Tokyo. Tape recording in author's personal possession.

Kennan, George F. *Memoirs 1925–1950*. New York: Bantam Books, 1967.

Kennedy, John W. "Tokyo: Indifferent to the Risen Son." *Pentecostal Evangel* (5 December 1999): 10.

Kennedy, Paul. *The Rise and Fall of the Great Powers: Economic Change and Military Conflict from 1500 to 2000*. New York: Random House, 1987.

Kim, Lieutenant Colonel Andrew H. N. "Japan and Peace-Keeping Operations." *Military Review* (April 1994): 22–33.

Kim, Samuel, ed. *The International Relations of Northeast Asia*. Lanham, MD: Rowman and Littlefield, 2004.

Kissinger, Henry. *Diplomacy*. New York: Simon and Schuster, 1994.

Kitaoka, Shinichi. "A Green Light for Japanese Peace-keepers." *Japan Echo* XIX, no. 3 (Autumn 1992): 42.

Kodama, Katsuya. "Non-Provocative Defense as a New Japanese Defense Policy." Paper presented at the International Studies Association Conference, Washington, DC, 17–20 February 1999.

Kodera, Jiro. Director, First International Economic Affairs Division of the Japanese Ministry of Foreign Affairs. Interview by author, 20 May 1998, Tokyo. Tape recording in author's personal possession.

Koh, B. C. *Japan's Administrative Elite*. Berkeley: University of California Press, 1989.

_____. "U.S.-Japan Security Cooperation and the Two Koreas." Paper presented at the International Studies Association 41st Annual Convention, Los Angeles, California, 17 March 2000, p. 1.

Kristof, Nicholas D. "A Big Exception for a Nation of Apologizers." *New York Times,* 12 June 1995, pp. A1, A4.

_____. "Japan Expresses Regret of a Sort for the War." *New York Times,* 7 June 1995, pp. A1, A11.

_____. "The Problem of Memory." *Foreign Affairs* 77, no. 6 (November/December 1998): 37–49.

_____. "Seeking to Be Tokyo's Governor, Politician Attacks U.S. Presence." *New York Times,* 26 March 1999, p. A12.

_____. "A Tojo Battles History, for Grandpa and for Japan." *New York Times*. Internet edition. 22 April 1999. Available at www.nytimes.com/library/world/asia/ 042299 japan-tojo.html.

Kubota, Seiichi. Professor, Faculty of Modern Culture, Tokyo Junshin Women's College (former journalist with the *Asahi Shimbun*). Interview by the author, 1 June 1998, Tokyo. Tape recording in author's personal possession.

Langdon, Frank. *Japan's Regional and Global Coalition Participation: Political and Economic Aspects*. Vancouver, British Columbia: Institute of International Relations, the University of British Columbia, 1997.

Leitch, Richard D., Akira Kato, and Martin E. Weinstein, eds. *Japan's Role in the Post-Cold War World*. Westport, CT: Greenwood Press, 1995.

Lohr Steve, Andrew Ross Sorkin, and Jad Mouawad, "Unocal Bid Denounced At Hearing," *New York Times,* p. C1, available at www.nytimes.com, and *The China Daily,* 14 July 2005, available at www.chinadaily.com.cn/english/doc/2005–07/ 14/content_460173.htm.

Luney, Percy R. Jr., and Takahashi, Kazuyuki, eds. *Japanese Constitutional Law.* Tokyo: University of Tokyo Press, 1993.

Madsen, Sandra. "The Japanese Constitution and Self-Defense Forces: Prospects for a New Japanese Military Role." *Transnational Law & Contemporary Problems* 3 (Fall 1993): 549–79.

Magosaki, Ukeru. "New Diplomatic Challenges in East Asia." Unpublished paper. Japanese Ministry of Foreign Affairs, 1998.

Maki, John M. *Japan's Commission on the Constitution: The Final Report.* Seattle, Washington: University of Washington Press, 1980

Markman, Robert. "A Whole Lot of Bull $*#%!" *Worth* (February 2000): 116–25.

Masaki, Hisane. "Japan, China Consider Upgrading Security Forum." *Japan Times,* Internet edition, 14 September 1999.Available atwww.japantimes.co.jp/news/news 9–99/ news.html.

Mastanduno, Michael. "Preserving the Unipolar Moment: Realist Theories and U.S. Grand Strategy after the Cold War." *International Security* 21, no. 4 (Spring 1997): 49–88.

McDonough, Peter, Samuel H. Barnes, and Antonio López Pina. *The Cultural Dynamics of Democratization in Spain.* Ithaca, NY: Cornell University Press, 1998.

Mendel, Douglas H. Jr. *The Japanese People and Foreign Policy: A Study of Public Opinion in Post-Treaty Japan.* Berkeley: University of California Press, 1961.

Mensing, John. Email comment on how Japan embraced defeat, 13 October 1999, H-Net/KIAPS List for United States and Japanese Relations. Available at H-US-Japan@H-Net.msu.edu.

Michio, Nagai and Miguel Urrutia, eds. *Meiji Ishin: Restoration and Revolution.* Tokyo: United Nations University Press, 1985.

Midford, Paul. "From Reactive State to Cautious Leader: The Nakayama Proposal and Japan's Role in Promoting the Creation of the ASEAN Regional Forum (ARF)." Unpublished Paper, Columbia University, Department of Political Science, 1998.

_____. "The U.S.-Japan Defense Guidelines: Balance of Power, Balance of Threat and Asian Reactions." Paper presented at the International Studies Association Conference, Washington, DC, 17–20 February 1999.

Ministry of Foreign Affairs (Japan). "Japan and the United States: Teamwork Today and Tomorrow." Ministry of Foreign Affairs (Japan) publication, February 1993.

_____. *Japan's ODA: Annual Report 1997.* Tokyo: Association for Promotion of International Cooperation, 1998.

Miyashita, Akitoshi. "Consensus or Compliance?: 'Gaiatsu' and Japan's Foreign Aid to China and Russia." Paper presented at the International Studies Association Annual Conference, Los Angeles, CA, 14–18 March 2000.

_____. *Limits to Power: Asymmetric Dependence and Japanese Foreign Aid Policy.* Lanham, MD: Lexington Books, 2003.

Miyashita, Akitoshi, and Yoichiro Sato, eds. *Japanese Foreign Policy in Asia and the Pacific: Domestic Interests, American Pressure, and Regional Integration.* New York: Palgrave, 2001.

Mochizuki, Mike M. *Japan: Domestic Change and Foreign Policy.* Santa Monica, CA: RAND, 1995.

Monji, Kenjiro. Cabinet Office of the Prime Minister, Office on External Affairs. Interview by the author, 11 June 1998, Tokyo. Tape recording in author's personal possession.

Morgan, Forrest E. *Compellence and the Strategic Culture of Imperial Japan: Implications for Coercive Diplomacy in the Twenty-First Century.* Westport, CT: Praeger, 2003.

Morgenthau, Hans J. *Politics Among Nations,* rev. Kenneth W. Thompson. New York: Knopf, 1985.

Mori, Eisuke. Member of the House of Representatives of the Japanese Diet (LDP). Interview by the author, 22 May 1998, Tokyo. Tape recording in author's personal possession.

Morikawa, Jun. Professor, Rakuno Gakuen University. Interview by author, 22 June 1998, Tokyo. Tape recording in author's personal possession.

Motomatsu, Takashi. Major in the Japanese Ground Self-Defense Forces and former commander of a SDF PKO mission to the Golan Heights, current station Planning Section of the Plans and Operations Department, Japan Defense Agency. Interview by the author, 5 June 1998, Tokyo. Author's notes in author's personal possession.

Mulgan, Aurelia George. "Strategic Update—Japan." School of Politics, University of New South Wales, Australian Defence Force Academy. Conference paper, 1999.

Nakagawa, Tomoko. Member of the House of Representatives of the Japanese Diet (SDP). Interview by the author, 16 June 1998, Tokyo. Tape recording in author's personal possession.

Nakajima, Kuniko. Former career diplomat with the Japanese Ministry of Foreign Affairs and currently a researcher with the Okazaki Institute. Interview by the author, 18 June 1998, Tokyo. Tape recording in author's personal possession.

Nakamura, Kenichi. Dean of Law, Hokkaido University (top Japanese researcher on the PKO Law). Interview by author, 20 June 1998, Tokyo. Tape recording in author's personal possession.

Nakamura, Yoshihisa. Colonel in the Ground Self-Defense Force and Professor at the National Institute for Defense Studies, Japan Defense Agency. Interview by the author, 28 May 1998, Tokyo. Tape recording in author's personal possession.

Nakanishi, Terumasa. "Japan's Place in the World." *Japan Echo* XIX, special issue (1992): 2–5.

Nakano, Minoru. *The Policy-Making Process in Contemporary Japan,* trans. Jeremy Scott. New York: St. Martin's Press, 1997.

Nathan, John. *Japan Unbound: A Volatile Nation's Quest for Pride and Purpose.* Boston: Houghton Mifflin, 2004.

National Institute of Population and Social Security Research. "Selected Demographic Indicators for Japan." Internet Web page. Available at www.ipss.go.jp/English/ S_D_I/ Indip.html.

Newland, Kathleen, ed. *The International Relations of Japan.* London: Macmillan, 1990.

New York Times. "Japan Discovers Defense." 26 August 1999, Internet edition. Available at www.nytimes.com/yr/mo/day/editorial/26thu1.html.

Nishihara, Masashi. Professor at the National Defense Academy, Japan Defense Agency. Interview by the author, 31 May 1998, Tokyo. Tape recording in author's personal possession.

_____. "Japanese Defense Policy: Issues and Options." Paper presented at the International Symposium on Japan and Its Neighbors in the Global Village: Current and Emergent Issues. Nanzan University, Nagoya, Japan, 16–17 October 1999.

Nishimura, Mutsuyoshi. "Peace-Keeping Operations: Setting the Record Straight," *Japan Echo* XIX, no. 3 (Autumn 1992): 50–56.

Nishimura, Shingo. Member of the House of Representatives of the Japanese Diet (Liberal Party). Interview by the author. 17 June 1998, Tokyo. Tape recording in author's personal possession.

Oberdorfer, Don. *The Two Koreas: A Contemporary History.* New York: Basic Books, 2001.

Oberdorfer, Don, and Hajime Izumi. "The United States, Japan and the Korean Peninsula: Coordinating Policies and Objectives." Working Paper, 14 April 1999, Available at www.seas.gwu.edu/nsaarchive/japan/donizumiwp.htm.

Obering Lieutenant General Henry A. III USAF, Director, Missile Defense Agency, Missile Defense Program, Fiscal Year 2006 Budget testimony before the Strategic Forces Subcommittee House Armed Services Committee, 15 March 2005.

Odawara, Atsushi. "The Kaifu Bungle." *Japan Quarterly* (January–March 1991): 6–14.

Ogata, Sadako. "The Changing Role of Japan in the United Nations." *Journal of International Affairs,* no. 27 (Summer 1983): 29–42.

Ogawa, Akira. Professor, Okazaki Research Institute, Tokyo, Japan. Interview by author, 18 June 1998, Tokyo. Tape recording in author's personal possession.

Ogawa, Shin'ichi. Professor, National Institute for Defense Studies. Interview by author, 11 June 1998, Tokyo. Tape recording in author's personal possession.

Oshiba, Ryo. "Japan's U.N. Policy in the 1990s." Paper presented at the International Studies Association Annual Conference, Washington, DC, 16–20 February 1999.

Oshitani, Hajime. Professor at Rakuno Gakuen University. Interview by author, 25 June 1998, Tokyo. Tape recording in author's personal possession.

Ota, Kazuo. "The Place and Role of Political Parties in Contemporary Societies in Connection with the HASTIC Production System: An Analysis of Japanese Political Parties." *Journal of Rakuno Gakuen University* 21, no. 2 (1997): 205–14.

―――. Dean, Rakuno Gakuen University. Interview by author, 6 June 1998, Tokyo. Tape recording in author's personal possession.

Overby, Charles M. *A Call for Peace: The Implications of Japan's War-Renouncing Constitution* (Bilingual Edition), trans. Kunihiro Masao. Tokyo: Kodansha International, 1997.

Oxford American Dictionary. New York: Avon Books, 1982.

Ozawa, Ichiro. *Blueprint for a New Japan: The Rethinking of a Nation (Nihon Kaizo Keikaku),* trans. Louisa Rubinfien, ed. Eric Grower. New York: Kodansha International, 1994.

Palka, Eugene J., and Francis A. Galgano. *North Korea: Geographic Perspectives.* Guilford, CT: McGraw Hill/Dushkin, 2004.

Paris, Gilles. "Le Japonais Kochiro Matsuura da succeder a Federico Mayor a la tete de l'Unesco." *Le Monde,* 22 October 1999 as cited by H-Japan, H-JAPAN@H-NET.MSU.EDU #1999–91 5–7 November 1999.

Parker, Jay M. "The U.S.-Japan Defense Guidelines and the Future East Asian Security Environment." Paper presented at the International Studies Association Annual Conference, Washington, DC, 16–20 February 1999.

Pempel, T. J. *Regime Shift: Comparative Dynamics of the Japanese Political Economy.* Ithaca, NY: Cornell University Press, 1998.

―――. "Structural 'Gaiatsu': International Finance and Political Change in Japan." *Comparative Political Studies* 32, no. 8 (December 1999): 907–32.

Powell, Robert. "Absolute and Relative Gains in International Relations Theory." *American Political Science Review* 85, no. 4 (December 1991): 1303–20.

———. "Anarchy in International Relations Theory: The Neorealist-Neoliberal Debate." *International Organization* 48, no. 2 (Spring 1994): 313–44.

Putnam, Robert. "Diplomacy and Domestic Politics: The Logic of Two-Level Games." *International Organization* 42, no. 3 (Summer 1988): 427–60.

Ramsdell, Daniel B. *The Japanese Diet: Stability and Change in the Japanese House of Representatives 1890–1990.* Lanham, MD: University Press of America, 1992.

Reischauer, Edwin O. *The United States and Japan,* 3rd ed. New York: Viking Press, 1969.

———. *The Japanese.* Cambridge, MA: Belknap Press of Harvard University Press, 1977.

———. *Japan: The Story of a Nation,* 4th ed. New York: McGraw-Hill, 1990.

Rhodes, John. Former Republican Congressman and Minority Whip from Arizona. Conversation between the author and the congressman during spring 1996 at the University Club, Arizona State University. Author's notes in author's personal possession.

Rose, Caroline. *Sino-Japanese Relations: Facing the Past, Looking to the Future.* New York: Routledge Curzon, 2005.

Rosenau, James N. *The Study of Political Adaptation: Essays on the Analysis of World Politics.* New York: Nichols Publishing, 1981.

Ross, Robert S. "Managing a Changing Relationship: China's Japan Policy in the 1990s." Paper presented at the Strategic Studies Institute, United States Army War College, Carlisle Barracks, 23–25 April 1996.

Rostati, Jerel A., Joe D. Hagan, and Martin W. Sampson III, eds. *Foreign Policy Restructuring: How Governments Respond to Global Change.* Columbia: University of South Carolina Press, 1994.

Royer, Kendrick F. "The Demise of the World's First Pacifist Constitution: Japanese Constitutional Interpretation and the Growth of Executive Power to Make War." *Vanderbilt Journal of Transnational Law* 26 (1993): 749–801.

Sackton, Frank, Major General United States Army (Ret.) and former aide to General Douglas MacArthur during the occupation of Japan. Interviews by author, 19 and 24 September 1997. Tape recording in author's personal possession.

Saiki, Naoko. Director, International Peace Cooperation Division, Ministry of Foreign Affairs. Interview by author, 4 June 1998, Tokyo. Tape recording in author's personal possession.

Saito, Shiro. *Japan at the Summit: Its Role in the Western Alliance and Asian Pacific Co-operation.* New York: Routledge, 1990.

Sakamoto, Masahiro. "PAX Americana II and Japan." Paper presented at the International Studies Association Conference, Washington, DC, February 17–20, 1999.

Sampson III, Martin W., and Stephen G. Walker, "Cultural Norms and National Roles: A Comparison of Japan and France." In *Role Theory and Foreign Policy Analysis,* ed. Stephen G. Walker, Chapter 7, pp. 105–22. Durham, NC: Duke University Press, 1987.

Sanger, David E. "U.S. and Japanese Told to Resolve Dispute on Trade—Blunt Warning to Both—New World Trade Chief Calls Conflict a 'Delicate Matter'—Nationalism Is Cited." *New York Times,* 14 June 1995, p. A1.

Sasaki, Yoshitaka. "Japan's Undue International Contribution." *Japan Quarterly* (July–September 1993): 259–65.

Sato, Hideo, and I. M. Destler eds. *Leadership Sharing in the New International System: Japan and the United States.* Japan: University of Tsukuba, 1996.

Sato, Yoichiro. "Toward a Non-Threatening U.S.-Japan Alliance." Paper presented at the International Studies Association Conference, Washington, DC, 17–20 February, 1999.

_____. "Modeling Japan's Foreign and Economic Policy with the United States." In *Japanese Foreign Policy on Asia and the Pacific*, ed. Akitoshi Miyashita and Yoichiro Sato. New York: Palgrave, 2001.

Scalapino, Robert, ed. *The Foreign Policy of Modern Japan.* Berkeley: University of California Press, 1977.

Scanlon, Charles. "Brief Return for Japanese Abductees," BBC, 16 October 2002, available at: http://news.bbc.co.uk/2/hi/asia-pacific/2331447.stm.

Scheiner, Irwin. *Modern Japan: An Interpretive Anthology.* New York: Macmillan, 1974.

Schmiegelow, Hendrik, and Michèle Schmiegelow. "How Japan Affects the International System." *International Organization* 44, no. 4 (Autumn 1990): 553–84.

Schoff, James L, ed. *Crisis Management in Japan and the United States: Creating Opportunities for Cooperation amid Dramatic Change.* Dulles, VA: Brassey's Inc., 2004.

Schoppa, Leonard J. "Two Level Games and Bargaining Outcomes: Why 'Gaiatsu' Succeeds in Japan in Some Cases but Not in Others." *International Organization* 47, no. 3 (Summer 1993): 353–86.

Selin, Shannon. *Asia Pacific Arms Buildups Part One: Scope, Causes and Problems.* Vancouver, British Columbia: Institute of International Relations, the University of British Columbia, 1994.

Shibata, Akiho. "Japanese Peacekeeping Legislation and Recent Developments in U.N. Operations." *Yale Journal of International Law* 19 (1994): 307–48.

Simon, Sheldon W. *East Asian Security in the Post-Cold War Era.* Armonk, NY: M.E. Sharpe, 1993.

_____. "International Relations Theory and Southeast Asian Security." *The Pacific Review* 8, no. 1 (1995): 5–24.

_____. "Multilateralism and Japan's Security Policy." *The Korean Journal of Defense Analysis* XI, no. 2 (Winter 1999): 79–96.

_____. *The Many Faces of Asian Security.* Lanham, MD: Rowman and Littlefield, 2001.

Sims, Calvin. "U.S. Resists Cut in Funds by Japan for G.I.'s." *New York Times.* Internet edition. 17 February 2000. Available at http://www.nytimes.com/yr/mo/day/ news/world/japan-us-troops.html.

_____. "Tokyo Chief Starts New Furror on Immigrants." *New York Times.* Internet edition, 11 April 2000. Available at www.nytimes.com/library/world/asia/041100japan-immigrants.html.

Smith, Geoffrey. "Japan Expanding Defense Role." *Washington Times.* 7 March 2000, p. 11, as cited by Northeast Asia Peace and Security Network Daily Report for Tuesday March 7, 2000, from Berkeley, CA. Available at NAPSNet@nautilus.org (NAPSNet).

Snow, Donald. *National Security: Defense Policy in a Changed International Order,* 4th ed. New York: St. Martin's Press, 1998.

Soeya, Yoshihide. *Japan's Dual Identity and the U.S.-Japan Alliance.* Palo Alto, CA: Institute for International Studies, Stanford University, May 1998.

Spruyt, Hendrik. "A New Architecture for Peace?: Reconfiguring Japan Among the Great Powers." *The Pacific Review* 11, no. 3 1998: 364–88.

Starr, John Bryan. *Understanding China: A Guide to China's Economy, History, and Political Culture.* New York: Hill and Wang, 2001.

Stevenson, Matthew. "Re-Reading Rosecrance: International Norms and the Trading State." Paper presented at the International Studies Association Annual Conference, Los Angeles, CA, 14–18 March 2000.

Storry, Richard. *A History of Modern Japan.* Baltimore, MD: Penguin Books, 1969.

Takagi, Yoko. "Japan's Foreign Policy: Japan's Decision Making of the Foreign Policy and the PKO Law [sic]." Research Paper for Dr. Linda Rawles, Grand Canyon University, 1998.

Takayanagi, Sakio, and Katsuya Kodama, eds. *Japan and Peace.* Mie, Japan: Mie Academic Press, 1994.

Takemi, Keizo. Member of the House of Councillors of the Japanese Diet. Current Cabinet Vice Foreign Minister and past House of Councillors Chair of Foreign Relations Committee and founding chair of the subcommittee on Pacific Affairs. Interview by the author, 25 May 1998, Tokyo. Tape recording in author's personal possession.

Takesada, Hideshi. Professor, National Institute for Defense Studies. Interview by the author. 5 June 1998, Tokyo. Tape recording in author's personal possession.

Tan, See Seng. "Constituting Asia-Pacific (In)Security: A Radical Constructivist Study in 'Track II' Security Dialogues." Ph.D. diss., Arizona State University, May 1999.

Tanaka, Akihiko. Professor, Institute of Oriental Culture, Tokyo University. Interview by author. 16 June 1998, Tokyo. Tape recording in author's personal possession.

_____. "Japan and Regional Integration in Asia-Pacific." Paper presented at the 40th Annual Conference of the International Studies Association, Washington, DC 17 February 1999.

Task Force on Foreign Relations for the Prime Minister, "Basic Strategies for Japan's Foreign Policy in the 21st Century: New Era, New Vision, New Diplomacy," 28 November 2002, Executive Summary (unofficial translation). www.kantei.go.jp/foreign/policy/2002/1128tf_e.html.

Taylor, Trevor, and Seizaburo Sato, eds. *Future Sources of Global Conflict: The Security Challenges for Japan and Europe in a Post-Cold War World,* vol. 4. London: Royal Institute of International Affairs and Institute for International Policy Studies, 1995.

Terada, Takashi. "The Origins of Japan's APEC Policy: Foreign Minister Takeo Miki's Asia-Pacific Policy and Current Implications," *The Pacific Review* 11, no. 3 (1999): 337–63.

Tow, William, Russell Trood, and Toshiya Hoshino, eds. *Bilateralism in a Multilateral Era: The Future of the San Francisco Alliance System in the Asia-Pacific.* Tokyo: The Japan Institute of International Affairs, 1997.

Tucker, Robert W. *The Inequality of Nations.* New York: Basic Books, 1977.

Urata, Kenji. "The Peace and Security of Japan." *National Lawyers Guild Practitioner* 44, no. 3 (Summer): 75–86.

Usui, Hideo. Member of the House of Representatives of the Japanese Diet and former Defense Minister and Vice Defense Agency Minister (career ministry appointment). Interviews by the author, 26 and 29 May 1998, Tokyo. Tape recording in author's personal possession.

Vogel, Ezra F. *Japan as Number One: Lessons for America.* Cambridge, MA.: Harvard University Press, 1979.

Walker, Stephen G., ed. *Role Theory and Foreign Policy Analysis.* Durham, NC: Duke University Press, 1987.

Waltz, Kenneth N. Man, the State, and War: A Theoretical Analysis. New York: Columbia University Press, 1954/1959.

_____. Conference comment. January 1999, Scottsdale, Arizona. Author's personal notes in the author's personal possession, January 1999.

Wan, Ming. "Spending Strategies in World Politics: How Japan Used Its Economic Power in the Past Decade." *International Studies Quarterly,* 39, (1995): 85–108.

Ward, Michael D., David R. Davis, and Corey L. Lofdahl. "A Century of Tradeoffs: Defense and Growth in Japan and the United States." *International Studies Quarterly* 39 (1995): 27–50.

Watts, William. *The United States and Japan: A Troubled Partnership.* Cambridge, MA: Ballinger, 1984.

Welfield, John, ed. *An Empire in Eclipse: Japan in the Postwar American Alliance System: A Study in the Interaction of Domestic Politics and Foreign Policy.* London: The Athlone Press, 1988.

Wittkopf, Eugene R., and James M. McCormick, eds. *The Domestic Sources of American Foreign Policy: Insights and Evidence,* 3rd ed. Lanham, MD: Rowman and Littlefield, 1999.

Wolf, Charles Jr. *Straddling Economics and Politics: Cross-Cutting Issues in Asia, the United States, and the Global Economy.* Santa Monica, CA: Rand, 2002.

Wolferen, Karel van. *The Enigma of Japanese Power.* Tokyo: Charles E. Tuttle Co., 1993.

WuDunn, Sheryl, and Nicholas D. Kristof. "Japan as No. 1? In Debt, Maybe, at the Rate Things Have Been Going." *New York Times.* 1 September 1999. Internet edition. Available at www.nytimes.com/yr/mo/day/news/financial/japan-debt.html.

Yamaguchi, Jiro. "The Gulf War and the Transformation of Japanese Constitutional Politics," *Journal of Japanese Studies* 18, no. 1 (1992): 155–72.

Yamaguchi, Noboru. Colonel, Ground Self-Defense Forces, Deputy Chief of Defense Planning Division, Ground Staff Office, Japan Defense Agency. Interview by author 2 June 1998, Tokyo, Japan, Tape recording in author's personal possession.

Yamamoto, Ichita. Member of the House of Councillors of the Japanese Diet. Interview by the author, 18 June 1998, Tokyo. Tape recording in author's personal possession.

Yamauchi, Toshihiro. "Gunning for Japan's Peace Constitution." *Japan Quarterly* (April–June 1992): 159–67.

Yanai, Shunji. "The Law Concerning Cooperation for United Nations Peace-Keeping Operations and Other Operations: The Japanese PKO Experience." *The Japanese Journal of International Law* 36: 33–75.

_____. Vice Minister Japanese Ministry of Foreign Affairs (Currently Ambassador to the U.S.). Interview by author, 20 May 1998, Tokyo. Tape recording in author's personal possession.

Yomiuri Shimbun. "Appropriation Sought for Refueling Aircraft," 21 July 1999. Internet edition. Available at www.yomiyuri.co.jp/newse/ 0722p001.htm.

_____. "Law on Constitutional Poll Needed." 9 August 1999. Internet edition. Available at www.yomiuri.co.jp/newse/0809ed16.htm.

Zhao, Quansheng, ed. *Japanese Policymaking: The Politics Behind Politics: Informal Mechanisms and the Making of China Policy.* Westport, CT: Praeger, 1993.

Zinberg, Yakov. "In Search for Alternative National Interests: Russo-Japanese Territorial Disputes After the Cold War." Paper presented at the 40th Annual Conference of the International Studies Association, Washington, DC, 17 February 1999.

Index

287

Wolf, Charles 281
World community 3, 58, 75, 103, 167,
    174, 181, 191, 195, 202
World Trade Organization (WTO) 107,
    252
World War II 3, 4, 5, 7, 8, 18, 19, 23, 24,
    25, 26, 33, 34, 36, 37, 40, 44, 48,
    50, 51, 52, 53, 55, 57, 58, 60, 63,
    65, 73, 88, 90, 98, 113, 114, 115,
    117, 129, 130, 138, 151, 159,
    168, 171, 179, 183, 184, 188,
    190, 191, 193, 194, 199, 202,
    203, 230, 234, 235, 236, 238,
    239, 240, 241, 243, 245, 246,
    251, 256, 257, 268, 269

WTO. *See* World Trade Organization

Yamamoto, Ichiro 182, 259, 281
Yasukuni Shrine 52, 53, 122, 159, 167,
    194, 232, 264
Yomiuri Shimbun 108, 109, 110, 136,
    145, 251, 252, 253, 254, 260, 261,
    262, 273, 281
Yoshida Doctrine 6, 7, 8, 36, 38, 58, 59,
    60, 65, 79, 80, 113, 130, 139, 195,
    230, 246, 247
Younger generation 8, 57, 84, 95, 97, 98,
    140, 189, 193, 199, 203

Zemin, Jiang 43, 158, 243

Kevin Cooney is an associate professor of political science and international relations at Union University in Jackson, Tennessee. He received his B.A. degree summa cum laude from Oral Roberts University (1988). His M.A. was in international relations and strategic studies and comes from Lancaster University in England (1989), where he attended on a Rotary Foundation Ambassadorial Fellowship. He earned his Ph.D. in political science from Arizona State University (2000). His doctoral dissertation focused on the changes in Japanese foreign policy since the end of the Cold War. Dr. Cooney teaches courses in international relations, comparative governments, international security, Asian politics, terrorism, human rights, and democratization. He has taught previously at the university level in the People's Republic of China, in Japan, at Western Oregon University, at Arizona State University, and at Grand Canyon University. He has also worked as an expert commentator for radio and television on American politics, international security, and East Asian affairs. Dr. Cooney's first book, *Japan's Foreign Policy Maturation: A Quest for Normalcy,* was published in 2002.